New Zealand journalist Chris Bourk
House story since 1984, when he
demise of Split Enz and his plans fo
of the first Crowded House album in
soon after its release. At the time he
Zealand's leading rock magazine (an⌐ ⌐⌐⌐ ₀₀₀ ₀₀₀ review copy).
Shortly afterwards, he interviewed the band on the night of their first
New Zealand concert, in an Auckland living-room. He has been a staff
writer and arts and book editor at the New Zealand *Listener*, and has
a degree in music history from Victoria University of Wellington.

CROWDED HOUSE

SOMETHING SO STRONG

CHRIS BOURKE

MACMILLAN

Pan Macmillan Australia

Grateful acknowledgement is made to the following for permission to reprint previously published material:

BPI Communications Inc.: excerpts from *Billboard* magazine. © 1987–1997 BPI Communications, Inc. Used with permission from *Billboard* magazine.

IPC Magazines Ltd.: excerpt from *Melody Maker*. © 1991 IPC Magazines Ltd. Used with permission from *Melody Maker*.

Mushroom Music: lyrics from 'Six Months in a Leaky Boat' – by Tim Finn/Split Enz © 1982, administered by Mushroom Music.

Lyrics from 'Weather With You', 'All I Ask', 'Chocolate Cake', 'It's Only Natural' – by Neil Finn and Tim Finn © 1991, administered by Mushroom Music. Lyrics from 'Voices', 'Don't Dream It's Over', 'Mean to Me', 'Something So Strong', 'Into Temptation', 'Better Be Home Soon', 'Private Universe', 'Distant Sun', 'Instinct' – by Neil Finn © 1984–1996, administered by Mushroom Music. Lyrics from 'Haulaway', – by Tim Finn © 1982, administered by Mushroom Music. Lyrics from 'Split Ends' – by Tim Finn & Phil Judd © 1972, administered by Mushroom Music. Lyrics from 'Leaps and Bounds' – Paul Kelly & C Langman © 1986 administered by Mushroom Music. All used by permission. Reproduction prohibited.

First published 1997 in Macmillan by Pan Macmillan Australia Pty Limited
St Martins Tower, 31 Market Street, Sydney

National Library of Australia
Cataloguing-in-Publication data:

Bourke, Chris.
Something so strong.

ISBN 0 7329 0886 8.

1. Crowded House (Musical group). 2. Rock musicians–
Australia–Biography. I. Title.

782.421660922

Typeset by Midland Typesetters
Printed in Australia by McPherson's Printing Group

CONTENTS

For my mother and the memory of my father

'The tyranny of distance,
didn't stop the cavalier
So why should it stop me,
I'll conquer and stay free
Ah c'mon all you lads,
let's forget and forgive
There's a world to explore,
tales to tell back on shore'
　　　　—Tim Finn, 1982

'Dust from a distant sun
will shower over everyone.'
　　　　—Neil Finn, 1993

Marching to a different tune • July 1984

'The weight of the past is quite overwhelming
sometimes. Indecisiveness is a hard thing to live
with. Sometimes you've got to take the plunge.'

—Neil Finn, 1984

On 16 June, 1984, Tim Finn told his friends in Split Enz that he had decided to leave the group. A few days later, the rest of the band assembled in the Melbourne home of its keyboardist, Eddie Rayner. They started preparing for a future without Tim, who had been the driving force in the group since its inception in Auckland, New Zealand, 12 years earlier. During the rehearsals, they worked on a new song by Neil Finn, who now faced the task of leading the band his older brother had founded, and carrying the bulk of the song-writing burden. The new song was half-written, really only a chorus which went, *'Something so strong / could carry us away . . .'*

But over the next couple of weeks, Neil decided it would be better if he started afresh, without the expectations that accompanied the Split Enz legacy. At the next rehearsal, he told the rest of the band – the reaction wasn't 'overly traumatic'. Paul Hester was the most mortified, having joined Split Enz as drummer less than a year earlier and now finding it had suddenly broken up. After the meeting, Neil took Paul aside and said, 'Don't worry, mate, it's you and me – we'll get a new band happening. Just the two of us.' Paul put his thumbs up and looked very relieved. For some time, there had been a joke between the two youngest members of the Enz, with Neil saying to Paul, 'We'll lose these old bastards and get our own band, a real band.'

A few days later they all met at the house of their manager, Nathan Brenner, to formalise the demise of Split Enz, and organise its swansong. It was a typical Enz meeting: hours of talk with little progress. But the plan was to release another album, without Tim, and embark on a farewell tour, with Tim.

Neil was the first to leave the meeting, and he drove off in his 1975 Peugeot 504, 'feeling that everything was full of portent, of deep significance'. As he approached Kingsway, a Melbourne thoroughfare, a car shot out from a side street. 'I barely saw it, and I ploughed into

1

it. The moment went into slow motion, my car was spinning around. I'd never been in a major crash, it was very extreme: you've got no control, no power, and you see everything.'

The other driver hit a power pole on the other side of the road. 'The dust settled, and we sat there,' says Neil. 'I thought, am I dead? No, I'm not dead. Am I hurt? No, I'm not hurt. I felt a bit weird in my neck, but moved my legs, so they were working. Two Greek guys came running up – a tram driver and his conductor – to see if I was okay. I said, I think so . . .'

At that moment, Eddie Rayner drove past in his 1961 Morris Major. Neil yelled out, 'Hey! That's my friend!' Rayner looked vaguely at the wreck, but kept going – Neil's car had spun around 180 degrees and was unrecognisable. 'The two guys looked at each other and said, "Are you *sure* you're okay?" I said, yeah, that was my friend.'

Then Noel Crombie, the Split Enz percussionist, drove by in his 1949 Triumph Renown. Again, Neil yelled out to his friend who, once more, obliviously drove by. The two samaritans, thinking Neil was delirious, only half-heartedly tried to stop Crombie.

Next, Nigel Griggs, the band's bass player, came along in his 1954 Fiat station wagon. 'Hey! That's my friend!' called Neil. Griggs didn't even look, not wanting to be ghoulish about an accident.

'The cars were all bizarre,' says Neil, 'and these two guys were thinking something was really wrong, that I had lost it big time. Not one of the others stopped, none of them realised it was me as I was facing the other way, and the car was so pushed in.

'There was something beautifully symbolic about the whole thing. I haven't figured out exactly what it meant, but it was a ritual parting of the ways.'

Drink to my journey • 1958-72

'We thought the novelty would wear off. Six months, maybe a year. Particularly when Split Enz showed signs of struggling.'

—Dick Finn, 1996

When Neil Finn married Sharon Johnson, on 13 February, 1982, Split Enz had just completed recording their seventh album, *Time & Tide*. Dick and Mary Finn, parents of Tim and Neil and their sisters Carolyn and Judy, travelled from their home in Cambridge, New Zealand to Melbourne, Australia for the wedding. It was late when they arrived, so a tired Mary Finn went to bed, while Dick stayed up and poured himself a shot of duty-free Johnnie Walker. Feeling mellow, he picked up a tape that his sons had left beside the stereo, and put it on. Out came a sailor's hornpipe, followed by the tenor voice of Tim in a parody of a sea shanty:

> *'I was born in Te Awamutu*
> *25th of June 1952 . . .'*

'What's this?' Dick muttered to himself. 'This isn't a song . . .'

> *'My mother and father's pride and joy*
> *Richard and Mary, drink to my journey . . .'*

It was 'Haul Away', the most autobiographical song Tim Finn had written since co-founding Split Enz 10 years earlier. To Dick, it seemed crazy. He went to Mary and said, 'Listen to this, there's something stupid on this tape, it's about us'. 'I'll listen to it tomorrow,' she replied.

Mary was born in Ireland, and immigrated to New Zealand at the age of two with her mother and younger sister. The family joined her father, Tim Mullane, a hard-working Catholic farmhand who six months earlier had moved to New Zealand. His former employer in

3

Ireland (a Protestant farmer who had quickly sold up and emigrated when he heard the IRA were after him) asked Mullane over to help manage his farm, and paid for his journey. The Mullanes settled in the province of Waikato in the North Island, managing dairy farms near the towns of Te Aroha and Putaruru.

While Mary Mullane's father 'had no ear', singing in tune came naturally to her very musical mother, Nora. Mary herself found that, after a year of piano lessons, she could lead party singalongs through the hits of the day. It was this talent which caught the attention of Dick Finn, a Waikato farmer's son who was studying accountancy after World War II. 'The thing that appealed to me most about Mary was she was very good at parties. She could play all the tunes by ear, and was a very good dancer, which we both enjoyed.' Dick used to request 'My Happiness', a 1948 hit for both Ella Fitzgerald and the Ink Spots (and the song which Elvis Presley recorded as a present for his mother, earning himself an audition at Sun Records). 'I suppose that was our tune,' says Mary.

Dick Finn's mother could also play the piano, but the family didn't have one in the home until a cousin – whom the Finns had helped through teacher's training college – bought them one to express her gratitude. 'I can still see the tears in my mother's eyes, the thrill she got.' At the age of about eight, Dick took piano lessons for a few weeks with an 'old German who was very musical but tough as nails'. But Dick gave up when his teacher whacked him over the fingers with his steel-tipped ruler for making mistakes.

That put him off learning the piano, but his interest in music intensified, particularly in the early years of the war when he was listening to the radio while studying for his accountancy exams in Wellington. When his brother joined the air force, Dick (who later served in the army, in Italy) returned to help run the family farm at Te Rore and study by correspondence in the evenings. 'It was hard work, but the radio kept my interest up.' One night he heard a song open with a dramatic cascading trumpet solo. 'I stopped work immediately, listened through and thought, my God, that's beautiful. Luckily the announcer said, "That's Buddy Berigan with 'I Can't Get Started'." I wrote it down on the flyleaf of my exercise book and I've been a fan ever since.' Berigan became the cornerstone of a well-rounded collection of big-band jazz by acts such as Ella Fitzgerald, Artie Shaw, Tommy Dorsey, Benny Goodman and Gene Krupa.

Before their marriage, Dick underwent three months of instruction to join Mary in the Catholic faith. Afterwards, the couple settled in Te Awamutu, a quiet country town of about 3800 people (1951 census) which services the Waikato farming district; the name means 'the river cut short'. Dick worked as an accountant, eventually establishing his own practice. They lived close to the town centre at 78 Teasdale Street, a spacious wooden house with fruit trees in the front yard and the unusual luxury of a small swimming pool in the back.

Brian Timothy Finn – he took his middle name in the early days of Split Enz – was their second child, in between Carolyn and Judy. A year after he started primary school at St Patrick's, the local convent, his youngest brother, Neil Mullane Finn, was born on 27 May, 1958.

Home movies of the Finns' childhood show an idyllic mix of wholesome activities: swimming and skylarking in the pool, backyard games, pet lambs, pedal cars and events such as the day the circus came to Te Awamutu. With his friends and family, Neil would 'hang out in the pool all summer', play tennis, go for the occasional horse ride and bush walk, and take long bike rides out to the village of Pirongia, six miles away. 'We'd stop at a milkbar, have ice creams and lollies, and ride home.' Throughout childhood he played rugby for the convent team, the position of halfback suiting his slight, nuggety physique.

The family orchard became a favourite place of Neil's, not just for the acorn and plum fights, but as a private refuge. As it got close to Christmas, when the plums started to appear, he would climb his favourite tree, lie back on an especially comfortable branch, then gorge himself on the sour fruit and spy on the neighbours. Later, this inspired a line in 'Private Universe' ('highest branch on the apple tree').

On cold Waikato winter mornings, with the harsh frosts and dense fog slow to lift off the rolling hills, Dick would coax him out of bed with a corny joke – 'almost, almost', instead of 'Neily' – and he'd run to the kitchen and jump into the drying cabinet, where Mary would have removed the racks so he could get dressed in warmth.

The pivotal influence on the boys' lives came after hours, when they observed and took part in their parents' parties. Seeing the adults 'go crazy' was addictive. 'We discovered fairly early on that when everyone had had a couple of drinks and started to sing, a lot of the barriers came down and kids got away with a lot more,' says Neil. 'So music was a powerful force.' Fuelling the revelry was not just Dick's jazz records, but the piano, with friend Colin O'Brien taking over from Mary. 'He was one of those guys who could play any song, or would have a go,' says Tim. 'He'd blaze away and the party would fire.'

The parties were especially frequent during the Finns' summer holidays at Mt Maunganui, a beach resort about an hour's drive from Te Awamutu. On the way, Dick and Mary would try and entertain the children in the back so they didn't get bored and start fighting.

Between 'I Spy' games and saying the rosary, they'd encourage singalongs on tunes such as 'Michael Row the Boat Ashore' and 'Cross Over the Bridge'. Mary's sister Bridie, and her husband George Goddard, would take a beach house nearby and the two families would get together at night. Each year, the Durning brothers, Matthew and Peter – Scottish twins who were Marist priests – would stay with the families, and their skilful two-part harmonies would lead the sing-alongs after dinner. ('Like most Catholic priests,' says Neil, 'they knew how to party.') As the children grew up, they were expected – in the Irish tradition – to do an item. It was the boys' Uncle George who insisted, cajoling 'Nugget' to take part. 'Neil was always quite willing, Tim was shyer – he had to be pushed,' says Mary. 'And afterwards George would make them go right round the room and shake hands with everyone.'

To Tim, the performances were tormenting. 'We used to be forced into it. Good naturedly, but definitely forced.' Tim would fight against it 'almost to the death', he says; Neil 'with less conviction. He was enjoying more being this little cute kid who could sing with his brother.'

'We'd get dragged out,' says Neil, 'and though we'd squirm with embarrassment, we'd really enjoy it.' Even Tim found that afterwards, the affection received made it worthwhile, if not easier. He describes the ritual as a 'gift' from his parents. 'We might have had the talent, but they helped to ignite it.' The duo's big number was 'Jamaican Farewell' – Tim taking the high harmony, Neil the low – while Neil's solo turn was always 'Terry', a maudlin hit for Twinkle in 1964 about a man who dies on a motorcycle. 'We probably got a bit from records and radio too,' says Tim, 'but it was the live presence of harmony singing that kicked it off.'

For five years Tim took piano lessons, having a breakthrough when his teacher Sister Raymond swapped the stultifying children's exercises with the jazz piece 'Alley Cat'. 'That was a liberation,' he says. 'She was great, she understood that there was this swing element to music.' Hearing Tim's enthusiasm, Dick suggested some lessons with the local jazz musician Chuck Fowler. 'He taught me all the chords, and then I could start improvising and picking out tunes and, I guess, eventually writing. So I thank Dad for that, to notice there was something going on and to steer it a bit.'

For Tim, hearing Eddie Hodge's 'I'm Gonna Knock on Your Door' was an 'epiphany' – he could relate to the adenoidal, boyish voice, which stopped him in his tracks. Watching Tim's progress and taking part in the rowdy parties gave Neil the desire and confidence to emulate his older brother. Just after he started at the convent, at the age of five, Neil won the school's talent quest with a rendition of 'You Are My Sunshine'. With 10 shillings as a prize, 'He thought he was made', says Mary.

New Zealand radio in the early 60s was government run, and bland, with pop limited to specialist shows such as the weekly *Lever Hit Parade*. Until the beat boom and TV pop shows began, the biggest local act was the Howard Morrison Quartet, whose hokey humour played on the 'happy-go-lucky Maori' stereotype. In the Finn household, the record player was a boxy gramophone with a heavy bakelite needle. Between them, Carolyn, Tim and Judy assembled a varied collection of 45s, which developed from childhood favourites such as 'Love Letters in the Sand', 'The Wanderer' and 'Green, Green' to the Beatles, Kinks and Rolling Stones as they became teenagers.

Tim would play with pots and pans, pretending to be a drummer. Later, it would be with a tennis racquet and a plastic wig, pretending to be a Beatle. A second epiphany took place for him in 1965, when the Dave Clark Five came to Hamilton, 18 miles north of Te Awamutu. Just entering his teens, Tim went with his elder sister Carolyn and his mother. When the lead singer, sitting behind the drum kit, began playing, 'My sister started screaming and ran down the front, and I realised that this music had a – I wouldn't have known how to put it then – but it had a sexual element to it. Up till then they'd just been tunes, and being haunted by melodies. That's when I became obsessed, and got into the romance of groups.'

With an age difference of six years, the relationship between the boys was one of mentor and pupil. 'I was happy to be the elder brother,' Tim told *Good Weekend* in 1987. 'I don't think I patronised him or insulted his intelligence. He was like my pet project; I loved having a younger brother who I could tell things to.'

Tim would fire up Neil and his friends with motivational speeches. 'He'd come in the room and say, "You guys can be anything you want to be", which was quite effective,' says Neil. 'Of course, later he applied some psychological significance to it. He said, to dominate me he had to make me idolise him. I think he was being facetious. In fact I did really – everything he was doing seemed very glamorous.'

Any fights between them didn't get as far as violence. 'I never got beaten up by Tim,' says Neil. 'In fact, I saved him in a fight once.' It's a favourite story: the time Neil rescued Tim in a playground brawl at the convent. 'I was being beaten into submission by this other kid,' says Tim. 'Neil was standing off to one side holding a tennis racquet. I cried, "Neil, Neil!" He came running over and started bashing this guy in the back with his racquet. We both ran home together.'

In 1966, when Tim was 13 and Neil seven, Tim headed off to Auckland where he had won a scholarship to attend Sacred Heart College. A long-established Catholic boarding school for boys, in the 50s the college had relocated from the inner city to Auckland's eastern suburbs. The brick buildings may have been modern and the grounds spacious, but the educational philosophy was a very traditional, Irish Catholic mix of drilled obedience and doctrinal spirituality. Sacred Heart is run by the Marist Brothers, whose approach at the time favoured strict discipline and a dogged concentration on the faith, vocations, academic prowess, rugby and cricket. Nevertheless, Tim thrived in the environment, despite his description in 'Haul Away' years later: *'Small fish, big sea . . . no more happy childhood days for me / Catholic condition, strength through exhaustion.'*

By the end of his time at Sacred Heart, five years later, Tim had won prizes for English literature, praise for his inspirational captaincy of the 2A rugby team, been a member of the idolised First XV and the senior squash champion. He took prominent roles in musicals – *Oliver* and *Trial By Jury* – and drama (the school magazine records his Edmund in *King Lear* as 'competent'). But most importantly, he met Mike Chunn, an Auckland boy who was, with his brother Geoff, a fellow Beatle fanatic. New musical horizons were opened in 1966 with the arrival of New Zealand's first pirate radio station, beaming in from a boat off the Auckland coastline. In the music practice rooms of Sacred Heart, the two Chunns and Tim Finn would seek to recreate the pop songs they heard, and the exotic sounds on *Revolver* and *Sgt Pepper's Lonely Hearts Club Band*.

'The Beatles were a huge, powerful influence,' says Tim. 'That group was pretty much the reason I'm doing what I'm doing today. They affected my life to that extent. They inspired me, they were idols and icons, all of that. Everybody, media included, wanted heroes and I was very much ready for hero worship. Wanting to be in a group, wanting to take drugs, wanting to wear certain clothes – all of that was due to the Beatles. In a certain way we fell in love with them, it bordered on the homo-erotic. There were a lot of other groups that I was into – the Kinks, the Move, other English bands – but the Beatles were it.'

Crucial in their motivation was the broad-mindedness of the music master, Brother Ivan Gannoway. 'Sacred Heart in the '60s was abuzz with creative and performing talent,' says Gannoway, 'more because of a whim of nature which saw exceptional people appear at the same time rather than the facilities.' Described by Chunn as 'a beatnik in disguise', it was Gannoway's championing of Dylan and the Beatles, and encouragement of live performance, which had the lasting influence on his pupils. One day in 1967 he conducted the whole school singing 'Strawberry Fields Forever' in assembly, and he gave his blessing for Chunn's group to organise class concerts. Stunning his peers with his singing in these rudimentary performances of pop hits was Tim Finn. The enterprising Chunn recorded the group on an old reel-to-reel, and played it back to him. 'He said, "Look, you can sing, you can sing",' says Tim. 'And I suddenly realised that I *could* sing, I had a voice.'

In the school holidays, the Chunn brothers continued their recording experiments, while the Finns went to their Mt Maunganui beach house. Surfing and snorkling would be more on Tim's mind than music, but he'd go to dances to hear local bands such as the Hi-Revving Tongues and the Fourmyula. 'At a certain time of the night I'd get pushed by cousins and friends, who would say to the band, we've got a friend who can sing – can he get up?' To his surprise, Tim found his renditions of Bee Gees or Beatles songs were well received. 'So I was very intoxicated and seduced by the notion of being a lead singer,' he says. 'Neil was more like beavering away, learning how to cut it as a musician. I guess he saw me as this glamorous older figure who was the lead singer. He was the guy who would play chords and learn records and, of course, write songs.'

The musical focus of each year at Sacred Heart was the Walter Kirby music prize, keenly competed for by solo and group performers. The first year Mike Chunn entered his group, with Tim singing 'Yesterday', they came third. The next year, they triumphed with Tim warbling a vibrato-heavy version of the Bee Gees' 'Words'. They said farewell to Sacred Heart in 1970, coming first equal with Simon and Garfunkel's 'Frank Lloyd Wright', observed by Mary and Dick Finn in the audience, plus Neil, who would start at the school as a third former the following year. That summer, Neil himself entered a talent quest at Mt Maunganui, but the judges preferred a cabaret singer from Hamilton yodelling 'Quando, Quando' to a 12-year-old's version of Arlo Guthrie's drug ballad 'Coming into Los Angeles'.

A couple of times the Chunn brothers came down to Te Awamutu with their friend Stephen Streat, and rehearsed in the Finns' living-room, with Tim singing. Neil, then 10, excitedly took it all in as they performed several Beatles' songs, the Bee Gees' 'To Love Somebody' and gave him an introduction to Hendrix with 'Hey Joe'. The group played at a party to farewell an American boarder at the Finns, just after the release of the Beatles 'White Album', with Neil keeping time on snare drum. Geoff Chunn recalls, 'Stephen would have worked out "Ob-la-di, Ob-la-da" on the piano, and we had no idea that Neil had probably figured it out the day before.'

Neil credits his father, who when young aspired to be a professional cricketer, with instilling in them a sense of competition and ambition. Like most Catholic boys, Neil thought briefly of becoming a priest; then it was an archaeologist, inspired by the *Tintin* books; then a fireman (having heard about his father, a volunteer in the small town's brigade, fighting 'the legendary Collingwood Farmers Woolshed Blaze of 1954').

Two years after Tim witnessed the Dave Clark Five, Neil had his own epiphany – watching the Beatles perform 'All You Need is Love' on television in a world-wide broadcast was 'amazing, it gave me the chills'. (For Neil's birthday in 1969, Tim gave him a membership in the Beatles fan club.) And when he heard Tim play 'Lara's Theme' from *Dr Zhivago*, Neil worked out the tune on the piano by ear. Later, he worked out a song on the guitar Tim brought back from Auckland – Herman's Hermits' '[Rise and Shine] Sleepy Joe'. By the age of 12, Neil made a commitment to himself: he would be a musician. Inspired by Tim's early efforts with Mike Chunn, he had already started writing songs. 'We never had to rebel to play music,' says Neil, 'so I could make up my mind at a fairly early age without being rubbished. Mum and Dad said fine.' To Mary, 'There was never any doubt that Neil would do music,' she says. 'Whereas with Tim, we thought, a professional life for him, for sure'.

That year, Neil wrote his first song: a tune to some words he found on the back of the first album he bought, *Catch the Wind* by Donovan: *'Precious little do we kiss the sun and drink the rain / We will find out that good can be bad and bad can be good ...'*

Shortly afterwards, Neil went up to Sacred Heart as a boarder. He threw himself into the college activities, hoping to find the same stimulation that Tim had. All the stories he had heard from Tim – about mateship, making music and mischief – made the college sound like a magical place. 'I was expecting, or hoping, that would happen to me. I was so eager to follow in Tim's path that the very first night, we had a pillow fight.' The dormitory master let them off getting the cane so soon; instead, he sentenced them to silence for a week.

But in every aspect of school life, he found he was following Tim's legacy. The music rooms were his main hang-out, where he would have jam sessions with allcomers, but it didn't seem to be as thriving as in Tim's descriptions. 'I was measuring my own experiences against Tim's. The whole scene didn't seem to measure up, though it's stupid to expect it to.'

Despite this, Neil got off to a good start. In his first year, he represented the college in the leading teams of his grade for rugby, tennis and swimming; he also came first in class, topping his form in English,

French, Latin and maths. In the music rooms, he found a rapport with a sixth former, Bernard McHardy, with whom he shared a love for Elton John's *Tumbleweed Connection*. Forming a quartet with Mc-Hardy's two brothers, they took on the Walter Kirby prize, in a year 'of unprecedented interest'. With their four-part harmony version of James Taylor's 'Carolina on My Mind' – Neil took the piano solos – they came first equal in the group section. In the school magazine's photo of the winners, Neil is listed as 'B Finn' – even a year after he had left, the legacy of Brian/Tim was dominant.

So too was the influence of Elton John, who brought a trio to Auckland in October, 1971. It was New Zealand's first international outdoor concert, and Neil had just bought his live album *11-17-70*. Mike Chunn took his younger brother Derek, and Neil, who were in the same class, to see the concert at the Western Springs ampitheatre. The crowd sat quietly on their plastic seats until John kicked back his piano stool near the end. 'It was a very simple move but the crowd went crazy,' says Chunn. 'I was on my chair, screaming, and so were Derek and Neil. We'd never heard anything that loud or that clear. It was very exciting.'

Meanwhile, in Auckland, Tim was a year into a Bachelor of Arts degree. After the restrictions of Sacred Heart, he revelled in the freedom of life at university. At the student hostel, he mingled with a creative and musical crowd which included a trio from Elam art school: Geoffrey (Noel) Crombie, Rob Gillies and Phil Judd. They began jamming in the music rooms, and dabbling with the counter-culture. 'My whole world turned upside down,' he says, 'there was so much freedom there, so many interesting people around who were daring and brave, anarchic and artistic.' Life as a student was never easier: it was the era of full employment, so finding summer jobs wasn't a problem. Student fees were almost non-existent, and exams didn't take place until the end of the year. The '60s having come late to New Zealand, radical behaviour was in vogue for the students: there was still a war in Vietnam to demonstrate against and national conscription to protest. Hair could finally be grown long and – at last – pot began to be available. Elsewhere in society, things changed slowly – in Auckland during this period, Germaine Greer was convicted for saying 'bullshit' at a public meeting (fine: NZ$25), and the musical *Hair* was taken to court for obscenity (case dismissed).

During the Christmas holidays, Neil entered the talent quest at the Mt Maunganui soundshell again and, while his family sat in the stands under blankets, took first place playing Carole King's 'You've Got a Friend'. He won NZ$100. Also that summer, Tim put together a loose ensemble of his university friends and entered a talent quest at the Te Rapa racecourse near Hamilton. Geoff and Mike Chunn played drums and bass, Rob Gillies the flute, Ben Miller was on bongos and Tim at the piano. Singing an original, 'Take it Green', they won NZ$500.

When Neil returned to Sacred Heart in 1972 for the fourth form, his disappointment that 'it wasn't like Tim's time' intensified. 'I became aware that I was following this path of Tim's, trying to have the same experiences he did. Also, the Brothers were relating to me as Tim's little brother, and I wanted to carve my own track.' Witnessing Tim's bohemian lifestyle when visiting his student flat on free Sundays intensified Neil's dissatisfaction. 'I encouraged Neil to be rebellious,' says Tim, 'to be the things I hadn't been. I think it got him very confused.' At the end of the first term, when Neil missed out on a place in the 5A rugby team, that was it: there was nothing more to aim for. He called up his parents in Te Awamutu and said he wanted out – he wanted to come home and go to the local college.

Mary was thrilled to have her youngest back at home for a few more years. Neil found he had a lot more freedom. Carolyn and Tim had left, so there were few distractions at home; and at the co-ed Te Awamutu College, he could have a normal adolescence. He learnt the piano with Mrs Nicholson ('a great teacher'), reaching grade eight, started practising the guitar seriously, and got involved in the local folk and drama clubs. Teenage life in Te Awamutu was actually a lot more lively than being at boarding school in the big city.

About the same time Neil pulled out of boarding school, Tim dropped out of university, to Dick and Mary's dismay. In hindsight, Neil finds their tolerance remarkable, considering his parents' values and expectations. 'Initially, Dad was pretty appalled. First, Tim didn't register for the army. Then, he dropped out of university. And when they found out he'd taken acid, it was a major freak-out.' One day, his parents tearfully told Neil that Tim was taking LSD, and they were going up to Auckland to see him. Neil slipped out to phone Tim and warn him, in case he was tripping when they arrived. 'I sort of watched all this from a safe distance, and got quite excited by it all,' he says.

Living at home, Neil's musical horizons broadened with the purchase of records by Neil Young, Crosby, Stills and Nash, Led Zeppelin, James Taylor, Cat Stevens and David Bowie. The family got a stereo when he was about 13, which made its way into his bedroom. 'Before I had headphones, I'd put my head on a pillow between the speakers and blow my mind. I had a routine when I was going to bed. At night I'd listen to "Revolution 9" and "Good Night" off the "White Album", then drift off to sleep. Complete mayhem, then the total lullaby. Gets you off every time.'

Bold as brass • 1972-83

'When you're from New Zealand you've got to try twice as hard to be noticed by the rest of the world.'

—Neil Finn on Split Enz, 1984

Flatting in Auckland with Phil Judd, Tim immersed himself in musical experiments. Judd was a revelation to Tim, an immensely gifted painter and a budding musician prepared to take risks. By the end of that year, the pair decided to form a band as an outlet for their new songs.

Split Ends was a folky combo when it appeared for the first time on Sunday 10 December, 1972, at the Wynyard Tavern, a café on the edge of Auckland University. Joining Tim Finn, Phil Judd and Mike Chunn were a classical violinist, Miles Golding, and flautist, Mike Howard; Geoff Chunn sat in on drums. Their first performance was over in an instant, their repertoire consisting of three original songs: 'For You', 'Split Ends' and 'Wise Men'.

Judd and Tim began writing together in earnest, and were surprised at the rush of songs which appeared. The pair were determined for the band and its music to be original; the songs were melodic but mercurial, with changing time signatures and no ideas lasting more than a few bars. By taking this uncompromising stance from the outset, the band had already characterised itself as unique.

As John Dix's history of New Zealand rock'n'roll, *Stranded in Paradise*, testifies, by the early '70s, there was no shortage of bands replicating the musical trends taking place overseas. The country had produced its own, often respectable, exponents of every pop genre, who would echo their heroes with increasing speed and accuracy. Achieving nationwide fame in the '50s was Johnny Devlin (New Zealand's Elvis, who outsold the man himself), followed in the '60s by the energetic, showy rock'n'roll of Ray Columbus and the Invaders, the R&B of the La De Das, and the Beatlesque pop of the Fourmyula. For an enthusiastic live audience, seeing New Zealanders making music mattered more than the originality of their work. But the more experimental underground scene was equally healthy, with acts such as the Underdogs, Human Instinct, Ticket, Blerta and Mammal exploring blues, psychedelia and progressive rock to cult audiences.

When private radio was legalised in late 1966 and the Hauraki pirates came on shore, the government stations responded by finally giving pop music substantial airtime. New Zealand had only one television channel (also government run) until 1975, so any pop show was guaranteed an audience. *C'mon* and, from 1970, *Happen Inn* were essential viewing, even if most of the acts were middle-of-the-road, lip-synching cover versions of overseas hits in the pre-video age. Even less hip, but just as avidly watched, were the televised talent quests *Studio One* and *New Faces*, on which the occasional rock band would awkwardly appear beside barbershop quartets and boy sopranos. The live scene was also growing, thanks to licensing law changes. A pub circuit for live music slowly developed, albeit one that demanded bands that were human juke boxes.

The New Zealand music scene developed in an isolated micro-climate; colonial attitudes and over-regulation resulted in an active, if derivative, musical culture. Ironically, the restrictions in broadcasting meant local artists were not swamped by international acts on TV and radio. But the ingrained 'cultural cringe' still meant their music was regarded as somehow second-rate to what they heard from England and America. Originality was a difficult, unrewarding battle in this environment, and any acts which did show promise quickly ran out of options in the limited market. Over-exposed and, in songwriter Hammond Gamble's phrase, 'stranded in paradise', they would head overseas. Usually, they would not get much further than Australia, and come home weary, humble and broke.

It was onto this stage that Split Enz emerged, romantic, naive, and stubborn. For the band's next gig, Carolyn, Judy and Neil Finn drove up to be in the audience. Neil recalled later, 'Back then I was still a pimply schoolboy but that performance and those first songs made a lasting impression on me. I went back to Te Awamutu and wrote Split Ends on my pencil case.' He also witnessed their poorly received set at the Great Ngaruawahia Music Festival. The Waikato audience, waiting for the headliners, Black Sabbath, had no time for Split Ends' effete, esoteric folk.

In the months that followed, Split Ends went on a national university tour, the main live outlet for original music. On stage, Tim emerged as the band's natural leader and – possibly due to nervousness – a dynamic, compelling frontman. By the tour's end, the group had expanded its audience but, ditching the acoustic players, made the first of many lineup changes. The band was no longer a folky combo.

Determined not to play the pub circuit, the band entered the television talent quest *New Faces*. Split Ends won its heat and when the final screened, the Finn family was watching in their Te Awamutu living room. Beside Neil on the carpet whirred a Super-8 movie camera, capturing the performance in the pre-VCR era. The judging panel placed them seventh out of eight: 'too clever' was the majority verdict. Phil Judd and Tim walked out; at home, Neil was almost in tears.

Early in 1974, Tony (Eddie) Rayner came in on keyboards. Rayner, who had briefly been at Sacred Heart College, a year behind Tim and Chunn, had proved himself a dazzling player in bands such as Cruise Lane (R&B) and Orb (progressive). However Phil Judd had developed a distaste for performing live. 'I hate it,' he told the Auckland rock magazine *Hot Licks*, 'it disturbs me.'

But the band established its live reputation with successively theatrical appearances at the Buck-a-Head concerts promoted by Radio Hauraki. Also, the name of the band was changed to Split Enz, to emphasise its New Zealand identity. The band spent weeks in preparation, Noel Crombie designing bizarre costumes and eventually becoming a fulltime member, playing percussion and a show-stopping spoon solo.

Their stage act was a psychedelic mix of art rock, *opera buffa*, Monty Python and old-fashioned music hall. Eccentric personas became a trademark; Tim began introducing songs with mock-Shakespearean soliloquies, and pranced the stage like a man possessed. Inside, however, he was still a shy performer – stage fright would mean his eyes were often jammed shut as he sang.

Split Enz became the essential local band to witness, and the critics' darlings. The rest of the country saw what the fuss was about on a well-received national university tour early in 1975. In March, Split Enz finally made the move which so many other New Zealand bands had done before. It was time to conquer other territories; they headed for Australia. By May, Split Enz was recording its debut album, *Mental Notes*. The members had also – Phil Judd excepted – decided to use their middle names: Brian Finn was now Tim Finn.

In the two years since leaving Sacred Heart, Neil had settled into a busy, more liberated life as a student at Te Awamutu College. He was adopted by Graham Hare, who introduced him to a close-knit group of friends, many of whom had been together since kindergarten. Neil was first noticed after breaking his arm playing rugby. 'We originally thought he was a bit of a wimp, but he was the strong one when it came to standing up to the teachers,' says Dean Taylor, a classmate of Neil's at college, and now a journalist with the *Te Awamutu Courier*.

In Te Awamutu, Neil was getting involved in musical activities of his own, performing at school and at parties, playing guitar when slipping away with his friends at lunchtimes (a routine which later inspired his song 'Kia Kaha'). Neil took part in a production written by the Te Awamutu Light Opera Society, *Henry Tudor's Flying Circus*, a medieval Monty Python spoof. He played the role of Culpepper, and also contributed a song.

Neil also attended regular meetings of the All 'n Some Folk Club. Run by Felicity Saxby, an outgoing mother-of-four, the club was the only place in the town where Neil could meet and play with other musicians. 'There was nothing else going on,' he says. 'So I would hang out with these folkies. I went to a couple of festivals, which were fantastic fun. Camping out with hippie-ish types, sitting around the fire singing old English folk songs.' Although his interest in traditional music was limited, it related to what he was hearing on his records at home, and his love of harmony singing grew. His schoolfriends also joined the folk club, 'though we weren't in it for the music,' admits Taylor. They enjoyed the regular beer drinking competition called 'flonking'. At a festival at Tauranga, while Neil was asleep, his school friends won a bottle of scotch whisky. Another party in Tauranga was an initiation for Neil: he secured his first kiss (made awkward by his broken arm) and smoked his first joint. 'It was full of seeds, so I didn't get stoned, but the seeds smelt fantastic and kept exploding. I felt like a million bucks.' Neil travelled up to Auckland to go to a Jethro Tull concert the day *Thick As a Brick* was released. 'Tim was really sheepish when we got in the car. He said, "Look Neil, we're going to this friend's house on the way. We're going to smoke some pot." I said, that's alright – I've already smoked it. He said, "What!"' This time, it worked. 'I remember bouncing down the road to the Town Hall, feeling I was on the moon. A really good concert.'

With the folk club he sang at Te Awamutu institutions such as the Waikeria borstal, the Tokanui mental home and at the Plunket Society for nursing mothers. For a few weeks, from a teacher in nearby Te Aroha, he learnt the fingerpicking and clawhammer guitar styles much used by Bert Jansch and acolytes such as Donovan. He developed an interest in classical music after Tim played him Dvoràk, Wagner and Bach.

Saxby introduced Neil to Rod Murdoch, a Waikato guitarist who was 10 years his senior and had broad tastes in music. Besides folk, Murdoch was interested in classical, soul and blues, and played in a rock'n'roll revival band. On weekends Neil began to travel to Ngaruawahia, a small town about 24 miles north of Te Awamutu, and jam with Murdoch. 'It was a valuable musical time,' he says. 'It was the first sense of getting in the zone and really communicating with another musician.' Meanwhile, says Taylor, 'Neil was fanatical about everything Split Enz were doing, going to concerts and telling us all about them.'

Split Enz returned to New Zealand in July 1975 for another national tour. As a support act in Tauranga and Hamilton, Neil and Rod Murdoch did a brief set. Tim stood at the side of the stage, impressed by the fearlessness of his younger brother in front of an audience.

Mental Notes was warmly received in both countries, though it made little impact beyond those who had experienced the band live. The elaborate, lengthy pieces were never destined for radio airplay or the singles charts. If the album had been made just a few years earlier – and in another hemisphere – it might be regarded as an art-rock classic.

Phil Manzanera of Roxy Music offered to produce an album for the band. The sessions were to take place in England; just going there would be the fulfilment of a dream. Before leaving, they embarked on an Enz of the Earth tour of Australia and New Zealand. Chosen as the support act in New Zealand was 17-year-old Neil Finn, who had just left school. He would slip through the curtain and, on piano, guitar and mandolin, perform a 20-minute set of his own songs such as 'Mother of Five', 'Platform Three' and 'Late in Rome' (the latter was written with Rod Murdoch and eventually released by the Enz as 'Serge'), plus the Beatles' 'Blackbird'.

'I remember how gutsy he was at that age,' says Tim. 'To play not just covers, but his own songs, in front of 2000 people. Neil always felt that being on stage was a natural space to inhabit. I don't think he went through that blind terror that I went through.'

In Dunedin, Neil was nervous enough to say 'Hello, Christchurch' to the audience. But in Christchurch, Jude Fahey, the young music critic on *The Press*, wrote:

'I would like to get it on record now that Neil Finn is a singer of great potential. Timothy's 17-year-old brother sang and performed his own material along with two or three Lennon-McCartney numbers. The standard of both lyrics and tunes was astounding. Barely out of school, [his] writing and use of voice is already quite sophisticated and sensitive.

'Brother Timothy considers him a born performer and adds, "I don't believe in performers necessarily making it just on their own merits. If I can help him I certainly will."

'We await more from Neil Finn.'

Neil says that at the time, he was 'awestruck, just completely embroiled in the whole Split Enz thing. Even if I wasn't Tim's brother, I would have thought those guys were incredible. It was an amazing way to get inspired.'

Split Enz arrived in London in April, 1976 to record *Second Thoughts*. Tim remembers Manzanera telling them, 'There's a huge hole, a gap in the music scene. Everybody's waiting for something to happen. You guys are going to be that.' Then punk exploded. 'The battle lines were drawn,' says Tim. 'You were either punk, or you weren't, and it was a very exclusive club. Split Enz was somewhere else altogether, so we got swept aside. But it was a brilliant time to be in London.'

By the end of the year, they were headlining their own tour and a cult audience had emerged which called itself Frenz of the Enz. But without experienced management, or an agency, and Tim and Phil no longer writing together, the band was actually going backwards. Debts were growing, as was internal discontent.

Chrysalis released the Manzanera-produced album in the United States and, after a New Zealand tour, Split Enz flew straight to Los Angeles. For the six-week American tour, Chrysalis rolled out the promotional machinery. The initial spotlight was exhilarating and promised much, but there was no single to generate radio play. Reality soon became apparent when the band began to outnumber its audiences. Missing his family, and tired of the exhausting, fruit-less grind, Phil Judd's commitment started to unravel. One night in Atlanta, Georgia, he left the stage in the middle of the set. Tim confronted him in the dressing-room. Judd – feeling cornered and under siege – punched him on the chin and declared he was leaving. He finished the tour with them, then the man who many saw as the heart of Split Enz was no longer part of the band he had co-founded.

Heading back to London, Tim became the main songwriter, and his new songs were unlike the multi-layered epics of *Mental Notes*. They were more like pop songs. Meanwhile, Mike Chunn returned to New Zealand to see his family.

Neil had left Te Awamutu College early in 1976 when the headmaster wouldn't let him specialise in music. Instead, he got a job working at Martin's Refrigeration, a local store selling electrical appliances, musical instruments and records. 'Charlie Pride and Klaus Wunder-lich were the two biggest sellers,' he says. 'I'd have to demonstrate home organs, which I thought were revolting things. Occasionally I'd be really bold and order a Gibson Les Paul – no-one would ever buy it, but I could mess with it in the shop.'

During the Enz of the Earth tour, Neil had talked with Mark Hough, an artist friend and acolyte of Phil Judd's. Hough suggested he come up to Auckland and move in with him and his girlfriend. Neil took up the offer, found a job at a record warehouse and, later, as a hospital orderly. Hough, an aspirant musician, was keen to collaborate. They began writing songs together, with Neil on the piano and Hough as lyricist. The songs were heavily influenced by the Enz, some of them 10 minutes long, with complex structures and many time changes.

The pair began rehearsing with Geoff Chunn on guitar, and Hough on drums. But their enthusiasm dwindled, and the group soon dissolved. A year later Geoff was asked to play support at a university concert. He called Neil: was he interested? Of course. 'Neil was a man with a mission,' he says. 'He would do anything to be on stage.' The trio reunited, adding Alan Brown on bass. Geoff found the Enz parallels 'a bit weird' – a younger Chunn, a younger Finn and, in Hough, a Judd equivalent – but the group had a good rapport. They called themselves After Hours.

At lunchtime on 13 March, the lights dimmed at the Maidment, a small theatre on the Auckland university campus. On the stage was a lampstand, armchairs, potplants – and Alan Brown, reading a newspaper. Neil, wearing hornrim glasses for effect, began with his short ballad, 'Fall Out With the Lads'. The quartet's sound was dominated by Geoff's guitar, which showed jazz influences, and Neil's rhythm piano in the style of Elton John and Carole King. The songs were all original, well rehearsed, carefully arranged and full of melodic hooks.

The concert was more like a recital, with the small audience clapping between items. The band was unaware that Mike Chunn was in the theatre, just home from the American tour. Back in the country only a few hours, he was impressed by the richness of the voices and the quality of the songs. Afterwards, he went backstage to congratulate them on their successful debut.

While in New Zealand, Chunn approached an acquaintance of Split Enz to be the band's new guitarist. Alistair Riddell had been the lead singer of Orb and, with his group Space Waltz, had won the TV talent quest *New Faces*. But Riddell wasn't interested – his career languished thereafter – and Chunn returned to London. The Enz began preparing their new songs for recording a new album. First, however, they needed to sort out the problem of finding someone to replace Judd. It was a daunting prospect: auditioning dozens of would-be guitar heroes. The winner needed to fit in musically *plus* comprehend the Split Enz aesthetic – and the album sessions were only two weeks away.

Chunn realised there was an easy way out, in fact it had already been talked about as a possibility: Neil Finn should join the band. Chunn argued that while Neil wasn't a great guitarist – he didn't even own an electric guitar – more importantly, he understood the Enz culture, was young, malleable and showed promise as a musician and songwriter.

Tim called his mother in Te Awamutu and asked her to get Neil to ring him. Neil called from Auckland shortly afterwards, and Tim put the question to him: 'How would you like to join Split Enz?' Neil replied, 'I'll have to think about it. I'll call you back.' Tim was a little surprised, but a few minutes later, Neil called again. He accepted.

Neil had After Hours to consider. That very week, they were scheduled to play a second concert at the Maidment. He went to tell Geoff Chunn his decision, who replied, 'I can't blame you. Go.' But, he says, 'Alan and I were crestfallen. We thought we'd found something beautiful.'

It was Monday, 4 April, when Neil got the call. He quickly arranged his affairs and got a passport. On Thursday, at the Maidment, After Hours played its second and last gig. (Brent Eccles, later of the Angels, replaced Hough on drums.) Then they headed to Harlequin Studios and recorded the songs for posterity. Geoff Chunn describes Neil as 'terribly excited, in a state of euphoria and organisation'. That night, Neil was on the plane to London. He was six weeks away from his 19th birthday.

A day after suggesting Neil, Mike Chunn decided that he, too, needed to leave the band, for family and health reasons. Split Enz now had an English rhythm section; in only a few weeks, the band had made decisive steps away from its beginnings.

For Neil, arriving in London seemed like a Monopoly board was unfolding before his eyes. When he met the others at a rehearsal room, he was 'still spinning from the plane trip', says saxophonist Rob Gillies. He was given a tape of the new songs, sent into Soho to buy an electric guitar, 'then he was right into learning all of Phil's bizarre guitar parts. He started harmonising with Tim and instantly the vocals leapt to a new dimension.'

Within days, the band began recording *Dizrythmia* with Geoff Emerick at AIR Studios, owned by Beatles producer George Martin. In the sessions, he surprised the others with his edgy guitar lines, which suited the sharper, more focused songs. In concert, Neil knew how to be a Split End – put on a pair of specs and leap about madly – but his guitar playing needed work. 'In the beginning, he was down in the mix, but not for long,' says Gillies. 'It was more important that he fitted right in.' Years later, Enz bass player Nigel Griggs recalled to the *Dominion*, 'Neil did about five years' work in the first year. But he had to. When he first joined nobody wanted to stand near him on stage.'

After the album was completed, the band flew out to New Zealand for a few weeks break. Tim and Neil went down to Te Awamutu and wrote their first song together, 'Best Friend'. In Auckland, Neil stayed with Paul Pattie, an airbrush artist and friend of Crombie's at university. Visiting the house one day was Sharon Johnson, who got talking with Neil in the kitchen. The same age as Neil, she had seen Split Enz from the Buck-a-Head days. Tim's English girlfriend, Liz Malam – who later became his wife – thought Neil and Sharon were a good match, so encouraged a date. The pair found an immediate rapport, and spent the next 18 months writing to each other. 'It was a courtship by a long communication, from a distance. We were both young, and idealistic about marriage and love and all that stuff.'

Dizrythmia was well received upon its release. While still clever, busy and well-crafted, its more accessible style suited the era. It looked as though the band had made their breakthrough, and increasing interest in their live shows seemed to confirm it.

But early in the new year, Chrysalis leant on Split Enz to produce a hit single before another album was recorded. It became a standoff; when the band refused, they were dropped from the label. Although this conveniently meant $150,000 in debt was written off, it resulted in Split Enz spending a year broke and frustrated, just when its live act had never been more focused.

In England, Neil was living on the outskirts of London with Noel Crombie. Their old cottage had a romantic address – 1, Appletree Dell, Dog Kennel Lane, Chorley Wood, Rickmansworth, Hertfordshire – but they had little to live on. The band was at its lowest ebb, but it was an exciting time for its youngest member.

Neil and Crombie started jamming together, recording into two cassette players. Crombie says that working on songs and sounds together in an 'indulgent' way gave him 'an inkling that Neil had a lot of good songs in him somewhere'.

Although the band played very few live gigs in 1978, they were on a creative wave, writing and rehearsing often, honing their more direct style. A grant of NZ$5000 from the New Zealand arts council kept them from starving; but with no management, the Enz were unable to secure another record deal.

A fan gave them some free recording time at a studio with David Tickle, an 18-year-old engineer who was said to be brilliant. The band and Tickle immediately clicked, and soon recorded a song, 'I See Red', which forcefully captured the punchy new Enz. It convinced Michael Gudinski of Mushroom in Australia to reinvest in the band.

'I See Red' was released as a single, and its tough, frenetic drive also captured the moment. It reached No. 12 in the Australian charts. The band stayed in the southern hemisphere, recording demos, writing songs, sustaining themselves with several short tours which confirmed the impact of 'I See Red'. However their followup singles, which gave Neil his first songwriting credits, both failed. 'Give It a Whirl', off their album *Frenzy*, was an uneasy mix of grinding punk guitar and cheerleading vocal, but the sparse dance-pop of 'Things', produced by the band themselves, revealed the direction Neil's songwriting was taking.

The band settled in Sydney, with Sharon coming over to join Neil in a flat with Tim and Liz Malam. Tim had already written 'I Hope I Never' and 'Poor Boy'; now the brothers spent their days writing songs. 'We'd give each other titles and go off to our respective parts of the house, then come back and see what we'd done,' says Tim.

Noel Crombie remembers the day Neil played through a new song to the others at rehearsal. 'He went *chug chug chug chug* on the guitar and everyone sat around fairly nonplussed. We thought, not a bad little song, we'll give that one a go.' The song was 'I Got You', and although it seemed a little trite to Neil, he was convinced by the others to leave it alone.

David Tickle was hired as producer and, coming straight from the simple power-pop of Blondie and the Knack, made sure they found a basic, uncluttered sound. With punk and new wave, pop music had rediscovered itself; once more, snappy, three-minute singles were the goal. For Tim and Neil, this meant a return to the pop values they had grown up with.

Everything finally clicked into place. The band had the right song at the right time, plus more strong contenders for followup singles. Shrewd management decisions made sure the opportunity wasn't squandered. 'I Got You' and the album, *True Colours*, were smash hits in Australia and New Zealand, topping the charts in both countries simultaneously. After seven years, Split Enz were the region's biggest drawcards ... and Neil Finn was suddenly a pop star.

In Britain, 'I Got You' reached No. 12 (10 in some charts), even getting a play on *Coronation Street*. The album eventually sold more than 700,000 copies worldwide and reached 40 in the US charts. But while the single made the Canadian Top 10, in the States it stalled just inside the Top 50. The band learnt about the realities of hitmaking in the US. All it would take to get into the Top 10, they were told, was to pay $100,000 to the independent radio promoters.

The followup album was finally released in April 1981, as *Waiata* in New Zealand and *Corroboree* in Australia, once again topping the charts in both countries. The lead song, 'Hard Act to Follow', was written by Tim; the singles, 'One Step Ahead' and 'History Never Repeats', by Neil. With each album, it seemed, the hits seesawed between the brothers. Wrote New Zealand critic Roy Colbert, 'The two Finns are beatling down the home straight, shoulder to shoulder, hurling diamonds at each other as they run.' The press was certain there must be rivalry between the brothers, and saw Tim's awkward onstage banter with Neil – intended as humorous, it came across as patronising – as evidence. But, Tim told the New Zealand *Listener*, 'Neil coming into the band has been fantastic. He had all these songs, eagerness, talent. Neil used to be my kid brother, now he's my equal. He can also cut me down to size easier than anybody, and more effectively. He sees right through my tantrums.'

Neil saw Tim's role in the band as the natural leader: 'He's good at motivating others. He can be a negative force within the band sometimes – he's quite moody and subject to bouts of depression. But in other ways, because he's such a tempestuous person, he inspires everyone else.'

Just after the release of *Waiata*, the lineup changed again: Noel Crombie was appointed drummer. Tim's writing was the strength of their next album, 1982's *Time & Tide*. The new songs were his most autobiographical: 'Haul Away' was his life story, 'Dirty Creature' revealed his anxieties, 'Six Months in a Leaky Boat' used the metaphor of the emigration to New Zealand for the striving to achieve. Finding success after years of ambition had come at a personal cost to Tim; his marriage to Liz Malam ended, his goals achieved, he was on the verge of a nervous breakdown.

Australia, New Zealand and Canada responded with their usual fervour to the album and the band's shows, and it looked as though the uplifting 'Six Months in a Leaky Boat' was breaking through on British radio – until the Falklands war started and, with the Empire's navy steaming towards the South Atlantic, the song was removed from the airwaves.

Split Enz had been on a rollercoaster for a decade, with the years of success even more arduous than those of frustration. Fatigue was setting in, causing bad decisions, and the relationship with Mushroom had deteriorated. The band took a break for a few months – but the period of time out kept getting longer.

In 1983, Tim embarked on a solo record with a group of stellar session musicians, recording songs which had been deemed unsuitable for the Enz. He particularly found a rapport with Ricky Fataar, a laidback drummer who, besides work with the Beach Boys, had been 'Stig O'Hara' in the Beatles parody band the Rutles. The album, *Escapade*, and its single, 'Fraction Too Much Friction', cruised to the top of the charts on both sides of the Tasman.

Meanwhile, Split Enz was in limbo. 'If we'd known we were going to wait so long,' says Neil, 'we probably would have done more with our time.' Neil did some production work with Karen Ansell, who had sung with the Reels and the Melbourne band Bang (featuring Nick Seymour on bass).

By the time they got into the studio, Neil had several strong songs ready, among them his most candid love song, 'Message to My Girl', and a song about parenthood, 'Our Day', which was imminent (Liam was born on September 24). Tim came to the sessions distracted. Demands caused by the success of *Escapade* had prevented him from concentrating on songwriting, but the album's title came from one of his songs: *Conflicting Emotions*.

I say we're having fun
• November, 1983

'My ambitions. Music: to become a leading drummer in the world and to have a successful pop group.'

—Paul Hester, school essay, 1967

For a lead singer, Tim Finn had always been conscious of the importance of drummers – ever since he was 14, and saw the Dave Clark Five, in which the singer *was* the drummer, sitting in front of the band. After the unsatisfactory recording of *Conflicting Emotions*, Tim lobbied for the Enz to recruit yet another drummer.

Neil rang Rob Hirst, Midnight Oil's drummer, and asked if he knew of anybody he could recommend. Hirst suggested Paul Hester, formerly of Deckchairs Overboard, who was then living in Sydney with Deborah Conway of Do-Re-Mi. Hester had recently been talking about his future to Hirst.

'I told him I wasn't into drumming anymore,' says Paul. 'Unless, of course, one of the big bands phoned him for an audition. If so, ring me and I'll go – as long as I don't have to lug my own gear, I'm in.'

A week later, Hirst got the call from Neil, and Paul was invited to Melbourne to audition. At the time, Paul was toying with the idea of getting into acting – his father had been involved in amateur theatre – and that very week he had actually got two parts, in a film *Coolangatta Gold* and a TV series about a young rock band called *Sweet and Sour*. He was to play the drummer in the latter.

'So I thought, will I pretend to be a drummer – or will I actually try and be a drummer?' He headed for Melbourne, his acting career on hold.

Unlike his colleagues in Crowded House, Paul Hester wasn't the youngest member of a family with something to prove. 'I'm just a bastard son of Mike and Anne,' he once said on Australian radio, 'I don't have any relatives. Once they saw me, they stopped.'

But like Neil Finn and Nick Seymour, Paul's interest in music had been nurtured by his mother. 'Anne Hester,' he says, pausing for effect, 'is marvellous. A jazzer, a drummer, a right-hander, a smoker.'

Anne Hester was part of the thriving Melbourne jazz scene in the 1950s and '60s, with many friends who were musicians, including Chris Karan who was later in the Dudley Moore Trio. She was a regular at the local jazz clubs where there would usually be jam sessions featuring any international players who were often visiting Melbourne then.

Although Paul's mother never played professionally, he says she has that crucial quality: she swings. 'Not many people swing anymore, but ol' Anne can swing.' His father, Mike, bought Anne a small snare drum and cymbal and she would play small gigs and parties. 'My Dad couldn't hold a tune to save himself. But he encouraged the family. He loved to talk while Mum and me were on the drums.'

His mother's kit was set up in the house, so Paul would have a go, and she started to teach him when he was about five years old. She began with brushes, playing on an album cover. It wasn't long before she bought him a kit of his own. Then, like the Finn brothers, he'd be dragged into performing at his parents' parties. 'They'd wake me up and get me to come down in the middle of the party. I'd play drums to one side of [Creedence Clearwater Revival's] *Cosmo's Factory*, and then go back to bed. Which is what later happened in bands – I'd take a nap before gigs and have to be woken up to go on stage. I like to play after I wake up.'

From about the age of nine, he was in a band called Electric Woodfish which did well in the talent quest in the primary school social. He always seemed to be in the limelight, in whatever he did. 'I act rather stupid just to impress my friends,' he wrote in 1967 school essay. 'I would rather be a quiet little kid who just sat there and did a couple of funny things but not act stupid.' Talking about the ebbs and flows of fame to *Juke* in 1991, Paul said, 'I remember going from Highvale State School in Melbourne – as the football captain, the cricket captain, the house captain and the best long distance runner in the school – and going to Glen Waverly High School and becoming the apron monitor in woodwork. It's all pretty relative.'

He was in a few bands at high school, towards the end of which the Hesters were living in the Dandenong Ranges, a rural area outside of Melbourne. There were a lot of alternative lifestyle communities dotted about the district, and from the age of about 15, Paul was mingling with 'old hippies, jamming with them at dances on the weekends'. Then, in 1977–78, when the punk explosion hit the Melbourne music scene, he joined a few punk bands, 'and that's when it got really exciting'. He was in the International Exiles, who were influenced by acts on the Stiff label: edgy power-pop, nothing over three minutes. They would support acts such as the Models and the Birthday Party.

The unpretentious ideals of the era suited Paul, whose two drumming idols were the no-frills legends: 'Ringo ... and Charlie. The skiffle-type pop drummers of the '60s with their funny little quirks.' Ringo Starr, who never played the bass drum during a fill; Charlie Watts, who never hit the snare and the hi-hat at the same time.

Meanwhile, Paul flitted between day jobs, holding more than 20 in a two-year period, including working on a chicken farm, at a dental factory making fillings, in a timber yard and even self-employed as a house renovator. 'The first job I did I ended up forking out $100 over what I got paid. It was for a sweet ol' granny. I think she saw me coming actually.'

In the early '80s, he joined a band called Cheks, who evolved into Deckchairs Overboard. After three or four years building up a fan base in Melbourne, it was time to expand, so the Deckchairs moved north to Sydney. 'That's where we lost our way. We made an EP, and started an album which we never finished. It was my first foray into the real music business – and I'd never lived in Sydney before, so it was fascinating. Going to all these clubs, seeing the seedier side of life. We got a bit side-tracked there for a while and after a couple of years I decided to leave. I went overseas for a big holiday, and gave up drumming.'

Ten drummers auditioned for the place in the Enz. Paul impressed the band with his work on the swampy, staccato 'Dirty Creature'. After three sessions with the band, they finally gave him the nod and he went back to Sydney to pack. While there he went into Festival Studios, and asked the engineer to play the master tapes of *Escapade*, mixing out the band tracks so he could focus on the drumming of Ricky Fataar, and discover the secrets of his simple style.

This impressed Tim, with whom Paul had found an immediate rapport. At the auditions, Tim had let on that he wanted Paul to get the job. So when Paul drove down to Melbourne, he moved into the big Caulfield house where Tim was living alone.

Joining the Enz was like becoming a member of a tight-knit extended family. So Paul took his back-seat role and checked out the group dynamics. It had been a while since he had been in a band which loved playing as much as the Enz. 'I thought they'd be too bored to rehearse with me.' Instead, the band spent 17 straight days preparing for the *Conflicting Emotions* tour.

They jammed at night until everyone was exhausted. 'It really taught me a lesson, that that's what kept the whole vibe going.' Paul was also taken aback by the competitiveness of the Enz, 'whether it be pool, bike riding, paper aeroplanes, just parking the car – anything. I'd never encountered such a competitive bunch of people before. It worked well with the music, too.'

The *Conflicting Emotions* tour revitalised the band, and climaxed with an outdoor show in Te Awamutu celebrating the town's centenary. Although their parents had retired to Cambridge, nearby, the Finn brothers were treated like prodigal sons, with a Maori haka taking place during Neil's tribute to his schooldays, 'Kia Kaha'. After the tour, Neil said, 'We came right back from feeling depressed to feeling really good. It was a lot of fun having Paul on the road. He's very vibrant and it was a really good thing for the band to have a new personality there. It was a great change. It made us feel good about being Split Enz again. But all during this time, you couldn't help but run through your mind all the alternatives, all the other things you could be doing.'

Tim, also, formed a solid bond with the new drummer. 'He was coming from the right place for what we needed at the time. It was really good for me. I was aware that the end was nigh and it was good to have this new kid on the block, wide-eyed and funny – he kept me up.'

Tim and Paul continued the role-playing they'd developed at home in Caulfield. 'We developed characters,' says Paul, 'Wrongie and Longie, two old gentlemen of the rock industry that were getting on a bit, gout was setting in. On the tour we tried to remain undressed and unshaven as long as possible in the day. We'd be in our hotel complimentary robes, ordering drinks up to the room. We had a competition to see who could ring each other up the earliest in the day to suggest a gin and tonic. "Perhaps we should burn one down before soundcheck, darling." '

In late January, Tim met Greta Scacchi, through the director of *The Coca-Cola Kid*, for which he was writing some songs. He was smitten, and his courting of her became a game as well. At their house Paul built a shrine to the actress out of photos in the *TV Week*, and when Tim found it he declared, 'Don't mock this, you'll ruin it. It won't happen.'

'Yes it *will*, Tim, it's going to happen.'

Paul was in an awkward situation. At home, Tim would talk about his experience with *Escapade*, and the inspiration he got from playing with other musicians, exploring funkier rhythms. 'It was like one of those soapies on TV,' says Paul, 'where you've got a child of 12 counselling the parents about their relationship. I was tempted to say to Tim, "Well, maybe you should go and be with this girl." I was certainly there for him . . . I'd have been out the door weeks ago.'

The band was keen to record again as quickly as possible. Tim wanted to use a big overseas name to produce, to revive the band internationally. But with no overseas label interested in *Conflicting Emotions*, it may have taken a while. 'We were prepared to do an album, whatever,' says Neil. 'We wanted to set a date. But it came to a point where we were rehearsing songs and it just seemed very vague. Tim just lost interest, I think. I suppose he'd experienced the flexibility of being a solo performer and enjoyed it.'

In 1995, Tim told Australian journalist Lawrie Zion, 'I was distracted by two things. One was the success of *Escapade*, the other was falling in love with Greta Scacchi. Those two things gave me a catapult into a new life. Without them I would probably never have wanted to leave the band.'

The band was stuck, waiting for Tim to make a decision. By June, 'Tim decided that he was probably causing more conflict than helping the band,' says Neil. 'We had a couple of rehearsals where he got really depressed. He'd obviously been thinking about it for a long time and the experiences of the year all built up and he just made his mind up one night. He rang us up and said he'd decided to leave, and I said, "Oh well, at least it's something definite." '

The band all went out to dinner, got drunk, and sang 'Bon Voyage' to Tim, who shed a tear. He then flew off to London to join Scacchi. The news of Tim's departure made headlines in Australia and New Zealand; it was greeted with sadness but not surprise. The rest of the band were determined to carry on.

About three weeks later, however, Neil began to have doubts. 'Was I committed enough to put another year, maybe two or three, into the band? It was also like the responsibility was on my shoulders to redefine this big thing: *Split Enz*.'

Neil went around to Eddie Rayner's house and poured out his feelings to the rest of the band. 'Eddie said, "That's exactly what I've been thinking for a long time, too." The others were less eager to end it, but they understood.'

The band made plans for a grand farewell tour through Australia and New Zealand, with Tim included. Then, without Tim, they recorded the last Split Enz album, *See Ya 'Round*. Included was Paul Hester's 'This is Massive', but most of the songs were by Neil. 'Fallout With the Lads' from the first After Hours concert in 1977, he reworked and renamed 'Voices': '*I hear voices leading me on / the wise and the strong.*'

The Enz With a Bang tour was a triumphant, emotional celebration for band and audience, a wake rather than a funeral. The last Australian gig was at the Festival Hall in Melbourne. Neil had a cathartic night, throwing off heavy metal solos throughout the show – and eventually throwing himself off the stage in a swan dive. 'The audience didn't catch me and I went crashing into the chairs,' he says. 'I remember going backstage between the set and the encore and just weeping. It was mental.'

Afterwards, there was a party at the Tropicana Club. Late in the evening, Neil was approached by Nick Seymour. 'He said, "I want to try out for your new band." I said, sure, anything – I'd had 14 tequila slammers. Nick brought me home. It was dreadful. I threw up everywhere.'

During the farewell tour, things started to fall into place for the future. Behind the scenes, working for the promoter Ian Magan, was Grant Thomas, the tour accountant. The entertainment business had always been a passion for Thomas. As a teenager in Martinborough, he'd been in a band with his brother Brent. 'I tried to be a musician, I knew I was no good, even though I loved playing,' he says. Together they went to see a concert in Wellington in 1968. On the bill were the Small Faces, Paul Jones from Manfred Mann, with the Who topping the bill. The Thomas brothers were sitting five rows from the front as the Who set about demolishing their expensive guitars and amplifiers, all impossible to get in New Zealand at that time. 'That night, I realised, I don't have the x factor,' he says. 'But I also realised they didn't end up on stage on their own. Behind the scenes something was happening. So I ended up managing the band Brent and I were in.'

Thomas went into a hotel management career, and was running a hotel in Invercargill when he first met Neil. The Enz had returned to the hotel after their concert to find a staff party in full swing. Most of the band ended up on stage, while outside, Neil was placing a dining-room table and set of chairs in the swimming pool. Next morning, Thomas had an argument with Ian Magan, who was adamant the Enz weren't the culprits. Shortly afterwards, Thomas ended up on Magan's staff, organising tours.

Out in the audience at the final Auckland show was Gary Stamler, a music attorney from Los Angeles. He had stopped off in New Zealand with his ·wife Peggy, after representing Eric Burdon in Australia. That evening, he read in the paper about the demise of Split Enz, a band he'd never seen, though he had heard one of their records. The Enz show was just about to start, so Stamler jumped in a taxi to the venue, where he bought one of the last tickets. 'That night I was very taken by Neil's performance,' says Stamler. 'I came away with a strong notion that Neil Finn had the ability to become an international pop star.' When he arrived back in Los Angeles, he told a close friend what he'd seen. Tom Whalley was an A&R man for Warner Bros Records. 'I don't know what this Neil Finn's obligations are,' Stamler said, 'but I have a strong instinct about him. I'd sign him in a minute.' Whalley replied, 'Tim Finn, Neil Finn ... I'd have to listen to the records. I don't know the difference.'

Just before soundcheck one night in Auckland, the rest of the band came across Neil and Paul, already on stage. They were jamming with Bones Hillman, who had been the bassplayer in Phil Judd's band the Swingers, and was later in Midnight Oil. 'That's when it hit me that the Enz were over, and we were off,' says Paul.

Before the tour, Neil said that he would definitely be working with Paul in the future. 'I'm keen to keep it small, because part of being in a band is accepting other peoples' stamp on your music. It's curiosity, I guess. I want to see how my ideas shape my songs. I like the idea of another band. But we haven't burnt any bridges, we're all still friends. We're all capable of coming together and playing together, which is a very secure feeling.'

Boys next door • 1958-84

'I originally saw pop music as my ticket out of wherever I was. If you were focused, you could put one foot in front of another and create a whole lifestyle, and a successful business, out of it, and it would take you around the world.'

—Nick Seymour, 1996

It was Nick Seymour's mother who was the musical parent; his father the enthusiast who encouraged the rest of the family. Frank Seymour, a school headmaster in rural Victoria, was a dedicated record collector. He had a large and diverse collection, with Gilbert and Sullivan at one end, the classics at the other. 'When he wanted to take the piss out of you, he'd always come back with a sung chorus from Gilbert and Sullivan, some turn of phrase which was very theatrical, almost camp,' says Nick.

His father's classical section was wide-ranging: Mozart, Beethoven, Tchaikovsky, Grieg, Mussorgsky, Saint-Saëns, Albinoni. He knew all the pieces well, and could always find a famous melody. On Sundays, he would fill the house with popular classics. 'You'd be dragging your feet around, saying, "Oh God, Dad's playing classics again," says Nick. 'He'd be in the lounge, conducting away, being totally pretentious, and he'd try and get you in there. He'd say, listen to this bit – and if you ever showed any interest in one tune, just one hook of a classic, he'd find another tune that was somehow related.'

Frank Seymour was in charge of the stereo – 'we weren't really allowed to bring pop music home' – and gave Nick his first record for a birthday one year. *Swan Lake*. For his father, it was an important gesture: a major piece to start a lifelong interest. 'I wanted Twister or a skateboard or something.'

Nick's mother Paula only had one record, by the Clancy Brothers, which she was as protective of as Nick's father was with the gramophone. 'It was weird, like "You're playing my record. You haven't asked me – why are you playing my record?"' The tunes Nick enjoyed on it were the traditional ballads such as 'A Jug of Punch', 'The Bold Fenian Men' and 'She Moved Through the Fair'. Hearing Nick play them, his dad would get out a Mozart or Beethoven air and showed what they'd done with the same melodies. His mother would sing all the missing words.

Nick was born in Benalla, and grew up in Beaufort, the small town in Victoria where gold was first discovered in Australia. At the end of their street lived Mavis Vinnycomb, a talented singer and pianist with a hairstyle that rivalled the wigs of Mozart or Dame Edna. Paula Seymour encouraged her children to take lessons with Mavis, so, from about the age of six, Nick would wander down the road and knock on the screen door with the large treble clef. 'I thought it was amazing,' he says. 'There were so many *objets kitsch* in the house, it was almost intuitive to her. Mavis Vinnycomb – she was a country woman piano teacher who was totally into this sanitised, almost Liberace piano style.'

Mavis Vinnycomb loved the Seymours down the road: a big family who enjoyed singing tunes from *The Sound of Music* and *My Fair Lady* and *Oliver*. 'She'd wander past and hear us singing in the house. Eventually we talked about it and she offered to accompany us if we wanted to sing anywhere. So we ended up doing parent–teacher nights here, country women's association gigs there, a couple of weddings.'

Nick, his older brother Mark, their mother Paula, and their sisters Hilary and Helen became the Seymour Family Singers, performing at functions in rural Victoria – even in front of the state governor on one occasion. (Paul Hester: 'You've seen *The Sound of Music*? The Von Seymour Family Singers. I'll say no more.')

For an Irish wedding, Mavis played the organ while Nick and Mark sang 'Panus Angelicus'. It was the first time they had sung a hymn in Latin, with medieval harmonies. The Seymours were practising Catholics in the Irish tradition ('Neil and I are both from pretty well-ordered Catholic families,' Nick once told *Q*, 'although mine was the kind that used to turn up for Mass late'), however they didn't send their children to the local parish school. 'They thought a state education was better for us than a Catholic school, where you learnt things like the Virgin Mary never used a washing machine, or you shouldn't chew gum in the toilets because you're feeding the Devil. Things like that . . . they had their wits about them.' Catholic schools also had limited facilities, and were overcrowded. 'Hence the expression, "I'm as full as a Catholic school." '

After secondary school, Nick attended the Victoria College of the Arts for a fine arts degree, majoring in printmaking. 'There seemed to be a lot more girls at art school than guys, and the type of guys there were romantic, charming individuals,' says Nick. The VCA is an institution founded last century, 'indulged by the old money of the

Melbourne gentry'. In its conservative early years, the VCA was pivotal in the Heidelberg School tradition, which transposed the art of the French impressionists to the environment of the Australian bush: eucalyptus trees and burnt, earthy colours.

It was the influence of Andy Warhol's Factory that led Nick to art school, however. The VCA was located in the heart of Melbourne, in the old public library, but Nick wasn't thinking about the Heidelberg School. In his mind, New York was the focus, and he had romantic visions of living in a big open loft space in the centre of town, 'a thriving urban environment, with a lot of street energy. That's what art school was all about, and a chance to wear flamboyant clothes.'

Thanks to the punk explosion in the late '70s, Melbourne did have the downtown culture Nick craved. A recurring theme in his paintings at the time were burning-down, tumbling cityscapes – images he later used on the *Temple of Low Men* cover and stage sets. He was emulating the German expressionists of the 1920s and '30s, whose paintings of urban decay seemed to be about the same energy he felt existed in Melbourne at the time. Sydney had been the economic centre of Australia for a few decades now, and Melbourne's aura of English gentility had been allowed to fade, while an influx of post-war Greek and Italian immigrants had given the city a multicultural, European flavour. 'And in Melbourne we considered ourselves a lot more European than we really were,' says Nick. 'Everyone was living in Berlin in one way or another. There was a sense of romance in Melbourne based on this strange European city mentality. In the early '80s, it was a very inspiring time to be in the city.'

Punk may have emerged from the working class in London, but almost everywhere else, the first to follow the revolution were the art students. In Melbourne, the catalyst of the punk scene was Nick Cave's band the Boys Next Door, which later evolved into the Birthday Party. Many were students at the VCA, or studying film at Swinburne College, 'so they wanted to have a certain style,' says Greg Perano, a close friend of Nick Seymour's who helped start Hunters and Collectors. 'It was a reaction to the T-shirts and jeans, pub-rock attitude. People wanted to be different, not to be elitist, but just to have an identity of their own. So the crowd would be in op-shop suits, rather than have 10 different colours in their hacked hair. It was more of a gentrified punk idea, a bit more sophisticated: more to do with literature and art and film. In that scene, you had to do something different to grab people's attention. The Boys Next Door were always sartorial, everyone paid a lot of attention to what they wore and who they were reading.'

'There was a boom of youth culture in Melbourne, somehow

younger musicians were empowered by the punk rock thing,' says Nick. 'The art schools were very supportive, there were always parties and venues, and bands pre-empting styles that have become mainstream now, everything from techno, garage music, electronic music to someone like Nick Cave. There were so many different styles of white music being produced in Melbourne in the late '70s and early '80s that people my age were incredibly arrogant.

'I was in a number of groups – you could be in those days – not playing much, just doing a lot of rehearsing, going to parties and gallery openings. The art school crowd and the music crowd were very inter-related.'

There were plenty of venues for bands in the inner Melbourne suburbs of St Kilda, Carlton and Richmond. 'It was a very lively scene,' says Paul Hester. 'On any given night there'd be 10 gigs to go to.'

The leading venue was the Crystal Ballroom, on Fitzroy Street in St Kilda. Formerly the ballroom of a luxury hotel built in the 1920s for people who wanted to have a seaside holiday on the St Kilda esplanade, it was a classy venue for an often squalid music scene. It hadn't been used for years so it was in good condition. At the top of the stairs was a huge ornate mirror, which broke one night when someone ran into it and knocked themselves out. Operated by an eccentric Spanish woman called Delores San Miguela, the Ballroom was plush, with a big stage, high ceilings and red velvet wallpaper.

'It was *the* venue,' says Perano. 'You'd probably go there a couple of times every weekend, if not Thursday-Friday-Saturday. Every band who came out of that era played there at some stage: the Birthday Party, Chris Bailey, overseas shows such as the Members, UK Squeeze, the Cure.'

The room upstairs was used for bigger acts; downstairs was another venue, more like the standard Australian bar. The two bars were meeting places for a diverse audience to see a diverse range of music. 'Downstairs there might be a pop group like the Reels, then on the same night you could go upstairs to see the Bad Seeds,' says Nick. 'And there would be a crossover of the audience: some of the same people who would watch Dave Mason singing "Quasimodo's Dream" would then go and watch Nick Cave killing a savage beast on stage.'

The downstairs room was also alleged to be one of the heaviest city bars outside of Port Melbourne. 'There were always fights outside, I remember a guy got shot once,' says Perano. 'But it never spilled over into the Ballroom itself, which was a very mellow venue. There was no heavy group of people who dominated the place. You'd walk in there and it was relaxing, comfortable. So it attracted all the young eccentrics around town.'

However the main streets of St Kilda, Fitzroy and Acland were rundown and sordid at the time. 'It was like King's Cross then,' says Perano. 'It was where everyone went to score; it was the red-light district where all the girls were. Police would often stop you on the way home, not really to harrass you, but to find out where you'd been and what you were doing. If you gave them the right answers they'd leave you alone.'

However the musical activity had a dark side. 'There were a lot of opiates around,' says Nick. Heroin was so pervasive in St Kilda then that the teaspoons in the cafés of Fitzroy Street would have holes drilled through them, to prevent them being stolen, or used for shooting up. A lot of people in the music scene got involved. 'They came from very nice middle-class backgrounds, and to use heroin was the height of decadence for them,' says Perano. 'Unfortunately they didn't think at the time it was going to be a lifelong problem. It destroyed a lot of people's potential careers.'

The musician junkies may have romanticised that they could live 'an opiated existence, read the right books and have a bohemian lifestyle,' says Nick, but in reality, it meant mixing with hardcore criminals. 'That criminal element was what almost destroyed the whole scene.'

For all the creativity and diversity of the city's music scene, Nick also says that many musicians were 'not as focused as I thought you needed to be. Melbourne was a very soft cushion that gave people a voice who wouldn't get one in cities that were harder to live in. It was very affordable. Heroin had a devastating effect on a lot of vital, vibrant free spirits.'

Among the early groups Nick Seymour was involved in were the Romantics, the Glory Boys, Horla and the provocatively named Scratch Record Scratch. He was briefly in Crime and the City Solution, who were originally from Sydney and an 'incredibly original band,' according to Perano. 'Quite eccentric but with very good songs. They would have fitted right into the Akron scene like Pere Ubu.' Another group, Plays With Marionettes, Nick describes as 'art-school theatrical – but with a dark energy rather than being humorous like the Enz.'

Perano got to know the Seymour brothers through the Boys Next Door scene. 'You're talking about a group of 150 core people, you met them all pretty quickly. Nick was very much part of it, Mark was still on the outskirts. He was a bit of a dag then really, being a schoolteacher. But he had a good feeling about him because he was really obsessed about playing music. Mark's first group, the Jetsonnes, were a very good pop band, but they didn't fit in. It was a tight little scene. You had to read Raymond Queneau, and know who Baudelaire was, Foucault and Verlaine. I remember someone had taken a discourse in Baudrillard and had translated it into English, and it was being passed around. I thought, this is bullshit. It was like, wait a minute . . .'

Creating your own outlets and occasions for performance was part of the ethos. Perano was involved in organising Little Band nights, which mixed the avant-garde areas of music and art. 'You'd put a little band together for the night, and go on for 10 minutes. There would be complete cacophonies of sound, but it was always entertaining. I had a band called Anne's Dance Marathon Band. We used to tape Hitler's speeches and church bells and horses galloping. I'd play the guitar with a teaspoon and smash glass on it, we'd have percussion, sax and violin – it used to drive people out of the room. The Oroton Bags were a girl group, Equal Local played weird instrumental cocktail music, like the lounge revival that's happening now, but this was in 1979.'

Perano spent 1980 in London, living in an Alderton squat with many other Melbourne musicians passing through – Nick Cave and Tracy Pew of the Birthday Party, Ian 'Ollie' Olsen of the Primitive Calculators and several members of Crime and the City Solution. When Perano returned to Melbourne, Nick Seymour was the first person he talked to about the music he'd seen. 'Greg had all these ideas,' says Nick. 'African-sounding percussion grooves using electronics, bands like Aswad, Pigbag, Shriekback.

'I convinced my brother Mark, who had a band called the Jetsonnes, to form a band with Greg, myself and a friend of ours, Geoff Crosby. Within about two months of working up a number of songs, Mark and I had a falling out – as brothers do – and he went back to the Jetsonnes with Greg and Geoff and formed Hunters and Collectors. Their first shows – basically the first two Hunters' albums – had that energy borrowed from the UK. Hypnotic, trance-like rhythms, created from electronic and percussion instruments, with a bit of bushman thrown in for good measure.'

If the Seymours hadn't been brothers, Nick would have been the bassplayer in Hunters and Collectors, says Perano. 'I always think "Talking To a Stranger" came from Nick as much as Mark. Because Nick was the guy with all the records, and that song is based on a track by the Orchestra of Love, on the Zee label out of New York.'

In the early '80s, when Hunters and Collectors was peaking, Nick was in Bang, who were 'funky with art-school leanings,' says Perano. Funk had become fashionable again. The inner-city crowd was listening to Parliament, discovering James Brown, while also taking in New York groups such as James White and the Blacks, the Contortions, James Chance. 'Bang had a real mixture of influences. Quite innovative, especially the rhythm section, Nick and Ollie Olsen, but they were let down by what went on around them. They didn't have an edge like Hunters and Collectors. It was pretty frustrating for Nick at that time, to see his brother being so highly successful, and in such an innovative group. He'd have loved to be in that band when it started.' Members of Bang later formed Big Pig and Boom Crash Opera, both of which had an art-funk emphasis.

The bands he was in enabled Nick to combine his obsessions of music and art. He would use his studio to rehearse, and to paint special backdrops for each important gig. It gave Nick a canvas to work on a large scale, and provided a theme for the performance. An inspiration for this multi-media approach was Noel Crombie, the percussionist/image-maker of Split Enz, who was friendly with a woman in Bang. 'I thought he was brilliant, really lucky,' says Nick. 'He was very clever, well informed on contemporary music and art around the world, and he had the opportunity to voice his own interpretation of that in this band Split Enz. And they gave him free rein. He's one of the biggest influences on my adult life.'

Crombie was the Split Enz member who mingled the most in this scene, once the Enz moved to Melbourne in late 1979. Paul says the Enz were viewed in the music scene as 'icons – they were this power around, but weren't seen terribly much'. The Enz seemed to tour constantly from this period, the summer that 'I Got You' became a massive hit. Nick, however, did know some of the band; at one point his girlfriend lived in the same flat as Crombie and Neil Finn. 'You'd run into them at parties and marvel at their experience and success and world travel,' he says. 'You had to respect them.'

Because of the touring, and the self-contained nature of Split Enz, it took a while for the band to feel part of Melbourne, says Crombie. 'We weren't connected, because we hadn't gone through several different bands, and have all those connections, as most musicians living in a city do.'

Neil went to the Crystal Ballroom a couple of times, but mostly, he says, 'I watched from the fringe, I wasn't part of a scene. I always felt suspicious. Maybe it's a smalltown reticence to buy into that sophisticated urban way of living. For some people it's a genuine thing, but for others, it's a pose, and it always seemed slightly pathetic to me. I was attracted to the imagery of it all, and I loved some of the music that came out of it, and the danger and recklessness was attractive. But I kept hearing of people falling foul of those scenes. I had a family, and that took care of my social life.'

Perano remembers members of Hunters and Collectors joining forces with Bang for a benefit gig at the Venue, on the esplanade at St Kilda, which drew 1100 people over two nights. 'That was some of the best fun I've ever spent on stage,' he says. It was a chance for many big local names – and for the precious – to let their hair down playing covers 'without people criticising them'. The Hunters horn section, plus Nick on bass, became the Big Bang Combo, supporting singers such as James Freud, Sean Kelly of the Models and Kate Ceberano. The songs were both hip and kitsch (hits by Tom Jones, Motown, Chic, Sister Sledge, Led Zeppelin and Thin Lizzy), the performances ironic and deadpan. Each act would dress appropriately for their song, and before they went on they'd have a team-talk singalong in the bandroom – a bonding technique common to both the Hunters and Split Enz – so they would be charged up when they hit the stage.

Crombie played drums and percussion at one of these events, and Neil Finn took part in another entrepreneurial extravaganza: the Big Choir. 'We were a big group of strange people who couldn't sing,' says Perano. 'Neil turned up to a couple of rehearsals we had in a church hall; I don't think he realised it was going to be such a shambles. But he went along with it. Half of us couldn't sing, in a conventional sense. And Neil and Tim had got to know Vanetta Fields, an incredible singer [a gospel backing vocalist on the Rolling Stones' *Exile on Main Street*, Fields was living in Melbourne at the time]. She came along and was appalled by it. We never professed to be slick, it was like a punk choir, singing "Pokarekare ana" and "Drunken Sailor". We tried to get Mark involved, but it was a bit light for him, he was opposed to the idea. For us it was a light relief from the intensity of what we'd been involved in.

'It was very naive, that spirit was a very Melbourne thing then. To avoid elitist prickery – it was, yeah, let's do this, it'll be really entertaining. Because Melbourne could be very elitist, that Boys Next Door scene, if you weren't accepted you were out. You had to eat humble pie to be part of that crew.'

Nick became an art director at Crawfords, a television production house which specialised in quality soap operas such as *The Sullivans* and *Carson's Law*. He would dress interior sets from period photographs, and find props by haunting antique and bric-a-brac stores in Melbourne. 'I was really into vintage clothing, so it legitimised my interest in going to op shops, basically.'

One of his tasks at Crawfords was to look after any livestock on the productions. This usually meant a few hens, but Perano remembers when they were flatting together on Acland Street, Nick would occasionally have to bring the animals home for the weekend.

'I came home one Friday night, looked out in the backyard and there are two pigs there. I thought oh, the poor things are off to the abattoir on Monday. At the time, I really wanted to form a band called Sex Pigs. So with Bruno Charlesworth, who lived downstairs – he's now a big entertainment lawyer in Melbourne – I spray painted *SEX* on one and *PIG* on the other. Then Nick came home and asked how the pigs were.

'They're okay – what's happening to them?'

Nick said, 'Oh, we're using them all next week for filming.'

'I went, oh fuck. No matter what we did, we couldn't get the stuff off these pigs. So he goes to work on Monday and says to the director he's got a bit of a problem.

' "It's about the pigs," said Nick. "Someone's written on them."

The director replied, no worries, that could happen to anyone.

' "No – it's bad," said Nick. "There's actually *SEX* written on one and *PIG* on the other."

'The guy said, "Well cover them up with dirt or something – we still have to use them." ' The shoot went ahead, including a scene in which a guy is leaning against a shovel, '40s workclothes on, and in the background a pig wanders across the set, *SEX* written across its back.

Perano suggests Nick was wondering what he'd do with his life at this point. 'It was an awkward stage, he'd finished art school, his vocation was obviously music, but he wasn't going to be successful at it.'

In the meantime, Nick concentrated on art directing, working quite conscientiously when he went freelance. 'I took it seriously, set myself up with a van and a toolbox. I put money into it, and was making reasonable money. But it got to the point where the hours – if I wanted to run it as a business – were in excess of what any of my friends were doing. I was always getting up early in the morning and being really punctual. Ironically, one of Neil's biggest gripes in the early days of Crowded House was that I'd never be on time.'

Nick worked on films and video clips. As a friend of the director Richard Lowenstein, he was art director on all the clips for Tim Finn's *Escapade* album. 'You'd employ your mates to do videos. I had the van, so would end up picking up all the camera gear and art department stuff.' Lowenstein later directed the videos for Crowded House's 'Mean to Me' and 'Into Temptation'.

During a break in the shooting of a film he was then working in, *The Leonski Incident*, Nick was watching television; it was the time of the final Enz shows in Melbourne. He was watching a rock show, and Neil Finn and Paul Hester were telling an interviewer about the band they were going to form together after the Enz. So he made sure he went to the party after the last Enz show, to buttonhole an inebriated Neil Finn for an audition.

Nick had to take a day off *The Leonski Incident* shoot to go to the audition. On the movie set, he learnt a couple of songs on the Finn/Hester demo tape he'd been given, with his bass, a Walkman and a pair of headphones. 'When I drove to the rehearsal studio I was so nervous. I played and played, then just got completely hysterical. I had to go for a run around the studio to calm down. I came back, did another two tracks, made a couple of jokes, then left.

'I possibly impressed them with my intensity. Because I was really on a roll, in the middle of this six-day-a-week shoot, with a lot of responsibility to make sure the actors had their props on call. Also, I was training as a makeup artist – I wanted to learn to do makeup and prosthetics, and for a couple of films had been working with a makeup professional. When I got the gig with Crowded House, he couldn't believe I was going to take it, and not go into makeup. He thought I was mad, "throwing away an amazing career in the film industry for a . . . a . . . band, a musical group!"'

The bands Nick was serious about at the time were Bang and Plays With Marionettes. When he told his fellow musicians that he'd like to be involved in what Neil Finn was doing after Split Enz, it brought out the conceptual art student in them. A couple responded, 'Those guys? You're selling out – those guys are commercial.'

Then the third, who came from the same philosophy, twisted it slightly, saying: 'No, hold on – I think he's buying in.'

A man with a mission
• February 1985

**'It's a bit scary, thinking about not being in Split Enz.
It is a very closed existence. But I'm looking forward
to finding out what it's like.'**

—Neil Finn, 1984

All Neil Finn knew about his future was that he'd be working with
Paul Hester. Beyond that was just speculation. He wanted a new band,
and wanted to keep it small: something a bit more manageable than
the Enz. He wanted his songs to sound the way he intended them.

But if musicians he felt he could work permanently with weren't
available, then becoming a solo artist was an option. 'I like the idea
of a challenge rather than safety – even if I fall on my face,' he said
as the Enz With a Bang tour began. 'I have enough optimism to think
I've learnt enough to avoid a lot of mistakes. And I'm lucky that the
public are familiar with my songs. I don't have to break any doors.'

First, he needed to record some demos. Paul came around to his
house at Osborne Street, in the Melbourne suburb of South Yarra, and
together they worked out a few songs. They decided to audition bass
players by getting them to work on the demos. They didn't fuss over
the demos at all; none of the songs were finished, none of them had
arrangements. 'We just went in and put them down. I'd yell out
"Change!" to Paul, and we'd go from verse to chorus. One take. Then
we got a few bass players in.'

They whittled the contenders down to just two. An early contender was Bones Hillman, who contributed a bassline to 'Can't Carry
On' which made it to the first album. But he was a little rusty, and
his style too similar to Nigel Griggs of the Enz, says Neil. 'I thought,
if it's going to be that style of bass playing, I may as well have Nigel.'
So Nick Seymour got the job, mainly because he jumped around a lot
and played well on 'That's What I Call Love'. 'When Neil said to me,
What do you reckon, Bones or Nick?' I put the word in for Nick,' says
Paul. 'He lived in Melbourne, and he was very keen.'

'I wasn't a big fan of his bass playing in those days,' admits Neil,
who had only heard Seymour play in the Melbourne band Bang. Neil
had produced a solo single by their lead singer Karen Ansell. 'He was

trying to be funky to the *nth* degree, and I'm not really a funk merchant. Nevertheless, he came in and there seemed to be a spark there. It's good to choose people who aren't obvious, then you get an interesting mix.' A few days later, Neil made his decision. Nick was in.

The pair thought they needed another member, so they tried out several guitarists and keyboard players. 'We auditioned some real dags,' says Paul. One guitarist seemed seven foot tall, and towered over Paul at the audition. He'd done his homework with their tape, though, and said to them, 'Okay, I've worked out this bit at the beginning – don't come in for five minutes.' He had more foot pedals than a bike shop and, for a five-minute display of ear-shattering pyrotechnics, used every one of them. Then called out, 'Okay, you guys come in now!'

'We sent him down the road,' said Neil later on Adelaide television. 'He's now making burgers.'

Both Neil and Paul were fans of the Reels, then in limbo, and, knowing that their guitarist Craig Hooper was at a loose end, they invited him for a jam. 'He was just *flash*,' says Paul. The quartet clicked; Hooper was very experienced, on the road and musically. 'He knew what everything was called, could read, write, program – he's very much a whizkid,' says Paul. 'He was a great foil for Neil.'

Stored in the Crowded House archives in Melbourne is one of the original demos Neil and Paul took to the world. It's on a cheap Maxell XLI-S 60 cassette, marked 'Neil Finn/Paul Hester'. Paul's 'That's What I Call Love' leads, a slight dance tune built on Nick's stepping bass and the Chic-style rhythm guitar riffs INXS were later to appropriate. Neil's voice is strangely thin and uncertain. 'Carry On This Way' is similarly slight, though the melody and Beatles backing vocals in the bridge are already in place for when it became 'Can't Carry On'. Hillman's driving bass is the strongest element.

'Walking On the Spot' opens with the metronomic rhythm of an early drum machine; the reflective melody is all there, but compared to the final version which appeared eight years later, the vocal is taken at an undignified jaunty pace. Some disturbing mid-80s effects turn it into a novelty song. 'On the Pier' has a droning melody and an Enz-like twitchiness to the backing; it deserved burying. 'Galfriend' grooves like *Undercover*-era Stones, with a melody similar to 'Tombstone'.

It's a chastening tape – almost amateurish and crudely recorded. 'The demos were very hastily assembled,' says Neil. After the quality of his Enz songs, any potential on that first tape is well hidden. It featured both Bones and Nick on bass.

This was what Paul and Neil had with them as they determinedly headed off in late February to dazzle the A&R men of the world's major record companies (originally short for 'artists and repertoire', an A&R person finds new talent for a record company, and liaises between the label and musicians on artistic matters). Or rather, the A&R men they managed to actually meet. Says Neil, 'We couldn't get to see everybody ... well, maybe we *could* have if we'd hassled. But there was a good vibe about Split Enz, which opened a few doors. I was relying on contacts I had already, which were minimal really.'

Neil was determined to sign a worldwide deal direct with an overseas record company, rather than an Australian branch. After his experience in Split Enz, he realised that if a major international company felt an act was their own, it made them work harder. Especially once they spent a lot of money getting them established, and wanted to recoup their investment.

In London they spent time with Tim and Paul caught up with Deborah Conway and the other members of Melbourne band Do-Re-Mi, who were recording their first album.

The first record executive they saw was Simon Potts, A&R for Elektra-Asylum, who had signed the Thompson Twins. 'This sounds good,' he said, 'I can get you Alex Sadkin, who has produced Talking Heads. He'd be perfect for this stuff. I'll give you a call on Monday.'

The band never heard from him – ironically, two years later they ran into him at Capitol, in Los Angeles, where he'd just been employed to head the A&R department. 'I thought he liked us but Neil was a bit more reserved,' says Paul. 'I couldn't work out why until years later I realised, that's what they're all like.'

The pair kept getting fobbed off as they headed west. Potts told them to see his colleague in New York, who said 'Yeah, I like your stuff but go and see our man on the West Coast.' In Los Angeles, Peter Philbourne of Columbia had a chronic stutter and a very nervous manner. He listened to the tape, talked about the Enz, and said he couldn't relate to bands with more than one singer.

What was the last band you signed?

'The B-B-Bangles ... b-b-but I like this ... yeah ... there's a kind of v-v-vulnerable guy in here. Yeah, I hear a v-v-vulnerable guy!'

Neil was pleased they had made the trip, 'though it could have been a waste of time'. They funded it with their meagre proceeds from the last Enz tour – or, in Paul's case, the little he had left after a disastrous investment in goat breeding. The pair had enjoyed themselves, seen a bit of Tim in London and recorded demos of 'Walking On the Spot' and 'Something So Strong' – but, most importantly, they got to know each other.

'Neil filled me in on the whole industry,' says Paul. 'He got us into all the meetings, and knew everyone because of Split Enz. I was just following him along like a shadow. We were at a hotel in New York one night and we were introduced to Diana Ross, Jerry Moss and Quincy Jones. Neil's there, they know who he is – the Split Enz chap – and I'd be saying, "I'm with him!" '

Everyone then went off to the Ritz Theatre, to see Sting's first solo gig since quitting the Police; Paul had his foot stood on by Diana Ross and met Andy Warhol. 'It was extraordinary,' he says. 'Andy Warhol's just standing there with this totally flat, cold look, staring down at the people from the balcony. He turned and was eyeing me and Neil up and down, like we were lollipops or something. He offered his hand like a wet fish. That was great – if anyone's gonna have a wet fish handshake, it's gotta be Andy. If he'd had a staunch handshake it would have freaked me out.'

By the time the pair arrived in Los Angeles, they thought a couple of companies had shown serious interest. 'But if the truth be known,' says Paul, 'no-one followed it up.' They had got some names of people to approach from Lars Sorenson, who had briefly been a tour manager for Split Enz. Now, Sorenson was nominally the manager of Neil's new band, though he wasn't in a position to underwrite it. But he gave them the names of a few industry players, among them Tom Whalley, a 32-year-old A&R man who had just joined Capitol Records from Warner Bros.

When Whalley got the call, the name Neil Finn rang a bell: this was the singer who had so impressed his friend Gary Stamler on his New Zealand holiday. So he invited them to come and see him. It was Whalley's first day in the Capitol Tower; he didn't even have an office yet. When Neil and Paul arrived, they all went into the office of Don Grierson, the head of A&R at Capitol, and listened to the demo.

'The *last* thing I wanted to happen in my first week at Capitol was to fall in love with something,' Whalley later told Bud Scoppa of *Music Connection*. 'I wanted to get settled first. I kept playing it and I loved it more and more, but I sat on it for a while and played it for some people at the label. I got mixed reactions, so I told Neil I wanted to hear some more songs if possible.'

Whalley also advised them to see a lawyer, who they would need when the time came to draw up a contract. He recommended one in particular: Gary Stamler, his good friend who had alerted him to Neil's existence. Stamler was an attorney in his 30s; among his clients had been Ringo Starr, Van Halen, Harry Nilsson (briefly: Stamler knew he couldn't continue long when after the first meeting he staggered home at 8.30am), Richard Thompson and Van Dyke Parks.

At the time, he was representing several Los Angeles bands, and that day, was at a rehearsal showcase for some record labels when he phoned in for his messages. His secretary ran through various names, finishing with, '. . . and Neil Finn called.' 'Neil Finn? Where from?'

'He's in LA, in a hotel, the Beverly Prestcott. He wants you to call.'

Stamler thought that was odd. When he returned the call, Sorenson answered and explained what they were up to, and that they'd just been into Capitol and seen Tom Whalley.

That afternoon, Neil, Paul and Sorenson met Stamler in his office. Neil did all the talking. 'He told me the story, that they'd been to London, New York, and LA. He'd found it a frustrating experience – I guess he thought it was going to be easier to get A&R people on the phone. He was just ringing up record companies and expecting people to jump at him. Virtually one of the only guys who did was Tom, because he was as surprised as I was to get a phone call from Neil Finn.

'So we had about a 30 minute meeting, talked, listened to the tape, found out a little bit about each other – and the next thing you know, he hands me a bunch of demo tapes and says, "You're it". Therein started the process of trying to get the band – the project, Finn/Hester, whatever it was – off the ground.' Stamler was now the band's attorney, representing them in negotiations.

Also in Los Angeles, they met with David Tickle who, since producing 'I Got You' and *True Colours*, had graduated to working with Prince. They listened to the demos on his car tape deck, with one of Prince's sexy backing singers in tow. Tickle and friend 'were vibing like crazy,' says Neil. 'That was the last thing we did before we came home. So, with the good response from Tom Whalley, we felt pretty good about the trip.'

Or ambivalent, according to Paul – the commitment at that stage was very tentative, 'handshakes and we-love-it – but we'd had all that before. So we went back to Melbourne and got the band together.'

In 1987 Neil told *Creem* magazine, 'We approached this whole band in a bit of a backwards way. We went straight for the jugular – for the record deal – before we did gigs, found a manager or anything like that. As the year progressed we worked the band into shape. So we weren't really a band when we got the deal at all. We made ourselves into a band in that ensuing year. I didn't want to sit on my arse for too long after Split Enz, and brood on everything. I wanted to get on with it.'

And he didn't want to go solo, 'because then I'd be missing out on the benefit of the conflict that a band creates. The last thing I want is to be surrounded by yes men.'

'Yes, that's right, Neil,' said Paul.

One step ahead
• May 1985

'A new band, a new era. 1985 will be the Year of the Road.'

—Neil Finn, May, 1985

On 13 March, 1985, Neil, Nick, Paul and Craig Hooper arrived at a Melbourne warehouse with their instruments and amps. The fledgling group had decided the quickest way to become a real band was to road-test themselves before entering a recording studio. They rehearsed for three weeks in the warehouse, and the quartet gelled. The adroit musicianship of Hooper eased the process, and the band found they wrote a song together in the first week: 'Recurring Dream'.

With no manager, Neil found he was making all the phone calls to organise the new band, which was yet to find a name. He contacted Grant Thomas, who had been tour accountant on several Enz tours, and worked for the Enz management promoting the Enz With a Bang tour. Finn told Thomas that there was interest in the band from America, but they wanted the band to play live before signing a deal. Could he organise a tour?

Thomas arranged a two-week tour of small towns on the east coast of Australia. Visiting his parents back home in New Zealand, Neil finally came up with a name. He explained on the public radio station Triple-J later in the year: 'I was lying in bed agonising over what to call the band when we toured and my mother came in and said, "Call it the Mullanes, Neil." And we did.' Mullane was his mother's maiden name, and Neil's middle name.

But who were the Mullanes? It was difficult to get the message across. Thomas had a poster designed to enlighten the public. 'We named all the guys: Neil Finn and Paul Hester, *ex-Split Enz*. Craig Hooper, *ex-the Reels*. Nick Seymour . . . and we didn't know what to say. The bands he'd been in were so small it wasn't worth putting their names on the poster. Everybody would have said, "Who??"

'So we put, Nick Seymour, *Frank and Paula's youngest.*'

If booking agents, promoters and pub managers thought they were onto a bonanza when they booked the Mullanes – with *Neil Finn*, formerly of Split Enz! – they were in for a shock. Despite the Enz connection, says Neil, 'We stiffed every promoter in the country.' Thanks to Thomas's accounting skills, however, the tour was structured so that the band didn't end up losing money.

They kept it small, travelling in just two cars, one for the band, one for crew. For Neil, it was the apprenticeship in grass-roots rock'n'roll that he had never served. He acted as tour manager, making a mental adjustment from the million-dollar gross, slick organisation of the last Enz tour, to dealing in mere hundreds of dollars of beer-stained bank notes.

'It was the bush-fire tour,' says Paul. 'We burned the whole east coast of Australia. A lot of the gigs up north in Queensland were really poorly attended. We had guarantees of $4000 – and there would be 150 people. Neil would have to go in and pick up the money each night, dealing with his poor old Catholic guilt while these guys were throwing hundreds of dollars onto the table, not even talking to us. Neil would shovel it into a bag, hide it under his coat and then have to walk out through the crowd to the car. People would come up to him, "Mate, how are ya mate, you were great!" And Neil would go "Great, great, thanks mate!" and scurry off, he was so worried about the dough.

'It was quite a thing for him to do. But he loved it, it was very confrontational, very honest. You get up, you play your gig, you entertain, then you go up to the man and get your money. After all those years in the business, Neil had never done that. I'd been in punk bands getting ripped off all the time, so I wasn't that fascinated.'

One night in north Queensland, a pub manager tried to short change them. 'Shame there weren't more people here,' said Neil, as the publican handed over $2000 backstage. Neil counted it, said thanks – but what about the other half? 'Whaddaya mean?'

'The contract says $4000,' said Neil. It was obvious he was going to stand his ground. The publican went to his safe, pulled out another stash – and threw the money at Neil, the notes spraying all over the room.

Each day, Neil would bank the cash and at the end of the tour Thomas did a reconciliation. An added expense was a bass guitar they needed to buy halfway through the tour. After all the bills were paid, the tour made just $250.

On one date in the tour, the Mullanes were booked to clash with New Zealand singer Dave Dobbyn's band DD Smash at the same venue. Mildura is a small town in the middle of wine-growing territory on the Murray River, at the border of Victoria and New South Wales: 'A town renowned for cask wine, appropriately,' says Dobbyn's manager at the time, Roger King. The gig followed one at the Yoogalli Hotel in Griffith, a town renowned for its marijuana farms.

It made sense to have a double-bill on 5 June at the Bridge Hotel in Mildura. But who would headline? Both bands had the same agency, but Dobbyn had the booking secured. Grant Thomas wanted the Mullanes to 'drop in over the date' – ie, take it over. He started an in-house battle at the agency. 'Both agents were ferociously saying their artist should be the headliner. My agent was saying, "It's Neil Finn – ex-Split Enz – Dave doesn't have the pulling power. It would be in his best interests to open". His agent was saying, "No way, it's my date – you open for Dobbyn." '

In the end, Dobbyn's band was the opening act, and after their set, their presence helped lift the numbers at the gig. 'The evening was very odd,' says King, 'I can remember turning up and seeing the four of them standing outside the motel, stoned and laughing, every-one thinking what on earth are we doing in this strange town. One small problem with Mildura: no-one had heard of the Mullanes *or* DD Smash. Not many punters at all, maybe 100 if we were lucky, in a very big room.'

But King remembers the Mullanes' performance: 'They were already working in Crowdie style. It struck me as exceptional music. We just stood there and loved what we were hearing. It was fun seeing Neil's initial foray into pub gigs – though because there was no-one there, he didn't really have to confront the sort of pub anarchy Dobbyn had so much.'

Nick remembers the Mullanes period as 'intense, positive but very enjoyable. Neil was hungry – *hungry*. He had to prove, not only was he the guy who wrote the hits in Split Enz, but he had to do it on his own terms, without the shadow of the other members supporting him.'

A typical show by the Mullanes included songs Neil wrote for Split Enz, early versions of Crowded House songs by Neil and Paul, Reels songs and a few crowd-pleasing cover versions. The set-list of a gig in Townsville on that tour reads: 'Hello Sandy Allen', 'Does Anyone Here Understand My Girlfriend?', 'Not Fade Away', 'Rawhide', 'Walking On the Spot', 'Love You 'til the Day I Die', 'Now We're Getting Somewhere', 'This is Massive', 'Recurring Dream', 'Can't Carry On', 'One Step Ahead', 'I've Seen You Before', 'Breakin' My Back', 'Return', 'That's What I Call Love'.

By the time they reached the main centres of Australia, the Mul-lanes had begun to develop the group rapport and spontaneous humour that became Crowded House's trademark. The band were glowing with enthusiasm in their first TV interviews, to the Adelaide rock shows *Trax the Music* and *Night Shift*. On *Trax*, the band came across like an unsophisticated bunch of bumpkins who had just walked off the street. They chewed gum and laughed at their own jokes. Neil's makeup (blonded hair, eye shadow) was offset by the cowboy motifs on his home-knitted jersey. Paul looked boyish in a turquoise satin shirt, Hooper drab in a woollen v-neck jersey; both had hair from the mid '70s. Nick's hair looked as if he cut it himself and he was wearing a plaid shirt. It was Nick's first TV appearance; he didn't say anything, just looked from camera to camera. Craig Hooper entered into the banter, saying that though the Reels hadn't done any gigs for about two years, they might make a record soon: 'Dave Mason and I still correspond.'

Neil: 'Lawyers letters, basically.'

Hooper: 'But I doubt we'll ever play live again.'

Paul: 'After two years off, they're a bit worried about overkill.'

Were they picking up any fans during their gigs in Adelaide?

'We're picking up everything in Adelaide,' replied Paul. 'We're having a ball. I've got a clinic to go to. Only joking!'

After their first gig at the Bridgeway, Neil and Paul returned to appear on *Nightshift*. Neil described how the new band was breaking in: 'We were a bit rough for the first few gigs but we're getting quite consistent now. We're having a good time on stage every night. Hooper's going nuts on the old guitar and Nick's thumping away on the bass. We have to hold young Nick down actually.'

Paul: 'Nick's a definite worry.'

Neil: 'He's not really been on tour before, though he's played in bands. And he comes into your room in the morning, so excited that a new day has started. He's jumping up and down on the bed. And we're just trying to get our eyes open.'

The *Trax* host asked them how the Mullanes sound compared to Split Enz.

'It's a very guitar-oriented sound, there are no keyboards,' said Neil. 'It's possibly more energetic, and heavier than Split Enz. It's great to see the audiences reacting so well to the new songs.'

But the Australian music industry was underwhelmed by the Mullanes. Michael Matthews, then senior promotions manager at EMI in Melbourne, remembers going to see them in a club in Collingwood, Melbourne. 'They were . . . rather boring, actually,' he says. 'And the name I loathed.' Greg Perano says the band was held back by Hooper, who, for all his musical technique, lacked the charisma and enthusiasm of the other members.

From Los Angeles, Tom Whalley called Peter Dawkins at EMI

Australia; like Capitol, a member of the EMI group. They had met at Warner Brothers, when Whalley had signed an Australian band, the Church. Dawkins was originally from New Zealand – in 1969 he had produced 'Nature', the biggest hit of the local pop heroes, the Fourmyula – but had been very successful in Australia since the '70s, signing the lucrative soft-rock acts Air Supply and Little River Band. He had also signed Dragon, expatriate New Zealand glam rockers whose knack for pop hits was matched only by their taste for heroin. Dawkins only realised this when, two weeks after their second single was released, the drummer died from an overdose.

'Tom asked what I thought of Neil Finn,' says Dawkins. 'Stupid question. Neil was always my favourite composer in Split Enz: to my tastes he was far more commerically oriented. He then sent me a tape. None of the songs turned up on the first album, but it was very impressive – very typical of the Neil style. I was all for signing on the spot, but Capitol – being Capitol – weren't quite sure. Tom had the vibe, but was trying to get the rest of his Capitol people into it.

'I suggested a joint venture. It was the word of the moment. I could see a lightbulb go on over Tom's head. First, he wanted to see the band. I wasn't so concerned, I'd always been a song person. If a band's competent, you know they're going to get better on stage as the success comes. It's very seldom a band will blow it, unless they're staring at their shoes, with nothing happening. With the experience of these guys, that wasn't going to happen.'

Meanwhile, in Los Angeles, Whalley received a second tape of demos, with a skeletal version of a song called 'Don't Dream It's Over', plus 'Love You 'til the Day I Die', 'Hole in the River' and the chorus of 'Now We're Getting Somewhere'. 'A pretty good bunch,' says Neil. 'That was what clinched it.' Whalley was very impressed – but then he got a phone call which undermined his enthusiasm in the band. A prominent player in Australian music publishing, called to say he had seen a couple of Mullanes gigs, and advised Whalley not to go near the group – they weren't very good.

The band were on the verge of getting signed to Capitol, and now Whalley cooled slightly. His head of A&R, Don Grierson, was still unconvinced, but they thought it unwise to be swayed by the negativity of one Australian. So Whalley flew out to Australia with Gary Stamler to witness a couple of Mullanes gigs.

They arrived in Melbourne late one morning and, being jetlagged, both decided to take an afternoon nap. Hours later, Stamler woke in a cold sweat. He looked at his watch, and got a shock: the gig was about to start. 'We'd flown all that way and were on the verge of sleeping through it. I called Tom up, who was really groggy, and said, you won't believe this – the gig starts in five minutes. We'll miss half of it even if we go right now.'

They threw their clothes on, caught a taxi, and arrived halfway through the concert. Both Stamler and Whalley were immediately struck by the scene: there was no buzz. 'We'd both come down to Australia thinking Split Enz were still regarded as a big band there, yet the crowd was so small and they were showing no interest in what was going on on stage. The audience weren't paying any attention, they were just . . . there.'

That puzzled them, though they thought the band played well. Afterwards they went over to Neil's house to discuss the gig; in the taxi on the way back to the hotel, Stamler fell asleep onto Grant Thomas's shoulder, exhausted.

A few days later, they saw another show at the Tivoli in Sydney. 'A similar room, a similar size crowd,' says Stamler. 'We were under-whelmed by the response.' Peter Dawkins accompanied them to the Tivoli, and was even less impressed. 'Perhaps I was concerned Tom wouldn't like them, so I was looking at some of the worse aspects. They were just developing the comedy routine which became their hallmark. But at that stage it wasn't very good – they dribbled on too much, trying to be funny. I thought, a little less humour and more meat and potatoes, I'm afraid. But Tom said afterwards, they were great, weren't they? And I said, yeah, yeah, forgetting my own reservations. As long as he was happy, I had no qualms that we could sell the band in Australia.'

That night in the hotel, Stamler and Whalley talked late into the night about what they'd seen. 'Tom was wobbly about the whole thing,' says Stamler, who still felt positive about the band and argued in favour of signing. The evening ended with Whalley going to Neil's room to say, 'I think we should do it.' The idea of a joint venture between Capitol and EMI Australia helped persuade the still-hesitant Grierson.

'At that stage, the Americans weren't falling over themselves to sign new Australian acts,' says Dawkins. 'Despite Men at Work, too many had fallen flat on their faces. There had been a whole spate of Australian managers going over to America to tell them how to suck eggs. And it hadn't gone down too well.'

Nevertheless, the EMI group was keen to develop an international roster, because for too long clever band managers had signed their acts to different companies in each territory. However, unlike CBS, EMI lacked experience in coordinated international marketing strategies.

The joint venture idea clinched the deal: EMI Australia put up a small amount of money, and kept its market share. Capitol put up the money for the rest of the world, with Australia receiving a percentage of the proceeds equivalent to its investment.

Stamler returned to Melbourne to discuss the contract. 'At this stage, Neil saw the project as one between him and Paul. All the early drafts of the contract were just with Finn, Hester and Capitol.' The Mullanes had done a few more gigs, and the subject of Craig Hooper came up. When Stamler said he felt Hooper didn't fit in, Neil agreed.

'It just didn't seem right with Craig,' says Neil. 'We didn't intend to stay as a three-piece, but we didn't find anyone who suited.'

Nothing was wrong with Hooper's playing, says Paul. Everyone got on well; it was too soon for the classic 'musical differences'. 'I think all of a sudden Neil found he had another band around him. Craig's more upfront about his ability as a guitarist than Neil, and maybe Neil felt he had too many people making suggestions. He could walk Nick and I through his ideas and songs, and we were happy to. But, after years of Eddie and the other influences in the Enz, he really wanted to see what he could come up with himself. It worked well live, but thinking about recording and the future, I think Neil wanted to have more space. I think that was the main reason he cut Craig.

'It was a sad day; poor Craig shed a tear or two. He loved being part of it. We had a rehearsal with Craig and Nick before going overseas to shop for a deal and said to them with a handshake, 'We're a band. We're going to get a deal – see you in two months.' It was sad, we had good times together – when you've toured with someone, you're like old soldiers who have served time together. But things were pretty focused and Neil realised his time was *now*, and he had to make some hard decisions if he was going to get that freedom for himself. We've run into Craig a lot since and it's good – there's no blood lost.'

Shortly afterwards, the Reels reformed, with Hooper on guitar. The day before Neil and Paul were to sign the contract with Capitol, Nick Seymour's name was added to the final draft. 'It was a reasonable first-album contract,' says Neil, 'similar to the deal Split Enz got towards the end. But in hindsight, some things weren't that great. The percentages in Europe were only about 10 percent. We never renegotiated, and considering it became our best market, that stuck in our throat.'

After cloak-and-dagger secrecy over the signing, Peter Dawkins surprised his colleagues by announcing EMI Australia's new act at their 1985 conference in Wollongong. 'It was a charge for everyone at EMI to have Neil on the label, because at that stage we had Pseudo

Echo and some acts that weren't happening. We were mainly selling comedians at that time: Rodney Rude selling 300,000.'

Neil and Sharon then took a month's holiday, starting with a week in London with Tim, who gave a showcase concert at the Rock Garden on June 26. Neil joined a band of guest musicians, to back Tim playing songs from Split Enz, *Escapade* and his forthcoming *Big Canoe*. Then, with Tim and Greta, they travelled to Italy. 'It wasn't a great holiday,' says Neil. 'It was one of those holidays where the details don't work out. We drove for about a day-and-a-half to get to Italy, and went to a place called Scarlino. It was supposed to be this old villa near the sea, but it turned out to be a dark, old baronial place looking out over a chemical factory. We had some good times, staying on the island of Gilio. But we regretted leaving Liam, who was then two.' While in Italy, Neil played Tim a new song he'd written, in reaction to the recent suicide of his father's sister. The song's title was 'Hole in the River'; the phrase had stayed with Neil after watching Shirley McLaine in *Irma La Douce*. He later recalled to Australian journalist Glenn A Baker, 'She said, "I'm going to throw myself off a bridge and make a hole in the river". The next day I was told that a member of the family in New Zealand had committed suicide and that phrase immediately sprang back. I wrote that song as a response to hearing that news. When you come across news like that you just think about the sort of emotions that churned inside to make that person take such an extreme step.' The song came very quickly, almost writing itself. Although Tim says 'the song isn't an issue in the family', Neil was always aware some of his relatives wished he hadn't written it; not till the very end did Crowded House play it while his parents were in the audience.

When Neil and Sharon got home from Europe, he was immediately off again – to New Zealand and back to the States.

A blind date with destiny
• September 1985

**'I get a shudder of disgust at the words Party Boys
... but it was good, all part of the preparation.'**

—Neil Finn, 1996

The Mullanes tour wasn't the only apprenticeship Neil served for Crowded House. He also made a hurried tour of New Zealand pubs in an all-star covers band.

Neil and Dave Dobbyn had occasionally talked about playing together. In the early '80s both had emerged as New Zealand's leading singer-songwriters. Both shared similar cultural and musical backgrounds: Dobbyn was two years ahead of Neil at Sacred Heart College in Auckland, and both grew up on a diet in which the Beatles and Bowie were staples. Although they didn't know each other at school, they would have inevitably worked together a lot earlier if Neil hadn't been plucked from Auckland in 1977 to join the struggling Enz in London.

That year Dobbyn and his former Sacred Heart classmates Ian Morris and Peter Urlich were beginning to get noticed for their band Th' Dudes. Unlike the punks in Auckland who followed local leaders such as the Suburban Reptiles and Scavengers in the sudden emergence of young bands in the late '70s, Th' Dudes made it no secret they wanted to be rock stars. Their heroes were the Rolling Stones, Bowie, Iggy Pop, Lou Reed and Mott the Hoople; their local mentors were Hello Sailor whose legacy in New Zealand was the development of a pub-rock scene that demanded original music and high production values.

In Th' Dudes, Dave Dobbyn had grown from a shy lead guitarist, hiding behind peroxide hair, to an irrepressible performer, stealing the show from the good-looking frontman Urlich. He became the Mr Personality of New Zealand pub-rock, bubbling over with charisma and talent. With his band DD Smash he quickly became the leading drawcard on the booming New Zealand pub circuit of the early '80s. His idiosyncratic songs, soulful vocals, fiery guitar work and skills as a showman won him a devoted audience and the respect of musicians, few of whom were considered his equals. But one writer Dobbyn respected was Neil Finn, even if he found that Tim and Neil had an 'aloof, even authoritarian air about them' in the Enz heyday. 'That was part of the whole deal,' he says, 'it was always assumed they were making the best music.'

Dobbyn moved to Australia in 1983, but never conquered the new territory. At home, his career was briefly derailed by a riot at an outdoor concert in Auckland, the weekend of the final Split Enz shows in December 1984. The devastation stunned the country (and took the shine off the Enz private party following their 'final' concert that night). The police charged Dobbyn with inciting a riot. Their case was defeated in court, but the incident cost Dobbyn dearly. It was almost a year before the case was decided, and the momentum of his career was gone. There was no point in touring his new album, *The Optimist* –and his legal fees came to NZ$30,000.

The solution was obvious: go out on the road. But to tour the large showband that DD Smash had become would have been foolhardy at that time. So Roger King, then Dobbyn's manager, revived a concept which was low-rent, low-budget, aimed at the lowest common denominator – and sure to make money. In Australia, a group of rockers who were past their prime had joined forces to become the Party Boys: a temporary amalgamation in which ageing stars played the hits, grabbed the money – and ran. King's cohort in the venture was Mike Corless, a gum-chewing wide boy who ran, with adrenalin and swearing, Auckland's leading booking agency for the pub circuit. 'There was immense interest in pairing Neil and Dave together,' says King. 'They'd talked about it, but nothing had ever emerged until this Party Boys idea.'

Shortly after the Mullanes tour, King phoned Neil, who was just about to leave for the United States to record what would become the debut album of Crowded House. 'He said yes, he liked the idea of a one-off tour through New Zealand with Dave'. Neil says that at this stage, he wasn't told that the group was to be called the Party Boys.

King didn't hear anything more until a week before the tour was to begin; the musicians had started flying in and everything was prepared. 'The phone rings: it's Neil. He's completely demented, absolutely livid, saying, "What is this fucking Coruba Party Boys thing?" I said, I've no idea. He said, "It's me, and Dave, and it's all over New Zealand."'

Corless had found a sponsor: a brand of rum favoured by young pubgoers learning to drink. 'Yeah, mate, it's sweet,' he told King. 'They're in, Coruba's in. They love it. They're covering all my costs, all my promo, all the posters are up.'

Well, King replied, Neil's doing his block, he's pulled out of the tour. 'It was a nightmare,' he says. 'I didn't know which way to run. It was about as tacky as it gets, and Neil was refusing to have anything to do with it. Dave just wanted to hide his head under a pillow until it all went away.

'To his credit – he could have blown us out of the water on it – Neil came back a day later, saying, hell – let's go ahead.'

So just before going to Los Angeles, Neil toured the New Zealand pub circuit playing cover versions under the banner of a sticky rum. A lifelong distaste for sponsorship was intensified, but the spontaneous, crowd-pleasing nature of the Party Boys was not unrelated to the act evolved by Crowded House.

Neil visited Dobbyn in Sydney to rehearse. 'The idea was to play a bunch of our favourite covers, and a few of our own,' says Dobbyn. 'He seemed quite uptight, I thought that was his character. I showed him a few songs we might do: the Rolling Stones, the Doors, the Monkees, Led Zeppelin. They seemed so un-Neil. I was looking forward to seeing him on a pub stage, seeing what sparks would fly when he was confronted with the audience that comes to see me.'

The band assembled in Auckland. On bass was Mike Chunn, founding member of Split Enz – an affable character with a broad pop repertoire. On drums was the enthusiastic Peter 'Rooda' Warren from DD Smash, like a heavy metal circus performer – solid as a rock, and about as funky. Warren and Neil didn't get on, says King. 'Neil didn't like his playing and found him rather brash. Rooda thought Neil was a wuss. The Party Boys, you started off partying and didn't stop till the end. That was what the first one was like. This was much more ... regulated. There was endless reworking of the set and analysis of the tour, which made Peter Warren even more pissed off. Chunn just remained sublimely indifferent and smirked his way through the whole thing, finding it funny and just loving being on the stage with Neil, I think.'

Neil gave his only interview during the tour to the *Christchurch Star*. 'One thing I've discovered about playing pubs – besides how to avoid flying jugs – is that people are not there to love you. It's up to you to give them a good time. I made a mistake at the first gig, and told the audience this was the first time I'd played [a New Zealand pub tour]. Some joker yelled back, "Why the f*** are you up there then?" I thought, fair enough, I won't be silly enough to say that again. The pubs are a whole new experience. It seemed a great idea at the time, now I'm not so sure. Somehow I can see this band breaking up fairly soon.'

From the moment the tour began, Neil started replacing a lot of the songs with originals by himself or Dobbyn. 'He was a taskmaster, too,' says Dobbyn. 'Every soundcheck was a rehearsal, which I was glad of, because we were a bit sloppy.'

Early on in the tour, a woman approached them after the gig in Hamilton. She told them her name was Annaliesje – the same as Dobbyn's wife – and that she was clairvoyant. She took Dobbyn's hand and said, 'You can't hold cold beer in these hands, you'll suffer for it!' Then she took Neil's and said, 'You've got to take care of your voice. Be very careful on this tour or something may go wrong with your voice.' She suggested remedies, and advised him not to drink. 'That's when Neil started to get panicky and paranoid about getting sick,' says Dobbyn. 'She wanted us to have no fun.'

When the band reached Palmerston North, Neil started to come down with flu, and he wasn't looking forward to an awkward situation he knew was imminent: he was about to meet a devoted Split Enz fan from America. The girl had never seen Split Enz live and had come out to New Zealand on a scholarship.

Neil described the encounter at the shabby Albert Motor Inn in the Australian magazine *RAM*: 'She had a real mission from God. She wrote to my parents and said that she *had* to meet me. I was doing this tour with Dave Dobbyn and she was going to come and see the show "dressed in a gold lurex top". If I didn't talk to her or was mean to her, that would completely shatter her – this is what she wrote.'

Neil arranged with King that the girl was let into the house bar after the show, 'So they could talk it through, and treat her well,' says King. 'There were certainly no amorous overtones to the thing at all.'

Neil continued: 'I had a really chronic flu, and didn't feel like talking to anybody, but thought, "Well, I'll go." ' They talked in the hotel's private bar for an hour. 'She was telling me about her life, how her friends had committed suicide, and her parents were divorced and how much my songs had helped her through all that – and it was like "Great, but it's not easy for me to comment on or help you now."

'But she kept saying, as is the wont of these people, "Look I'm not here because I am a groupie, but because of the songs and everything." After a while I just had to leave, I was so sick. Two hours later, I came back to see if she had left or was still in the bar, and there happened to be this poet there called Gary McCormick, a vaguely known New Zealand poet.'

A fervent New Zealand music supporter, McCormick has become a household name in New Zealand. His bloke-ish humour has seen him evolve from poet to standup comic at rock gigs to television frontman. McCormick recalls that he was alone in the house bar because a heated discussion between the band and King had taken place, and they were in no mood to socialise. The young woman 'just seemed like a fan,' he says. 'Nothing was going on that I was aware of.'

Neil: 'So they're dancing with each other and they're really getting down, and I thought, "Oh no, what's going to happen? He'll take her to bed and she's going to feel really bad about the whole thing."'

Dobbyn remembers Neil's face turning ashen, and shortly afterwards found him in King's room. 'It seemed to spin Neil out,' says King. 'It topped it off, his own angst about the future, being on this dodgy tour, and the whole nature of everybody's behaviour. He was in a fair state of disarray. He felt he couldn't carry on with the tour. His anxieties overwhelmed him and he was tearful and upset. Dave spent a long time with him talking it through.'

Dobbyn: 'There was Neil, sitting in one of these horrible motel rooms, crying. He hadn't let on to us how depressed he was, though you could tell he was worried. I said, what's going on here? And Rog said, "He's pretty down, mate. He's worried about his life, marriage, money, the band, and he thinks he's got some horrible illness." We managed to cheer him up a bit so he didn't die in his sleep.'

Three hours before another show, King got a phone call. 'It's Neil, croaking. "You'll have to get me a throat specialist, my voice is packing in." Then Dobbyn's voice went out in sympathy. So I had to pack them off to a throat specialist who opened up his rooms to examine their throats.'

Dobbyn: 'Neither of us had had a problem with our voices before, and here was this German ear, nose and throat specialist saying, "You should stop sinkink for a munz." We still had two weeks to go and managed to get through, but with a touch of animosity to the clairvoyant called Annaliesje.'

But things had clicked musically. By the end most of the cover versions had been thrown out of the set, and Dobbyn remembers rehearsing 'Can't Carry On' and a few passages inspired by the Palmerston North incident, which later appeared in 'Mean To Me'. 'Neil was blown away because things would happen between the two of us. As guitarists we'd naturally knit together, so from that point on I always knew we could work together.'

The tour finally returned to Auckland to play the Mandalay, a club for about 1000 people. 'It was another packed madhouse of a show, and the PA blew out *twice*,' says King. 'Dobbyn, whose parents were there – I think it was the first gig his parents had come to – he completely lost it, stormed off the stage and left it to Neil. He was absolutely consummate at that moment, taking over, keeping the audience going, singing a capella, getting them to sing along while Dave had his flip out backstage. Here was Dave – the person with all the pub-rock experience, who really understood the crap that goes on in low-rent pub shows – totally fazed because of his parents. And Neil saved the day completely. It could have got ugly, there were a lot of people there and long silences. But Neil held it all together.

'And so we duly pressed the cash into Neil's hand. About five grand. Which was really going to change his life in the States.'

A caravan in the hills
• November 1985

'We couldn't believe we'd get that far so quickly. We found ourselves in LA, with a budget.'

—Paul Hester, 1992

Having survived the Party Boys experience, Neil flew back to Melbourne to see his family briefly, before returning to Los Angeles alone. It was time to look for a producer for the debut album. Both band and record company wanted someone well-known, but were coy about who they were after. 'Noddy from the Bay City Rollers,' said Paul.

They were seeking a big name, someone with a track record of producing guitar bands. But none of the current A-league of producers were interested in the unknown, unnamed entity from Australia. Among those approached were Keith Forsey (Billy Idol), David Kahne (Rank and File, Romeo Void) and Chris Hughes (Adam and the Ants, Tears for Fears). Forsey was always 'in the shower' whenever Stamler or Whalley phoned, the others declined. It looked as though David Tickle would get the job by default.

Days before the commitment was made to go with Tickle, Whalley called Stamler. 'I'm sending an album over for you to listen to,' he said. 'It's by a band called the Del Fuegos.' When Neil and Stamler listened to the rootsy East Coasters' second album *Boston, Mass.*, they thought it was okay, but couldn't see the relevance to their imminent project.

Whalley explained that while he was at Warners, the company had wanted to sign the Del Fuegos. 'But I saw a show and they were a *mess*. There were maybe one-and-a-half real songs in the whole set. But when I listened to their album, they're like *real songs*. I saw the producer's name and figured, this guy Mitchell Froom must have done everything that's good about the record.

Boston, Mass., in fact the Del Fuegos had 'humbly dedicated to our hero, Mitchell Froom'. Whalley arranged a meeting with Froom, and gave him the Finn/Hester demo tape. His response was rapid, Whalley later told *Music Connection*: 'Mitchell called me up the *next morning* – he had gone through the 10 or 12 songs that were on the tape, and he had a critique of *every* song, and he was on the money on every single one of 'em. And I said, "There is *no doubt* that this is the guy."'

Tickle was put on hold, while Neil went over to Froom's apartment. They spent half a day making music together, and Neil returned to Stamler's excited by the rapport they'd discovered. Finally, he'd met a real producer, one with enthusiasm, and very specific ideas for songs. 'He was very impressive,' says Neil. 'I liked the little reel he had of his own music, though I didn't relate to the Del Fuegos record particularly. But I knew there was something in there. And he had a very dry sense of humour.'

The respect went both ways: Froom was knocked out by the demo tape, which he thought didn't start well, but halfway through came 'Don't Dream It's Over' with just Neil on guitar. From there, the tape just got better. 'Maybe people who heard it only got through a few songs,' he says. 'I couldn't believe every producer in town turned it down. I was just struggling to get started when I got the tape and I thought, "Boy this is fabulous, incredible – there are all these great bands out there!" But of course, never again do you get a tape like that.'

At the time, Froom was in his early 30s and his career had finally started to gain momentum. It had been a good year already: he had played keyboards on between 40 and 50 albums, among them Elvis Costello's *King of America*, the Bangles' *Different Light*, the BoDeans' *Love & Hope & Sex & Dreams* and Marshall Crenshaw's *Downtown*. Froom grew up in Petaluma, a small town in northern California, and studied classical piano, pipe organ and harmony at university while playing in rock'n'roll bands in the San Francisco Bay Area. 'Really miserable stuff, but you have to learn somewhere,' he says. 'I wasn't one of those people who was brilliant right from the start – Stevie Winwood, say, singing "Gimme Some Lovin" at 17.' He is grateful that his early 'humiliating' experiences never got recorded.

Froom reluctantly moved to Los Angeles, where his break from 'bad, bad groups' came when he composed and performed the soundtrack to a low-budget movie, *Café Flesh*. He recorded it on an eight-track machine for under US$2000, and the score was later released as an album on Slash called *The Key of Cool*. Slash gave him the job of producing the Del Fuegos debut *The Longest Day* with a bargain-basement budget: Froom delivered it for just US$30,000, and the follow-up, *Boston, Mass.*, for US$50,000. Through his work for Slash, Froom became known as an adaptable, highly musical keyboardist. T-Bone Burnett hired him to play organ on the Los Lobos single 'Will the Wolf Survive?', which led to the work with Costello, Crenshaw and the BoDeans.

He quickly established a reputation for authenticity and a willingness to experiment. Froom explained his approach to production to *Rolling Stone* in 1986: 'Cut the crap; get rid of extraneous elements right away. Keep as many generic elements out as possible. Make sure the song is right and understand the emotional level on which it works. And then, to make a song interesting, I like to think that there's the 'wild element' – what Brian Jones did for the early Stones – where you go for something unusual, but it *still works*.'

Neil and Froom spent three days together working on the songs, the latter expanding on his ideas. He suggested a more soulful feel for 'Don't Dream It's Over', came up with a bass part and the organ solo. Neil thought, this is great, it's happening. Froom's minimalist keyboard style was refreshing after the flamboyant verbosity from Eddie Rayner in the Enz.

Now that Neil had met Froom, however, he was confused. 'I remember him sitting on the living-room couch, nervous and unsure,' says Stamler. 'He was switching back and forth: Should it be Mitchell? Should it be Tickle?' So Stamler suggested Neil call Tim for advice. 'I'd never met Tim, didn't know what their dynamic was, but something had to break the ice. He would have sat there all day torturing himself with the decision.'

Neil called Tim, and told him about Mitchell; both had already experienced Tickle. Tim said, if it was his record, he'd do it with Mitchell. That tipped the balance, however Neil had all but committed to Tickle. A delicate situation was resolved when Tickle offered to be engineer. 'It was set, it would be a great collaboration, the best of both,' says Stamler. Tickle said he didn't care about getting percentage points on the album, and that they could use a studio he had already booked. He was offered more money than Froom, to acknowledge he had more experience.

After six weeks back home in Melbourne, Neil once more flew to Los Angeles by himself for pre-production with Froom. During this period he stayed with Stamler and his wife Peggy in their condominium at Santa Monica, writing more songs for the album while there. A song with the original working title 'Roll Back the Ocean' was completed, having become 'Tombstone' at Tim's suggestion when the brothers were looking at Etruscan ruins during the holiday in Italy.

Another which made the first album was 'World Where You Live', the theme of which came to Neil in the middle of the night. He slept in the second bedroom, 'high above the kitchen'. At six o'clock each morning he would be woken by the 'unnecessarily loud' orgasmic screams of a woman having sex in the next-door condo. He would come down to breakfast and say, 'She was at it again this morning. It's a very peculiar sexual timetable.'

While visiting a local musician, Neil was offered a substance which at the time was still legal: ecstasy. 'It's called "the love drug",' he was told. There was a demo studio in the basement and, suitably inspired, Neil went down to write some songs. 'I spent about two hours, playing constantly,' he says. The memory of it slightly embarrasses him now. 'And I seriously thought I'd written about 15 songs, words and music, no problem. I taped the whole thing, and in the morning I found out I'd been turning the same side of the tape over and over. Maybe I missed some great stuff – but there were 45 minutes left, and it was all complete crap. Terrible, woeful stuff. I enjoyed the experience, but never felt compelled to do it again.'

Nevertheless, says Neil, stories get distorted and a few years later an Australian singer-songwriter was justifying massive ecstasy use to a mutual friend. You shouldn't wreck yourself, he was told. 'Hey man,' he replied, 'Neil Finn wrote the first Crowded House album on ecstasy!'

The real fun – and the real work – began a few weeks later when Paul and Nick arrived in Los Angeles. Neil arranged for a limousine to pick them up from the airport, to give them the 'classic LA experience', Nick in particular, as it was his first time in the United States. Nick, 'beside himself with excitement', responded appropriately, putting his head through the sunroof of the limo to scream, 'I love LA!' all the way to Hollywood.

Their accommodation was a two-bedroom art deco bungalow in the hills overlooking Hollywood found by Connie Froom, Mitchell's wife. It was owned by a woman named Kay Armor, whose fastidious concern about the house's upkeep led Neil to say that they were three sound engineers moving in rather than musicians. Although it was one bedroom short, it was within their budget and close to the studio. Neil and Nick got the bedrooms, while Paul slept in the hall. But, to his delight, the well-decorated house had 'a huge TV and a beautiful couch and a big kitchen'. He immediately discovered that Californian pot and television were made for each other. Sunday was their only day off, and Paul would settle in and quickly became addicted to basketball and the outrageous gall of the TV preachers such as Jimmy Swaggart. 'They had received the *sacred word of God* and these guys were selling it,' says Paul. 'They were adamant *God had rung them* – not today, but *the day before yesterday* – and now you could have the *sealed word of God* in an envelope for $50, tax deductible.'

Paul describes their home life as 'intense, but great – like being in the Partridge family on acid'. The trio quickly established their roles in the household. 'I was like the mother,' says Paul. 'I cooked, cleaned and did the shopping. Neil was Dad, who took care of finances and did a bit of management. Nick was the scout-leader, who everyone thought was tough and capable. He had a fix on everything and quickly made sure we had a car.'

Neil would have an early-to-bed, early-to-rise routine, while Nick and Paul would often watch TV until dawn before going to bed. So they would be hard to raise in the morning. Like a dorm master, Neil would crack the whip each morning, wanting to get to the studio, but to no avail. 'Nick and I would play the naughty boys,' says Paul. 'Nick would yell out for a cup of tea, and Neil would begrudgingly oblige. It was the only time of the day you could get Neil running around after us. The rest of the time, he'd be in charge.'

The house on North Sycamore is tucked beside a narrow, winding road near the Magic Castle and a Japanese restaurant called Yamashiro's. The band became natural converts to the all-night lifestyle, watching *Late Night with Letterman* after work then whipping down to the 24-hour supermarket at Highland and Franklin in their third-hand Chevy Caprice. To Paul, it was 'consumer paradise'. Nick was mocking up ideas for the album cover, and Capitol gave him an account at a local art shop, where they stocked up on boxes of pencils and sketchbooks. When not hitting the bright lights of the big city, they would spend evenings at home, making cups of tea, looking out at the skyline, drawing. If they weren't feeling inspired, there was always Hester to entertain them – bored and fussy, he'd flick lint into the corners of the room with a tea-towel.

Nick did, indeed, love LA. The clubs, the bars, driving on the right-hand side of the road, 'all that sexy stuff'. In downtime, he'd cruise to Malibu Beach, or visit the Huntington Beach pier to see where the surfing legends of the '60s took their woodies to the waves.

The gregarious Nick's social radar brought them in contact with a steady flow of bizarre characters. 'LA is full of them, and Nick would go out into the night and come back with the weirdest tales, and of course Neil and I were up for it in those days,' says Paul, who was introduced to an exotic world when he befriended a gay girl. Through word-of-mouth they would hear about unlicensed warehouse clubs holding rave parties. 'We'd go downtown at one in the morning to a big, underground place where there'd be illegal booze, and performance art happening and the most incredible looking people. Hollywood Babylon, really. We'd be out all night, dance, get pissed and have a fantastic time. Then we'd have to record the next day.'

Occasionally the party would end up back at North Sycamore. Neil would work late, then get home from the studio and find his home invaded by 'eccentric hordes of people gathered from the bottom rungs of LA lowlife'. Half a dozen people might be in the garden in their pyjamas, drinking gin, or a group of strangers sliding down the stairs on trays. Australians visiting LA would join in. Film-maker Evan English was staying in a greasy hotel on Sunset, and would enthrall them with stories from his research for *Ghosts of the Civil Dead*, which involved visiting LA high-security prisons. He later directed the videos for 'Something So Strong' and 'Nails in My Feet'. New Zealand-born singer Jenny Morris, then backing vocalist with INXS, remembers a crazy night when their tour passed through, where everybody partied with Hispanic band the Cruzados. Neil told her he'd spent all night writing songs, only to wake up in the morning and find they were really bad. 'I remember feeling happy about that: even Neil Finn does that!' Dave Dobbyn recalls the drunken phone-call he received from them during the party, while he was hard at work in Sydney on his biggest hit 'Slice of Heaven'. His friends had all been to a sell-out INXS show at the Palladium – and he was at home, writing a song for a cartoon about a sheepdog.

Among the locals who befriended them was the photographer Dennis Keeley, who shot all the baroque early publicity stills of the band. 'He was a fantastic guy, sweet and gentle,' says Paul. 'But every time we came back to LA it seemed he'd just been mugged. One time he was in his car. Then it was down by the beach. And one night he woke up in his bed in the middle of the night with a man standing over him holding a gun.' The band got used to hearing helicopters overhead during the night, and were woken by gunshots so often they stopped worrying about their life insurance and took bets whether it was a .45 or a Luger.

'We touched base with lots of odd people,' says Paul, 'so we had some weird parties. And a bit of a lost weekend in the middle of it all, when Neil returned to Melbourne. Debauchery reigned for 10 days or so. I completely lost my way, I don't know about Nick.' Like dial-a-pizza, top quality Californian pot would be conveniently delivered by 'the Rabbi'.

The band spent over four months at North Sycamore, and it was in this claustrophobic environment that they got to know each other properly. In 1987 they analysed each other's personality for Robert Lloyd of *Spin*.

Neil on Nick: 'He likes to experience everything that's going on. He hates missing out on anything. I couldn't handle giving myself to that many situations. It would exhaust me. Rather than go out every night, I'll go back to my room and just listen to a tape or read a book, because I like having my own time. But Nick is willing to give himself to anybody who comes along. He had LA sussed within three weeks. It's different paths to the same knowledge – Nick's path is to experience everything, get to know everybody.'

Nick on Paul: 'I think he has a major chemical imbalance. He's always at extremes. He has his totally over-the-top, very funny, intense periods, but when he's really down, everybody has to suffer with him. But he's remarkable when he's on the ball. He can keep an audience totally entertained. I don't think he likes touring. He's domestic. He likes his space, and his tea, and his cleaning utensils. His vacuum, his freshly laundered tea towels, his clean kitchen surfaces.'

Paul on Neil: 'In Split Enz, everybody had an animal to describe his personality. Neil was the ant. To a large degree, he is still very antish. Like, 'Where's the stage?' There it is. 'Right!' And he'll march straight onto it. He's a real noble sort of musician, Neil. I can imagine him as a knight or something. He can't sleep or relax if some one thing is bugging him, until he nuts it out. He'll come to you and talk it over. Make an apology if he thinks it's due, or tell people off, but in a fair way. Neil's always striving to do the right thing. But then, he likes to be a tear-ass, too, go crazy. Because he suppresses a lot of things, and people like that have an incredible explosive point. And he's the eternal songwriter. It's in his blood.'

The trio assembled at a rehearsal studio in Burbank. The complex catered especially for heavy metal bands; in adjacent rooms big-hair aspirants in hard rock regalia would do showcase gigs for record companies. Neil, Paul and Nick would sit in and watch the bizarre spectacle. The bands would cavort and wail with full productions, lighting rigs, powerful PAs, dry ice, the works ... but instead of an audience of 10,000 there would be two or three silent A&R men, who could be spotted at the other end of the room by their cigarettes glowing in the dark. The only noise between songs would be the claps and cheers of a few girlfriends.

Preparations completed, the band were ready to begin recording when David Tickle changed his mind about the arrangements. Explains Neil, 'He's a bit of a star, old David, and he started dicking us around.'

'He basically walked out,' says Stamler. 'Neil was screaming at him as he went. We were about to start work.'

At the last rehearsal, Tickle had arrived with his lawyer and brought up the topic of a percentage. Froom says it was a tense scene. 'He was saying to Neil, don't you remember how good those records we made together were? We were mystified. It was like, what's the problem? We're giving you more money, you said you didn't want points. He replied, "I didn't say points, I said *point*." Then it got extremely ugly.'

Neil told him where he could stick his point, and Tickle stormed out of the room. Now the band had one week to go before starting their first album, but no studio and no engineer. Stamler suggests the points issue was a red herring, that Tickle's ego 'got the better of him' and he had second thoughts. To Neil, it was a setback, but also a relief. 'Mitchell couldn't relate to him at all,' he says.

Froom called Larry Hirsh, with whom he had worked on Elvis Costello's *King of America*. Capitol offered them the B-studio in the Tower; Frank Sinatra and Nat King Cole had used the room in the 1950s. Hirsh was only available for the recording of basic rhythm tracks, then more engineer problems began.

Froom describes the recording sessions as 'fraught'; no fewer than five engineers eventually worked on the album. Recording shifted to Sunset Sound Factory, though the first engineer hired didn't show up. A personality clash quickly developed with his replacement. Neil describes Dennis Kirk as 'a Buddhist chain-smoker, obsessed with putting some radical effects on every sound that came out of my guitar. You ended up with a sound that had nothing to do with the song whatsoever. I started to get really pissed off.'

Recording was constantly interrupted by phone-calls from Kirk's girlfriend, and the band would stand around gagging while he turned the music down to coo into the receiver, 'Oh I know, baby doll, look I'll be home soonie ... oh, I love you too.' Then Froom noticed him writing swastika symbols next to Neil's fader on the mixing desk. He had to go.

Things calmed down with the recruitment of Tchad Blake, who had worked with Froom on music for a play. At the time Blake was just getting started as a sound engineer, after playing guitar in some 'horrible bands' in his 20s. 'My roots come from British progressive music,' he says. 'The rougher stuff, like Van Der Graaf Generator, early King Crimson, weird stuff like Hatfield and the North, and film music by Nino Rota.' His rapport with Froom began when he lent the fledgling producer the *Barbarella* soundtrack.

Froom describes Blake as 'eccentric in a really good way, he brings an interesting perspective on board'. Also Blake's manner was similarly down-to-earth, a rare quality in the engineers-as-rock-stars then strutting around LA. 'They just weren't cool as people: Tchad was most like a person you enjoy hanging out with.'

The recording of the debut album was an exuberant but anxious time, says Neil. 'The record was actually very difficult to make. I was pretty tormented by it, being in the studio the whole period, while Nick and Paul were having a ball.' Froom remembers the trio arriving with great energy and spirit ('Nick was on Mars, he was so excited') but occasionally the mood in the studio was tense. Looking back, he says a lot of it was because 'none of us knew what we were doing'.

Froom and Neil's weeks of pre-production, and the band's Burbank rehearsals, meant the recording proceeded rapidly. The sessions at Burbank, where they concentrated on the rhythm tracks, also gave them an idea of arrangements. So, by the time the group arrived at the studio, they were just going for good takes – and trying to get an engineer to stay for more than a couple of days. They were motivated by Froom's musicianship, and a shared desire to make an honest, direct album that sounded like a band playing together. It quickly became apparent that the lack of a big-name producer was actually an asset. Instead of having a lavish production imposed upon them – with results that sounded like a Mister Mister, or Starship, or any of the other bland rock fodder around at the time – the band developed its own identity.

Paul's drum tracks were the first to be recorded. Having worked out the various rhythms and feels in rehearsal, they just needed to be captured on tape. A reminder that they were recording in Hollywood came early, when the call went out for the drum doctor. Paul's kit had been acquired from a firm which specialised in hiring drums to the LA studios. Included in the service was daily maintenance. Paul quickly got used to a scene that would have seemed extraordinary back in Australia: each morning, before the session began, 'the drum doctor' arrived to check the kit, put on new skins if required, and polish it up. Another reminder that Paul was in consumer paradise. 'If I was playing and one of the drums went out of tune, I could ring a beeper number, and this guy would arrive to fix it. They insisted on it, as part of the service. I'd be playing away and Tchad would say, that tom sounds a bit funny. So it'd be like, "Down tools – I better make a call." '

The band and Froom quickly became aware of the influence their different cultures had on their music. For the first time, Neil was recording with someone who grew up with authentic American rock'n'roll. 'Neil didn't know what the blues were about, or anything about Elvis,' says Froom. 'They grew up on the Beatles and the Bee Gees, and didn't hear the authentic thing till later.' However for him, some of the great pop records were those which were trying to be R&B, but were one generation removed. 'The Beatles were very much an R&B band,' says Froom, 'and I guess the first Crowded House album was their R&B album: rhythmically it tried to feel good in that kind of way, in pop music.'

Neil acknowledges his own background 'has more of a British pop sensibility' and suggests that if the band had produced the album themselves, the arrangements would have been more complex, but the songs may have suffered. Froom's firm direction turned them into stripped, raw-boned pop.

This became apparent when 'Love You 'til the Day I Die' – with its pretty melody written on mandolin – changed into the edgiest cut on the album. Then Froom completely altered the groove of 'Something So Strong', which began life as a slow, dirgelike ballad. But the album already had too many ballads, so Froom had the idea to give it an upbeat groove, adding his Hammond B3 organ and a driving bassline. The result was a sunny mix of pop and R&B, Squeeze meets Booker T and the MGs. He also suggested a few chord changes, and ended up with a songwriting credit. 'He totally transformed it, and it was quite exciting,' says Neil. 'It was a big musical discovery period for me. Mitchell's obsessed with not accepting anything that's fake. That's his big thing, but in some cases he was overbound by that American tradition. Coming from where we do, you can mix things up, there's no right or wrong.'

Froom put his foot down, though, when it came to the recording of 'Now We're Getting Somewhere'. The song was written as a shuffle, and Froom wasn't happy with the feel Nick and Paul were getting. The band were still learning to play the song and, says Froom, for bands which don't play a lot of shuffles, it's the hardest thing to play. (Played slow or fast, a shuffle rhythm has an eighth-note pattern which skips on the backbeat. Randy Newman feels *his* career has suffered from his addiction to the shuffle: 'Musicians don't like it, drummers don't like it, and even people don't like it,' he said in 1996.)

Paul describes their attempts as 'a bastardisation of a shuffle – more like Melbourne swing'. So Froom called in the experts, the stellar rhythm section he'd recently worked with on Elvis Costello's rootsy *King of America*: Jim Keltner and Jerry Scheff. Together or separately, the pair had worked with an encyclopaedia of rock'n'roll legends, including Elvis Presley, the Beach Boys and John Lennon.

'It was an extremely black moment,' recalls Froom. 'We'd rehearsed the song for three or four days, just trying to get it to feel like anything. I was trying to explain the way to play a shuffle – and I could only explain it so far. Maybe I should have brought in a few records. But we tried cutting it again and again, and I just said to Neil, the song is either off, or I can get some people in that can play it in a cool way. Let's just try it.'

Neil wasn't about to say no, says Froom: it was a musical experience and, besides, they needed the song. 'Mitchell was atuned to the best elements of American music,' says Neil. 'I wasn't familiar enough before that to appreciate what a good shuffle was or a good soul groove.' Paul and Nick, however, were dark on the idea. To them, the slickness of West Coast session musicians was an anathema – and besides, what if it was a single and they weren't on it? 'Look, let's just try it,' said Froom. 'Maybe it'll be positive.'

Paul remembers the disappointment that he and Nick felt: it was as though they had failed. Reluctantly they agreed, 'for the good of the song, as a team kind of thing', says Paul.

Attitudes thawed as soon as Keltner and Scheff arrived. They quietly introduced themselves, sat down in the control booth, and started to tell a few stories. Scheff talked about being in Elvis Presley's band, Keltner on recording with Phil Spector and John Lennon during his lost weekend. Soon the old salts were holding court.

'We were like kids, it was wonderful,' says Paul. 'And Jim leans over and says, "Can I have a toke on that?" Sure! Go ahead!'

They listened to the demo, and Keltner looked over towards Neil and said, 'You know, that reminds me a little of John Lennon.'

'And Neil *loved* that,' says Froom.

Paul was taken aback when Keltner said, 'Look, I understand your position. Thanks for letting us play on your record.'

By this time, the band couldn't wait. Keltner and Scheff determined that the song was a 'three-beer shuffle': by the third Corona, they'd have it down.

When they started the first take, the band realised they were hearing the antithesis of slickness. 'Jim plays in a much more eccentric way than Paul,' says Froom, 'not like a studio guy at all. And Jerry Scheff played beautifully. In the solo section, it's the bass notes that make it open up. It sounds as if the harmonies are getting richer and richer as it goes by. A *great* feel.'

'It was a magical moment,' says Paul. 'And Nick and I actually got to sit and watch. That really charged us up after that, we were on a high.'

Neil was so stimulated by their playing, he got most of the vocal right first time, throwing himself into cathartic screams at the end. Nick pulled out his video camera. Listening back to the take in the control booth, Keltner started playing along with his brushes on a table. Tchad Blake set up a mike and, faded into a calliope melody from Froom's keyboard, the song had a new introduction. By the time the six-pack was finished, the song was done.

'When things go well in the studio, it's almost like your ears are wide open,' says Froom. 'You hear everything that's good, you're not worried. It was a very good day. Everybody was happy.'

As the sessions continued, says Paul, they realised how much they gained from the opportunity to meet Keltner and Scheff. 'Just watching Jim play was exciting. He got about four or five sounds out of the snare, just by the way he hit it. And he hit things really soft and sharp – and he had these *beautiful* wrists. He confirmed everything I already believed in.'

Now they were getting somewhere. Until then, the trio had been unsure of themselves, of whether they were, in fact, a band. And Froom felt the same way, says Neil. 'He was overly cautious about letting us have our head.' So he brought more visitors into the studio: a couple of singers from San Francisco (one of whom happened to be Joe Satriani) for backing vocals, and a session guitarist, Tim Pierce. 'I made a mistake,' says Froom. 'But then, I was new to it. I figured, there's a guy in LA I know who's got all the equipment – and in those days, sonic power was the thing. And Neil didn't rate himself either. Now, I think he's one of the best pop guitar players I've ever worked with.'

With all these other characters on board, Neil thought the idea of them being a band was becoming meaningless. 'I got really antsy about it,' he says, 'we had a few testy moments. I systematically took off the record most of what Tim Pierce played, and I don't think we used any of the singers. Because they sang with American accents, I couldn't stand it, it drove me crazy.'

But Neil shared some of the Froom's sentiments; back home on North Sycamore he shared his doubts bluntly with Paul and Nick. 'He sort of laid down the law,' says Paul. 'Saying, "Look, even though we are a band, we're not *really* a band yet. We haven't had anything go wrong yet, we haven't suffered the bad times or shared the good times. You guys have to realise it's hard for me to imagine this as a band."'

His colleagues were shocked, 'We'd been in 150 bands in the punk scene, changing every couple of weeks,' says Paul. 'Luckily I'd got the gig in Split Enz and it helped me see things as they really were. Nick came at it cold, while I was more cautious. I knew that more was going on than we were aware of, so I was willing to accept anything Neil had to say and go along with it.'

To Nick, 'it was kind of scary. But I later realised it was just Neil, articulating a set of strict guidelines he'd set for himself when he had any doubt. But the actuality of it wasn't really like that: there was still very positive room to build a relationship. Neil wrestling a few demons was something I didn't think I was in any place to offer any assistance. I was forging my own relationship. He was governing the rules, but I knew there was still a creative association and input I could have.'

It was a volatile time, but only once during this period did it become a physical confrontation ('there was one every record,' says Nick. 'Maybe not the second one: that was an easy, armchair kind of gig.'). As would become the norm, it began over something insignificant and forgotten. 'I remember Neil standing over Paul, who was sitting in the kitchen. He had a guitar over his head and was threatening to smash him with it. But not. And Paul not backing down or acting scared. It was total schoolboy stuff.'

When things had calmed down, they went down town 'to tie one on, to get over it', says Paul. 'And that's how we ended up with the take to "Don't Dream It's Over". It was the attitude everyone went in with that morning. It was quite an emotional time. It was hard for Neil being away from his family but at the same time, totally intriguing.'

The band came in to the studio, feeling a bit blue and hungover, and decided to have a crack at it. 'We immediately got this beautiful tempo, with this sad tragedy to it,' says Paul. 'It was the other magic moment of the record.'

The song had always been considered hot property, from the moment Neil wrote it. He was staying with Paul at Tim's house in Melbourne, having a few days away from his family. 'It was nothing serious, I just needed some space to get some work done,' he says. When some friends of Paul's arrived that he didn't feel like talking to, he shut himself in a room. In less than an hour, the song was there. When he got back to his house at Osborne Street, South Yarra, he made a demo. Over the steady scratched guitar rhythm he double-tracked a gentle vocal, then added a rough electric guitar break and some percussion: a pencil tapped on an electric heater.

Recording went just as smoothly, only requiring a couple of takes. Then they played it back, listening to it again and again, no-one saying what everyone thought: there was something special about this song. In the corridor outside, musicians and engineers working on other sessions gathered to listen. 'We were all singing along,' says Blake, 'going, *man* that's a great song.'

For Froom, it was a real ballad: it started one place, took a journey somewhere, then returned. You could take your time with it. 'The only other option,' he says, his eyes flickering with contempt, 'seemed to be a power ballad – which are so obnoxious I can't bear them.'

A few elements make the song special to Froom: the opening hook, the simple guitar rhythm, the scratch-and-flick riff known throughout New Zealand as 'the Maori strum' which leads every singalong. In pre-production they decided to add a bassline that gave it a languid R&B groove. And then there was the ecclesiastical organ part . . .

'I had this idea, my *one big* idea,' says Froom. 'Most people who play keyboards – particularly organ players – always want to do "Whiter Shade of Pale". It's such a great pop tune. There was already some dark synthesiser in the background, but my idea was to come in at this funny place, where there's a measure of 2/4. The whole song is in 4/4, there's a measure of 2/4, then in comes the organ, in such a way and a place that it gives it a slight shock value. It feels *so good*. That was my idea: to have a classical melody like "Whiter Shade of Pale", then continue the melody at the end of the solo, as if it was all of one piece.'

Not just any organ: it had to be a Hammond B3, the bulky wooden instrument essential on soul stages and gospel altars, with the spinning Leslie speaker giving it more vibrato than Mahalia Jackson. Froom had been honing his Hammond skills recently on *King of America* and in Costello's temporary, all-star band of 1985, the Confederates. 'I'm not taking any credit for bringing back the Hammond,' says Froom, 'but that was the idea.'

Froom also dusted off a Wurlitzer electric piano during the sessions for the first album, to use on 'World Where You Live'. 'When we made the record, those instruments were very unpopular,' he says. 'I called SIR – Studio Instrument Rentals – to rent a Wurlitzer and a Clavinette, and they said, "Is this a session for the Smithsonian Institute?" They couldn't believe anybody would want them, when there were *synthesisers* available.'

Froom's part ensured the song had the timelessness essential to make it a classic, and Neil was excited by what they had achieved. 'I'd never really experienced a Hammond organ being played properly before,' he says. 'That's the problem with keyboards, they don't last like a real instrument, they don't have the dynamic or the emotional range. People thought they were amazing, suddenly these vast vistas of sound opened up, but they're so identifiable with periods, and they're changing so fast.'

Recording the vocal on 'Don't Dream' went smoothly, though Froom thinks Neil was still finding his voice at the time, 'like trying on a suit of clothes'. Certainly he was surprised by the power of some of his vocal performances. 'He did a lot of incredible screaming on that record – I think a lot of it was angst. He was extremely worried. He would have relaxed more if I'd been a person of greater experience.' Among his regrets are two songs from the early demos which Froom feels he failed to capture successfully in the studio: 'Can't Carry On' and 'Walking On the Spot'. (Eddie Rayner co-produced with Neil the version of 'Can't Carry On' which appeared on second editions of the debut album.)

It was an anxious time: there was a lot at stake, and a lot to prove. For the first time, Neil was leading a band, giving others the directions. Not that they always listened – Paul was prone to down sticks for a cup of tea. Nick says that, while he had 'total licence' in his bass playing, 'I wasn't being told what to play, but I was lucky to get what was there out of my lack of ability. Mitchell's an incredible virtuoso on the keyboards, he can play virtually anything. He probably thought I was a bit of a Luddite. Certainly, Neil's ability in the studio was still a lot more savvy than ours.' Still, the musical naivety had its compensations, inspiring the 'happy accidents' which turn into creative ideas. Nick mentions the ending of 'World Where You Live' as an example. The 'to the world, to the world' refrain emerged when he didn't know what to play next, and went off on a journey of his own. 'Paul realised I was off with the pixies, then gave me the signal to resolve, to play the last beat. It ended up being a good combination of chords to finish the song.'

Nick says the sessions were 'a real test of Neil's mettle. He possibly touched on the fear of meglomania during that record, where he got very scared and had to look inside himself to see what his motivation was. He really screamed a couple of times on the record, singing like he really meant it.'

Neil reasoned it was the desperate edge of Hollywood, 'a good environment for conflict, for emotional energy. When it came to the singing I was ready to scream my lungs out.'

The tension continued when it came time to mix the album. Scott Litt, highly regarded for his work with REM, was brought in to mix for three days but Froom and Neil didn't like the results so he was let go, too. This caused more unpleasantness: Litt's manager called Froom's manager to say, how dare they, and that Froom would never work again. Stamler may have found him shy and awkward when they first met, but Froom's determination was easily the equal of Neil Finn's.

Back in Melbourne Neil played the rough mixes '20 or 30 times a day for about a week and drove Sharon crazy'. It was the first chance for Neil's colleagues in the Enz to hear what he'd been up to in LA. It seemed so *American*, particularly the male backing vocals in the choruses: 'Don't *dream* it's *overrrrr*.' Stamler remembers getting an anxious phone call from Neil in Australia: 'At that point he was panicking that we'd made the wrong record.'

Back in Los Angeles, Michael Frondelli was hired for the final mix. With so many engineers, it was a difficult job as the tapes were not well organised. 'We were extremely stressed out at that point,' says Froom. 'There were things about the record that were fun, but it's one of the few times Neil has ever gained weight, he was so stressed. Tim was making a record [*Big Canoe*, in London] with a great sound engineer, and Neil was worried his brother's record would be of higher quality.'

Stress levels were so high that when Frondelli started mixing, no-one noticed the whole record was accidentally mixed one or two per cent slow, adding to the melancholic sound of 'Don't Dream It's Over'. 'That's how amateurish we were on many levels,' says Froom.

The trio entered the studio with no name, and no concept as to who they were. They left with an album, a sense of identity – but still no name. Mullanes went quickly and without an argument. No-one could get a handle on it. Was it an Irish folk group? Italian? Were journalists going to quip they were the Mundanes? Malaise? Dullanes? 'There were a lot of bad uses for the name,' said Neil. Capitol were bringing a lot of pressure on them to make it 'Neil Finn and the . . .' which he was ambivalent about but that made the others a little queasy. Paul explained, 'That was underwriting the whole recording process. Nick and I got to wondering, what is this – a band, or Neil? Neil was saying, well you can't just expect to be a band because we haven't done anything yet. He'd been in LA on his own before we got there, he'd been doing everything, so there was nothing for him to get sentimental about. Fair enough. But, Neil Finn and the Tearaways? I didn't want to be a Tearaway. And by the end, we wanted to go against that pressure from Capitol: we wanted a band name.'

'We had to put up a convincing argument as to what our position was in the relationship,' says Nick. 'It was always that way. The rows would be incredibly intense when they exploded, but they never came to violence. We were cohesive enough never to be treacherous to each other. The treachery of the music industry, especially Hollywood, where it's almost a rule of thumb, was such an easy path to follow if you didn't want to face confrontation and put your cards on the table.'

Froom was typically blunt. The rapport between band and producer was so strong by the end of the sessions, he was asked to join. He replied: 'Only if we can be "Neil Finn and the Losers". I'd like to be a Loser.'

They even went to the local library to find a solution. Looking through books at random, Neil came across a phrase which was suitable for the album's title. It seemed to reflect the lifestyle they'd been leading: Crowded House. But their ideas for a name just made Capitol choke. Largest Living Things was the leading candidate; others included Krakatoa Chorus, Barbara Stanwyck's Chest and even the Record Company. There was a lot of indecision, and it was just before the deadline for the cover art that they took the easy option. 'Crowded House sounded strange to a lot of people, but so does every band name when you first hear it,' says Stamler. 'It certainly fitted.'

Hollywood & Vine
• April 1986

'In the entertainment business, imagination is a most valuable quality; it can take shape in a hit record, or in a dramatic structure, like the Tower.'

—Capitol founder Glenn Wallichs

The futuristic Capitol Tower quickly became a Hollywood icon when it was completed in 1956. Although the building has only 13 storeys – the maximum allowed in Los Angeles at the time – its architecture and musical history have given it an almost legendary status. One of the earliest circular office buildings, it looks like the Leaning Tower of Pisa rebuilt in the age of Sputnik. The architect was Welton Becket, who had designed Hilton hotels in Cuba and Egypt. The Tower's resemblance to a stack of records was assumed to reflect the activities taking place inside. Reinforcing the impression is the spindle emerging at the top (the light on the 82-foot spire flashes out the word *Hollywood* in morse code). But Becket chose the building's innovative design merely for cost efficiencies: being round, it is easier to heat, has better light – and there are fewer steps between offices.

The construction of the Capitol Tower made a statement about how far the company had come in only 14 years. Capitol was founded in 1942 by Hollywood record store magnate and music buff Glenn Wallichs, plus two prominent lyricists, Johnny Mercer ('Lazybones', 'Blues in the Night', 'Skylark') and Buddy DeSylva (a film studio executive who contributed to minor songs by Al Jolson, Jerome Kern and George Gershwin). It was a risky time to start a record label: the US had just entered the war, there was a shortage of shellac to make discs, and the musicians' union had imposed a ban on recording. But by the mid-'50s Capitol was the leading contender among independent labels taking on the 'big three', Columbia, RCA-Victor and Decca, all of which were based in New York.

Walk into the foyer at 1750 Vine Street, near the corner of Hollywood Boulevard, and the gold records on the walls testify to the label's achievements. The earliest hits came from the Nat Cole Trio, Freddie Slack, Peggy Lee, Mercer himself and children's records. In the '50s, the label was home to Nat 'King' Cole as a solo artist, Stan

Kenton, Tennessee Ernie Ford, Les Paul and Mary Ford. Frank Sinatra's career was resurrected when he left Columbia for Capitol and recorded classic albums such as *Songs for Swinging Lovers* with producer Nelson Riddle.

So successful was Capitol that in 1955, the major English label EMI bought an 85 per cent controlling interest in the company. For US$8.5 million, EMI acquired a champagne catalogue, a share of the lucrative American market – and a Stateside outlet for its own artists. (EMI upped its stake to 100 per cent in 1979.)

The Capitol building may be round, but the label was square: timeless, middle-of-the-road pop was its forte. Despite signing Gene Vincent, whose 'Be-Bop-A-Lula' went Top 10 in 1956, Capitol neglected rock'n'roll until the early '60s, when the Beach Boys became one of the label's most enduring and successful acts. Then, in 1964, EMI insisted Capitol release an English group the American label had originally turned down: the Beatles. Thanks to an extensive marketing campaign (demanded by Brian Epstein), Capitol achieved what was considered impossible: it broke a British act in the American charts.

The phenomenal success Capitol enjoyed with the Beatles carried the label through the '60s. So when the band broke up in 1970, the company was in trouble. In its 1970–71 financial year, despite successes with acts such as the Band and Grand Funk Railroad, Capitol lost US$8 million after taxes. Having the cash-cow of the Beatles had meant the company hadn't reacted to the rock explosion as vigorously as Columbia and Warner Bros – and the same unhip corporate attitudes remained from the '50s. The label was to spend the '70s and '80s catching up.

In 1971, Capitol founder Glenn Wallichs was retired and dying of cancer. But he convinced EMI to send one of its leading executives out from London to restructure the company. When the 37-year-old Bhaskar Menon arrived in Hollywood, most in the Tower thought his mission was to sell off Capitol; indeed he quickly sacked staff, cut back the artist roster and sold peripheral businesses. But the urbane Anglo-Indian was a record man rather than a business school graduate. He took the company apart to virtually start again from a much smaller core. By 1973, Capitol was back on its feet, with hit singles from Helen Reddy, Anne Murray, the Steve Miller Band, plus hit albums from Glen Campbell and Grand Funk Railroad. The year also saw multi-platinum sales of the Beatles 'red' and 'blue' compilations, Top 10 albums from all four ex-Beatles – and the arrival of a new English moneyspinner in Pink Floyd's perennial *Dark Side of the Moon*, which the company distributed for Harvest.

By the late '70s and early '80s, Capitol's biggest acts were long-established, mainstream artists such as Steve Miller, Bob Seger and Tina Turner, the latter two finally enjoying widespread success after years of struggle. Although the Knack reached double-platinum sales with their cheeky 'new Beatles of the new wave' campaign, the joke wore thin quickly. Of the few new acts which broke through in the early '80s, only Duran Duran, Billy Squier and Iron Maiden achieved consistent success. Capitol was still an anomaly in the music business: bigger than a boutique label but smaller than a major. With a sense of its own history – and two esteemed songwriters as founders – the company culture was still more musical than entrepreneurial, its approach more conservative than streetwise.

Both the physical design of the Tower and its musical legacy has an impact on the atmosphere inside. 'The building being round, the offices don't really have corners,' explains Julie Borchard, who joined the company in 1987. 'You're constantly working around the floors, from marketing, to promotion, to design. And there's this history you feel – the richness of the catalogue was never ignored.'

The members of Crowded House learnt their place in the pecking order when they arrived to start recording in one of the Capitol studios on the bottom floor. Security wouldn't let them into the carpark. 'We're Crowded House,' Paul told them. Crowded who? 'We're the new band.' But they quickly made themselves at home in the Tower. 'We were in there every day, running around, up and down the lift to the A&R department,' says Paul. 'We knew all the secretaries, we'd go out with them and find out who was doing what, who was in who's pants and in who's pocket. Guys had all the big jobs and the women were secretaries, assistants and PAs. Basically, the women did everything and the men bullshitted on. We learnt a lot – basically who not to upset.'

Nick and Paul quickly discovered the boundary when they threatened to go up and see Bhaskar Menon on the top floor – to give him a takeaway curry. 'He was the chairman of the board, appointed by the Beatles,' says Paul. 'No-one got to see him – he was the ghost who walked.' A horrified Tom Whalley made a panic phonecall to Gary Stamler to bring his band to order.

It wasn't only the band who were adept at 'working the building'. While they charmed the staff with their antics and affability, Stamler understood the culture and protocol within the Tower. 'He worked the company just right,' says Walter Lee, head of promotions when Crowded House signed to Capitol. 'He knew how to stroke egos, massage personalities, knew how to deal with all the repetitive people, how to stoke fires, how to keep it going. He didn't over do it, he didn't undersell it. He did it just right.' Stamler's familiarity with the staff (he had represented some of them in contract negotiations) had its disadvantages as well, says Paul. 'He could go in anytime and talk to anybody, which was good. But if we wanted to do something a bit quirky or offbeat, Gary would have more concern than was necessary.'

Nick Seymour in particular developed a rapport with the staff, as he stayed on in Hollywood after the record was finished to design the sleeve. The design department gave him his own office to work in, as well as the account at a local art shop. While he was 'stinking out the seventh floor' with his oil paints, and knowing few people in LA, he socialised with the staff after hours, going to gigs or dinners, 'basking in this opportunity to get to know these people', he says. Consequently, says Julie Borchard, Nick built 'a relationship and vibe with most parts of the company'.

Among them was Bill Burks, the head of creative services, who knew where the best bookshops and galleries were in the city. Nick thought artist Sue Coe should be commissioned for the cover of the debut album, 'showing the three of us in some obscure spatial arrangement in a little room, along the lines of a David Hockney operatic set'. Burks and Nick tossed ideas and names back and forth, trying to settle on an artist or image that suited them both. 'He knew the ballpark, I convinced him I had a picture in mind,' says Nick, who mocked up an illustration from various photos of the band. Burks asked Nick to paint the cover himself.

Tommy Steele, later head of design at Capitol, says, 'Here was a band member who was actually a good painter and had some vision. You hope for that – a David Byrne or a Lou Reed or someone who has the aesthetics. We always felt a little handcuffed working with Nick until he came in – and he'd have this amazing painting which would blow you away. He's not a graphic designer, so that was what we would try to contribute, to make it work as a cover.'

But seeing the results, the executives further up the Tower 'just did not get it', says Nick. They didn't think his ideas were commercial enough. 'They said, "What's this? This is not *rock*." This was in Hollywood, in 1986, when Poison, Wasp and Guns N' Roses were big. They really wanted an alternative cover. We dug our heels in. Every record, there's been some controversy about the cover.' Capitol relented when Neil – who, as songwriter, they took the most seriously – said that the band's relationship with the record company would suffer if they didn't use Nick's cover art.

'There was a lot of confusion in Capitol about the "image" of the band,' says Paul. 'Any idea they came up with, we were a bit suss about. Nick had never dealt with corporate America before. Boy, did he get a rude shock. There are so many people you have to run things by, and they very rarely have an opinion. They never say, you can't do that – but everybody has to feel like they're involved.'

Crowded House had the music; what these clean-cut Anzacs needed was a *look*. Something a little more exotic than their earliest publicity photo: white shirts, rolled-up sleeves, and a Friday-night trim at the barber. After all, strutting down Sunset Boulevard was their competition in the mid-80s: the *hair bands*, rock'n'roll wannabes in poodle bouffants, spandex trousers, leather vests, cowboy boots, metal studs, mascara and tattoos.

With his art-school aesthetic, Nick slipped easily into the Noel Crombie role. 'What I liked about Split Enz was they had *outfits*. We needed a specific image so people would remember us if they saw us. My idea was to instil a familiarity.' The costumes which emerged – pegged trousers, short-cut matador jackets, hand-painted with baroque curlicues and filigrees – were carried through the album cover, promo shots, stage sets and videos. 'I wanted it to have the integrity of folk art, like the Reverend Howard Finster: hand-written, a bit cheesy but kind of cute. It worked. I wanted it to be a little more sexy than it was, with a slight Musketeers bravado, but you couldn't get Neil and Paul into anything too flamboyant.'

At the time of the first Crowded House album, music videos had recently become crucial in the marketing of an act. Head of the video department at Capitol was Mick Kleber, an erudite polymath with an unusual background for the LA rock business. He had gone to Harvard on a naval reserve scholarship, so after graduating in 20th century American culture (with a special interest in the lavish musicals of Busby Berkeley) he served seven years in the Marines. He did a tour of duty in Vietnam, then was seconded to Washington, where he was an aide in the White House during the Watergate years. When Nixon announced his resignation in 1974, it was Kleber who introduced him to the worldwide television audience, 'Ladies and gentlemen, the President of the United States . . .'

After working on media projects for the 1976 US bicentennial, and as Don McLean's road manager for a year, Kleber moved to Los Angeles and became a music journalist. He joined Capitol Records as a creative director where, because of his television experience, he was well placed when the video explosion occurred in the early '80s. 'Originally we were this little experimental unit, not even in the Tower but across the street. Then all of a sudden we had money and nobody else did.'

It took a while for cable television to infiltrate middle America, but after Michael Jackson's 'Billie Jean' clip, music videos and the MTV channel boomed. At the time, it was thought the major networks would program video shows in primetime, and that fans would buy the clips for home use just like records, so investment in rock videos was at an all-time high. It was the era of huge budgets and extravagant production values.

Crowded House however were keen to keep costs down and have the videos made in Australia, as they were wary of Capitol's American perspective when it came to image-making. 'The feeling I got from Neil,' says Kleber, 'was that this band had come out of a theatrical tradition, that they had a retinue of creative people in Australia and New Zealand at their beck and call. They wouldn't have to spend an enormous amount of money to make a viable video.'

Kleber was doubtful, as he hadn't seen anything out of Australia that could compete with American videos. 'But we also weren't sure "World Where You Live" was going to happen at radio anyway, so didn't want to spend a lot of money at that point. We wanted to wait and save money to spend on "Don't Dream It's Over".'

Noel Crombie was enlisted as art director on 'World Where You Live'. 'Neil had this legacy of the Split Enz presentation,' says Crombie, 'but I think he and the others were wary of making it too Enzy. They were in this middle ground: of wanting an image, but not one that was too strong. They deliberated on it an awful lot.'

'World Where You Live' and 'Mean To Me' were filmed simultaneously at the Melbourne Showgrounds. In between shots, the band would run between the two sets. Directed by Ray Argall, 'World' featured the band in a cluttered room which moved on its own axis. Hoping to convey a feeling of disorientation, Crombie built the set on a rig he had used for a TV programme about the Australian aviator Charles Kingsford Smith. The colourful, stylish video opens with Neil inviting the audience into a topsy-turvy house crowded with furniture. Inside, the band is playing with enthusiasm; with their natty suits and Nick's double-bass, they could be a mariachi rockabilly combo. By the closing scene, the band have shifted to being the entertainment at a '50s country dance.

The clip for 'Mean to Me' is a lot more humble. It reunited Nick with the director Richard Lowenstein, with whom he had worked on the videos for Tim's *Escapade* album. By 1986, says Nick, Lowenstein 'wanted to focus on film-making and felt he was a bit long in the tooth for videos. Ironically, he makes a lot of commercials now.' The camera spins around the band as they perform in an empty warehouse; the grainy footage is livened up with brightly coloured scribbles and casual scenes of the bandmembers at home. While Neil sings earnestly, Nick mouths 'I love you' to the camera. During the video shoot, Paul met a tape operator, Mardi Summerfield. The pair soon became a couple.

Back in Hollywood, Kleber and his colleagues at Capitol were disappointed by the early Australian clips. They were charming, and quaint, but didn't have the 'explosive moments' needed to gain any notice on MTV at the time. They were particularly unhappy with 'Now We're Getting Somewhere', filmed later in mountains near Melbourne for under Aus$5000. Scenes of Crowded House carousing in the snow are interspersed with handheld footage of the band on stage (with Gill Civil on keyboards).

To Capitol, the video seemed amateurish and, worse, a rip-off of the Beatles in *Help!*. 'Not that the Beatles are sacrosanct, but when *they* were flopping around in the snow, it seemed totally fresh,' says Kleber. 'I thought it was the wrong way to go. It was like, are you saying you're the new Beatles?'

In retrospect, the spoofy nature of the video was exactly the personality the band were to convey in the States, and the fashions in video-making have since encouraged low-budget, homemade clips. 'But then, it didn't seem like an attempt to be competitive. We wanted to go to MTV and say, Crowded House: not only is their music great, but their videos are fantastic. That's what we achieved with "Don't Dream It's Over".'

The clip for the band's breakthrough single was directed by Alex Proyas, who has since become a successful film director (*The Crow*). Kleber had been impressed with an INXS video shot by Proyas and his company Meaningful Eye Contact, which featured long Steadicam shots of the band in a desert. When Crowded House balked, Capitol insisted. 'We said, "If it's not Alex Proyas, then there's no video: spend your own money",' says Kleber. 'We knew they wouldn't go with that, as they'd resisted us spending money on the earlier videos.

'I found Proyas to be like Hitchcock, not glamorous but a really intriguing filmmaker. I'm really glad we held our ground. When the video came in, I couldn't have been more thrilled.' It was professional, but captured the character of the band: it was credible.

The clip begins with the smashing of a cup and saucer, then the camera glides through a house showing the band in various domestic scenes: Neil playing guitar, Paul vacuuming, Nick looking through a family album. Images for the video came from discussions Proyas had with Neil and Nick; sub-titles explain the connections to the bandmembers' childhoods, and among the props are home-movie reels, religious paraphernalia and kitchen utensils. It finishes with the band in rehearsal, then Neil puts on an overcoat and walks out into the countryside.

'Something So Strong' was also directed by an Australian, Evan English, but the band have mixed feelings about the excruciatingly wholesome clip. 'It ended up looking like a commercial for margarine,' says Nick. The action takes place in a barn. Drenched with golden sunshine, the band perform the song to an audience of healthy, smiling girls who dance among the hay bales, and tease Neil with flowers and paper planes. An envious male extra dances with the washing line, then climbs on board a tractor, taking Paul with him. It finishes with a surprise bucket of water being thrown at Nick. 'It was anti-glamorous,' says Kleber. 'Those women would never have been cast in the US. They looked like *real women* – not actresses. And that worked to its advantage. It said, these guys were real, not fake.'

The intention of English, a radical left-winger, was to 'tap into the soft, white underbelly of middle America,' says Neil. 'He wanted to penetrate the heartland of niceness, and subvert it once we'd got them. I think it looked a bit much like a toothpaste commercial myself. But certain people you'd never expect really liked that video. Elvis Costello for one. That really surprised me.'

To Paul, the clip was 'bordering on the edge. I don't think it went far enough. I think it should have been a priest on the tractor, taking young boys for rides ...'

The big schmooze
• June 1986

'I had to play until about three in the morning for all these pissed record executives. It was the best thing I did to vibe people up.'

—Neil Finn, 1996

Back home in Australia, on 31 May, a cryptic message was written on a blackboard beside the modest stage in Melbourne's Middle Park Hotel – *Split House*. Later that night it was a full house: 1000 people were packed into the small room. Word had got out, Split Enz was hastily reuniting for a one-off performance. But the extra surprise was the support act, the debut of Neil Finn's new band. It had almost taken place in early April, when the still-unnamed band was booked to play a benefit gig for Greenpeace in Auckland as 'Neil Finn'. Instead, Split Enz donned their costumes once more to join Jackson Browne, Graham Nash and Neil Young on the bill.

At their Melbourne debut, Crowded House – joined by Eddie Rayner on keyboards – gave a short, punchy set, occasionally interrupted by tuning problems and confusion about which song to play next. Neil Finn had an increased confidence on stage, wrote Byron Smith in *Juke*. He was revelling in playing his new material off their debut album ('That's What I Call Love', 'Hole in the River', 'Love You 'til the Day I Die', 'Now We're Getting Somewhere', 'World Where You Live'), the release of which was imminent. 'He squeezed every possible ounce from the songs, like a kid with a new toy.' Thrilled with his guitar sound on stage, Neil told *RAM* he felt like taking a solo every song.

If it had been any other band on next, Crowded House would have been a hard act to follow. Neil Finn didn't need reminding as his closest friends joined him on stage for an informal but enthusiastic two-hour romp through the Enz greatest hits. It was their second gig together in the eighteen months since the Enz With a Bang shows but, wrote Smith, 'the brothers' vocals blended, as always, like milk and honey'.

Crowded House quickly endeared themselves to their Australian label. The Melbourne offices of EMI became like their second home.

As they had done in the Tower, they charmed everyone in the building. 'That's why we got stuck into the project – we loved them as people,' says Michael Matthews, EMI Australia's long-serving promotions manager. 'They'd come in and visit, not for any reason, they might just be in the area. It was very clever of them to do that, as a PR gesture. So many bands criticise their label, which is counterproductive.'

The Melbourne office had the idea of throwing a 'crowded house' party to launch the band. 'It wasn't a concept that required a brain surgeon to think up,' says Paul Martinovich, later the head of EMI Australia, 'but it was our most successful launch ever.'

Matthews's assistant David Hunt provided the venue, his stylish two-storeyed terraced house in the hip area of Albert Park. It was made for parties, and tasks were shared among the EMI staff as if it was a family gathering. They put spotlights in the trees, covered the backyard with awnings, decorated the living-room, hung banners across the front porch, brought in crates of beer and heated up pies and sausage rolls in the oven. The only hired hands were a couple of bouncers on the door; a radio station contest brought in a group of fans to join the guests from the media and music industry.

The band set up in the corner of the small living room. The house was so packed, says Matthews, 'as people came in the front door we had to push some out the back. With just their acoustic set-up they sounded fantastic. Usually with industry people, they come, they drink, eat your food, do some drugs, fart and then piss off. No-one listens to the music. But this was like having your own ragey party with all your mates, and having a really top-notch band performing at it.'

'They blew the place to pieces,' says Martinovich, 'The adrenaline rush from everyone was incredible. It gave them a good feel for the band, they were casual and relaxed, a band you could bring home.'

It worked so well the band repeated the act at a ratings party for local radio station Eon FM, playing in the atrium of their building. Then branches of EMI in the other Australian states had their own Crowded House parties. In the era of techno pop and equipment overkill, such casual, accessible, impromptu gigs hadn't been seen for years. Crowded House called it their 'busking' routine; almost five years later, MTV borrowed the idea for a show, and called it *Unplugged*.

In Los Angeles, inside the Capitol Tower, Jeremy Hammond, a product manager at Capitol, was well disposed to the band before they even had a name. He remembers receiving an early publicity picture of the trio: they had black trousers, white shirts, rolled-up sleeves. Good keen men. In the era of Prince, Billy Idol and Duran Duran, it was refreshing: they looked cool, like regular guys. But as Neil ran through a few ideas on what they were going to call themselves, Hammond tried to show enthusiasm, but was gagging inside: 'The Largest Living Things? God help us, no! Crowded House? The French will never be able to pronounce it: *crooded hoose.*'

Hammond was one step ahead of his colleagues when it came to support for the band: he was born in New Zealand. When he was 12, in 1968, he moved to England with his parents. In 1977, in the small city of Guildford, 30 miles south of London, he wandered into a show by a band called Split Enz. He'd never seen them, or heard their records, but knew they were New Zealanders. 'They were brilliant. After the show, they were all in the pub next door celebrating Neil's birthday. I introduced myself. They were ordinary guys, said have a beer with us.'

Hammond was so impressed he was tempted to start a Split Enz fan club at the time, although they had very few fans in England. He did join the music business, however, and in 1980 was working for CBS Australia when *True Colours* went through the roof. He had always held on to his laser-etched vinyl copy of that album, and remained a fan.

So when Tom Whalley told him about this band he didn't want to sign on his first day, Hammond didn't need convincing to get in behind. He was given the job of marketing the band.

'I listened to the album, which I thought was amazing. They were remarkable, they really wanted to go out there and do a show, and present themselves in a unique way. There was an interesting chemistry between them: Neil, always the consummate artist, temperamental, melancholy, and very driven. Nick was the bohemian and Paul should have been in the Marx Brothers.

'In meetings they had a firm direction on what they wanted to do visually, with the packaging, videos. Nick was doing the artwork, which was risky, but he had a strong vision. The company was hesitant because it was very conservative and their ideas were a little offbeat. The head of sales would be saying, it's not commercial, but Don Zimmermann, the president of the label, was very open-minded.'

Capitol's original press release described the 'unique history' of the band members: '*Neil Mullane Finn* emanates from the volcanic regions of New Zealand. Born in 1958, he was raised in the small rural town of Te Awamutu. After breaking several bones playing rugby as a youngster, he gave up sport for a more gruelling musical career. In his spare time, he studies volcanoes ... *Paul Newell Hester* was born in Melbourne, Australia, in 1959. The proud offspring of convict ancestors, he is the son of Mulga Mike Hester, the legendary bushman of the Northern Territory of Australia. Paul once had the distinction of having 20 jobs in two years, a fact no doubt responsible for his uncanny ability to make absolutely anyone laugh. A great mimic with a passion for tidiness, he owns goats in New Zealand that he's never seen ... *Nicholas More Seymour*, born in Benalla, Australia, in 1958, also has convict ancestors ... Welcome to the Crowded House. It's a house you'll find crowded with delight.'

Hammond knew promoting the band was going to be difficult: if they didn't manage to get something on radio quickly, it was all over. The record company was very promotions driven, but not when it came to nurturing artists from scratch – and this band was only available in the States for short periods of time. Also, some senior executives in the company did not share Whalley and Hammond's belief in Crowded House. There was a positive reaction to the debut album, but some doubt whether it contained a hit single.

In the rigidly formatted radio market in the States at this time, the two main formats for new music were CHR (contemporary hit radio, or Top 40) and AOR (album oriented radio). But Top 40 was the crucial force. College radio wasn't important yet, and few alternative radio stations existed. It was also the era in which, when it came to getting singles on radio, independent promoters held all the power.

Record companies would pay an independent promoter to gain radio 'adds' on a single – songs added to stations' playlists. It's a shadowy system, a way of distancing the companies from direct payola in which programme directors are paid for airplay with money, drugs or other enticements. But the 'indies' had a stranglehold on Top 40 stations: you couldn't get a single away without them (as Split Enz found out with 'I Got You'). And their services were expensive, costing up to US$250,000 to get a song significant airplay. 'So record companies had to decide which records they were going to get behind, because the financial consequences were enormous,' says Stamler. 'If they got a song up the charts and it didn't stick, they'd blown a quarter of a million dollars. They needed to know they had a hit song which would generate sales.'

However in March, 1986, all the major record companies had grouped together to boycott the independent promoters. This followed embarrassing revelations on NBC television, which alleged links between some of the 'indies' and the Mafia. Ironically, the person the programme concentrated on, Joe Isgro, was filmed having lunch with Capitol's head of promotions, Walter Lee. There was nothing illegal or clandestine about their association – they were both doing their jobs – but the secret filming of the flamboyant Isgro, and the other connections the programme made (for example, with Mafia god-father John Gotti) left the impression that the practice of independent promotion was suspect at best. 'These guys lived like Arab sheiks,' says Lee. 'One of them had a stable of 40 racehorses.'

As Fredric Dannen reported in his acclaimed music business exposé *Hit Men*, while the NBC-TV revelations were embarrassing, 'much of the record industry rejoiced in private'. Now they could self-righteously insist that the record business wasn't corrupt, and put the cripplingly expensive 'indies' out of business. Within weeks, the major record companies ostentatiously started their boycott.

With a lack of conviction from the promotions department about possible singles on the debut album, it was unlikely the indies would have been hired for Crowded House's first release anyway. In July, the company sent out a promotional EP to AOR stations, with 'World Where You Live' as the lead track, and 'Something So Strong' and 'Mean to Me' as fillers. If the song worked at AOR, they would then try and cross it over to Top 40 stations.

But the brooding 'World Where You Live' attracted no interest from AOR radio. With all Capitol's promotional emphasis at this time being towards getting radio play, the company was at a loss on what to do next. 'About three months into the release of the album, the climate at the company – beyond a few real believers – was that there were lots of problems with the record,' says Stamler.

Hammond became an in-house cheerleader for the album at Capitol. He knew they had to do something off-beat to spark interest in the record. In the meantime, they did get some encouragement from retailers and reviewers, which kept them going for the first six months. In particular, Charles M Young of *Musician* magazine was an enthusiast, and excerpts from his review were used in an advertising campaign. He wrote that the *Crowded House* album had given his life a purpose – to make people buy it.

'They have written five out of 10 songs on their debut album that Paul McCartney should sell his children to have written. We're talking your basic gorgeous melodies here, melodies that almost no-one is writing anymore because almost everyone is concentrating on recycling old riffs through all the latest technotwaddle.

'So I'm just telling you for the permanent written record that "Don't Dream It's Over" is the best ballad of the year, with no expectation that anybody is going to do anything about it.'

Capitol had been reluctant to make 'Don't Dream It's Over', the entrancing ballad which had won so much critical acclaim, their first release off the album. The attitude was, you don't release a ballad as your first single – and with an organ solo, 'Dream' was so retro . . . 'This was in the era of synthesisers and British pop such as Tears for Fears and Duran Duran,' says Stamler. 'It didn't fit. And people would run for the hills at something a bit different.'

In the meantime, Hammond was leading a private campaign for the band. 'The head of promotions at the company was reluctant to do anything, even service songs to programme directors,' he says. So he took matters in his own hands. Without telling the radio promotions department at Capitol, he arrived uninvited at a radio convention with a box of *Crowded House* cassettes inside his jacket. At cocktail hour, he went around the programme directors, introduced himself, and gave each of them a copy of the album. 'This is a band we love,' he said. 'Take it home, have a listen, it's just for you.'

Three weeks later, Hammond was hauled onto the mat of the Capitol head of promotions, Walter Lee. He showed Hammond a letter he'd received from the programme director of the soft-pop station Coast 104. 'It was like a critique of the album,' says Hammond. 'He wrote, Dear Walter – one of your guys, Jeremy Hammond, gave me a cassette of this band. I think it's good, it has potential.'

Lee said to Hammond, what is this, do you want my job? 'He was aggressive, threatening me over it. But I could sense . . . he also liked my cheek.'

Hammond was a fan of Dierdre O'Donoghue, a personality DJ who had her own show on KCRW in Los Angeles. 'She played great music, and had a killer sexy voice, deep and gravelly. I thought she should be playing Crowded House.' He sent O'Donoghue the album, then several days later phoned the station, requesting they play 'Don't Dream It's Over'.

'I rang in about three times, like some kid. Then one night it came on. I went nuts. It was the first time it had been played in America. This was even before the Loop in Chicago. It didn't mean a lot, it was a public radio station, but it was a small breakthrough. These private victories kept us going – the record wasn't getting much help internally – but lots of people in the lower ranks were right behind it.'

Although Zimmermann, the president of Capitol was supportive, there was no evidence that the record was going to make an impact, so the company was reluctant to spend any more money. They had paid for two low-budget videos already, 'World Where You Live' (which received occasional airplay on MTV), and 'Mean to Me', the first single in Australia (where it reached No 26) and New Zealand.

Capitol agreed to bring Neil over to the States for one last promotional trip – on his own. They weren't prepared to pay for Paul and Nick to go.

Adding to the difficulties was the increasing unreliability of Lars Sorenson, whose effectiveness as manager had been deteriorating for months as other issues and financial problems distracted him.

Grant Thomas passed through Los Angeles at this time, after representing an Australian artist in New York. He had dinner with Stamler, who sounded him out about his availability: 'We've got a few problems in Australia – would you be interested in getting involved with Neil?' Thomas wasn't sure, he had a lot of respect for Neil, but he remembered a few stand-up arguments they'd had in the Enz days. A couple of days later, Thomas was in Auckland when he got a call from Neil asking if he would look after the Australian end. Having been in America a lot recently, Thomas hadn't even heard the record. Neil sent a copy over, and Thomas called back: 'Count me in.'

Neil then flew to Los Angeles to start the solo promotional visit – his first since the album had been released – and, at LA airport, found his tickets and hotel bookings hadn't gone through. When Sorenson unsuccessfully tried to pay for the airline tickets with a JC Penney card, Stamler and Neil split the costs between them on their credit cards.

At this point, Gary Stamler officially became the manager of the band. He had virtually been doing the job for months. Others approached for the job in the States and Australia didn't seem to have the right commitment or rapport. Up to then Stamler had worked mainly as a music industry attorney in Los Angeles, negotiating contracts for artists and executives. Stamler jokes that Paul Hester liked his connection with Ringo Starr; Neil, the fact that the final Split Enz show in New Zealand had made such an impression.

'I was very reluctant, feeling at this stage Neil needed a manager with more experience. I didn't want to risk blowing it for him. Those arguments became less persuasive when Neil said, well you're doing it anyhow. As I recall, I wasn't asked, just told. Neil said if I didn't do it, he was going back to Australia and that was that for this record.'

Stamler recalls this as 'a dark period. Neil was very depressed. I remember him calling me from the different cities he was in, by himself. Very clearly there was no momentum in the project at that point.'

Although Neil describes the beginning of the solo trip in August 1986 as 'a washout', he says it eventually got results. 'I got to Toronto, having not slept for 48 hours, and I had to do 20 interviews in one day.'

It was Hammond's idea to take him to Nashville, where Capitol was holding its international conference of product and marketing managers. 'Tina Turner was there,' he says, 'and people in the company from around the world. So I asked Neil to come – not to play – just to be there. I went out on the town with him and we returned about 10 o'clock when I knew everybody would be in the bar, drunk.

Neil had his acoustic guitar with him, and Hammond set him up on top of a table, using the bar's PA and microphone, which he tied to the back of a chair. 'He did an impromptu performance for about 50 Capitol people till one in the morning,' says Hammond. 'He had the whole place rocking, singing everything – the album, requests, Beatles songs, the Bee Gees – everyone was drinking, having a great time. I remember seeing his strumming hand afterwards – he had no plectrum – and his hand was blood red, he'd ripped the tops of his fingers off playing the guitar.'

Capitol's international marketing reps were knocked out, particularly Kick Van Hengel, based in Los Angeles, and Heinz Henn, of EMI in London. They suggested the band should go to Europe on a small-scale promotional tour – an idea the US company had already rejected for their own country. Neil returned to Australia and said to Thomas, 'This guy wants to take us to Europe, Heinz Henn's his name, you're our manager, let's go.'

In late August, 1986, Capitol released the single of 'Don't Dream It's Over'; a few days later, the band and Thomas were off to Europe. That the budget was extremely tight (the company was reluctant to provide a ticket for Thomas) worked to their advantage. Crowded House developed their 'busking' routine – playing small, packed rooms with just acoustic guitar, bass and snare drum, using practice amps for a PA – and charmed everyone.

'It was the great schmooze-on in Europe,' says Paul. 'We scratched away on a budget of nothing, using Grant's credit card and coercing people at the record company to let us do our laundry in their homes. We'd double, triple, quadruple up in rooms, with our socks and undies hanging everywhere. We'd get drunk at the record company's expense, eat their food and travel around in a mini-van, getting lost in traffic.

'We ended up on the *Riva del Guarda*, this Italian TV variety show that went out to 30 million people, with Belinda Carlisle and Chrissie Hynde on the show. We found ourselves in a disco where we got this soul train happening, with the Go Gos taggin' on, and the big black guy from the Pretenders who kept slapping Nick on the arse. We were like the *happening guys*. Neil was breakdancing on his head. Nick pedalled through the lobby of the hotel late one night, pissed as a fart, with a rose in his mouth. All these label people were sitting around and he was yelling out *"Viva Italia!"* We overwhelmed people the first time we went to Europe.'

In countries where they couldn't speak the language, the band started to take the folksy 'busking' set onto radio shows, breaking down the language barriers – and the rigid playlist formats. 'Talking through an interpreter was a very slow process,' says Nick. 'I think it was in Holland where we said, Look, the best way to describe anything about the group is just to sing a couple of songs.'

A stylish restaurant in Knightsbridge was the setting for the London showcase, at which Tim Finn joined them on stage. 'Heinz implored everyone to go, and it was very impressive,' says Malcolm Hill, promotions manager at Parlophone UK. 'That's when everyone realised what they were trying to do.' The band flew around – to Helsinki, Stockholm, Milan, Madrid, Munich – with the record company working out their itinerary and accommodation day by day. In London, on the morning of 23 September, the band was told they'd be playing at the Hard Rock Cafe in Stockholm that night.

The band was unaware their acoustic set was before another showcase, by the Swedish heavy metal group Dalton. Nick remembers the café was almost empty when Crowded House took the stage: 'Behind us was a full heavy metal drumkit, with two gongs, a double kick drum, cymbals aplenty, and the only people in the audience seemed to be leather-clad men and women.'

Swedish teenager Stefan Warnqvist also attended, his mother having heard on the radio that two members of Split Enz were playing in town, in an Australian band called Crowded House. Warnqvist, a passionate Australian music fan, had never heard of the band, but insisted on going. Accompanied by his father, he wore a jersey his mother had knitted with the *True Colours* cover design.

Crowded House left their table in the café and stepped on stage. 'Good evening,' said Neil 'We're from Down Under, and I'm from New Zealand.'

Warnqvist remembers they mainly performed songs from the debut album: 'The acoustic performance, the small venue, and the fact I was less than a metre from the stage, made it very intimate. And the songs, which I hadn't heard before, were really great. The band members really seemed to be enjoying themselves, thus affecting the audience to do the same. They smiled and joked a lot. Apart from their own songs, they also performed a superb version of Talking

Heads' "Road to Nowhere" and Buddy Holly's "Not Fade Away". In "Love You 'til the Day I Die" they spontaneously added the chorus of "I See Red". In one of the last songs, "Something So Strong", they played a verse from "Six Months in a Leaky Boat" – both Tim songs, I noticed.'

The heavy metal audience loved it. Nick still can't believe the response. 'We're singing acoustically, and we won them over. Before Dalton came on, we got an encore, and the crowd was really happy. I don't remember what we did, or how – maybe we played "Stairway to Heaven", or endeared ourselves by somehow sending the thing up. It was a bizarre moment, I thought, hell: we can work any room in the world!'

Afterwards, a waitress got the band to sign a poster for Warnqvist, who then plucked up the courage to say hello. But if he was excited to meet them, it went both ways: the band were thrilled to find a fan. They had noticed his *True Colours* jersey, which is why they dropped in the Split Enz songs. Hester asked Warnqvist if his mother would knit him a jersey too, gave him a copy of *Crowded House* and promised to send *See Ya 'Round*. Neil apologised for his croaky Rod Stewart voice, and they talked about Split Enz news. Nick said, 'We performed with Tim in London. He wants to join Crowded House now. He wants to play again with his brother, to make a classic album together.'

'It had been a perfect evening,' says Warnqvist, 'a fantastic gig, a signed poster, a signed LP, and a chat with all the band. And they were all really nice guys, with no hint at all of any rock star divas.'

The campaign wasn't without its upsets, however. In Milan, the morning of the *Riva del Guarda* show, Neil and Paul had a heated argument over something neither can remember. 'It was a huge screaming match,' says Paul. 'Even the Italians stopped and watched.'

It got as far as Neil holding Paul up by his collar against a wall, threatening to thump him. 'Paul was left in the square opposite the hotel, fuming,' says Neil. 'He was kicking a tree, and a policeman comes up and demands to see his passport. He didn't have it on him, so he ends up being strong-armed into the hotel to find it.'

'Something about Milan,' says Paul, with a wry smile. 'We always had a bit of a blue there. All that hot tomato in the pasta sauce.'

The band also caught up with Tim in Italy, where he was staying with Scacchi on a film-set. He caught a train to Milan to join Crowded House on their weekend off. They went to a studio to record a song called 'Everything to Live For'. The song came about when Neil was approached by a couple of Australian street kids, who were given Aus$60,000 by Dire Straits to make people more aware of teenage drug problems. The intention was to add a large choir in Australia and release it before Christmas. 'We've got a good working relationship with Tim,' Paul told *Music Connection* shortly afterwards. 'Whether it becomes a big feature or not is another thing. It's there – it's a shame not to use it.'

All the way around Europe – the band visited 25 cities in a month – Thomas battled for funds. 'It was a nightmare, a trip of desperation,' he says. 'The guys weren't that comfortable, because at that point the record seemed to have misfired, could even be construed as a stiff. No one had heard it, or bought it – things were at a really low ebb. The company wanted to energise the thing, but were arguing about per diem expenses. They said, "Don't worry, the local branches will look after them, breakfast, lunch and dinner." Neil had some money from the Split Enz tour, but Nick and Paul weren't flush. So I was using my American Express card to get cash as we went around Europe, so the guys could pay for cigarettes and guitar strings. Eighteen months later the company reluctantly repaid the bill.'

'It was like running a political campaign on no money,' says Paul, 'but we made ourselves heard, that's for sure.'

Two nights after playing Belgium, Crowded House arrived in Auckland, New Zealand, after a gruelling 27-hour flight. In Belgium, the showcase was in a club called the Bierodrome; on the other side of the world the venue was a modest brick bungalow on Paritai Drive. The house, then rented to an EMI receptionist, is only a stone's throw from the city's most exclusive homes: out the window is a sensational view of Auckland. Usually, Monday nights are quiet in Auckland, so the city's music industry and media flocked at late notice to see the first New Zealand performance of Crowded House.

Half-a-dozen goldfish swam inside a bowl, perched on top of a speaker. Sixty people were packed onto the lurid floral carpet in the living-room, a table groaning under a cornucopia of hors-d'oeuvres and cans of beer, and all the other furniture had been shifted outside. At one end of the room, in front of the fireplace, was the entertainment: Crowded House. Neil Finn had brought his new band home. 'This is great,' he said. 'We've just arrived back, and we're straight into a classic Auckland party.'

The only thing organised was the beer and the nibbles. The band's set was as chaotic as a spontaneous living-room party after everyone comes back from the pub. Crowded House quickly won the room over with their harmonies and affability; the Steinlager disappeared as the crowd sang along, demanded requests, danced to Neil's energetic strumming and Paul's brushes. As the party peaked, Neil broke a guitar string, then another, battling on until he finally broke a third. Time for a refill while local record company rep Chris Caddick raced back to the band's hotel in town to grab a spare guitar and strings. After they ran out of their own songs – which few at the party had heard, though the album was five months old – they played Split Enz tunes, and paid tribute to their Anzac compatriots with Hunters and Collectors' 'Throw Your Arms Around Me' and Dave Dobbyn's 'Whaling'. Then they moved on to favourites from any woolshed bash: 'Hit the Road Jack', 'Kingston Town' and Kiwi country novelty 'Love in a Fowlhouse'.

Afterwards, the party continued while the band gave an interview in the bedroom to local magazines *Shake!* and *Rip It Up*. They were still running on the adrenaline of 'the big schmooze-on' in Europe. Nick was so thrilled at what was happening to him, he was as exuberant as an excited three-year old. They made jokes at each other's expense, told stories of their overseas travels, and talked optimistically about the future. They would be back around Christmas time, promised Neil, though the small crowds for Tim's first solo New Zealand tour (for *Big Canoe*) were a worry. Asked if Crowded House would hit the pub circuit, 'Yeah, we don't mind the idea of that at all,' said Neil.

The enthusiastic reports from the showcase tour of Europe convinced the Americans that the same style of promotion should be done in the States, where the *Crowded House* album had already been spotted in discount bins. For the LA showcase, the band returned to the scene of their hi-jinks earlier in the year. Just above the 'crowded house' on North Sycamore is Yamashiro's, a large Japanese restaurant in an old Oriental-styled building with a magnificent view of Hollywood. Six months after the album's release, Capitol booked the restaurant to launch the band, in a showcase for press and radio programmers.

The album may have had little reaction, but all those months charming every level of the Capitol Tower meant Crowded House was the hot ticket in Hollywood. Also, there had been a run of ecstatic reviews – in the wake of Young's piece in *Musician*, *Spin* and *Pulse* had joined in the clamour. The *Spin* review, by Brian Cullman, read, '*Crowded House* is the best record I've heard this year ... and "Don't Dream It's Over", a sister song to John Lennon's "Watching the Wheels", is one of the few recent love songs I've heard that doesn't sound like it's being sung to a mirror.' Tom Gorman ran excerpts from all three in the influential industry tip-sheet *Radio & Records*, beneath a glum photo of the trio and a headline, 'At first nobody listened to Crowded House either – will you?'

There was a traffic jam of cars in the winding, narrow road leading up to Yamashiro's, and those who got inside weren't disappointed by the embullient, fresh performance by the unknown band. 'It was like our deb ball in LA,' says Paul. 'For some reason there was a real buzz. We'd been living there for four months and made a lot of friends as we tore about town. We were the little Aussie battlers and the Kiwi chap, these weird guys with funny accents – real small and real cute – and we jammed the place out. It was the perfect thing to do, a wonderful night. All the bigwigs from Capitol were there, and they thought it was great.'

With Mitchell Froom on keyboards, Crowded House played in the restaurant's garden courtyard, and ended up cracking jokes and singing while cavorting about the bonsai trees and lily ponds. The media were knocked out. So too was the promotions department of Capitol. 'Everyone in the band was a *wack*,' says Tom Gorman. 'They made friends with all the radio and retail we brought in. Because seeing the band was believing in the band. The minute you saw them you knew they were something special.'

Capitol head of promotions Walter Lee became a convert that night. He had a few drinks and at the end of the show got up and told everyone present – press, radio, his own company – 'We're going to break this band! I *guarantee* they'll have a hit.' Jeremy Hammond's jaw dropped.

'We all got drunk and went back to the hotel,' says Paul. 'There was a jacuzzi and I remember the scene at about three in the morning. Nick's in there with Don Zimmermann, the president of Capitol Records, and a few babes. Don's got a big cigar and a gold chain and he's going, "Nick, you know, that's the thing about the Middle East – it's always shut." And Nick's going, "That's right, Don" – just talking politics, man to man – it was like Nick had finally found a friend and it happened to be the president of Capitol.

'And I look in the other room and I see Neil – typical – up till all hours, sitting on his bed running through some songs he's just come up with. And Gary Stamler and Tom Whalley are there, and a few assorted dregs on the floor in a post-party coked stupor, all looking at him as if he's God. He loves to sing and any party you go to – Tim's the same – it gets to a point where they've had enough socialising and it's time to get the vocal chords going. So I just shut my door, I didn't want to know, but it seemed that we'd conquered something there.'

Next morning, Lee was nursing a hangover when Zimmermann came into his office. 'You *guarantee* a hit?' is all he said.

The nights of busking and banter were now the modus operandi of Crowded House; they repeated the formula across the United States in a restaurant goodwill tour. They charmed Minneapolis, Cleveland, Boston – like a dine-and-dance act they accompanied seafood meals in Seattle and Indian curries in New York. The latter restaurant was called Nirvana, and situated at number one Times Square, the building with the flashing news sign. The stage was 50 floors above, against a floor-to-ceiling window.

'Don't Dream It's Over' had been out for three months, with no real results. The showcase gigs in the States were well received by everyone who saw them, but they didn't generate much in the way of sales. But, more importantly, Capitol was now united in its support for Crowded House, although, as far as the single and debut album were concerned, industry convention said it was getting too close to Christmas. That's when the record companies release albums by all their heavyweight acts, and new artists get swamped.

For several months, virtually nothing had been done, says Stamler. 'In a lot of people's minds – in the senior levels of the company – the record was already finished. Jeremy Hammond and Tom Whalley and others were trying to keep the fire burning, but not senior people. Paulette McCubbin and Tasha Mack were perpetually calling the small stations, trying to keep the record alive. But there was nothing really to hang anyone's hat on.'

Crowded House was also running out of money. It got to the point where Neil and Stamler decided to chase a publishing deal. But, because the record didn't show any promise, the offers were all 'low-ball deals', says Stamler. 'Out of desperation, we finally agreed to take a deal from EMI Music in America. But then the publishing company told me the deal was withdrawn, because the record had stiffed.'

Stamler found out later that, after his approach, EMI Music had approached Capitol and asked what their plans were. A senior executive at Capitol said there were none – don't make the deal, because the record was finished. 'I got really angry at that,' says Stamler. 'I asked, "Are you in the publishing business or chasing records? Does Neil Finn mean anything as a writer? Goodbye." But I also heard loud and clear that a senior executive at the record company had said this record is done.'

Neil would occasionally get despondent about the lack of progress the album had made. Thomas remembers how difficult it was to get Neil to leave on promo trips: 'I never knew until the last minute whether Neil would show up at the airport.' Stamler still has a tape of a message Neil left on his answerphone in LA, saying the project was dead, he was giving up.

In the States, the album had sold about 25,000 before Christmas 1986. But Australia had slowly been responding, thanks to a series of small club dates and showcase gigs which brought them some radio support. Kerry Byrne, now of EMI New Zealand, remembers Neil whooping it up in the corridors of EMI at Brisbane, when he heard 'Mean To Me' had reached No 26 – it was Crowded House's first significant chart placing.

The profile of Crowded House was rising in Melbourne, as they cooperated with almost any promotional schemes thrown their way. 'I enjoyed working that first album so much, because we had almost total control,' says Matthews. 'You'd go to the band thinking, they're not going to wear this – knowing what serious young insects bloody Split Enz were, very arty, very serious – but with the Crowdies, it'd be, "Yeah, great idea." Neil spoke as if he'd lost a big weight off his shoulders. He was getting back in touch with working with the label, getting out there amongst it.

'They were like little Beatles. They clung together like shit to a blanket. In interviews, they'd have cues, and Hester would hop in and take it to another plateau. Nick was the arty one, the one who socialised. Neil was the family man, who wouldn't go out unless he had to. Nick had an important role beyond playing bass, he was mixing with the rich and famous, the glitterati and the actors and artists. A great ambassador for the band. When other touring musicians came through, he'd get friendly with them, and that all helped create Crowded House on the international scene. And Paul was more than a capable drummer, who had a great gift. Between the three of them they had the Beatle/Monkees happy-go-lucky thing, and made great music.'

In late December, things started to gain momentum; the band was asked to be the support act on the Orchestral Manoeuvres in the Dark tour of Australia. 'The two bands didn't really go together artistically, but there was a buzz about OMD,' says Thomas. 'Clearly they were going to get full houses. We all agreed it was better to try and flog someone else's audience than struggle on our own.'

OMD was big by the time the five-date tour happened, and the tour brought more radio play for Crowded House. 'We gave 'em a good run for their money, too,' says Paul. 'They had all these computers and lasers, and they often broke down, and people would be up and down.' The band all travelled in one car, with a single roadie, Geoff Lloyd. 'We were simmering,' says Lloyd. 'OMD couldn't hold a candle to us. With all their equipment failure, they never got a chance to get it going. I wouldn't be surprised if they went home and broke up.' The tour opened on New Year's Eve, at the Sydney club Selina's. Before a sellout crowd of about 3000 people, Crowded House stole the show from OMD with a triumphant set. Tim Finn joined the band on stage to sing harmonies. 'That was like a shot in the arm,' says Paul.

Backstage after the show, the band was presented with its first gold record for 35,000 sales of the *Crowded House* album in Australia. The embers were starting to flicker again. 'We had a great party that night,' says Paul. 'We bundled into the car and went back to the Cosmopolitan Motel in Bondi.' In a room overlooking Bondi Beach, the Crowded House family toasted themselves with pizza and champagne: Neil and Sharon, Tim and Greta, Paul and his girlfriend Mardi Summerfeld, Nick on his own. The same night, Australia could watch Crowded House see in the new year on the TV show *Rock Arena*. The band had pre-recorded it (with Eddie Rayner on keyboards) a couple of weeks earlier, so the bonhomie is a little forced, but you can almost smell the freshness of the songs: 'Something So Strong', 'Now We're Getting Somewhere' and 'Don't Dream It's Over', which receives little reaction. Neil plays 'Auld Lang Syne' like Hendrix, then segues into 'Recurring Dream'.

The night in the Cosmopolitan was a big celebration, says Paul. 'It was really coming to something. But after that, it just went *boom*.'

When the world comes in • January 1987

'It's pretty stupid comparing us to the Beatles, really. I mean, there were four of them. There's only three of us.'

—Paul Hester, 1987

Neil felt the band had turned a corner with their New Year's Eve show. Through January, they continued touring after the stint with OMD. Playing keyboards was Gill Civil, a woman picked by Nick and Paul while Neil was away. Her experience included time as an accompanist at a ballet school, but she struggled with rock'n'roll. Other keyboardists were auditioned, but eventually the call went out for Eddie Rayner. For 10 years he had been the musical linchpin of Split Enz, as essential to their sound and success as the Finns' songs had been. (He was considered so vital to the band that when he fell sick during the *True Colours* tour of New Zealand, and missed a show, each member of the audience was refunded $4.) But despite being close friends, both Neil and Eddie were reluctant to come together again because they wanted to get on with life after the Enz. Eddie had just finished some session work for Paul McCartney's *Press to Play* album, a creative disappointment as he had to play exactly what he was told.

Shortly after Eddie joined 'as an employee', word came through that – four months after its release – 'Don't Dream It's Over' was starting to get significant radio play in America. The first steady support had come from LITE 105, an alternative station in San Francisco where, despite the song being more romantic than its usual hard-edged fare, it received such a good response from listeners that programmer Richard Sands kept it on the playlist for months.

But isolated stations around the country have little impact, so it looked as though the single would fizzle out before getting started in the charts, despite the determined efforts of the Capitol promotions staff. Then Stamler had an idea. The boycott of the independent promoters hired to lobby radio programmers was still in place, and Capitol was sticking rigidly to its stance. 'Some of the companies were dealing with the independents through the backdoor,' says Walter Lee. 'We were not one of those companies. When Bhaskar Menon, the chairman of Capitol-EMI says, *do not do this*, you don't. We had a great deal of respect for him; I certainly would not have dreamt of going behind his back.'

Gary Stamler knew that the indies were still the key to breaking a single, but also realised Capitol wasn't interested in using them. Thinking of the NBC-TV programme, he asked Walter Lee to meet him in private. At a restaurant called Carlo & Charlie's on Sunset Strip, Stamler told Lee his idea. 'I said I was willing to take on the promotion of the record myself. We'd had good feedback on "Don't Dream It's Over", so there was nothing to lose – it was our last chance. I said, I want to hire these guys, I don't know what it's going to cost but I bet you it's almost nothing, because they're desperate for work.'

Stamler was prepared to invest up to US$10,000. Lee, already burnt by the TV programme and under strict instructions from Menon, was nervous about it but thought it might work. 'I said, go for it – but keep me out. I walked Gary through it, gave him the phone numbers and told him the system.'

Four independent promoters were hired at about US$2500 each to work the single for a short period, a tenth of what it might ordinarily cost. Then Stamler had another idea, which went against music industry norms: the promotion would begin in early December. Usually, singles by new artists are swamped in the buildup to Christmas. 'I thought, we'll strike while everything is shut down, we'll have a head start when 1987 begins.'

The idea was kept secret; only Lee knew at the record company. Any success that might occur would look as though it was achieved by the promotions department, who were genuinely excited by the song and were working hard on their own campaigns, in ignorance of what was going on behind the scenes.

Neil's response to the idea was sceptical, says Stamler. 'He'd basically mentally checked out on the record. He said, "I may be one of the world's pessimists, and you're one of the world's optimists – but don't expect me to do anything more to support the record." He wasn't going to step foot on American soil unless the single was in the Top 40.'

The plan worked. As 1987 opened, the usual glut of records was released, but 'Don't Dream It's Over' was already getting noticed. In December, 1986, WHTZ-FM ('Z100'), a key New York station, began playing the song, then another influential New York station, WPLJ-FM; other regions followed. Then MTV started playing the video regularly. The record company began pushing the single again, four months after its initial release. 'Capitol was very supportive,' Stamler told *Musician*, 'but the indies gave it the extra nudge to get it over.

When the label saw the single starting to happen, they ran with it.'

Stamler went to some lengths to keep the arrangement secret (from the record company more than anyone else). He held meetings in his car, handing over the money in places like the parking lot of a chinese restaurant. Neil was kept informed about what was happening and, he says, 'I had no reservations about it whatsoever. I'd become realistic about the way the music business in America worked to think it was par for the course.' In Split Enz days, he remembers an A&M promotions man who was a caricature: dressed like a pimp, girls on each arm, a big car to drive, 'going around dishing out cocaine to all the radio programmers. It was revolting, but you get used to it. "This is America, man, this is how we do things." There are some things we did that I'm sheepish about, but not that. Independent promoters were at their peak then. Unless you were prepared to use them, their were certain stations you couldn't get on.'

On 17 January, 1987, the single entered the *Billboard* chart at 85. That week, Crowded House played to 500 people on the roof of the Myers shopping complex in Melbourne. 'The band was firing,' says Geoff Lloyd. 'They'd done 30 shows in Australia, the banter was happening, and the band wasn't burnt out. They were still pretty raw, but they'd learnt to *flaunt the imperfection*.'

In the States, the single kept rising, reaching 44 in the 14 February chart. Stamler rang Neil to ask if the band was coming. He had already taken the precaution of booking them as the support act on a Bruce Hornsby tour. Neil agreed: they were on their way. Geoff Lloyd remembers him coming into Kramers, 'a horrible pub in Melbourne. He said, "We're going to America – are you coming?" It was straight out to the carpark to burn one.'

But the day before the band was due to leave, a close friend of Sharon's was killed in a car accident. 'That was a real leveller,' she says. 'Things go well, you're on a high – then you go tumbling down. It was a toss-up whether to go, or stay for the funeral. Everyone said, just *go*.'

The band flew to Los Angeles, accompanied by Sharon and Liam, plus Eddie Rayner. When they arrived, the single was at 38, and Paul had his carry bag stolen – containing all his personal effects – as they were checking into their hotel. The promotional rollercoaster got underway. A limo took them to *The Joan Rivers Show*, where they seduced the hostess, and her studio audience, with 'Don't Dream It's Over', followed by a relaxed, witty conversation on the couch. The band had hit the ground running, winning over everybody with their charm, humour and spontaneity, on stage and off.

Next came an appearance on *Solid Gold*, 'one of the things I *am* sheepish about,' says Neil. When they were introduced by Marilyn McCoo, Eddie complimented her on her dress, made from shredded leather. 'It'll be good when it's finished,' he said. McCoo's introduction read, 'Throw another prawn on the barbie – here's a group from Australia', until Neil managed to get her to add 'and New Zealand'. The *Crocodile Dundee* clichés were hard to fight, though the band was surprised when journalists believed the old Enz yarn that they went jogging with sheep under their arms.

A few days later, on 25 and 26 February, they headlined at the Roxy in Los Angeles. Capitol staffers did their job hyping the opening show. The next day, KEZY-96FM deejay Michelle gushed on her morning show:

'It was one of the best live performances I've seen this year, the music was really up and rockin'! There was everything from audience singalongs to a food fight – the band started it! These guys will be major in no time at all. I highly recommend going to the show tonight, if there are tickets left. Among the people in the audience, we spotted Val Kilmer, a few members of REO Speedwagon, some of the girls from the Bangles, Colin James Hay from Men at Work, Slim Jim Phantom of the Stray Cats with his wife Britt Ekland (remember she used to be married to Rod Stewart?) … I have a feeling this is probably the last time anyone will have an opportunity to see them at such a small place. The show was so good that the audience wouldn't leave, and the band kept coming back for encores. Finally the fire marshal kicked us all out!'

Chris Willman was only a little more sober in the *Los Angeles Times*: 'Is Crowded House the great white hope of power pop? Opinions *do* seem to be running in that direction … any band that can wax truly sensitive on love and mortality *and* instigate a food fight within a 10-minute period is ripe for all the success Crowded House is chalking up.' Willman spotted leftover elements of prog rock, of folkie hootenannies, but most of all, of Paul McCartney 'at his *Abbey Road* era best · … the group manages to conjure up those comparisons without wearing the slightest Beatlesque affectations on their sleeves. The Roxy show had too many diverse touches – including a great deal of spectacular, jazzy piano noodling from sideman Eddie Rayner on keyboards – and the band has too winningly casual and self-deprecating a stage personality to allow any harping about possible derivation.'

Afterwards, Joe Smith, who had replaced Menon as the chairman of Capitol-EMI, went up to Eddie and asked what it would take to make him a permanent member of the band. Eddie said he had wanted his family on the road with him, and more money. Smith replied, 'Bring the family over! How big a truckload of money do you want?' 'So I hung about,' says Eddie. 'It's nice to be wanted – and the band could do no wrong at that point.'

Crowded House joined the Hornsby tour in Houston, Texas, arriving just before soundcheck with their equipment lost in transit. The Hornsby people came through, lending them instruments. 'Once they heard the band, people bent over backwards to help us,' says Lloyd. 'Everyone was on a high – we were on the up escalator.' It was that night he realised things were about to catch fire. 'The audience reaction was a little awkward, they were looking forward to Hornsby coming on. All of a sudden, Neil goes, "Hey now, hey now . . ." and you can see people nudging each other. *This is them.*'

Crowded House hopped on and off the Hornsby tour, playing small dates in between. The band and its entourage were all on one bus: Sharon and Liam, Eddie's wife Raewyn Turner and their boy, nannies, roadcrew, management. To the American crews, the band's style seemed a bit 'touchy feely', says Lloyd. 'But the band never suffered from that negativity of being a one-sex road band.' Their tour manager was Ted Gardner, an Australian who had gone to the US with Men at Work, and stayed there (he later helped establish the Lollapalooza festival). Gardner had just come off a heavy metal tour, and was still in macho mode. Lloyd, an old friend, pulled him aside and said, ' "Naah, mate, we're a cuppa-tea-and-a-joint kind of band: no bourbon and cocaine, no women, nothing like that. They don't attract them, they attract fans." Ted calmed it down. He had just the right amount of zest and push.'

Routines quickly developed. At soundcheck, a pot of tea and, for those inclined, a joint. In the dressing room, after a nap, Paul would sit back with a newspaper, have a smoke, 'and try and upset everyone with sarcasm'. He would see Neil, pacing, checking set lists, conferring over details: 'Very scout-leader'. Eddie would be preening, finishing every night with the same quip: 'Oh Eddie, I don't know how you do it, after all these years.' Nick would get changed several times, and check everyone's costumes, 'like a mad Italian designer at a fashion show. "What! You're wearing *that*?" '

After their gigs, the work wouldn't stop. The bandmembers would have to rally their energy for a 'meet-and-greet'. 'It's just a blur,' says Paul. 'I was into it for a while. We'd say, what is it: a play'n'wave or a meet'n'greet? Because play'n'waves were the ones we wanted to hear about.' Meet'n'greets would require shaking hands and back-slapping '20,000 radio celebrities, competition winners, radio programmers, record reps, retail reps, radio reps, dignitaries, pikers – and maybe there'd be someone you'd actually want to see, who you'd miss! Play'n'waves, you'd stick your head in the door as you were leaving, wave, then get on the bus and get the hell out!'

At the functions, Sharon and Eddie would sit in a corner and laugh at the nonsense. 'We'd say, those poor bastards,' says Sharon. 'It's hard work, and they'd get exhausted. Management used to push them to the limit, persuading them to do stuff. On the first tour they were all up for it, but you could see it taking its toll.' Neil's voice would deteriorate from all the talking, and he would nurse it with a potion of lemon, garlic, ginger, honey and a dash of gin.

On the bus, the extended family would sit in a row, giving neck rubs to relieve each other's stress. With the band using club PAs, the crew was on the bus too; at the front was a crèche for the nannies and children. 'It was a really supportive group,' says Paul. 'We'd never had a customised bus before – beds, lockers, all that stuff – and we were up for it, really adrenalised.'

As their profile grew, celebrities started to take an interest in them. Elton John sent the occasional bottle of champagne backstage; turning up to say hello were then-hot actors such as Rob Lowe and Justine Bateman, musicians such as the Bangles, Todd Rundgren, Dave Mustaine, Aimee Mann and Sting. During a talent quest the band held at New York's Bottom Line club, four audience members sang Split Enz songs, the winner being an operatic version of 'Six Months in a Leaky Boat' by a black woman. Afterwards, Sting asked to be introduced to the band, and entered the dressing-room singing, 'Hey now, hey now . . .' Neil responded with 'De do do do, De da da da' – only to realise later that Sting thought he was sending him up.

By early March, the video for 'Don't Dream It's Over' was on high rotation on MTV and the single at 23 and still climbing. 'The momentum just swirled,' says Stamler. Neil told New Zealand journalist Colin Hogg, 'When it got to 26, I started to order more room service, make longer phone calls back home. When it got to 23, I thought, "Uh oh, this is serious."'

The band continued its small club gigs, on the east coast and in Canada. As the single entered the Top 10, they had a formal meeting in Minneapolis to discuss the future. Present were the band members, their record company, agent, their managers, Gary Stamler and Grant Thomas, their tour manager and crew, even Mitchell Froom. It struck Paul that it had only been two years since he and Neil travelled around the world with their cassette, wondering what would happen. 'I was thinking about how we brought all these people together,' he told Spin. 'I felt pretty good about everybody. It was extraordinary.'

On 28 March, with the single at number seven, they arrived at Daytona, Florida, to play the 'MTV Spring Break', when university students let down their hair during semesters. The band performed on a stage between two giant inflatable Budweiser cans. To the musicians, it was a nightmare, *Animal House* come alive: 'American males doing their mating thing,' says Eddie. 'Macho, homophobic, xenophobic . . . they're quite scary. They're big, drink a lot of beer, smoke dope, ride around in convertibles, scream their tyres, yell at women and intimidate smaller men.'

Also present were the Beastie Boys, who tried to emulate Crowded House and busk their hit '(You Gotta) Fight for Your Right (to Party!)'. But they couldn't work out the chords, so Nick took their acoustic guitar and showed them. 'It's just like "Smoke On the Water",' he said.

Crowded House's flexibility had made them a hot item on American talk shows as the single kept rising. 'We could play acoustically, and we gave them a bit of stick, which no-one was doing then,' says Neil. Joan Rivers had them back on, and invited Dame Edna Everage as well. Nick was in awe of the Australian icon, who was wearing a monumental purple wig, and a cockatoo on each shoulder. They serenaded her with a saucy version of 'Throw Your Arms Around Me'. Jane Pauley on *The Today Show* couldn't cope when they departed from the script. Another show had them performing on top of a car at a '50s drive-in, with rollerskating waitresses whizzing around. Even Johnny Carson expressed an interest . . .

The band was in New York when the news came through: 'Don't Dream It's Over' had reached number two in the American charts. 'Suddenly the impact sunk in,' says Grant Thomas. 'Until then, you'd been slogging it out, trying to advance the cause each week. I'd be on the phone all night, talking to the rest of the world. It was hard work, it wasn't a party.

'I remember lying back on my hotel bed, thinking, holy shit, we're in New York, with a hit single. Suddenly, the top-level photographers wanted time with the band. Limos were available, whereas six months earlier when we did the showcase in New York, we rode the subway to the gig.'

Billboard Top 100 • 25 April, 1987

1   'I Knew You Were Waiting' – Aretha Franklin & George Michael
2   'Don't Dream It's Over' – Crowded House
3   'Sign O' the Times' – Prince
4   'Looking for a New Love' – Jody Watley

5 '(I Just) Died in Your Arms' – Cutting Crew
6 'Nothing's Gonna Stop Us Now' – Starship
7 'La Isla Bonita' – Madonna
8 'The Finer Things' – Steve Winwood
9 'Midnight Blue' – Lou Gramm
10 'With or Without You' – U2

When the next chart was due to come out a week later, the band was on a flight to Albuquerque, in a beaten-up plane that looked as if it only just survived World War II. 'There was a crack in the window beside Sharon, and gaffer tape everywhere,' says Neil. 'During dinner we pointed it out to the stewardess, and she looked pretty worried. Five minutes later, the window blew with a big bang.'

The stewardess urgently told everyone nearby to take their bags and move to the back. The plane dropped to 10,000 feet, over the Rocky Mountains. 'We were freaking out,' says Sharon, 'flying low in case everything sucked out.'

By the time the plane limped to Albuquerque, 'We were all shaken up,' says Neil. 'We got off the plane and within a minute, I was surrounded by burly plainclothes policemen with guns and handcuffs. They demanded my ID. They were looking for an escaped prisoner and I fitted the description. That's when I knew we hadn't gone to number one. There was *no way*.'

Neil phoned Gary Stamler, who said that the single had dropped to number three. Cutting Crew's '(I Just) Died in Your Arms' had leapt to the top, with Jody Watley rising to second. As Crowded House drove from Albuquerque, heading for a few days break, they heard 'Don't Dream It's Over' on the radio, and the news was confirmed.

'It wasn't that traumatic,' says Sharon. 'It had been one of those hysterical days.'

Despite the 'national treasure' status of Split Enz in New Zealand, the country's radio programmers had ignored the debut album of Crowded House. Before Christmas, only 3000 copies of the album had been sold in the entire country, and it was appearing in discount bins. Only in Hamilton, near Te Awamutu, did a station give the 'truly sacred ring' of 'Mean To Me' a regular spin. It was not until 'Don't Dream It's Over' was heading towards the US Top 20 that any of the major stations showed any interest. New Zealand acts were all but shut out of radio playlists at the time, with programmers slavishly following the overseas trends in *Radio & Records*.

In February, Neil had said to the country's largest newspaper, the

New Zealand Herald, 'It's chronic. New Zealand radio is responsible for killing New Zealand music as far as I'm concerned. I don't care particularly about us. It's not going to bring tears to my eyes if the album doesn't happen there. It's a shame for the bands who are living there and relying on New Zealand radio to expose their music. They're just getting nothing.'

On 30 March, the *Herald* made the issue its lead editorial: 'Some things, sadly, never change. That Great Kiwi Clobbering Machine still stalks the land when the mood takes it. And New Zealanders still show a strange reluctance to recognise the talents of fellow citizens until they win accolades abroad ... here at home, Finn wins recognition second-hand, as New Zealand's rock stations, whose reluctance to play locally made records is swiftly becoming legend, frantically "discover" Crowded House.'

Once the single got played, it quickly shot to number one in New Zealand; the song had already peaked at number eight in Australia three weeks earlier.

'It would have been nice to go to number one in the States, but it didn't seem to matter that much at the time,' says Neil. 'I didn't enjoy the success as much as I should have. Part of it was guilt, I suppose. I was thinking about Tim and the rest of the Splits.' With his own band, Neil was achieving the goals he and his brother and their closest friends had worked so hard towards. *Big Canoe*, Tim's follow-up to *Escapade* – released at the same time as *Crowded House* – had attracted little interest.

Later in the year, Tim told Australian journalist Robin Hill, 'I won't say that I didn't suffer when all this success happened to Neil recently. It didn't surprise me, [but it was] the success I dreamed about with Split Enz. So I had mixed feelings for quite a while. So many people were saying, "Isn't it great? Isn't it great?" And, of course, it was great, and I was very proud and pleased, but I was also envious, I suppose. So it took a while for that to settle down and to see it all in perspective.'

Both realised how the other felt, says Neil. 'We dealt with it at the time. I gave him a call and suggested he come out on the road in America while the record was going off.' Tim flew in to New Orleans, and joined Crowded House on stage at a few shows. 'I think it really helped get it settled in his mind,' says Neil, 'rather than watching it from a distance. He felt like he was part of it to some degree.'

At its peak, the single was selling 40,000 copies per week in the States.

But at Capitol, Jeremy Hammond had a major regret: that no-one had thought of adding a sub-title to 'Don't Dream It's Over', as most people were going into record stores and asking for the 'Hey-Now' song. It would have made the difference between topping the charts and coming second if the single's label had read, 'Don't Dream It's Over (Hey Now)'.

Once 'Dream' was on its way, thoughts turned to a followup single. 'Something So Strong' had already been pressed, but Capitol wanted to reissue 'World Where You Live' after many from the Tower witnessed a sensational rendition of the song when the band returned to the Roxy in early April. 'There was a groundswell of opinion that we'd chosen the wrong second single,' says Stamler. Either song was ready to go; there were, after all, plenty of copies of 'World' left in the warehouse from its previous release. At the last moment Stamler found himself on the phone with Capitol president Don Zimmermann, pleading the case for 'Something So Strong'. 'Ironically,' says Stamler, 'I was calling from the same bedroom in which "World Where You Live" was written.'

Arguing against him was the head of promotions, Walter Lee. When Zimmermann gave 'Something So Strong' the nod, Lee called Stamler and joked, 'If this thing works, you're a genius. If it doesn't work, you'll probably blame the record company anyway!' Helped by its wholesome video, 'Something So Strong' walked onto radio stations, quickly reaching number seven. By that stage, Lee wasn't around to enjoy its success, having been sacked from Capitol. To inspire his promotions staff, he had taken to brandishing an electric cattle prod.

The band spent three months in North America on its first tour, with houses growing as their profile was kept high on radio and MTV. The album eventually peaked at No 12, spending 24 weeks on the US charts. Canadian audiences, with their history of support for Split Enz, were especially enthusiastic.

During the tour, Neil received a letter from the young woman who had inspired 'Mean To Me' during the Party Boys tour. 'She was pissed off I wrote a song about her,' he said. When they later met, she explained that she'd been offended by the way he'd explained it in an interview. 'I don't want to make a mess of anyone's life and songs can be very powerful,' he said to the Melbourne *Herald*. 'It's a bit daunting sometimes.' (The woman also wrote to Gary McCormick and asked, 'Have you heard our song?' He hadn't, but listened to it after being alerted to Neil's account in *RAM*. 'I couldn't work it out,' he says. 'Was I being mean to her? I was stunned by Neil's reaction. It was a major surprise.')

At the end of the tour, the band headed over to Europe for press and a show at the Montreux Rock Festival. In this pre-*Unplugged* era of slick technopop, they were surprised by how unusual their natural approach and busking routine seemed to the European press. Nick was aghast when a journalist said to him, 'You know, I think I prefer bands playing live to miming.' Topping the bill at Montreux were David Bowie, the Communards and Tina Turner. Crowded House ended up being filmed backstage for MTV, having a rap duel with Run DMC on the 'Our Father'. 'It turned into a toasting competition,' says Neil. 'We were absurdly white and stupid but ended up looking reasonably cool because they were being too serious about it.'

When Crowded House appeared on German television after the festival, looking cool was never a possibility. They were asked to mime 'Don't Dream It's Over' on a variety show, and found themselves slotted in between a man who hypnotised chickens and a group of Japanese drum dancers.

In June, the band had a short period at home in Melbourne. But there was no rest. To thank those who had shown the earliest support, they gave another 'crowded house' party at the same place the first showcase had taken place, a year earlier. It was so packed the crowd couldn't clap, just yell for more as the encores kept coming after an hour-long set: 'Whole Lotta Love', 'Morningtown Ride', 'Anarchy in the UK'. They also made an appearance at the party to celebrate the first release of *Sgt. Pepper* on CD. EMI Melbourne had gone all-out to establish the right atmosphere, hiring a recording studio, decorating it with flowers, burning incense and a trippy light show. Hash cookies did the rounds as 'A Day in the Life' blasted out of a large PA.

The New Zealand public got its first chance to see Crowded House in July, when a national tour got underway. Neil Finn was lauded like a conquering hero, though at a press conference there was nervous laughter when the question of New Zealand music on radio was brought up. Paul leapt to his feet and started massaging Neil's shoulders, as if for a boxing match. 'Come on, Neil,' he said, 'tell 'em what you told us.' The town hall concerts were packed with young fans, singing along to the lines, '*And the sound of Te Awamutu had a truly sacred ring.*'

On the Australian tour which followed, they used the opportunity to introduce two of their favourite acts to the sellout crowds. R&B trouper Joe Camilleri's Black Sorrows were a little mature for the audience, and Dave Dobbyn's material unfamiliar, but the apathy of the crowd evaporated when Crowded House got on stage. 'Just the sight of Neil Finn ducking out of the wings was enough to send the massed thousands into a frenzy of screams and cheers that grew in intensity with every song,' wrote Terri Robert in Melbourne's *Beat*. (Ironically, it was Dobbyn who had the biggest hit at the time, with 'Slice of Heaven', the theme for the animated movie *Footrot Flats*. The jaunty song spent four weeks at number one in Australia, after an eight-week spell at the top in New Zealand. The radio freeze-out at home was circumvented by saturation play in cinemas as part of the movie's promotion.)

Crowded House went back to North America in late August. Paul almost immediately made an impact by streaking on stage in Victoria, British Columbia. 'I lost my marbles,' he wrote to the fans' newsletter. 'I totally forgot that I was naked when I walked on stage while Neil was singing a solo spot at the piano.'

But their penchant for sponteneity briefly turned sour in Salem, Oregon. Before the show in a fairground, the band had been given a big pile of posters to sign. Afterwards, their roadies were packing away the gear, getting help from the local crew, when suddenly the mood changed. Genial assistance turned aggressive, remembers Lloyd. 'They start saying to me, "Your band shouldn'ta done what it did." It turns out someone had signed on the posters, *Fuck Ronnie* and *Ron & Nancy Do It*. It also turns out the place is owned by Ronald Reagan's best friend in the county. His other best friend is the sheriff.

'It's our little drummer boy. The shit hits the fan, there were these *incredible* bad vibes about. They pull down the roller door, so we can't get the equipment out. They've got guards around the bus and want to send it out of the arena. We're up shit creek. We can't get the police. Why not? Guess who is a friend of the police?

'They want to stop us from playing the next day, and hold our equipment overnight. The band are held up for two hours, the kids are distressed. There's a lot of backpedalling, apologies, they're let go. We're waiting for our truck to arrive, and they've left 40 security guards on. When the truck driver arrives, he says the whole town's talking about it.'

Luckily, the next day was a travel day. The truck was still banned from entering the fairground; so Lloyd had to buy a ticket to get in and retrieve the gear. 'It had all sorts of repercussions,' he says. 'The Hornsby crew got to hear about it, and they rang up our tour manager, pretending to be the FBI: *"Is this Chopper Borges?"* Yes. *"I believe you're on the road with an Australian group called Crowded House?"* That's correct. *"We also believe that this group Crowded House wrote some subversive literature in Salem, Oregon.''* We did have some problem with them . . .

'There's about 15 minutes of this, all on tape. Chopper's saying, "Look, sir, I've known these guys for about four months now, and in my mind they're not the kind of people that would want to bring down a government . . .'' '

'The big schmooze' and life on the bus were losing their novelty, but the return tour to the States was made more stimulating by the presence of Paul Kelly as support act. Since they started, Crowded House had been featuring the occasional song by Kelly, the poet laureate of Australian rock'n'roll, in their busking set. When it came to shared upbringings and cultural experiences, says Nick, 'We found we had a lot more in common with Paul Kelly, Dave Dobbyn and Mark Seymour than Radio Birdman or Nick Cave.'

Each night on their two weeks together, Paul Kelly would come out on stage and he would say, 'Good evening, ladies and gentlemen: welcome to the South Pacific Invasion.' Crowded House would invite Kelly and his band the Coloured Girls back during their encore to sing 'Throw Your Arms Around Me', the Hunters and Collectors song which had become an anthem to them. On the last night Kelly toured with Crowded House, in Washington DC, wives and stagecrew also joined in. Aferwards, the bands had a farewell singalong, surprising each other with their knowledge not just of Beatles and Beach Boys songs, but also Irish ballads such as 'The Parting Glass' and Brendan Behan's 'The Old Triangle'. 'We were blown away that we all knew that song,' says Nick. 'I knew it from my mother's Clancy Brothers record, and that's when Neil realised that Paul Kelly has a repertoire from his upbringing very similar to his own.'

'Paul Kelly and Nick grew up with the more rootsy, rebel-songs tradition,' says Neil. 'We grew up with the expatriate version: "When Irish Eyes Are Smiling".'

If the 'up escalator' was exhausting, part of the reason was the band's affability. Stamler occasionally felt this made them too familiar with the record company. 'They were in danger of losing their aura, because they were so outgoing. They were their own best salespeople, they seduced the building, the public, the industry. That image – warm, funny Paul, their witty, intelligent pop – captured the States by storm.'

The band learnt to say no – when Capitol proposed the band have their own Monkees-style TV series, or when a promo person gave Neil a list of every major record retailer in the country to phone and thank

– though Paul was always ready to inject some anarchy. 'The hysteria level rises as people are tired and stressed,' says Neil, 'and the humour would get particularly silly. Paul was fantastic. The biggest relief of doing promotion was that we could send it up.'

If they couldn't make fun of what was happening around them, there was always Nick, a style-aware night owl who made the other two look like domestic gentlemen. As the most conscientiously social and exuberant of the trio, and lacking Neil's experience or Paul's lightning wit, Nick was usually the fallguy. Neil explained the reason to *Vox*: 'Nick's father was the headmaster at his old school, and he used to get picked on because of that. He was the butt of everybody's jokes, and that's stayed with him. It's almost like he expects to get some stick, so that's exactly what happens. There have been times when we've gone too far, and he's felt that he's had enough.'

Nick was so enthusiastic, says Lloyd, 'he was like a puppy sometimes'. On the band's return tour, the entourage had expanded so a second Silver Dream bus was needed for the crew. 'Nick gets onto our bus, we're goofing off, smoking doobs, watching movies, playing Uno, and all of a sudden, Nick says, "I *love* it here with the crew. *This* is where it's at, not on the band bus where it's all boring and families." He started to sing that Bon Jovi song, "*On a steel horse I ride . . .*" We fell about, saying, "Nick, *this is day 92.*" '

Nick was still finding his feet in the band. The 'clangers' he made while playing live upset Neil's concentration, and in the studio, he took a while to find a bass part. But it had been a good year for Nick – after years scuffling around in bands, he was touring the world, had fallen in love with an American girl, Brenda Bentley, had even exported a 1961 T-Bird convertible back home to Melbourne.

'We were having a good time, it was over the top,' says Neil. 'Pretty exhausting, but we had the energy for it.' Limos arrived so often, they gave up turning them down. They began flying first-class, but stopped after a few months due to the expense and, says Neil, 'the discomfort from over-eating. For the amount of travelling we did, though, business class was justifiable.'

'As things blow up, there's a tendency for a frenzy to set in,' says Neil. 'You sense there are people barking at your heels, wanting to get every last dollar out of it. I find myself recoiling from that, and think, let's be dignified about this – but that's not the way it happens in America.

'We should have just jumped on it. It's a New Zealand trait to be embarrassed about being too noticed or too successful. But I was feeling a little perplexed and guilty, because it wasn't Split Enz. I was conscious of all the guys back home, and Tim in particular, watching it become massive. My enjoyment was undercut a bit by my concern about not sharing it with any of them.'

As the tour closed, 'Now We're Getting Somewhere' was released as a single. But Neil was thinking about the next album. He had already worked out several songs for it while on the road: 'Sister Madly', 'Mansion in the Slums', 'Never Be the Same', and one written from a woman's point-of-view, 'Better Be Home Soon'.

Love can make you weep • November 1987

'*Temple* was going to be even bigger. "Better Be
Home Soon" was gonna come in big time, and "into
Temptation" was the closest thing to perfect.'

—Paul Hester, 1996

The Finn brothers went public in Los Angeles on 29 February, 1988.
Before Christmas, Tim had recorded his solo album with Mitchell
Froom producing; now Neil was in the middle of sessions for *Temple
of Low Men*. He was getting log cabin fever after a month in the Sunset
Sound Factory, so the brothers took time out to appear live-to-air on
Deidre O'Donoghue's late-night show on station KCRW. 'We haven't
played together in public for a long time, except for the odd party in
New Zealand,' said Neil. 'We've played together since I was seven,
so we needed a break. But now we've got plans to do an album
together in the next couple of years, aiming at a two-part harmony
sound that hasn't been heard for a while.'

It was a loose, indulgent fireside singalong, with both Finns presenting new songs and taking requests from listeners for Enz obscu-
rities. Early in the set came 'Throw Your Arms Around Me', with Tim
taking the lead voice, and Neil weaving a high harmony line around
the melody. 'Mark Seymour and I have a running battle about that
song,' said Neil. 'I think Crowded House do a better version than
Hunters and Collectors. There's a lobby for Tim and I to record it –
we'll do it on our duo/solo record.'

They ran through 'Charlie', 'Poor Boy', 'Dirty Creature' and
'Message To My Girl', unveiled 'Show a Little Mercy' and 'Better Be
Home Soon'. Tim described 'Fraction Too Much Friction' as 'a painfully white attempt at reggae'; its sunny pop bounced along to a Maori
strum until they lost control in the middle eight. 'Neil sabotaged that
one! Deliberately!' cried Tim. 'It's your song – you should know it,'
came the retort.

A spirited romp through the Everlys' 'Bye Bye Love' collapsed
under its own exuberance, with Tim signing off, 'It's that famous Finn
brothers' sound – two voices sing as one.'

While in town, Tim visited Crowded House in the studio to add harmonies to 'Love This Life' and 'Better Be Home Soon' for *Temple*.

Compared to the first album, the recording of *Temple* had gone very smoothly. There were no dramas; everyone was on a high after two hit singles and the MTV award for best new video artist. 'It was though this train was on the track to stay,' says Stamler.

Recording had begun in early November, 1987. Froom and Blake flew across the Pacific for the first sessions, in Melbourne's Platinum studios. Stamler followed a few days later, and he was recruited by Froom to bring a very special microphone, a rare antique Telefunken 251 designed for recording voices. Sunset Sound wouldn't courier the relic, it had to be carried by hand. When he arrived in Melbourne, Stamler decided to wind Froom up. He took the treasured mike out of its luxurious case and replaced it with a US$10 model. Then he watched through the studio window as Froom opened up the case in the control room. A look of horror passed across his face. He beckoned Stamler in.

'Th-th-this is the m-m-mike they gave you?' he stammered.

'I don't know, Mitchell, I didn't open the case. Isn't it the right one?'

Froom was speechless. His eyes said it all: the project was doomed. Stamler quickly produced the antique, he'd gone too far: never joke with a perfectionist.

Nevertheless, Froom says *Temple of Low Men* was a 'painless' record to make. 'People have the idea that the second record was a misery and the first was joy. The first was hell and the second was joy. With the first we were trying to work out what the band should sound like. More electronic? Did they want to be a band like Talking Heads is a band, or like the Pet Shop Boys? How to approach it?'

But now, they were truly a band – and they were on peak form. 'Neil had really found his voice, so the singing went much quicker. The band had this huge amount of confidence, they were playing really well because they'd done all that touring. Paul especially, after all those months with the brushes, plus watching Jim Keltner play "Now We're Getting Somewhere", he got a new relaxed swing thing happening with his regular drumming.'

Froom noticed how far the band had progressed at the soundcheck of a gig in which he was part of the band. 'We were playing "I Feel Possessed", and when I hit the chorus, they were playing so well, it was like they could do no wrong. There was such a vibe there, and I thought these guys really, really know how to play together. It was something else, and still fresh and vital.'

There were six weeks of recording prior to Christmas. They were the smoothest, most stress-free of the band's career. Once again, however, Neil found he was bearing the burden of not just song-writing but – with Froom – the arranging. He missed the team approach to creativity that had been so healthy in the Enz.

One of the first songs Neil brought to the studio was 'Into Temp-tation'. To Froom, it remains 'the best record Crowded House ever made'. He was staying at Tim's place, where he had some keyboards set up. 'Neil came over and when I heard that melody, the chorus melody . . . once in a while you work on a song that, if you play it a certain way, it sounds like classical music. That was definitely one of those things. So beautiful, I thought, *man*, this is really something else. Most people that come up to me, that are in the music business, or musicians, that's what they say to me: man, *that* is a record.'

It was all but complete when Froom heard it. All it needed was another bridge, the piece Neil had written was too long. They cut it in half and started it in the middle, so that when the bridge begins ('*We can go . . . sailing in*') it flows seamlessly out of the chorus before it. Seymour's first reaction was to hear a classical motif running through the song, and the soulful feel required by its chord progres-sion seemed beyond any rhythm they could give it.

Froom based the string introduction on the melody of the chorus, using a different key. He played all the strings himself on a Cham-berlain, a '60s keyboard based on the Mellotron's principle, using tape loops of real instruments.

Froom had recently bought a Chamberlain in pristine condition, as it had been used only in a recording studio. If anything is respon-sible for giving the album a 'Beatle' sound – other than Neil and Froom's natural inclinations – it's the Chamberlain. The saxophones on 'Kill Eye' aren't just any saxophones, but the type used in 'Good Morning, Good Morning'. The flutes and string section in 'Into Temp-tation' are the flutes of 'Strawberry Fields Forever' and the string section of an early Moody Blues record. Froom also used early syn-thesisers on *Temple*, but both he and Finn preferred the 'wacked out, wobbly' inconsistences of the venerable Chamberlain, which give it an emotional quality.

Paul found the raw, strident 'Kill Eye' the most exhilarating to record. 'Think of it as a name for the TV set, and you'll have an idea of that song,' explained Neil. 'It's about the nightly horror of watching the world destroy itself on TV.' Whispering 'I beg you . . . forgive me' at the beginning is Jimmy Swaggart, pleading to all of America for absolution. It was taken from a news report after his fall from grace with a prostitute. Blake miked up a didgeridoo for the song and, with

Nick, went to a lot of trouble to add natural sound effects to the end. The pair got up at four o'clock one morning and went into the bush to record the morning call of the magpie. Nick wanted the specific Australian sound from his childhood: 'We ended up with crows, a bit of a kookaburra, cockatoos, blowflies and bellbirds. We had a whole potpourri of Australian wildlife. But, when it came to mixing the record, in this smelly little studio in New York, Neil was the only one present. Because he's from New Zealand, he didn't realise the significance of any of the birds. We missed out on the bellbirds and magpies and ended up with bloody cockatoos and blowflies.'

Critics reviewing the album never failed to note the influence of McCartney on 'Into Temptation' and Lennon on 'Kill Eye'. The Beatle comparison was a compliment that Finn found flattering, but it was beginning to irritate him. 'It's time I was staking my own territory. On the next album, I'll look at diffusing that. It hasn't been anything I've consciously gone for, but I know it resides in me, because people mention it so much. I'm prepared to cop that one, but I'm going to do something about it.'

However, escaping the influence of the Beatles meant Neil would also avoid writing songs like 'Into Temptation', although he agreed it was the best song on the album. But he felt he hadn't exploited his own uniqueness, such as his fragmented and pictorial style of lyric-writing. From now on, he said, he would be less concerned about having lines make literal sense, than the sounds of words and the strength of their individual images.

An example was the throwaway lyrics to 'Sister Madly', which began life as 'People That You're Standing On'. Driven by upbeat brushes and a brisk walking bass, it was the band attempting 'bastardised jazz', says Neil. The lyrics were stream-of-conscious, with the chorus ('Sister madly, waking up the dead') relating to the Finns' sister Judy waking up in the middle of the night. 'We used to share a room at one point. She used to have really bad nightmares, just before she sat big exams. I'd wake up, she'd be screaming at the top of her voice. It would freak me out completely.' (Judy Finn points out that Neil, too, talked in his sleep when young.)

This was the song which needed the antique microphone: Froom wanted to capture a 1940s, Andrews Sisters sound to the backing vocals. For the solo, the first intention was to use Toots Thielemans, the virtuoso harmonica player and whistler, whom Froom had recently witnessed stealing the show from the all-star Quincy Jones Big Band. 'I wanted to twist the song, let it go wild.' Thielemans was unavailable, so he called upon the English guitarist Richard Thompson, who was managed by Gary Stamler and whose *Daring Adventures*

Froom had recently produced. It was the beginning of a warm association between the folk-rock legend and Crowded House. 'He was a great second choice,' says Froom. 'He came down and played two solos, then got it.'

It was one of the band's favourite songs to play, and they were invigorated by the flair of the eclectic, idiosyncratic Thompson, who finished the song off with an extravagant flanged chord. 'He's one of those rare people who has got incredible technique but plays like a kid,' said Neil.

'When You Come' was another song the band already loved playing live, so the recording was straightforward, with Paul building the dynamic of the song to its erotic crescendo on tiny hi-hat cymbals suggested by Blake. Froom's contribution was to emphasise the contrast between verses and chorus, and the Phil Spector-like flourish at the end from children's toy bells. 'I just loved it,' says Paul, 'it's very sexual. It's great that it's when *you* come, not when *I* come. It means you have something to do with it, and I like that.'

'In the Lowlands' – 'about that state of mind when you're heading somewhere and you know what's waiting for you isn't very pleasant', says Neil – gave them the most difficulty in the studio. It was tried in a number of different ways, with Neil changing the lyrics at the last minute. But, says Froom, 'We never got the verses right. In my mind it's a bit like Morrissey, where it almost sounds like the vocal and the music don't match each other, it's floating over the top. We almost lost it, and only stuck with it because we needed the pace. Again, it's a shuffle, the dreaded shuffle.' Froom almost sighs: 'Shuffles are a fantastic art form,' he says.

'Mansion in the Slums' was written during the band's first stay in Los Angeles, and recorded quickly, having been performed acoustically on their first US tour. Neil describes it as a 'tongue-in-cheek collection of random notes about having success and what is meaningful or not in life. It's about how people there are trying to embrace a hippie lifestyle, while having all the mod-cons.'

Discussing 'Mansion' for the fans' newsletter Nick was reminded of the mishaps he kept having with the jacuzzi in their rented house. Life in the Hollywood hills may have given Neil a guilt trip, but Nick still relished their luck. To Neil, 'Love This Life' was self-explanatory, but it reminded Nick of being back in Melbourne after the adrenaline rush of the first album's success had finally calmed down. 'It was an incredible, hectic year, and we were home, just relaxing. I had a little motor scooter, and was zipping from home to rehearsal each day . . . and I remember thinking, this was a fantastic experience.'

Neil was aware that any emotional highs would be balanced by melancholic periods. He breezily said he liked the idea of presenting the teenagers who loved the romantic, uplifting spirit of 'Don't Dream It's Over' with the challenging, darker material of *Temple*. Froom, whom Hester had nicknamed 'the Gloomster', admitted to *Musician* that people had commented on the darkness of the album, but strangely, 'not many people have said how funny it is. It strikes me as funny, even if it is a bit on the black side.'

At the time, the first single seemed to choose itself. They would go out with the ballad: the classic simplicity of 'Better Be Home Soon' seemed unstoppable. It had been in the band's live shows for months, the exquisite melody haunted everybody who heard it – and the song's theme was universal. 'It's written from a woman's viewpoint,' Neil told the club newsletter. 'She's saying, you haven't got much time buddy, you'd better show up soon or else you're in trouble.' It seemed that Froom's minimal arrangement could only help, especially with the Hammond B3 organ solo reinforcing the connection to 'Don't Dream It's Over'. This was just a coincidence, says Froom. The first time he heard the song was when he was playing a promotional gig with the band. His B3 was on stage, it sounded right when they jammed on the song, so they stayed with it. 'When you play something and it works, you don't think any further,' he says. 'After that we studiously avoided it – it was more of a concern to avoid any formula.'

The confidence everyone in the Crowded House camp felt about *Temple of Low Men* was contagious. 'Neil was in a very peppy, spry, happy-go-lucky mood during a lot of that time,' says Stamler. Everyone was so enthusiastic about 'Better Be Home Soon' when it was finished at Sunset Sound, they started to play games about its potential. 'We thought it was going to come in big-time,' says Paul. The question wasn't, will this reach number one – but how long will it stay there. Three weeks? Four? They even considered taking bets.

Neil says that when he's finished a song, he never really knows if he's written a hit. 'But "Better Be Home Soon" is probably the closest. I knew that one was – in its simplicity – going to be hooky. It's probably the simplest song I've ever written, and the most like a generic pop hit I'll ever write.'

'Better Be Home Soon' was everybody's choice, says Stamler. 'Everybody got swept up into the same conclusion: this was going to be a number one single. It was the logical successor to "Don't Dream It's Over".'

Stamler had tried to talk the band into recording 'Throw Your Arms Around Me', the Hunters and Collectors song which had been so popular live for Crowded House. For him, the band's 'unwillingness or inability' to record the song was the only confrontational issue that emerged during the recording of *Temple of Low Men*. Stamler felt it was an 'uplifting, positive, magical song, the one which would carry the torch from album one to album two. It had become a trademark for Crowded House – to fans it was almost a certain single.' The song, Neil admits, is 'a hit waiting to happen for someone. We probably should have done it, but whenever we started to record an album, we never had the vibe for it. I can't think of a logical reason why we didn't do it – probably because Gary wanted it so much, and we were being perverse!'

After the sessions in Melbourne and Los Angeles, it was Easter by the time the album was mixed. Neil wanted the final mix to be done by the doyen of the profession: Bob Clearmountain, who polished the Rolling Stones' 'Miss You' remix and Bruce Springsteen's *Born in the USA*. Neil, Stamler and Capitol's Tom Whalley went to the Hit Factory, New York, to oversee Clearmountain craft the record into a work of clarity and warmth. It was a mature, consistent album, of originality and substance. The music people had done their work: how would the industry respond?

Stamler and Whalley were staying in the same New York hotel when the album was finished, very late one night. At about three in the morning, they went to a delicatessen to have a sandwich. 'There was something troubling the both of us,' recalls Stamler, 'though neither of us said anything. Clearly, there was this unspoken concern. I don't know if he said it, or I said it. But somebody said, "Are you thinking what I'm thinking?"'

'You mean, that we don't have a single on the record?'

'Yeah, that's what I'm thinking: we don't have a lead track.'

Both went to bed troubled by their misgivings. The next morning, Whalley called Stamler. 'He was trying to be a cheerleader, saying, 'What are we concerned about? This is going to be unstoppable, it's a brilliant record. We're agonising about nothing, something will surface, something *has* to surface. It's Crowded House, right?'

'Tom and I convinced each other: it was a great record. We were needlessly concerned that we didn't hear that single. It's Crowded House, radio will bend for them. We didn't state it that way, but that was the theory. So we just let it go.'

Never be the same
• May 1988

'Finn has neglected the only thing he has to offer the
world: perky hooks.'

**—Robert Christgau, the self-styled 'dean of rock
critics', on Temple, 1988**

In April, 1988, *Billboard* magazine announced the most successful
songwriters of the previous year. Topping the list was Lewis A Mar-
tinee (who wrote 'Point of No Return' and 'Seasons Change' for
Miami disco trio Exposé), followed by U2 and Michael Jackson. Neil
Finn was 10th on the list, ahead of Madonna and Bruce Springsteen.

Crowded House reassembled in May to take *Temple of Low Men* to
the world. The first gigs after the recording of the album were before
1400 people packed into the hallowed Melbourne club, the Venue, just
before it was demolished by the city council. The band then quickly
played a few warm-up dates on Australia's east coast. On keyboards
was former New Zealander Mike Gubb, who had played with Mental
as Anything. Eddie Rayner was unavailable; his wife Raewyn Turner
had recently given birth to their second child and, with Auckland
songwriter Brian Baker, his duo the Makers had an album coming out
on Warners. 'The album had a lot invested in it,' he says, 'and they
gave it a push, but it didn't sell a cracker.'

An appearance on the Saturday morning television show *The
Factory* introduced some of the *Temple* songs to the Australian audience. The show is chaotic, but the band earnestly performed and
answered questions from the young fans. A teenage girl asked Neil if
he competed with Tim. 'We play tennis,' he replied, then admitted,
'If he writes a good song, I feel I have to write a better one. We don't
compete in an ugly way, but in a caring way, to quote Dame Edna.'

The trio gave a spirited rendition of 'Sister Madly', accompanying
themselves only with handclaps, like a barbershop quartet. 'That's one
of the more flippant numbers on the new album,' said Neil. 'The rest
of them are dark and morose.' Soulful versions of 'Better Be Home
Soon' and 'Throw Your Arms Around Me' seemed to go above the
heads of their young audience. But there was nothing half-hearted
about the band's performance, despite their obvious dissatisfaction

129

with the lack of organisation. On the way out, Paul gave the fingers to the producers, calling out, 'You're real professionals. We love you.'

In mid-June, 'Better Be Home Soon' was released in the United States as the first single, followed by the album a fortnight later. The band had joked throughout its recording that the working title was *Mediocre Follow-up*; when the album came out, they went to great lengths to explain the title *Temple of Low Men*. It came from a phrase written on the side of a church in Los Angeles, said Nick. The band had seen it just after Jimmy Swaggart's public apology, and the phrase seemed to comment on the 'nouveau consumerist spiritualism' being sold on religious television. In fact, admits Paul, the phrase is a term for female genitalia. Nick and Paul had found it in a dictionary of slang, along with 'In the Lowlands'. 'Neil would be trying to finish the words to some beautiful song like "Don't Dream It's Over" and Nick would rush in and say, "Guess what *lowlands* means." We never told anyone at Capitol, they just said fine, they could throw a few religious icons in there. We ended up catching a few people out who said, "Yeah, great title – I've seen the church you're talking about."'

Critical reception to *Temple of Low Men* was favourable, with a few predictable exceptions (London's *Melody Maker*, Robert Christgau of New York's *Village Voice*). Most critics perceived a change in mood, seeing the album as a dark comment on the price of success. Last time, wrote *Rolling Stone*'s Anthony DeCurtis, the band sang, 'Now we're getting somewhere'. The new album was the story of what happened when they arrived . . .

'Success appears to have made Finn feel more vulnerable, less sure of himself and even a tad bitter. Fortunately, Finn is so skillful and articulate a songwriter that he manages to freshen up the clichés of loneliness at the top. [He] renders the darkness at the heart of this album convincing and compelling . . . *Temple of Low Men* is not as immediately winning a record as *Crowded House* but it's smart, mature and honest.'

People reviewer David Hiltbrand said, 'While Finn's mood seems to have slipped into a sadder, minor key here, it is clear on songs like "Into Temptation" that we are in the presence of true pop artistry.'

The *New York Times'* Stephen Holden wrote that Crowded House was one of the cleverest descendants of the Beatles, their personal signature refreshing the familiar style and mining 'an especially fertile middle ground between pop romanticism and art-rock whimsy.' Holden described 'Into Temptation' as the most distinguished song on the album, with 'a melody whose long, stealthy gait recalls "Hey Jude" while its climbing chromaticism and bold modulations are worthy of Cole Porter . . . [Finn's] songs are alive, the expressions of a thinskinned, hyperemotional singer and songwriter thrashing out his problems right in the moment.'

In the Australian edition of *Rolling Stone*, Ed St John wrote, 'It's unequivocally an excellent album brimming over with a brand new selection of beautifully constructed, post-modern domestic pop songs. It's instantly listenable.

'Without sentimentalising his emotional life, Neil Finn is making a clear statement in these songs; a statement about his need for a stable home life and family that doesn't grate with his jaunty, hummable melodies.'

To the press in New Zealand, Neil said he was sick of reviewers analysing the lyrics of his songs, and in future he was determined to be more obvious and, hopefully, positive. Yes, there had been a down side to the spectacular success of the previous year, but he was reluctant to talk about it, not wanting to be another whinging rock star. He told journalist Graham Reid, 'I don't think anybody should feel sorry for me because anything that's happened which is hard to deal with, I've created myself and been well rewarded for.

'But you do create a monster, and become aware you're part of the machinery and totally implicated in the vacuousness of the whole thing. Without wishing to put it too strongly, sometimes I feel like wanting to apologise for the entertainment industry as a whole – except for our performances.'

To *RAM*, Neil said, 'I am a hustler. All the stuff that people don't see is pretty agonising – getting ready for records, writing and making them. I agonise over it until the moment the record comes out . . . Sometimes I get megalomaniacal and want everything to be exactly as I say, but you've got to compromise to some degree.' He joked to *Smash Hits* that Nick and Paul would probably describe him as 'a maniacal egocentric dictator and I'd describe them as, *um*, limp vassals'.

New Zealand's *Rip It Up* asked if he was a strict bandleader. 'Bloody strict, mate,' he replied. 'No-one turns up late in this band. I've always been fanatically punctual, probably all the time, while Paul and Nick are incredibly late all the time. It's the one continuous irritation I have to live with. But it's not ridiculous. I suppose that because I write the songs I have much more concern with the way they turn out. Nick and Paul are happy to play, get into it, and try and avoid as many interviews as possible.'

In the crucial week of the album's release in the States, Crowded House was in Europe for their first proper tour of the Continent. Despite the tour only lasting two weeks – and travelling with them on the bus were Neil's family, and Nick and Paul's girlfriends – it was a struggle. 'That tour was a lowpoint,' says Neil. 'I was having a very difficult time with the whole thing at that point, trying to keep being the fun-loving bunch of lads from Down Under.' It was a stressful time for the family, even though an old friend, Jane West, was there as nanny and, says Sharon, 'the other guys were good about Liam – and it was good for them to have that environment'.

Causing added anxiety was the breaking in of a new keyboardist after the dazzling Eddie Rayner. Mike Gubb is more of a traditional keyboardist than Rayner, with a rhythm-and-blues, piano and organ background. 'Mike coped with some aspects very well,' says Neil, 'but having come from Eddie, who was a technological whizkid, with expansive sounds and detailed work, it was difficult.' Stage tech Geoff Lloyd remembers Gubb being 'good fun, and a great piano player, but he didn't have the confidence that Eddie had. The shows were loose compared to others, as they were still honing the new stuff.'

The short tour finished with two well-lubricated shows at the Town & Country Club in London where, to Neil's relief, a show of hands revealed that more than half of the audience was English, not expatriate Australians and New Zealanders. Then it was off to Japan for a week of intensive, regimented promo work. While there, Neil called Eddie: Gubb wasn't working out. The band filmed a video for 'When You Come' (a simple travelogue of the trio performing in the streets of Tokyo, directed by Paul Elliott) and performed shows in Osaka and Tokyo. 'The gigs were incredible,' says Lloyd. 'The crowd sat down the whole time, then went apeshit at the end. It was weird.'

They then swapped the neon lights and exotic food of Japan for the outback of Australia, with warm up dates in Alice Springs and Darwin, both rarely visited by rock acts. Back on keyboards – temporarily – was Eddie Rayner. Since the American tours, apart from his work with the Makers, Rayner had written and compiled the soundtrack for the Australian comedy *Rikky and Pete*. The project was a family affair; to play his music, Rayner brought in Schnell Fenster, a group which had recently been formed by Split Enz alumni Phil Judd, Noel Crombie, Nigel Griggs and Melbourne guitarist Michael Den Elzen. Crowded House offered one of its oldest songs, 'Recurring Dream', for a driving sequence.

Although Rayner was still the band's first choice as keyboardist, his limited availability had become a problem for the group. Neil joked to *Rip It Up* that 'We beg on our knees to have him come and tour with us. We should have got him to play on the record, then he would have been available. Now we've realised – probably too late – that he's an incredibly valuable person to have around.'

To Rayner, it was just a matter of priorities; his young family and own projects came first, and he had done more than enough touring with the Enz. 'Crowded House never had to cajole me into playing with them, I loved playing with them,' he says. For 10 years Rayner's skills had been providing crucial support to Neil; in concert he was like a musical safety net. But when his availability became uncertain, the issue began to 'play psychologically on the integrity of the unit', says Stamler. 'His schedule began to become more important than the band's schedule. Subtle games were being played, to Neil's disadvantage. We needed to make a change, or else the band was never going to be able to tour without referring to Eddie Rayner's schedule.'

During the Australian tour, Neil discussed with the *Auckland Star* Rayner's impending departure before the band moved on to the US: 'Eddie's so much ingrained in the whole thing now, he knows all the songs and all the little bits and pieces we fart around with in between the songs. It's not a brilliant prospect rehearsing a new player.

'It's just that Eddie is a lot less inclined to be spending a lot of time in America – to tell you the truth none of us are that excited about going there again.'

The climax of the Australian tour was a five-night, sold-out season at Sydney's State Theatre. One of the great picture palaces, the State is an architectural fantasy built in 1929, richly decorated with mosaic floors, marble statues, lavish chandeliers and bronze doors. The grand, elegant setting was appropriate for a triumphant series of shows which can be seen as the peak of the early Crowded House. The band were received as conquering heroes, returning with an album that was almost symphonic in its richness, and confidently displayed in a show of musical and theatrical sophistication.

Each night the theatre was filled to capacity with 2000 fervent young fans, many of them dressed in suit jackets, painted with elaborate Crowded House designs painstakingly copied from the band's early costumes. For this week, it seemed Crowded House had inherited not just a few chords and values from the Beatles, but the phenomenon of Beatlemania. As the concerts began, the screaming of the audience threatened to overwhelm the band. At each show, Neil stopped the music after a few songs to say, 'There's nothing like a good scream.' The audience then shrieked as one, eyes tightly shut, fists clenched. 'Come on!' Neil taunted them, 'is that all you've got?' The band then covered their ears as the screams whistled around the theatre. 'Louder! Let's get this screaming out of your systems! Because I want you to know, we hate it. It hurts our ears.'

The band deliberately avoided taking the easy route to satisfying the young audience, opening with 'Hole in the River' or 'When You Come', with Neil performing alone for a verse before the curtain lifted to reveal the band. The stunning set was taken from Nick's cover design: crêpe-paper flames leaping from burning buildings, turning the theatre into a vision from an expressionist nightmare. With laser lights and ultra-violet effects – plus the kaleidoscopic variety of Rayner's keyboard playing – the concerts were an audio-visual extravaganza.

The band tested the audience throughout with masterly shifts in dynamics and new interpretations of familiar favourites, all carried off with humour and spontaneity. The theatrical approach allowed sombre moments to be interspersed by goofy coordinated routines, without losing the dignity of the music. Neil's singing had reached a new level of assuredness, improvising with confidence, always con-scientiously projecting his voice. 'Something So Strong' and 'Now We're Getting Somewhere' were rousing crowd-pleasers but also a spirited demonstration of white soul; 'Sister Madly' had arrived as a central setpiece of the encores, with unexpected detours into Paul Kelly's 'Leaps and Bounds' and 'The Last Waltz'. But the evenings of colour, entertainment and risk-taking were brought to an emotional conclusion with graceful renditions of 'Better Be Home Soon' – already the 'Sailing' of a new generation – and 'Into Temptation'. Then, inheriting another theatrical tradition from Split Enz, all four band-members came to the front of the stage to dramatically bow together like well brought-up choir boys.

For Rayner, the shows had been a virtuosic swansong, his last in Australia with Crowded House. His eclectic flamboyance suited the theatre's ostentatious architecture. Always able to effortlessly segue between pianistic styles – a Rachmaninoff arpeggio might become a Jerry Lee Lewis glissando, or an Edwardian music-hall romp – with the addition of sampling keyboards, it was as though Rayner was let loose in a music shop. Pushing buttons furiously, he added musical colour to the songs: flute, saxophone, accordion, a Stax horn section, a string quartet, barrelhouse piano, calliope, Hammond organ, even a crowing rooster (at the line 'always waking up the dead').

On the last night, as the crowd were leaving the theatre, Paul and Neil bounded back on stage. Neil took to the drumkit while Paul, stripped to the waist, went into a crazed rap to farewell one of the family: *'We're making records, Ed's making babies / It's been fun, But it's coming to an end.'*

After a week in which they had been the toast of Sydney, Crowded

House immediately flew to New York for a concentrated stint of promotion. The band had been reluctantly anticipating the lengthy US concert tour which was planned to start once 'Better Be Home Soon' reached the Top 40. They already knew, however, that the high expectations held for the song were misplaced. Two weeks earlier, the single had peaked at 42 in the *Billboard* charts, and it was now on its way down. The album didn't fare much better, reaching 40 for two weeks before sliding away.

In Canada, the song had reached number one; in Australia and New Zealand, number two. But in the States, something went wrong with the song which Neil regards as the closest to a sure-fire hit he has ever written. At the time, the earliest measure of a single's success was how many 'adds' (additions) to radio stations' playlists it received in the first week. 'Better Be Home Soon' received far less 'adds' in its first week than Capitol's promotions department had projected. 'That was a danger sign from the beginning that this record needed some help,' says Gary Stamler.

'Man, that record was hard going,' says Jeremy Hammond. 'Radio is such a fickle business in America. You can have an incredible song – as that one was – but it was darker, while radio wants touchy-feely, warm records.' Programmers at adult pop, Top 40 and urban (black) stations had played 'Don't Dream It's Over'. But when they heard 'Better Be Home Soon', some said it sounded like a country song. (It actually received some airplay on a few country stations.) With the initial reaction of programmers to 'Better Be Home Soon' so disappointing – or going in the wrong direction – Capitol soon stopped promoting the song to radio.

In the 18 months since 'Don't Dream It's Over' had been a hit, there had been many important changes inside the Tower. Music industry veteran Joe Smith became CEO in 1987, and found the company was losing money and 'needed a complete overhaul'. 'It was an enormous job,' he wrote in *Off the Record*. 'It was a company with great values that had been suffering over the last few years and required some major reorganisation and restructuring to get it back to where it was.'

Smith succeeded Bhaskar Menon as chairman of the parent company, Capitol-EMI; David Berman had replaced Don Zimmermann as president of Capitol; since the departure of Walter Lee, the head of the radio promotions was now John Fagot. Despite the maxim that executives don't like inheriting artists their predecessors have signed, all were dedicated to making Crowded House a success. 'They were the most loved band on the label,' says Hammond. 'We were all poised to take them to the next level.'

In April, 1988, Smith told the Capitol staff, 'We have to outhustle, outwork, outthink everyone else on the street.' But with so many changes in key positions, there was no longer a focused approach to marketing and promotion. 'There was a real mix of cultures at the time,' explains a Capitol source, 'with an executive team who came from all these different labels. So they were still evolving together. Some of them came from companies much larger than Capitol, with much bigger artist rosters, who put out a lot more records. So they didn't come from a mindset that when you got that first rejection on a single, you just put your head down and went back in.'

When the promotion of 'Better Be Home Soon' went awry, it was clear the song needed help. Once again, calling for 'help' meant hiring the independent promoters to push the single to radio programmers; by mid-1988, the furore about the use of 'indies' had faded. The promoters were again wielding their influence, and most of the majors were again using their services. The most prominent exception, however, was Capitol Records. Just before the release of 'Better Be Home Soon', Berman and Fagot had taken a very public stance that they would not deal with the independent promoters, criticising them in the music trade magazines.

'It was corporate policy,' says Hammond. 'There was a decree from on high that no-one was to hire any independents.' The emphatic anti-indie policy at Capitol 'put a wave in the system,' says Tom Gorman, who was in the company's promotions department at the time. 'It said that anything that wasn't completely obvious wasn't going to make it on its own. And I wouldn't call "Better Be Home Soon" an obvious record.'

Gary Stamler points out the irony: 'With "Don't Dream It's Over" we had helped put the indies back in business. There was no way I could have operated the same sort of scam.' Grant Thomas thinks the single was 'artificially strangled', a combination of the turmoil at Capitol and the company's provocative stance towards the influential 'indies'. A resigned Neil says, 'Who knows? In 20 years I could be talking to some guy on a beach in Acapulco, and he'll say, "I was programme director at such-and-such a station. Do you know what really happened with that song?" . . .'

The single stalling at No 42 was only the first hiccup: apart from positive reviews, few other areas of marketing planned for the album clicked. Without radio play, there was no reason for MTV to play the videos, which were unremarkable; plus the band was not yet available to tour. 'So some fans who liked Crowded House didn't go back to them for *Temple*, partly because many of them didn't know it existed,' says Julie Borchard, Hammond's assistant. 'They discovered Crowded House off the radio, not from print.'

As 'Better Be Home Soon' fell from the charts, Neil said to Steve Pond of *Rolling Stone*, "It pisses me off, considering that everybody was so 100 per cent convinced that it was the right song to put out because it was a dead-certain smash. I was quite wary about putting it out first, because I feel it's not representative of the rest of the record.'

He saw the single's failure as 'further confirmation to me that the best thing I could be doing now is probably being at home writing songs instead of frantically tearing around the world trying to give the record company what they need in order to get a hit record.'

But for a week Crowded House hit the promotional circuit in North America, giving interviews to radio and press, appearing on MTV as guests, giving well-received club shows at CBGBs in New York and the Whisky in Los Angeles. They performed 'Sister Madly' on the David Letterman show, and appeared at the MTV awards in LA to present the best new artist award to their successors: Guns N' Roses.

Crowded House was to have been central to the awards show, but once they saw the banality expected of them, they decided to back off and minimise their participation. Instead, while sitting in the audience, they played 'Better Be Home Soon', Neil dedicating the song to Sharon and Liam at home. 'I was really fatigued and ready to go home,' he says. The goodwill the band had earned at MTV may have evaporated that night. After the show, Neil gave an interview to *Spin* journalist Michael Azerrad in which he criticised the vacuous nature of MTV and the awards. He also gave a dispirited interview to MTV's Randee, which never aired. Randee asked if the show was as much fun as last year's. 'No,' said Neil. Why not? 'I'll tell you what's going to be fun is the next two months, when we're going to be having a holiday. That's going to be fun.'

Neil decided to cancel the imminent *Temple of Low Men* US tour. 'I wasn't feeling that great and was feeling a lot of stress,' he says. 'The spectre of months and months of touring was looming up in front of me and I was starting to lose the vibe. Blowing out the American tour would probably be marked in commercial terms as a pivotal point. But even more importantly, we were let down by the record company. They weren't working very well, they were saying, "Shit – we don't know what to do, the band aren't here, the record is stalling ... *panic*." '

After the disappointing result of the single, Capitol felt a substantial tour was crucial. 'Hit singles sell albums,' explains Jeremy

Hammond, 'tours establish artists *and* sell albums – though not as many albums.'

The band went back to Melbourne, to have its first lengthy break after three intense years. 'It was crunch time,' says Paul. 'We stayed in Melbourne for quite a while. I remember I was quite happy to have the time off.'

Two more tours of America were booked, then cancelled. 'At the eleventh hour,' says Stamler, 'I'd get a phone call from Neil in the middle of the night, saying "I can't do it, pull it out." '

The band needed to 're-energise and refocus', says Neil. 'The whole experience of being a globe-trotting, high-profile, fun-loving outfit from down under was starting to wear a bit thin. It felt like we were becoming a parody of ourselves. The last thing I wanted to do was paint ourselves into a corner.'

The break was a chance to concentrate on having a normal family life, which the years of ambition and success had prevented. (In 1991 Paul told *Juke*, 'The most simple way to put it is, we sacrificed a lot of promotion for that album to get our private lives in order.') It was also an opportunity to rethink the future for Crowded House. During this period, Stamler remembers spending an 'enormous amount of time with Neil on the telephone, dealing with someone who was in personal turmoil. A lot of radical thoughts had entered his head about his future, he was confused. It was a very stressful time.'

Choosing the next single was one of the decisions causing problems. Neil didn't want to release 'Into Temptation' as a single, even though it was the most acclaimed song on the album. It was hardly the sunny pop hit they needed, and he was already tired of the prurient interest it had caused.

People assumed his songs were confessional, he told New Zealand's *Rip It Up*. 'I feel a bit vulnerable because of it, in the sense that people would relate it to my own life. And I suppose I have concern for my family in that respect. It's not pleasant for them sometimes to see the way people perceive my songs, and that's a pressure in itself. But I seem drawn to it ... out of a concern to sound like I mean it, it's easier to dip into my darker emotions.'

Neil talked about 'Into Temptation' to the Australian magazine *Countdown*. 'Sexuality is treated flippantly in a lot of songs these days,' he said. 'To me – and maybe this is because I am a Catholic – fidelity is a big thing, and anything that steps outside of this brings in a whole range of incredible issues. That is what attracted me to taking that song the whole way.'

In the fanclub newsletter, Neil explained, 'It's about needing a bit of a hug ... with your mother. Wanting to get back into the womb.

It's about temptation and guilt, something that everybody knows a little bit about.'

Paul quipped to Australian journalist Toby Cresswell, 'You know it's dark and there's something brooding in that Catholic guilt. He has to play these songs to us first off and they're like, primal. We're looking at him going, Neil! Do you really want to say that?'

To take the heat off Neil, Paul said in the club newsletter, 'I do admit that some of the lyrics on the new album Neil found scribbled on things in my guitar case, or in my suitcase on the road. I don't want to raise the issue now, or go on about it – whatever Neil finds or can craft into a song, I think that's a good thing – but I'd just appreciate now and then that I was acknowledged.'

Years later, on BBC's Radio One Neil explained the song's 'mundane background'. He'd been in a hotel in Timaru, New Zealand, late at night, watching a team of rugby players having a drinking session with a group of netballers. As the evening wore on, they started to pair off. 'They started to wander into each other's rooms,' he said. ' "*You opened up your door, I couldn't believe my luck*" came from that. It's not exactly a romantic story.'

In the meantime, 'Sister Madly' became the follow-up single in Britain, 'When You Come' (which had been Neil's first choice) in Australia. In LA, Capitol promotions staff started to get airplay for 'Never Be the Same' on album-oriented radio stations, hoping it might cross over to pop radio, and become a single. Unhappy with that idea, in December Neil agreed to release 'Into Temptation'. 'By then it was almost a last resort,' says Stamler, 'it never had the opportunity it might have had if it had followed "Better Be Home Soon" earlier.' The simple, band-in-rehearsal video by Richard Lowenstein didn't help. While Neil looks suitably sombre, Nick and Paul start to snigger as the clip progresses; finally they manage to coax a smile out of Neil.

'Into Temptation' made no impact on the American charts, and it would be nine months till it was followed by the equally unsuccessful 'I Feel Possessed'. Slow but steady sales meant that by the end of 1988, *Temple of Low Men* had sold 500,000 copies – a gold record – in the United States, but a disappointing result after the million-selling debut. It had been widely acclaimed, but was a victim of circumstances, appearing when neither the band nor the record company were functioning well.

'The public were used to this band being their own best salesmen,' says Stamler, 'seeing them out and around, actively promoting their record in the US. They portrayed an image that the American public was obviously taken with. So on top of what many perceived to be a dark record, without a seemingly uplifting, poppy single, we had a band which was conspicuously absent during the release of the record. The public were confused, the record company didn't get the help they needed from the band – principally because of Neil's situation – and he became rather sullen in some interviews. So the whole presentation of the record, and the band around it, was radically different from the first album.'

'*Temple* should have been massive,' says Mitchell Froom. 'It came at a very bad political time for Capitol. There was six months around then that they didn't have anything on the radio, anywhere. I remember Bruce Springsteen calling up Joe Smith, the president of Capitol, and saying about *Temple*, "How could you lose this record? What's wrong? This record is *great*."'

Just get an electric guitar • January 1989

'There was an amazing balance on stage. Neil was the straight guy, Paul was the funny one, Nick the bemused spectator who'd come in every now and then. I never said anything. There was enough talking going on.'

—Mark Hart, 1996

Crowded House took three months off, broken only in mid-December by a benefit gig in Sydney for Ethiopian famine relief. During the show they had the task of accompanying Australian singer Jimmy Barnes performing songs such as 'Have You Ever Seen the Rain', 'Many Rivers to Cross' and 'Throw Your Arms Around Me'. With Barnes's vocal style resembling two cats fighting, Crowded House's backing had the enthusiasm of a covers band at a wedding.

The band's vacation came to an end a week into 1989, when they embarked on a tour of New Zealand. Eddie Rayner returned on keyboards, and also on the Tour of Low Men bill was Schnell Fenster. With all the Split Enz connections taking part, and a relaxed schedule over nearly three weeks, the summer tour had the atmosphere of a family holiday. As the bands and their crew travelled through the country, they lobbed water-bombs and eggs at each other's vans.

But the two bands had polar-opposite approaches to pop music. Schnell Fenster's songs were obscure, and its sound was forbiddingly dense and guitar-heavy, whereas Crowded House performed their accessible pop even more light-heartedly than usual. Paul's antics and the spontaneous talent quests were fresh to the New Zealand audience. Noel Crombie was amazed that although the two bands had the same number of songs in their set, Schnell Fenster played theirs in 50 minutes, while Crowded House took about two hours.

In several centres, the inevitable onstage reunion occurred, with Crowded House evolving into Split Enz during their encores. With Neil, Paul and Eddie, plus Noel Crombie and Nigel Griggs of Schnell Fenster, Tim Finn appeared in Auckland to whip through favourites such as 'Six Months in a Leaky Boat', 'Dirty Creature' and 'I See Red'. Enz co-founder Phil Judd didn't take part, being in the odd position of not knowing the band's most popular songs, which had been written after he left. The tour concluded at the Founder's Theatre in Hamilton, a venue of special significance for the Enz alumni. Just 18 miles north of Te Awamutu, Hamilton is the nearest city to the Finns' hometown, so their appearances in the comfortable theatre take on a prodigal-son atmosphere. Tim and Neil rewarded the locals' affectionate reception with an impromptu singalong of 'Tom Dooley', 'Marie' and the Enz novelty 'Hermitt McDermitt'.

The Tour of Low Men was the last for stage tech Geoff Lloyd, whose delight in the music was being hampered by Grant Thomas's frugality when it came to paying expenses. Lloyd found his own replacement in Paul 'Arlo' Guthrie, with whom he'd worked on a Chantoozies tour. 'The band fell in love with him,' says Lloyd. 'He could play the guitar, use all the machinery, didn't smoke pot and always remained Arlo, one of the original nice guys. He could play guitar like ringing a bell, and found his niche with the Crowdies.'

After the tour with Schnell Fenster, Neil finally felt able to face an American tour again. But with 'no heat' in the music industry for *Temple* or Crowded House, Stamler had a difficult time getting promoters in the United States to book a substantial tour. So it was decided the wisest thing to do was concentrate on their strongest markets – Canada, where 'Better Be Home Soon' had been a hit, and a few dates in the northeast and west coast of the States.

Eddie Rayner had agreed to play keyboards on the tour but, just before the tour began, his father's health deteriorated after a long illness. Rayner flew from Melbourne to New Zealand and spent a few days with him before he died.

Crowded House was stuck, just as they were poised to re-establish themselves in North America. It was a Tuesday night when Stamler called freelance keyboardist Mark Hart in Los Angeles and asked what he was up to.

'Not much,' said Mark. His regular gig Supertramp was off the road.

Do you want to go on tour with Crowded House?

'Sure – when?'

'It starts Friday night in New Jersey,' said Stamler.

The pair knew each other from the early '80s, when Stamler represented Mark's band ComboNation in a pitch for a deal with Warners. Ironically, it was Tom Whalley who was signing them to Warners – and it was through ComboNation that Stamler had first heard of Split Enz. He'd been given one of their albums as a Christmas present by the lead guitarist of ComboNation, whose wife worked at A&M. That was why the ads for the final Split Enz concerts had caught Stamler's eye during his New Zealand holiday. Mark had already had some contact with Crowded House a few months earlier, when Rayner was again unavailable and the band were auditioning keyboardists. He had met Nick in a coffee shop for breakfast, and got as far as learning the first three songs off *Temple*. They hit a rapport, but when the tour was cancelled the audition didn't happen.

Six months later, it was Tuesday night and Mark had 48 hours before he was to catch a flight across the States to Madison, New Jersey. The three songs he had learnt for the audition were forgotten long ago, and he didn't even have copies of the albums.

He spent Wednesday running around like someone possessed, getting things prepared for his six-week absence. From Nick's girl-friend Brenda, he picked up a live tape of the band, with Rayner playing keyboards. He paid a few bills and bought a Walkman, some manuscript paper and the band's two albums. The number of parts he was to cram astounded him. He found it was all up to the keyboard player: organ, piano, horns, string parts. In fact, everything that wasn't guitar, bass and drums was his responsibility. 'And, being the fastid-ious, pedantic, precious person that I am, I thought God, I have to learn this stuff! It freaked me out.'

He phoned Stamler and said, 'I can't do it, I can't do it! There's too much. I can learn the songs but there is so much arranging, where do you start?' Hearing Mark's concern, Stamler got Froom to make a reassuring phone call. He said, 'Listen, just play the songs. If you can throw in a few horn lines here and there, that's fine, but they're not going to be precious about all that. As long as you don't play wrong chords and keep the feel going. Catch any major cues you have to do, and you'll be fine.'

Next morning Mark met Neil and Paul as they landed at Los Angeles airport. He remembers Neil's new haircut made him look very extreme, like a marine.

'Hi – I'm Mark. Your new keyboardist.' Neil and Paul chuckled. Mark was shaking with nerves. He didn't realise the band had had a nightmare trip across the Pacific, having taken some extra strong hash before leaving. At the stopover in Honolulu, Neil was paranoid about being mugged in the men's toilets, and thought every announcement over the intercom was bad news about his family. He was particularly annoyed that Paul managed to sleep through the flight, while he sat up, grinding his teeth.

On the flight to New Jersey, Mark took on board his Casio key-board, Walkman, manuscript paper and tapes. He was jammed beside the tour manager in a central seat in economy, and hooked up his Walkman headphones so that he could listen to the band's tape in one ear, his Casio in the other. He made a huge mess, loose manuscript sheets were falling everywhere as he listened, wrote out the parts, checked them to make sure the notes were correct, scribbling the barest instructions to himself: E, G, A, B, *guitar riff* ... chorus, verse, *keyboard solo with horn sample* ...

It was dark by the time they got to New Jersey. Mark went straight to his hotel room and wrote more charts. He got up at five o'clock the next morning, feeling panicky, and started again. The first rehearsal was at a long soundcheck the afternoon of the gig. Rayner had left his keyboard rig with the band, and Arlo took Hart through the complicated settings. 'I was a total stranger, and I'm pretty shy – I had no-one to confide in.'

Stamler travelled with the band to New Jersey. 'Neil was sceptical of Mark's ability to cut it, to digest all those complicated parts,' he says. 'In fact, he wasn't sure how an American would fit into the band, if he'd have the right vibe. Just before they started, Neil said to Mark, "Don't worry too much, we'll just play two or three songs with you and we'll just busk the rest of it, so there won't be any pressure on you."

'But as the soundcheck/rehearsal unfolded, Neil was amazed, even shocked at how well Mark was doing. Nick would walk over to me periodically, grinning from ear to ear, saying, "Neil's really excited – he can't believe it." They ended up playing nearly the whole set.'

Support act that first night was Rick Danko, bassist and vocalist with the Band – one of Mark's heroes, although the rest of Crowded House didn't know who he was. Danko thought Mark was a roadie, and asked for help to fix his equipment. 'It was a really heavy night for him,' says Mark. 'His son was in hospital in a coma, and subsequently died. But Danko couldn't be at the hospital, because he had to do this gig. I felt really bad for him, but couldn't watch him play: I was in my own secret anxiety hell.'

A reporter from *Rolling Stone* was backstage before the show, but Mark was too nervous to talk to anyone. Nick presented him with a painted 'Crowdie cossie' from the band's new wardrobe case. 'It was funny, they were really proud of it, they'd never had one before. It's a roadcase with four drawers for the four dwarves: Nick, Paul and Neil, and then one blank. The gig went okay, and I guess they were pleased because afterwards Nick went over and painted my name on the spare drawer. I felt really vindicated, accepted.'

From that first gig, Mark was in the band. 'He was the right guy, there was never anyone else,' says Paul. When Eddie Rayner rang a few days later, his father's funeral completed, he was told they were happy with Mark. Rayner had said he didn't want to join the band, 'and at that stage, "I don't want to join the band" is what I meant,' he says. But it was a long time before Mark could regard himself as a permanent member. Crowded House just wanted to get through the tour, before taking a break to record the next album.

It was a breadbox shaped like a piano that began Mark Hart's musical career, in the kitchen of the family home in Fort Scott, Kansas. He remembers playing with it, wishing it sounded like a piano, but nothing happened. Then his grandmother bought his family an actual piano, and, a few months after his brother and sister began lessons, Mark started as well. He was six.

He got a shock at his first lesson. His teacher, Mrs Pinkston, gave him a few tests to see if he had perfect pitch. He didn't, and his ego was bruised. Lacking a concept of rhythm was also frustrating, but he'd managed to teach himself the first piece in the *Modern Method* primer: 'A B C has a boat, round and round the corner floats . . .' He played it as fast as possible and asked about D, E and F, to see if Mrs Pinkston was impressed. She wasn't, and the next few years of lessons weren't always pleasant.

When he was nine, Mrs Pinkston ran a contest to see who could practise the most, and this appealed to Mark's competitive nature: he wanted to beat his brother, who was three years older. As he built up his routine from 15 minutes a day, he realised he was actually improving; this practice thing really worked. He got up to an hour each day, soundly beating his brother in the contest. 'It made him practise more, too,' he says. 'It was very funny. Then I quit.'

The Beatles conquered America in 1964, when Mark was 12. His brother had a guitar, albeit broken, and once more Mark opened up the *Modern Method*, teaching himself 'Home On the Range'. This riled his brother, but they formed a band together, even though they only had one amp and one guitar. The next Christmas his brother was given another guitar, a flashy multi-pickup model their mother bought from a radio store. Their music teacher, Marc Marcano, who had emigrated from Venezuela to Kansas, suggested they'd go a lot further with decent instruments, so she treated them both to US$80 Fenders. With good guitars, the boys practised with enthusiasm, and Mark was once again excited by the piano, stimulated by Marcano's rendition of Herbie Hancock's 'Watermelon Man' and his skills at boogie-woogie. Mark's future was set, though the lessons only lasted one summer, the year the Beatles progressed from *Rubber Soul* to *Revolver*.

Fort Scott, Kansas, was a town of 10,000 that had originally been a cavalry outpost on the edge of the frontier. The soldiers – dragoons – were there to prevent fighting among the different Indian tribes who had been pushed out west. The local tribe, the Osage, were a giant race who through selective breeding had reached a very tall average height. Feared by all the other tribes, they were enlisted by the cavalry as peacekeepers. European settlers pushed the Osage south into Oklahoma, bringing with them disease, which quickly killed off those who remained.

Radio WHB on the AM band out of Kansas City was the station Mark and his friends listened to while growing up. This inspired a lot of bands in the small town, such as the 007s, and the Aardvarks, which featured Marc Marcano. But to see anybody well-known, you had to go to Kansas City. There, Mark witnessed the Animals as they peaked, and one time his own band was driven there by the drummer's mother, to see a package show. On the bill were Gary Lewis and the Playboys, Sam the Sham and the Pharoahs, Bobby Hebb, plus the Yardbirds featuring Jimmy Page. For a 14-year-old, it was unforgettable.

An influential friend of Mark's group was Chris Kunkle, known around town as 'the hippy'. He had very long hair, walked around barefoot – radical enough in Fort Scott in 1967, but Kunkle had also been to New York, where he picked up albums by Cream and Jimi Hendrix. That altered the perspective of the Hart brothers band, then playing soul covers to perfectly coiffed high-school seniors at prom nights. Soon 'In a Gadda Da Vida' was part of their set.

Mark got out of Fort Scott to study classical piano at a small university in Pittsburg, Kansas, before going to Kansas City, like so many other musicians, to study jazz piano. After a few years, a friend training to be a director at film school in Los Angeles persuaded Mark to move to the west coast. 'Being a director, he's very manipulative, so he got me out to California. Not against my will, but I felt I was being taken by the tide,' he says. 'It was just as well I did, as I'd gone about as far as you could go with a rock band in Kansas City.'

It was 1979 when Mark arrived in Hollywood. He drove down Vine Street, and near the Capitol tower a huge banner was stretched across the street: 'Get the Knack'. The skinny-tied quartet had just been signed by Capitol. They were to be the new wave's new Beatles.

ComboNation didn't go anywhere, although the drummer Billy Thomas ended up in Vince Gill band. Mark scraped together a living playing sessions, while auditioning for veteran acts such as Foreigner and the Four Seasons. He always seemed to miss out – until the middle of 1985, when he got a call from Supertramp. They wanted him to play keyboards and sing on a European tour. A few months earlier, his wife Stephanie had given birth to their second daughter. 'I couldn't get a gig, then all of a sudden I went from nothing to *a real pay cheque*, playing several concerts in Paris, with 15,000 people at each one. It was amazing.'

Mark hit a rapport with the easy-going band, who were 10 years past their *Crime of the Century* prime, but were good to work with. It was the complete opposite of the spontaneity he was to encounter playing with Crowded House: all their concerts had exactly the same set, so you could almost time them by the minute.

In North America, though, it was more depressing. It had been seven years since Supertramp's last hit; the vibe for the band had long gone. Two months into the tour, Mark's wife called him: 'Channing's in hospital'. Their youngest daughter, now 10 months old, had a rare bacterial infection. She was on a respiratory machine for a day before she died.

Mark left the tour and returned to Los Angeles for a week, then went back on the road, joined by Stephanie and their eldest daughter Courtney. 'It was awful,' says Mark. 'We were in a haze at the time, unable to talk, depressed and numb. They were with me for about a week. I had to continue the gig, but I was just going through the motions.'

Supertramp's next leg was a European tour, on which the band-members were joined by their wives. Mark spent time in Paris and London with Stephanie and their daughter, but after they left, 'I was still in the same trance. I was so down. Shaking all the time, stomach problems – I was just wasting away.' He left the band and returned to the erratic employment of Los Angeles session work, not playing with Supertramp again until 1988. They were in hiatus when Stamler's call came through.

Mark Hart's first Crowded House tour was an intense six weeks, winding its way through the snow across Canada to the west coast, finishing up back home in Hollywood. But any tension was restricted to the gigs; the band were a tight-knit group of friends, playing at their best. 'I did notice they were pretty highly strung,' says Mark. 'Neil has mellowed quite a bit since then, but I remember him coming off stage all tense, yelling at the crowd from sidestage to "Clap more, you bastards!" – really angry that they didn't appreciate us enough to call for an encore.'

But Mark recalls it as one of the happiest periods for the band, because it was just them on the tour bus, the four musicians, a tour manager and the driver. Everyone got along; Mark introduced them to a health routine. After each gig he would microwave oatmeal for the others. Then it would be time for bus jogging. In the middle of the night, the band would jog up and down the aisle the length of the bus as it crossed the Canadian plains. They'd listen to a tape taken from the soundboard of their gig that night, jogging on the spot in the lounge as the concert roared from the speakers. Then out would come a set of playing cards for their nightly game of Uno.

'I was the instigator of all this activity, because I was new to the band,' says Mark. 'Oatmeal, jogging, cards, listening to tapes – that's how rock stars spend their time.'

Roger McGuinn, of '60s folk-rock icons the Byrds, joined the tour in Seattle as support act for the Californian dates. He and his wife kept to themselves for the first few days; computer buff McGuinn was already hooked on the internet. When Mark met him, he said, 'Nice to meet you Jim. Oh it's Roger? Weren't you Jim?' McGuinn explained that in the '60s he'd been involved in a religion based on 'other worldly things'. Devotees had to change their name to something to do with space exploration. So Roger was from radio communication: roger and out. He said, 'Well, it could have been Rocket.'

A bond soon developed between McGuinn and Crowded House. 'The Byrds were only 18 or 19 when they had their worldwide hits,' says Paul. 'So he'd been through the mill, you could tell. But he loved our music, and we loved his stuff, too, and soon we started jamming with him at soundchecks.' During McGuinn's set, Crowded House would join him on stage; they relished the opportunity to share harmonies on the Byrds' hits 'So You Want to Be a Rock'n'Roll Star', 'Eight Miles High', 'Turn! Turn! Turn!' and 'Mr Tambourine Man'.

'It was beautiful,' says Paul. 'We got really close to him and his wife. He had this untouchable, happy thing going down. He was a clean-living dude, keen on eating almonds, enjoying playing and travelling with his wife. We found out later they were reborn Christians. But he was cool – there was no evangelism going on.'

The Los Angeles critics raved about the band's shows at Pantages Theatre, near the Capitol tower in Hollywood. Richard Thompson was in town and performed on 'Sister Madly'; the 'Byrdhouse' set was recorded and later released on the 'I Feel Possessed' CD single. Gregory Sandow of the *Herald-Examiner* – a hip elder statesman of LA rock journalism – loved their 'half-ironic asides' to pop music of a distant era: the Everly Brothers, Harry Belafonte and George Formby. He also enjoyed the cameo appearances by McGuinn and Thompson.

'What about the grace with which the band played host to two artists from the past? There was no irony here, only wholehearted human respect.' Chris Willman in the *Los Angeles Times* loved the 'classicist beauty' of their chord progressions – and the chaos that occurred when Neil went walkabout in the balcony of the theatre. 'More than capable of carrying on without him, Paul Hester, one of the funniest men in rock, improvised with a sad retelling of *The Brady Bunch* as dysfunctional family.'

The last dates on the long-delayed US *Temple* tour were among the most memorable the band ever played. Anarchy reigned at a steaming hot concert performed at the University of California, San Diego (while in the gymnasium next door, a college team was breaking the world record for the longest continuous water polo game). Paul cooled down the crowd with buckets of iced water.

At the next show, in Santa Barbara, the atmosphere was frenzied, the band delving into the absurd end of their repertoire, weaving 'The Sound of Music', 'Walk on the Wild Side', 'The Brady Bunch Theme', 'Whole Lotta Love', 'The Girl from Ipanema', the traditional Irish ballad 'The Parting Glass' and Van Morrison's 'Irish Heartbeat' in among their own songs.

Spirits were so charged afterwards, that the band angrily interrogated Stamler on the bus back to LA: Why hadn't the tour been longer, and gone into the major US markets? Stamler had taken the advice promoters had given before the tour, but now agrees. 'We should have bucked the tide of professional sentiment. We should have played the other 20 or 30 markets. It was a huge mistake.' He also remembers Roger McGuinn being shocked at the passion the band displayed. 'He was astounded at the conversation that occurred, saying, "and I've had *a lot* of experience with astounding conversations in the Byrds, believe me".'

The following night, Crowded House were in schmooze mode on familiar turf: Hollywood. They took the evening off to attend a showcase gig at the chic China Club off Sunset Boulevard. Tim Finn was launching his first solo album on Capitol Records, produced by none other than Mitchell Froom.

Hollywood's hip were in attendance; the small room full of 200 people in black leather and teased hair, impenetrable shades and (the males) with stubbles just so. At the bar was Paul Kelly; in the shadows, Roger McGuinn; working the room, Nick Seymour.

But centre stage was Tim, wearing a shirt made out of Polynesian tapa cloth, flicking his long curly hair out of his eyes, strumming an acoustic guitar with intensity. Beside him was Neil, also with an acoustic, though not doing much except grinning proudly. Shunning the limelight behind them was the serious-looking pickup band: Froom filling out the arrangements on organ and bass pedals, Richard Thompson weaving exquisite acoustic guitar leads. (He also sang his own song, 'Waltzing's For Dreamers', at Tim's request.)

The songs on Tim's self-titled solo album were the best yet in his solo career, which had stumbled since leaving the Enz. He had followed the jingle-like soft soul of *Escapade* with *Big Canoe* in 1986. With a sleek, high-tech production, and lyrics written by a London playwright, *Big Canoe* came across as aloof and sterile. This new album was more humble, its songs sincere and substantial, and produced with humanity and warmth by Froom. Now Tim needed the FM programmers present to be swayed by this performance.

Tim was tense and earnest, his band deliberately subtle to avoid scene-stealing. The strongest reaction came from the hardcore of Enz fans present, who were thrilled to hear punchy, acoustic renditions of 'I See Red' and 'Six Months in a Leaky Boat'. Eventually the scenesters' background buzz of LA mellowspeak was broken by Tim's energetic, passionate performance; he threw himself into his music. Paul helped Alex Acuna on percussion, and the Finn brothers traded spirited harmonies on South Pacific standards such as 'Throw Your Arms Around Me'. After the encore, 'How'm I Gonna Sleep?' appeared on the video screen, featuring scenes of Greta Scacchi pirouetting in silk on the black sands of Karekare Beach, and Tim cruising through downtown Auckland with a few Maori mates. With references to Taranaki and Te Whiti in the new song 'Parihaka', plus 'Six Months' patriotic catch-cry '*Aotearoa . . . rugged individual*', it seemed a Kiwi invasion had landed on Sunset Boulevard.

The next day, inside the A&M studios, Froom described his experience of hearing the Finn brothers sing together for the first time. 'It was magic, about all you could ask. It would be great if they could do things together. Simple stuff, just for the fun of it. The ideal way would be if they got a band together, and a bunch of songs, then recorded it live – have the whole thing done in a few weeks.'

Black shapes gather
• April 1989

Were things at a pretty low ebb in 1989?
**Was that when Nick took his vacation? His, ah,
forced leave? Yeah. I guess we'd done a lot of work,
and it had been a very busy few years. Then we had
time to think. We were probably thinkin' too much.**

—Paul Hester, 1996

While the others flew home, Nick and Brenda made their way to New Orleans, to be married 'southern style' by a judge in the French Quarter. Paul kept the fans posted in a newsletter: 'Flash! New Orleans: Nick Seymour marries his childhood sweetheart of a couple o' months, Miss Brenda Bentley. My beautiful love blossom, Mardi, is still hangin' around me, so I guess I'm sort of behaving myself. I do most of the cooking and cleaning – you know, I wouldn't have it any other way. So our life is going along great. I hope life's being good to you all, as I know it can be a real shit sometimes.'

Meanwhile, Neil took the chance to get as far away from the music industry as possible. For some years he and Sharon had been sponsoring a child in Zimbabwe, so when the international aid organisation World Vision asked him to visit strife-torn Mozambique, he readily agreed. Over 4.5 million people were facing starvation due to racial and tribal conflicts. Neil spent nearly two weeks away, visiting refugee camps in places such as Gile, where one small waterhole served 36,000 people, and Gingoe, where young children were bloated from malnutrition and debilitated by disease. He expected to be shocked, and guilty about his helplessness in the face of such need. But instead he found it an uplifting experience. When he returned, instead of giving graphic accounts of the suffering, he spoke of the spirit of the devastated people. 'It was hard not to be affected by the sights and sounds of starving people, but the fact is they do still laugh and sing a lot just like "regular" people,' he said. 'They have incredible dignity and I found it very hard not to feel small when faced with that.' To feel a little less helpless, and to leave something behind even if it was only smiles on young faces, he performed several songs to a bemused response.

Crowded House was in limbo when Neil returned to Melbourne. The disappointments surrounding *Temple of Low Men* had disillusioned him about the music industry and Crowded House itself. The decision not to tour when it was released hadn't helped, but it had seemed more important to spend time at home rather than fruitlessly promote an album which Capitol had mishandled. There were still many strong supporters of the band in the company, including the current president, David Berman, and chairman, Joe Smith. 'They were both really good people,' says Neil, 'but the company wasn't working very well.' The restructuring of key staff had an impact on the marketing of *Temple*, and the status of Crowded House at the label was further undermined when Smith sacked their A&R man Tom Whalley. 'So we were battling on with Capitol, which had a weakened system,' says Grant Thomas. 'The band knew they would make another record, but they were damaged. They were badly hurt by America falling over on them. When you get a kick in the teeth, you've got to reel a little from it.'

While the band members had an extended break from each other, Neil struggled with the task of writing songs for the third album. When the band recovened at Platinum Studios in Melbourne to record some demos, his dissatisfaction intensified. The sessions didn't go well, and Neil saw Nick's bass playing as a cause. The faltering musical chemistry intensified lurking problems caused by their differing personalities – Nick is gregarious and style conscious, Neil private and aloof from trends. For the band to keep going, Neil thought a line-up change might be the answer.

'After *Temple* we went through a bit of an identity crisis,' says Nick. 'It's the classic reaction to success. It was so sudden for us, at times it could be really destructive, and scary. We didn't have much time to get a sense of ourselves reacting to it. I think I was ready to enjoy life a lot quicker than realising what mattered was the preservation of the band. The enjoyment, the gratification, was a lot more enticing than keeping the band on track. We ended up getting so self-conscious about what our next move would be, we alienated each other.'

At the time, Tim was out on the road in the States, touring his solo album with a classy band which included Mark Hart on keyboards. Accompanying them was Gary Stamler, now managing Tim as well as Crowded House. Stamler remembers being present when Tim got a phonecall from Neil during the tour: 'All Tim kept saying was, "So you're going to make the cut?". Tim hung up the phone in the hotel room, looked at me and said, "Neil's going to do it". I said, What do you mean? "He's going to fire Nick, make the cut." '

Above: Neil Finn at St Patrick's Convent, Te Awamutu, age 7. *Finn family*

Below left: Tim and Neil Finn on the Gold Coast of Australia, 1965. *Finn family*

Below right: Nick and Mark Seymour in the Big Bang Combo, Melbourne, 1982. *Nick Seymour collection*

Opposite page clockwise from top:
Nick Seymour, left holding the baby in Bang, Melbourne, December 1982.
Nick Seymour collection

Paul Hester's first day at school, 1964. *Paul Hester collection*

Melbourne, 1980. Tim and Neil Finn in Split Enz, at the filming of 'I Hope I Never'.
Frenz archive

Above: Split Enz say *See Ya 'Round*, 1984 (L-R): Noel Crombie, Neil Finn, Paul Hester, Nigel Griggs and Eddie Rayner. *Frenz archive*

Left: Split house. Neil and Tim on the night of Crowded House's debut gig, Melbourne, 31 May 1986 (Nigel Griggs at right).
Peter Green

Above: Paul, Neil and Nick in Hollywood – an early publicity shot by Dennis Keeley, June, 1986. *EMI*

Opposite page, clockwise from top: The old triangle. Neil, Tim and Paul Kelly lead the singalong, Washington DC, 19 September 1987. *Neil Finn collection*

A photo opportunity knocks with Jane Pauley on *The Today Show*, April 1987. *Nick Seymour collection*

USA, today. Paul on the bus, 1987. *Nick Seymour collection*

'One of those situations'. Nick at the 'MTV Spring Break', March 1987. *Nick Seymour collection*

Above: New York, just like I pictured it. Nick and Neil, 1987. *Nick Seymour collection.*
Below: Full house, United States, 1987. *Nick Seymour collection*

Left: The Finn brothers live-to-air for the first time at KCRW, Los Angeles, February 1988. *Jeff Soldau/Crowded House archive*

Left: Tchad Blake, Nick Seymour and Mitchell Froom at the Temple of Low Men sessions, Melbourne, 1988. *Nick Seymour collection*

Below: Busking for MTV in Central Park, 1988 (Tim was passing through New York). *Mardi Summerfeld*

Above: Mark and Nick Seymour, at the Concert of the Decade, Sydney, 31 December 1989. *Peter Green*

Below: Tim joins Crowded House, 1991. How Auckland Star cartoonist 'Bondy' interpreted the news. *Neil Bond*

HISTORY NEVER REPEATS...

Above: Paula Seymour joins her son on stage at the 'Chocolate Cake' launch, Melbourne, 1991. *Nick Seymour collection*

Right: Celebrating *Woodface* with Capitol top brass, 1991. From left: Gary Stamler, Hale Milgrim (Capitol), Nick, Jim Fifield (Capitol),
Neil, Richard Thompson,
Joe Smith
(Capitol),
Paul.
*Hale
Milgrim*

Above: Jeremy Hammond of Capitol with Tim, 1991. *Hale Milgrim*
Below: Nick at work on the *Woodface* cover art, Melbourne, 1991. *Peter Green*

Above: Paul leads the Cook Islands log drummers, Karekare, January 1993. *Kerry Brown*

Right: Neil, Karekare, January 1993. *Kerry Brown*

Top: At the desk, Karekare (from left): Nick, engineer Greg Hunter, Mark, Youth, Paul, Neil.
Kerry Brown

Above: Neil and his parents Dick and Mary Finn, Karekare, 1993.
Kerry Brown

Left: Youth at Karekare, January 1993.
Kerry Brown

Above: The sceptic and the existentialist. Neil and Youth, Melbourne, 1993.
Neil Finn collection

Below: Peter Jones and Nick, European tour, 1994. *Sharon Finn*

Left: Liam (centre, top) and Elroy with members of Ngati Ranana, UK tour, May, 1994. *Sharon Finn*

Below: Photo-call at the Corner Bar, Melbourne, 20 November 1996. Back row, from left: Geoff Lloyd, Craig Bird, Nick, Liam Finn, Mark, Bill Cullen. Centre, from left: Sharon Finn, Neil, Paul, Peter Green, Jules Bowen. Front, from left: Grant Thomas, Angus Davidson, Elroy Finn, Mardi Summerfeld, Sunday Hester. *Kerry Brown*

Left: The Capitol tower, Hollywood, Los Angeles. *Chris Bourke*

Below: Paul, rehearsing for the farewell concert, Melbourne, 1996. *Kerry Brown*

Bottom: Stage techs Paul 'Arlo' Guthrie and Dugald McAndrew, 1996. *Sharon Finn*

Next page: The final soundcheck: Neil at the Opera House, Sydney, 23 November 1996. *Tony Mott*

Stamler had been aware that Neil was often at odds with Nick, but hadn't realised it was so serious. Shortly after the recording sessions began, Neil called Nick and asked him to come into the studio early. 'He'd had a massive dry patch,' says Nick, 'and invited me in to have a talk. I went in a half-hour early and he said, "I've agonised over this, but I think I'm going to have to look for a new bass player." I said, what's the reason? – and he said, "You're just not pushing my creative buttons anymore."

'I said, "You believe you could just find another bass player to replace me, and maintain the Crowded House music and character?" He said, "Yes, well, that's up to me, if I want to go down that road." '

'Oh well,' replied Nick, 'that's how it's going to have to be.'

'I could see he wasn't going to change his mind,' he says. 'He was very resolved.' For some time, a saying of Neil's – although intended in jest – had been unsettling Nick. 'It had been a threat before, that if I didn't toe the line I would be "up the street with no pay". If I complained about certain things, he used to always have that stick to wave in front of me. I'd never heard this expression before, so I just assumed that what he was getting at is that he would sack me.'

Paul says it was very emotional when it happened. 'Nick cried and we hugged each other and he told us he loved us, and we said we loved him. It was very intense. And Nick went his way.'

A few days later, Stamler got a call from Neil, who told him that Nick was out of the band. 'I was to immediately put out the word in the US that we were looking for a new bass player, to send him some photographs, and start setting up auditions.'

Both Stamler and Mitchell Froom thought the decision was unfair and not right for the band, and were determined to change Neil's mind. Sharon Finn agreed. 'That was hard,' she says. 'I was sad when he decided that. I thought, no, that's not right.'

Froom's response was to phone Neil and argue the case for Nick. Meanwhile, Stamler held off placing advertisements in the music papers. However, in Melbourne, Paul sided with Neil. 'Basically, he called the shot, and I backed it up,' he says. 'Nick was having a hard time. They were just trying to find their space with each other and I think Neil got fed up with it. He didn't want it to be a hassle. So Nick got booted out. There was a bit of natural posturing going on. It wasn't like an incident, or that Nick had done something terribly wrong. It was kind of awkward.'

'I was frustrated musically,' explains Neil, 'and also, personality wise, we clashed over some things, and I thought it was time to branch out. I felt a lot of the weight of the musical side on my shoulders. The Enz was a much more collaborative band, everyone was much more involved. So I felt a bit alone, and pissed off about that aspect of it.

'At the time, it was frustration with the way Nick played. From my point of view, I can say that's my objective reason for it. Though he'd get there in the end, and play something brilliant. But I may have been less inclined to tolerate certain personal traits and characteristics because of the long touring, too. I was a bit fed up with the whole thing. We started rehearsing, did a few demos, and I got a bit annoyed at the way he was playing, and I got a bit . . . reactionary.'

For a period of about a month (Neil remembers it being two weeks, Nick a month, Paul 'a few months'), Crowded House continued recording demos without Nick. Neil invited Mark Hart over to play keyboards; he went with some reluctance, having become a good friend of Nick's during the tour earlier in the year. 'In September of '89, I went down to Melbourne for the first time,' he says. 'Nick was no longer with the band. It was weird. I was staying at Paul's house, and Paul hadn't spoken to Nick since Neil had sacked him. I thought, that's odd. I wanted to go and see Nick, because I was in town and he was just living down the street from Neil. So I went over there one night, and I could tell they were kind of stunned still. There was a certain sadness in the air. But I didn't really want to talk to him about it.'

Nick and Brenda were keen to show Mark around Melbourne, as were Paul and Mardi, so they agreed to go to Anglesea together to see some kangaroos. 'That was the first time Paul had seen Nick since he'd been sacked. That's what really hurt Nick more than anything: nobody ever called.'

Mark recorded with the band for about two weeks. 'We had this other guy, Joe somebody. A really nice guy – but a bit too tall – and a bit too eager to please. He just didn't have . . . Nick's a special bass player. For all his faults – he has memory lapses, he has a hard time staying focused – but he really comes up with good parts. He genuinely reflects his desire to make the song better. He's got a great feel, he and Paul can play wonderfully together. It's a really special rhythm section. And those songs somehow suffered from not having Nick around.'

The band had made a start on 'Whispers and Moans' with Nick present; the other songs demoed without him included 'a couple of Finn classics', says Paul. 'It's a shame they got away. They were killers.' Among them were 'Time Immemorial', 'Legs Are Gone', 'Good Luck Morning', 'I Love You Dawn' (Sharon's middle name) and Paul's song 'My Tele's Gone Bung'. Apart from 'Whispers and Moans' on *Woodface*, only 'Dr Livingston' ever received a proper release (as an extra track on several singles). 'In hindsight I wonder why we didn't use them as half the record,' says Neil, 'but no-one ever got to hear them. There were a couple of real beauties that we didn't do.'

Several bass players were tried out in Melbourne, while in Los Angeles, Stamler waited for the situation to resolve itself. He took many phone calls from Nick, who was anxious to know how he could change Neil's mind.

'Nick was very much on the outer at that point,' says Grant Thomas. 'But that's it with bands. Getting marriages to work these days is a nightmare, and there's only one other person there. In a band, it's a relationship that is tied four or five ways.'

'Neil had been on the road for a long time, since Split Enz,' says Paul. 'The ongoing touring was taking its toll. Also, he was having a family. I don't know how he coped. He was in a situation where he had to please a lot of people, all the time. His responsibility to his family was his first concern, then he had a huge responsibility to this band which he'd created. And through the band, it'd be management, the record company, the whole shebang. It's very hard. So Neil was constantly on the phone. And meanwhile, his life is going on in front of him.'

As the impasse dragged on, Stamler got a call from Neil. 'He got very irritated with me, as he knew my agenda was to get Nick back. He said, "I bet you haven't talked to one bass player in all this time. I bet you just want Nick back in the band." I said, that's pretty accurate.'

Nick says he eventually realised that 'to come back from the abyss', the solution was up to him: 'To his credit, Grant Thomas told me, "There's only one person who can do anything about this – and it's you". I had to go in there and have it out with him, re-establish it. I was scared to do it, but I had nothing to lose. As far as Neil was concerned, the band was him, when it suited him – and this was a time when it suited him. He had to be made to realise that the band couldn't operate as Crowded House without me in the fold.'

To make his pitch, Nick called Neil up and asked if they could meet for a drink. Neil: 'We had a big session one night at the pub, he did a very good job of convincing me that I'd been hasty, and I changed my mind. There must have been something that made me recognise that this was a band – it might fuck with it to pull him out.'

'I pointed out some serious misgivings that I had about the band,' says Nick, 'and I accused him of completely blowing it, of making a major career blunder: he'd underestimated the resolve of the three of us in the band. He accepted that, and we were reunited. That was a turning point for me, in pulling me back down to earth, and remembering who I was. When Neil confronted me with not wanting to be in the same band as me anymore, I had a pretty good look at the reasons he would come to that conclusion. And I dug my heels in, stood my ground. It was the first time I'd done that.

'We talked a lot of sense, and decided to pursue the band together. But Neil was still looking for other things, looking to where he was getting his inspiration for songwriting from. He was placing more pressure on me to contribute musically, but when it came to actually doing it, presenting ideas, you'd still be greeted with a defensiveness from Neil.

'The biggest problem we had was that familiarity had bred a contempt of each other's music. And when that happens, when you're trying to jam with somebody, and there's an energy that is stopping you trusting the flow of the music, you really don't have any kind of relationship. I don't remember what could have stifled that other than just ego, silly egos.'

The conversation led to a 'redistribution of respect', says Nick. Playing the perennial fallguy had been damaging. 'I was always happy to appear to be goofy and willing to sacrifice credibility for the sake of humour. I'd compromised myself by allowing that to happen. It was my own fault.'

As a perturbed observer, Mark Hart sees that Neil and Nick are 'poles apart in personality, in the way they see things, conduct their lives – but you don't have to be exactly the same to be in a band.' He was relieved when Neil called to say Nick was back in the band. 'I said, "Oh – that's good." And Neil was silent for a second. I thought I'd said the wrong thing.'

Crowded House returned to the studio, but didn't revisit many of the songs that had been worked on in Nick's absence. 'Nick could never really come at those songs,' says Paul. 'I think there was an element that just rejected them, because we'd knocked them up without him. Then Neil started writing songs with Tim, and Neil focused on those. They were generating a lot of positive vibes.'

Internally, Crowded House may have been in disarray, but the band's relationship with Capitol Records was about to be dramatically restored. In mid-1989, with the departure of David Berman, the company was once again searching for a new president. In the meantime, Joe Smith – the CEO of Capitol's parent company, Capitol-EMI Music – was acting as interim president. He met with all the managers of the major acts on the label, trying to soothe any problems that had developed while the label was without a leader. It was while discussing Crowded House that Gary Stamler gave Smith an idea for a suitable candidate: Hale Milgrim of Elektra Records.

Smith, who had been president at Elektra, replied, 'You know, that's the first suggestion anybody has made that makes any sense at all.' Before the meeting was over, he booked a ticket to New York to discuss the position with Milgrim. A few days later, Stamler was summoned to New York to negotiate Milgrim's contract.

At the time he was approached by Capitol, Milgrim was senior vice-president of marketing and creative services at Elektra. His career in the industry began in his teens, when he worked at his parents' toy shop in Palm Springs. Milgrim asked his father to loan him US$3000 to develop a music section in the store, and later, while attending university at Santa Barbara, he worked part-time in a record store. After graduation in the late 1960s he joined the staff of Discount Records in Berkeley. As the store was the main Berkeley outlet for tickets to the legendary San Francisco rock venues the Fillmore West and Winterland, Milgrim was in a prime position to maintain his music obsession.

In the mid '70s, Milgrim moved to LA to join the staff of Warner Bros and, in 1984, Elektra in New York. Along the way he was instrumental in several prominent marketing success stories: Devo's flowerpot campaign, the Cure, Simply Red, Anita Baker and 10,000 Maniacs. What linked these artists was the disinterest shown in them by radio; Milgrim helped break them through marketing rather than airplay. The success of the Gipsy Kings was typical of Milgrim's approach. He got the record heard in upmarket outlets such as restaurants and hair salons. Stamler says that whenever he was in New York, and going out to dinner, Milgrim would give him a Gipsy Kings CD for the restaurant: 'He developed a mailing list of the places yuppies frequented. That's how the record got off the ground.'

In his 1996 book *Off the Charts*, music business journalist Bruce Haring says Milgrim was 'an anomaly in the increasingly corporate world of the music industry, a stone-cold music fan whose personal warmth and enthusiasm for new sounds made him one of the business's most beloved characters.'

Milgrim was not only an industry mentor to Gary Stamler, but also the cousin of his wife, Peggy. From the time Stamler began managing Crowded House, Milgrim had helped with advice and ideas for the band, a relationship acknowledged by a Christmas card that Milgrim keeps in his room of memorabilia. Drawn by Nick, it shows Milgrim answering two telephones while wearing two hats: one is marked 'Elektra', the other, 'Crowded House'. 'So we had one of the best marketing talents in the history of the record business on our side,' says Stamler. 'He was on the outside, looking in, helping me with retail, offering all the things he did so well at Elektra.'

Milgrim had been a fan of the band ever since receiving an early tape of the first album; when he saw them during the Bruce Hornsby tour in early 1987, he was sold. 'I just couldn't believe the vocal harmonies, the melodies, the lyrics. They got straight to the heart. I remember thinking, this band, if they continue growing, they're going to be amazing. Never once did I think I'd be working at Capitol Records and working with them. I was hoping, if I built a relationship with them, that maybe in the future I could get them to Elektra, because I wasn't thinking of leaving.'

Paul describes Milgrim as 'incredibly enthusiastic, a real music fan, a hugger in the true Californian sense of the world. We'd always see Hale at gigs, he was terribly supportive of us, talking us up in the industry, very much part of things in America for us even before he worked for Capitol. He was an ally, someone to talk to when you had your campaign. I'm sure he helped Gary do things from time to time, and hence Gary helped Hale get sorted at Capitol.'

If the band wasn't having an immediate hit, Milgrim advised Stamler, they should stay out on the road as long as they could. He said, don't worry about radio airplay – it will come if it's going to, but you can't force it. 'The band could build a very strong base of fans with or without radio, just by continuing the slash and burn: working with the record company, continue going into the retail stores and doing press – which is probably what drove them crazy after a while. I said to Gary, as long as they had the energy and weren't getting pissed off or upset, they should continue. I think my only input was I kept telling Gary, stay on the road.'

Milgrim joined Capitol when the company's fortunes with its established acts was on an upswing. The careers of Tina Turner and Heart had been revived with great success, and Milgrim was soon to benefit from the groundwork done during the Berman era when Bonnie Raitt, Bob Seger and Hammer achieved spectacular results in 1991. But he was aware of the need to develop a roster of new artists, and nurture them as long-term prospects rather than short-lived pop hits. This strategic approach, of course, is also the most expensive, with minimal returns expected until several albums have been released.

One of the first things Milgrim wanted to do when he arrived at the Tower in late October, 1989, was revive interest in Tim Finn's solo album, sales of which had stalled shortly after its release six months earlier. 'I couldn't let go of the Tim record,' he says. 'So we went back out and did an unbelievable tour. Tim worked his butt off, but we really didn't accomplish what we wanted to with that record. He'd given us a record with the right songs on it, which should have got more radio airplay than it did, but at least Tim was working on the road. I felt we were building something for the future.'

Everything gets turned around • October 1989

'Quite often I'll bring Neil a theme or a title, one idea, and he'll start playing it and we'll both steer it through. When you get writer's block, that's often what's missing. If you've got talent, you can always come up with a tune or chord.'

—Tim Finn, 1996

In Spring, 1989, Neil and Sharon were awaiting the arrival of their second child, and were about to move into a house in Shirley Grove, East St Kilda, which they had bought a year earlier. About a 20-minute tram ride from the central city, East St Kilda is the heart of Melbourne's Jewish community, with synagogues and schools dotted among the leafy streets and large old homes. Nick lived at the entrance of Shirley Grove, two minutes from the Finns' new home near the end of the cul-de-sac. The area is a quiet residential haven between two of Melbourne's major thoroughfares, Dandenong Road and Alma Road. The Finns' house had dual access, backing onto Murchison Street. Prior to Neil Finn's arrival, the street's most celebrated citizen was Albert Jacka, the first Australian awarded a VC in World War I. He is buried in the St Kilda Cemetery, the tall crosses and obelisks of which peer above a hedge and brick wall, to be visible from the upstairs windows of the neighbouring houses.

The property Neil bought was a large block of land – two-thirds of an acre – with a substantial Edwardian wooden home, a tennis court and many tall trees in its grounds. When the Finns took possession, it was 'unliveable', having not been maintained for over 40 years. Buying such a large property – at an affordable price – was a lucky find in East St Kilda. Neil had missed the auction where two developers had bought it for less than the land value, around Aus$500,000. They couldn't agree on what to do with it, so quickly offered it for resale. 'We paid an extra 50 grand and got it,' Neil said in *Cleo*. 'It seemed perfect, we wanted a big piece of land because we'd bought a dog. We've got a *huge* mortgage. It's a great incentive to keep earning money. When people get successful they lose interest in making music. I've got an in-built reason to keep making music . . .

fear.' ('People assume the money just starts flowing, but it takes ages,' says Neil, 'and then there's taxes and running expenses.')

Neil also bought a nearby property in Murchison Street, a double storey art-deco brick dwelling, split into two apartments. He installed some recording equipment in the sun-room of the upper apartment, which has a distant view of the cemetery.

Crowded House had virtually been in mothballs through the winter of 1989. As spring began, Tim Finn arrived back in Melbourne. He was pleased to be back; although he was still with Greta Scacchi, he had just returned from a miserable trip to New York, and from a disappointing response to his album with Mitchell Froom.

In early October, with Shirley Grove still undergoing renovations Tim and Neil went to the nearby flat and started writing songs for the Finn brothers record they had talked about for so long. They hadn't written together since 1977, when they worked on 'Best Friend' in their parents' house while on holiday from the Enz; any later collaborations combined pieces they had developed separately. This time, says Tim, 'We were very conscious of going in to write songs that would suit harmonies.'

In the Murchison Street flat, 'We just had an amazing burst,' says Neil. 'We felt relaxed, probably because we hadn't seen each other for a long time. I was in a high state of anticipation with Elroy coming [Neil and Sharon's second child], and we weren't doing much with the band. Tim really enjoyed being back.

'We started playing on a few things, singing out loud and strumming the acoustics really hard on a couple of bits we already had around. I threw a new verse into a song of his and we went, 'Oh – that worked well.' Then we found ourselves jamming with our voices. We were throwing things around in a very uninhibited fashion. Someone would find a harmony, and then a melody would appear, and we'd seize that.

'Because there were two of us, we wouldn't give up and go and have a cup of tea. We'd say, "That was good, let's finish it now." Then we'd go home and say, that was a great day – we've written two songs. Once we had a couple of days like that, we had the feeling every day we went in: well, we're going to write another couple of songs today, wonder what they'll be.'

'Weather With You' was the first song they worked on. 'We just took it from there,' says Tim. 'After two weeks we had about 14. It was pretty exciting – the first time we'd ever done it.'

The chorus line had been nagging Tim for some time: 'Everywhere you go, you always take the weather with you'. He also had the opening line, 'Walking round the room singing "Stormy Weather" . . . ' – but it was a few days before he thought of putting the two together. When they started, they had no other lines for the verses, the chorus or middle-eight section. 'In terms of parts,' says Tim, 'I had more ideas for the song than Neil, but it wouldn't have been the song it ended up being without Neil.' The address '57 Mount Pleasant Street' is merely a positive-sounding image that emerged from Tim's subconscious; their sister Judy used to live at Mount Pleasant Road in the Auckland suburb of Balmoral, though not at number 57.

After a couple of weeks, they decided to record some demos on Neil's eight-track Tascam in the Murchison Street flat. They called Paul to come over with his brushes, 'to play along and have a bit of a sing'. Over about a week, they recorded 'Weather With You', 'In Love With It All', 'There Goes God', 'Chocolate Cake', 'How Will You Go' and 'All I Ask'; plus songs that were put on hold, such as 'Prodigal Son' and 'Catherine Wheels'.

'We worked pretty full-on,' says Paul. 'It was great – I was in the eye of the storm of the Finn brothers. It was an incredibly enthusiastic period. I'd set up this clunky drum kit with a cardboard box and a polystyrene cymbal. With the brushes I got this great little sound going, they had their acoustics and a couple of electric guitars. We just bunged these things down one after another, all singing along, and adding a little overdub here and there. It was fantastic, a great few days of work, I couldn't believe how much fun it was. Neil was engineering, we were all closeted into the sun-room, fagging on madly, just going for it. And there was this weird background to it all, you'd look out the window over the cemetery on Alma Road.' (Also at this time, Neil wrote a song called, 'Cemetery in the Rain', a surprisingly joyful song with a glam groove.)

The torch song 'All I Ask' 'popped out of thin air,' says Tim. 'Admittedly it's really spare – there's not a lot going on in the lyrics – but we sang it and played it at the same instant. It had just been a line in one of my journals – *all I ask is to live each moment free from the last*. I'd said it to Neil one day, and we just performed it, played the tape back, and realised we didn't really need to change anything. In fact we had to learn it off the tape. This was after we'd been going a few days and had a good head of steam. We didn't have to talk about it or think, we just did it. Normally we'd work on it a bit more, but we loved it the way it was, like a prayer or a hymn.'

Among the other songs worked on at this time were 'It's Only Natural', 'Four Seasons in One Day', 'Tall Trees' ('I didn't have a lot to do with it,' says Tim, 'I just helped steer it through'), 'Prodigal Son', 'The Sound of Truth' (a rootsier version of Tim's 'Always Never Now'), a very raw 'Strangeness and Charm', 'Throw Your Arms

Around Me' (with Tim playing simple piano, and Neil a ringing guitar hook). The demo of 'How Will You Go' has an a capella opening from Tim and all the harmonies of the finished version are intact. The song was pieced together from elements the pair had already written: the verse was Tim's, from a chord sequence he had written in the mid-70s but had never known what to do with; the chorus was Neil's.

With Sharon Finn about to give birth to Elroy any day, there was a sense of urgency to Neil, says Paul. 'He wanted to get this work done because he knew he was going to go into baby mode, and he'd be needed. He worked his butt off.' After it was all over, the trio listened to the tapes, playing all the songs back to back. 'It was amazing. Whenever you do a song, you think it's the best thing you've ever done. But this was the first time Neil and Tim had done it *together*. This was special. It had this thing about it: is this as grand as we think it is?'

After their listening session, they got up to leave. 'Neil couldn't move, he was lying on this couch, completely exhausted,' says Paul. 'He'd driven himself to the extreme. He said, you guys go – I'll just lie here for a minute. Tim and I let ourselves out, and he just stayed there. It seemed kind of tragic, leaving him there after we'd done this stuff.

'It was an interesting time for Tim and Neil. I was glad to have been there to see a little bit of it go on. Songwriting's a natural thing, you can't force it. Tim and Neil writing together had never really taken place, it must have been a great moment for them to have together, to do what they'd been thinking about for a while.'

'It was a fantastic period,' says Neil. 'I really enjoyed it. But it immediately made life more confusing. I started thinking, maybe we should steam ahead with this, and make the Finn brothers record. But I thought if we did that, it would be the end of Crowded House. Because we'd already waited a long time to record. I was unsure. In fact, this marked a long period of agonising. I couldn't decide what the fuck to do. The irony was, there was this amazing burst of songwriting, but it made life hell for quite a long time because it split my loyalty.'

In the meantime, Neil wrote in the club newsletter, 'It's baby time! My stunningly beautiful wife Sharon gave birth last Wednesday 25th Oct to a bouncing 7lb 8oz boy and the Finn household is joyfully awake to the sounds of gurgling, burping and just the occasional cry once more. Thanks to those of you who sent messages of encouragement during the year!

'I guess it's been a slow year on the public front for the Crowds but believe me, we have not been idle. New songs sprout from the fertile ground of home sweet home, so look out next year for not one but two albums, a new Crowded House disc and what's more, a Finn brothers offering: two-part harmonies all the way. Writing with Tim has been so much fun that we wonder what took us so long!'

The only song the band recorded and released during 1989 was a version of the Zombies' 'She's Not There' for the George Ogilvie film *The Crossing*. On New Year's Day, Tim and Neil were seen performing two songs they had recorded for New Zealand television, 'Parihaka' from *Tim Finn* and an oddity they had recently written: 'Chocolate Cake'.

At the time the '80s turned into the '90s, however, Split Enz was back in action, at Darling Harbour in Sydney. Neil had the idea to reform the band to top the bill at the New Year's Eve 'Concert of the Decade', which featured Crowded House and Hunters and Collectors. The Enz and Crowded House then turned it into a quick tour by adding a few warm-up dates with Boom Crash Opera; five years after the Enz With a Bang tour, the Enz were still Australia's biggest drawcard. The day after Christmas, the bands assembled in Sydney, and went out to a Japanese restaurant where Nick started the karaoke, singing a Supremes hit, before Michael Hutchence of INXS mimed to Kylie Minogue.

The next day, they bussed 270 kilometres to the first gig at the Mudgee Country Paradise Resort. They returned to Sydney during the night. Everyone was woken the next morning by their vibrating beds. Shortly afterwards a note was slipped under the doors of the band members' rooms: at 10.28am there had been a massive earthquake at Newcastle, just north of Sydney. The venue they were to play in that night, the Workers Club, had collapsed, killing a truck driver on the tour, John O'Shannassy, and trapping one of the roadcrew in the rubble. The toll could have been worse: the crew had driven from Mudgee that day, so stayed an extra hour in bed.

The Newcastle concert was postponed, and the tour continued at Surfer's Paradise, where the bands played to 12,500 people – including the Finns' parents – inside a circus tent next to the Seaworld resort. The Darling Harbour New Year's Eve gig was similarly massive, drawing 18,500 people. Hunters and Collectors paid tribute to the Enz with a spirited rendition of 'What's the Matter With You' at soundcheck – but at the concert, staked an early claim by finishing their set with a rousing 'Throw Your Arms Around Me'. Paul announced the arrival of Crowded House by cartwheeling on stage. The band launched into 'Mean to Me' as the security guards sprayed cool water over the steaming crowd. Mark played keyboards, and stage tech Paul 'Arlo' Guthrie added guitar to 'When You Come'. 'Forget that crap about Crowded House splitting up,' Peter Green wrote in the club newsletter, 'It was a happy band that entertained tonight.'

As the clock struck midnight, thousands of balloons and streamers fell to the ground. Liam Finn, dressed as the Joker, screamed 'Happy New Year!' into a TV camera as a large red satin sack hobbled on stage. The sack burst open as Split Enz leapt out in fluorescent coloured costumes. Tim yelled '1990!' to open a show that was an energetic tour-de-force. He flung his long mane of hair about as he paced the stage, while Noel Crombie chased the band members around during his spoon solo. The crowd sang their way through a set of ageless hits, brought to a close when Mark Seymour and Deborah Conway joined the band on stage for an anthem like reprise of 'Throw Your Arms Around Me'.

In the late '80s a small nightclub in Greville Street, Prahran, called IDs became a favourite haunt for Melbourne musicians. It was intimate, and the crowd was there to listen, rather than talk, while musicians performed out of their usual contexts. Run by Dror Erez, a recent immigrant from Israel, IDs was the place to see musicians such as Paul Kelly, Mark Seymour or Chris Bailey doing solo shows. In late 1989, Erez put together a stellar band for Bailey. The rhythm section was Paul and Nick, with Mitchell Froom (visiting Melbourne for pre-production on the new album) on Hammond organ and Erez himself on piano. 'I was just looking around at everybody, it was like I was tripping. Crowded House are one of my all-time favourite bands, and here I was, playing with them.'

Tim and Neil were keen to try out the songs they'd written together, so they approached Erez to book his club for a warm-up gig on 11 January, 1990. It would be a special night: Tim and Neil would unveil the 'brothers' songs, and the support act would be Mark and Nick Seymour, rarely seen on stage together.

'Somehow – maybe it was my fault – word got out,' says Erez. 'At that time the place could fit 350, so I guessed it would be full. The newspapers and radio stations were talking about it. Next thing, the musicians gave me a door list of 250 people – so that means only 120-150 people can buy tickets.' At four o'clock on the afternoon of the gig, queues were forming in both directions down Greville Street. 'There were about 1200 people standing in the street, and from these, only 100 are going to get in. We started to ring radio stations in a panic, saying "Don't go to Greville Street, it's out of control." I remember Mark and Nick arriving, looking around saying, "What are we going to do?" It looked like there was going to be a stampede. Next thing I got the police – it's the only time I've ever had the police do a good thing for me – and five minutes later, six police cars arrive and they ask the crowd to leave.

'The gig itself was unbelievable. It was a testament to Melbourne's musicians. The audience was everybody you'd like to see at a gig. For me – because I'm not an Australian or a New Zealander – it was like winning the Tattslotto.'

The Seymour brothers opened the show with versions of 'Do You See What I See' and Steve Harley's 'The Best Years of My Life'. 'Nick and Mark played the fighting brothers to a hilt,' Peter Green wrote to fans, 'and Mr and Mrs Seymour were there as well, bopping to the crowd.' When it became Tim and Neil's turn, they unveiled the fresh 'Chocolate Cake', joined by Paul 'in a very good mood', wrote Green. The song was 'already a favourite. The new songs come across as a new dimension to previous works by both brothers. Tim and Neil also surprised with cover versions of 'In the Summertime' [Mungo Jerry] and 'Come Up and See Me' [Cockney Rebel], before closing with the Split Enz encores, 'Sweet Dreams' and 'Six Months in a Leaky Boat'.'

(Eighteen months later, Dino Scatena wrote in *Juke*, 'Anyone present at the small club where the brothers introduced the songs to the world early in 1990 knew there was something very special in the air.')

A month after the IDs gig, the Split Enz/Crowded House tour came to a belated conclusion with two more gigs. With Hunters and Collectors, plus Boom Crash Opera, they played at an outdoor show to 15,000 people at the Myer Music Bowl in Melbourne on 16 February. And two days later, a rescheduled Newcastle concert took place, as a benefit gig in aid of the earthquake relief fund. Forty-five thousand people saw a show which mixed the finest and loudest acts in Australasian rock music, Split Enz and Crowded House being joined by Midnight Oil, the Angels, Jimmy Barnes and Noiseworks.

It was time to get started on the third Crowded House album, so Mitchell Froom went to Melbourne for pre-production and the Finn brothers songs written before Christmas were put on hold. 'I wasn't entirely convinced that I had the songs worked out and ready for the album,' says Neil. 'I had all these songs I'd written with Tim in the "can't touch" basket, while I felt I had writer's block with Crowded House.' Neil played Froom the songs he had done with Tim, and they briefly discussed doing them as Crowded House songs – but abandoned the idea as too difficult. 'I knew they were a really good bunch of songs, so I was slightly disturbed by that.'

The recording of what eventually became *Woodface* was a long, convoluted and expensive saga, a tale of two cities and five different recording studios. The sessions began in early 1990 with pre-production at Platinum Studios in Melbourne, shifted over to A&M in Los Angeles, returned to Melbourne and Tim's new home studio, Periscope, then finally went back to LA for work at Sunset Sound Factory and Ocean Way.

Froom's technique in pre-production is to record ideas onto an old battered JVC ghetto blaster with a built-in mike. 'It compresses the hell out of everything and you can hear whether you're making a good noise or not,' he explained to *Sound on Sound* later. 'You can completely focus on the songs and their arrangements, without technical distractions. With Neil, most of the time we'd just get the basic structure of the songs and then the band would take it from there.'

One night in Platinum, everyone loosened up, got mentally adjusted, and made a lot of psychedelic noise. Paul remembers Froom in hysterics over the mixing desk while the band jammed to 'I'm Still Here' and 'Ugly Sheila'. 'I was lying on the floor on my back, playing guitar, and Neil was playing drums. There were people around I didn't even know. It all went down.' ('I'm Still Here' turned up hidden in the fadeout of *Woodface*; 'Ugly Sheila' 'never made the light of day,' says Paul. 'It was a little bit blue for the record, I think.')

The same day, they had a breakthrough with 'Fall at Your Feet'. Neil had brought the chorus with him to the sessions, but had struggled to find a satisfactory verse from a variety of old half-written ideas. Blake recalls the moment Froom solved the problem. 'He said, "Am I crazy?" then sat down at the piano and put these two totally different songs together.' The band immediately recorded the basic tracks with acoustic guitar and drums, and the bridge emerged while jamming through the song. 'It was all done in a day, very easily,' says Neil.

Froom says that the best songs are usually written in one piece, in five minutes. 'Fall at Your Feet' was the exception to the rule. 'It's a great song, there's something about it that is very affecting. Obviously that chorus was something I was really fixated on. It was just beautiful and I was upset that we didn't get it.' The original verse he describes as 'uptempo and terrible: the idea was the verse would be shouted out, then it would mellow out on the chorus. I was searching for the answer to that.' Blake says Froom's musical memory is extraordinary; a couple of days into a new album, he'll know the mechanics of every song. 'I don't know if he's got staves in his head, but it's like he sees the chords and the music. We'll be talking at lunch, and someone will suggest an idea, and he'll say, "That G# won't work – you need a minor seventh." He's amazing.'

Pre-production over, the band returned to a crowded house in Los Angeles. When they were going to be in the city for an extended stay, they preferred to rent a house short-term, rather than be in a hotel. Hale Milgrim and his wife Anne had been renting a place on Woodrow Wilson Drive in the Hollywood Hills, while trying to buy a permanent home in Los Angeles. When they moved out, the band took over the lease. With an address sorted out, they put in an order with 'the Rabbi' in Hollywood to make sure some pot was delivered upon their arrival.

The Woodrow Wilson house 'was quite a step up from Sycamore, believe me', says Gary Stamler. But there were still only two bed-rooms. Tim Finn was staying with the band at this point, having visited Scacchi in the States, so he and Neil shared one of the bed-rooms. Paul got the other one, and Nick slept on a sofabed in the living-room. 'In the mornings,' says Paul, 'Neil would get up first – as usual – and make the pot of tea. There was a stereo system that had speakers right through the house, and he'd wake us all by putting on a classical piece and turning it up full. So you'd be shaken out of bed by Wagner or Bach, really early in the morning.

'Nick and I used to take great delight in getting into bed together in the mornings, having cuddles and drinking tea. Tim and Neil would be appalled – they just couldn't bear the thought of us in bed together without any underpants on. The Finn brothers would react against it, and Nick and I would push it a bit more each morning. It would all get a bit ugly and Tim and Neil would be a bit, you know, distraught. We had this thing going where we all called each other Cledwyn. So it was a very tight family environment we made *Woodface* in. We'd go down to work in the studio every morning, the four of us. It was a very happy time. Tim wasn't actually in the band, but he was around – and it just seemed really easy for him to come down to the studio and hang out.'

On 30 March, Tim appeared with the band in the filming of an early *MTV Unplugged* programme, which at this early stage featured the host, songwriter Jules Shear, sitting in with the band. They did a gorgeous gentle version of 'Four Seasons', with Mitchell Froom on piano (he lost an argument with the producers about whether his Hammond organ was 'unplugged'). 'The album should be out in Sep-tember,' Neil told the audience.

In the studio, Neil could hear a new, focused attitude in Nick's bass playing. However, the *Woodface* sessions caused a lot of tension between Neil and Froom. 'This is the record we had our biggest falling out over,' says Froom. 'At the time I was coming out of the low point of my entire career. I felt like the records I was doing were really difficult, and weren't very good. I really needed to be shaken up.

'As far as I'm concerned, Neil was ready to produce himself – in his mind. He probably appreciated what I might bring to the record, but he really felt he wanted to do it. And why should he be confined by the same group of people doing things the same way?'

The first casualty was Mark who, after going out to record demos in Melbourne in September, and playing in Crowded House on the brief Split Enz tour over New Year, was looking forward to recording with the band in his own city. The night before the earthquake, at a meeting at Crowded House's Sydney hotel, he was asked to join the band as a full member. 'They wanted another member of the band,' says Mark. 'Someone they could count on, who wouldn't be an itinerant keyboard player who might come and go. It was too much stress finding people. I said, sure, I'm flattered, I'll do it.'

But at the end of January, he got a call from Neil. 'He said, "Well Mark, we talked to Mitchell and he doesn't think we need another player, he sees us as a trio, and then you add things to that. He doesn't want to mess up the dynamic of the band."

'I'm sure Mitchell didn't have anything against me personally – it was just the idea of having another guy in the studio playing more parts. And having *ideas* and *suggestions*. It was going to make it more complicated, which it does. I don't think you should dictate to a band if you're the producer. But it's done all the time. As a way of recompense, they said they would send me a tape of rough mixes, so I could maybe work out a few parts, and come in and have a go.'

By the time Mark came to the studio with the ideas for keyboard parts, 'everything was done,' he says. 'I played through my ideas, but Mitchell would say, "That's pretty good, but I've done something there." It was really depressing. I was on the spot, having to prove myself. There was no place to add anything, it was finished.' It would be a long, tough year for Hart. He was asked to play on a Peter Case album, but then Froom was hired as producer. 'Peter rang to say, "Sorry Mark, I guess I don't need you." So I was still out of work.'

The band settled in for six weeks at the legendary A&M studios, an imposing mock-Tudor complex that was built by Charlie Chaplin in the 1920s to be United Artists film studio. 'We got quite into the place,' says Paul. 'There were all these expressionist paintings around the walls by [A&M owner] Herb Alpert, who fancies himself as a painter. So Nick would spend his days turning them upside down and sideways to see if anyone would notice. They would stay like that for months. It was the biggest studio I've ever seen. It was great, there were lots of people coming through.'

They felt like they were in the Mecca of the recording industry. While the band were there, Bob Clearmountain was mixing for Bruce Springsteen, having just gone through an ordeal with Guns N' Roses. 'They had spent millions of dollars,' says Paul. 'He'd done like 17 mixes and they'd rejected them all. All this stuff was going on around us. The remnants of the LA rock scene were hanging around all the time. Living Color were in one room, the Stranglers in another. The boys from Kiss were there – Gene Simmons and Paul Stanley – doing some sorry-arse song.'

All that emerged from the early sessions in Los Angeles were 'As Sure as I Am' and 'Fame Is', plus the rhythm tracks for 'Whispers and Moans', 'Four Seasons in One Day' and 'Dr Livingston'. Several songs which had been demoed in mid-1989, with either Nick or Neil on bass, made it no further ('Flowers in Bloom', 'I Can't Face It').

'A lot of the sessions got stranger and stranger,' says Froom. 'It became a thing where I thought, okay, I'm just not going to say anything. If he wants to do it, he should just do it. Obviously that didn't work at all. I got through a week of sitting around and getting almost nothing done, so I thought, I'll just do my job. The thing that was surprising about it was, when we worked together – even under really bad circumstances – there was still some great stuff that came out of it. To my mind, the really great things came out during that black period: "Fall at Your Feet", "Whispers and Moans", "As Sure As I Am", "Four Seasons". We made some great records, even though the vibe was bad! But enough of it came together, it was just feeling dry. I think he was wearing himself out. Occasionally it's time to make a change.'

The band returned to Los Angeles with the intention of finishing the record off at Ocean Way. Neil's family came too, staying in Hollywood near the original crowded house on North Sycamore. The stress intensified, to the point where Neil developed stomach problems. 'Then I came back to Melbourne and thought, "I'm not happy – this album isn't finished yet." I didn't think we had enough songs, and I wasn't happy with a lot of the songs we did have. I couldn't finish the lyrics to certain songs. It was agonising.'

Froom says that, essentially, it was a finished record, though Neil – as with every album – wasn't that satisfied with it. 'After the second album, he thought maybe the first one was better. And this third album was coming off a big disappointment.' The band returned to Melbourne, where Neil was keen to take a break from Crowded House and get stuck into the Finn brothers album. Meanwhile, Tchad

Blake did some rough mixes of the Crowded House sessions. On 23 June, 1990, the results were delivered to Hale Milgrim, then only a few months into his reign as president of Capitol Records. With Tom Whalley gone, Crowded House no longer had anyone in an A&R role.

Crowded House • Capitol Records
Final Mixes & Roughs • 23 June 1990

Side one	Side two
'Whispers & Moans' final	'Dr Livingston' rough
'Anyone Can Tell' final	'As Sure As I Am' rough
'Fall At Your Feet' final	'Italian Plastic' rough
'Fame Is' final	'Sacred Cow' rough
'Four Seasons in One Day' final	'She Goes On' rough
'Left Hand' rough	'Fields Are Full of Your Kind' rough

Milgrim didn't think the record was finished; he thought it was missing the one special song they needed – and, overall, it didn't have the quality of the first two albums. It was an awkward situation for Milgrim, who had always had a close rapport with the band when he was 'Gary's relative' at Elektra – a trusted industry adviser outside of Capitol.

Although Stamler was surprised that Milgrim was prepared to be so frank, so early in the album's gestation, he felt the same way. So he encouraged Milgrim to call Neil and say the record wasn't done.

Milgrim diplomatically says the phone call 'wasn't a positive experience. I don't think any creative artist wants to be told by a record company to come up with another song. I'm not an A&R man, I don't feel I can sit down and say what's wrong with a song. But I know if it has potential to go to radio or retail. I felt bad, because I wasn't being articulate enough with him. I wasn't saying I didn't like the songs. Just, "If there's another song you've got that has the potential to give us a major hit, it'll make all the difference in sales." If he needed more time that was no problem, there was no gun to his head. It was a very important album.

'Neil's response was, like, you tell me what to write then. I think he was very frustrated – which I was too, it was the first time I had to get into this type of situation with someone I respected. I'm a big believer in positive reinforcement. I wasn't saying the songs were shit:

they were great. Just that, if he took more time and wrote a couple more, maybe there would be one that would be perfect for Top 40 radio. It was a tense period for both of us, it lasted a couple of weeks.'

Stamler was in Milgrim's office when he made the call. 'The conversation wasn't pleasant at all,' he says. 'It was probably one of the most unpleasant Hale has ever had with an artist. Neil was extraordinarily upset. I got a call from him later that day, telling me about the conversation he'd had with Hale, asking me where I stood. I told him I basically agreed with Hale, so that conversation became unpleasant as well.

'He said he'd never had a record rejected in his life, we didn't know what we were talking about: "I don't need you – you're supposed to represent me, I don't need your opinions." A crazy conversation, he was very upset with me. He didn't want to talk to either of us again, sort of thing. Goodbye.'

A few days later, Stamler got another call from Neil. 'It was a shell-shocked voice at the end of the phone, devoid of emotion, saying he'd re-thought it and maybe he would take a shot at writing more songs.'

Nick described the original third Crowded House album to *Pulse*: 'It would have been more like *Temple of Low Men*, in that the songs came out of band jams rather than being completely written by Neil ... we started feeling we didn't have enough of a variety; it lacked uptempo songs. You only got one side of Crowded House; it wasn't a great example of our frivolity or our pop acumen.' In other words, translated *Pulse*'s Brett Milano, no single.

While they were in Los Angeles, Tim had had a small studio built at his house in Melbourne, which he called Periscope. Originally intended to be a room for writing and recording demos, it became a fully fledged studio through a lucky break. Setting up the studio was Paul Kosky, a 22-year-old engineer/producer Tim had met at Platinum. Kosky went to an auction of a Sydney recording studio which had gone bankrupt, and bought a lot of top quality equipment for a 'ridiculous' price. 'We only had the budget for an average home studio, but ended up with one that was very unique, with a very pure quality.'

Although small, Tim's house was perfectly set up to become a studio. A bedroom became the control room, and short cables were run under the floor to the sunroom, which became a double-glazed live recording room. There were also plenty of other spaces to record in: the lounge, bathroom, kitchen. The desk was a 32-channel Wheatstone. Kosky – who got his start in the Australian music industry as a 14-year-old radio DJ – spent three months building the studio, finishing at four in the morning the day the sessions were to begin.

Neil thought it would be therapeutic to inaugurate the new studio together and record the Finn brothers songs they had written six months earlier. 'We had a really good time for a couple of weeks, doing proper versions of the demos,' he says. Ricky Fataar came down from Sydney to drum, Neil played bass and they produced themselves, with Kosky engineering. They quickly put down satisfactory versions of 'Weather With You', 'There Goes God', 'All I Ask', 'Chocolate Cake', 'How Will You Go' and 'Tall Trees'.

There was a lot less pressure on these Finn brothers sessions than the recent disappointing Crowded House recordings in Los Angeles. Because Tim owned the studio, they could take their time. In the event, things gelled very quickly. 'Within the first week, everybody was beaming,' says Kosky. 'There were moments everybody had tears in their eyes, they were so happy with the music that we'd captured. For both Tim and Neil it was really exciting, because Neil had just come from a record he wasn't that happy with, and he wasn't sure what he was going to do. And Tim hadn't made a record he was so excited about for so long.

'If we wanted to spend two weeks on a song, we could. And we did. But "Weather With You" came together in about eight hours, which is amazing. We ended up keeping many of the guide performances because they were so good – usually in a small studio you can't record everything well, because you don't have enough good mikes. The majority of the song was recorded live, bar a few overdubs.'

The guide vocal tracks ended up being on the final record, and recorded simultaneously, with Tim at the piano and Neil in the control room. 'I've never experienced two people being able to sing together so beautifully,' says Kosky.

According to Neil, though, 'It's actually not a simple thing for us to work out. Although singing together is extremely natural – it's something you think is just going to be there – but you find that, when you do work on it, you can make it better, and hone it.'

The sessions had an improvisational air to them because the studio had just been built, so the usual facilities weren't available. The track everybody was most excited about was 'Chocolate Cake', says Kosky. 'It was wild, it was like nothing else Crowded House had ever done. Whenever we put up the tape everybody really enjoyed it, it was really fresh and it had humour to it. Whoever was playing on it would say, this feels great.'

'Chocolate Cake' had come from an anecdote of Tim's. He'd been in a New York restaurant when he heard a large woman ask, 'Shall I have another piece of chocolate cake – or the cheque?' 'I liked the phrase,' says Tim, 'and wanted to write a song which hammered that theme, but Neil took it right off into a few other areas. He came back with the Andrew Lloyd Webber line. Liam gave Neil "hairy legs", he had a little song about "Here comes Mrs Hairy Legs, she's under the bed." There were mad things flying around, a hodgepodge of images. That song really surprised people. There was a body of thought that Crowded House shouldn't be doing satirical material.'

But it was Tim's torch song, 'All I Ask' that went most smoothly. Most of it was recorded in only one take, and Tim took quite a bit of convincing to leave it be, says Kosky. 'Neil and I were ecstatic, jumping around with excitement at how beautifully Tim had just sung it, and Tim had no idea it was so good. He was ready to go back and try and beat it.' Mark, in Melbourne for two weeks, wrote a guide arrangement for the strings. Sharon Finn – who had designed a mosaic of a periscope for the studio's main wall – sang backup vocals on 'All I Ask'. 'There was very much a family feel all around for that whole recording,' says Kosky.

After the Finn brothers sessions, Crowded House had a short burst of recording again, completing a version of 'Italian Plastic' (which Paul describes as more like the Velvet Underground), and 'Left Hand', both of which were never used. (Mark played a melodica on 'Italian Plastic'; he also contributed to early versions of 'Four Seasons', 'All I Ask', 'Chocolate Cake' and 'It's Only Natural.')

Compared to the brothers' project though, it was a struggle. Nick remembers the album's obligatory confrontation: 'Paul was out on Hawthorne Road, storming across the tram tracks of this major four-lane road in Melbourne, yelling at Neil from the middle, "Why don't you do the fucking drums yourself?" I was in the lounge room having a little snicker over it, like being in a family when your brother's having a fight with your older sister.'

'Then we got to the end,' says Neil, 'and I started to get really schizophrenic. I ran into a bit of a mental crisis – just for a change. I started to get anxious, thinking, What am I going to do now? The Finn brothers sounded really good, but I had to finish the Crowded House record. That was the priority, so the Finn brothers record was going to get lost.'

Tim and Neil started discussing the possibilities. What if Crowded House used 'Chocolate Cake' and one or two others that were suitable, and were needed. 'Tim felt a bit weird about not being involved in them,' says Neil. 'He didn't know if he could let them go. He should have done!

'He saw me getting really anxious, and said, why don't I join Crowded House and we can just incorporate the thing into one. It wasn't an issue that we'd take the songs for Crowded House. But at the time it was like, if we wanted them, we had to take Tim, too. Which is kind of mental when you think about it later. We could both have done some of them. They would have lived as songs and it would have been fine. But we had to up the ante by saying, it's all or nothing.'

Tim says Neil was 'completely torn' by the dilemma of having to try and write a single, while feeling the brothers' songs were untouchable. 'Now, he wishes we had just divided the songs up. It would have been impossible at the time, as we were both so much a part of those songs. I wanted to be a part of them, to be singing on them and in the videos. I was excited by them, too. That's why I didn't just let go and say, well you have them.

'Neil was trying to write a song so they could finish their record, which they were dying to do. But he couldn't write. He said to me one day, "I can't write, I've got nothing to say, I'm dead, I'm finished." I was so appalled by that that I felt obliged to say, well, we will just have to merge.

'It wasn't a burning desire of mine by any means to join Crowded House. It wasn't a career move. It was tearing Neil apart, and I felt I couldn't hold out on the material. It had to be one or the other. For me, it could have gone either way, but for him there was only one choice: he could either do Crowded House or the Finn brothers.

'So, one day in the kitchen, almost as a light-hearted thing, I said, "Ah, well, I'll just join the band – then we'll do all the songs." And Neil, I'd never seen him like it. He was ecstatic, walking around the house pumped up, really excited. It was a great release for him. But straight away I was thinking, mmmm – what have I done? The next day I asked him what he thought, *really*. And he said yeah, we have to do it now. While I was having these secret conversations with other people, saying, "What have I done? I don't want to do this." '

Similarly, Neil wasn't '100 per cent sure'. In an unpublished interview from 1992, he told Mike Chunn what a confusing period it was for him. 'My loyalties were split, and I had this unresolved thing with Tim. It was like a continuation of when Crowded House was having its success with the first album: I felt I owed something to Tim. Which is a very stupid thing to feel, because it doesn't do any good to either party. It's not a generous way to be, the best way is not to care. But I was concerned because his records weren't happening, and I felt being in England wasn't good for him. Even though he was in love with Greta, he seemed stifled: the massively successful actress and the struggling songwriter. It didn't seem right. So I was overly conscious of his well-being and also guilty because it seemed like everything had gone well for me. Complicated brotherly stuff.

'So during that period when he was back and we were writing those songs, I thought it was very important that we do them – so the Finn brothers could be successful together.

'But of course I was a misery at home, total hell to live with. It overwhelmed me for a while. I got nervous complaints, a strange stomach, bad skin. But when Tim did join, deep down I wasn't sure. The next day I went through another major anxiety attack. For a couple of years there it seemed like there were very difficult decisions to make.'

'We basically told Nick and Paul that Tim was joining the band,' Neil says, with a wry laugh. 'They looked rather crestfallen, but reluctantly went along with the thing.'

Grant Thomas remembers the band discussing the idea when they were driving to a gig outside of Melbourne in spring, 1990. 'The boys were contemplating it: should we bring him in? In the end they just said, fuck it, let's just put him in the band. But there wasn't much pro-and-con discussion. Neil was obviously pushing it more than the others. I think there was an element of guilt on his part that he was robbing Tim of some really great songs. And also that this vision of their album together was being thrown out the window if these songs ended up with Crowded House. It was like stealing somebody's kids.'

When things had settled down, and he was starting to promote *Woodface*, Neil admitted that Paul and Nick had been sceptical. 'They're nervous about me coming to them with massive ideas that they haven't been privy to. I do tend to drop bombshells on them a little bit. And this was another one. They were probably slightly nervous about there being a Finn brothers' power bloc, that it might affect the chemistry of the band, that it might seem like Split Enz revisited, which no-one wanted. After a day or so, when we listened to the songs we'd started, they got excited as well. They were swept up by our enthusiasm.'

'Nick was cautious,' says Paul. 'He initially made me feel a bit cautious, too. We both felt that, even though Tim and Neil were sitting there saying, "It's up to you guys – if you can get together, then we'll do it." But as if Nick and I were going to say *no*.'

Paul regretted the demise of 'Curly, Larry and Moe', but wasn't so perturbed, as he had worked with Tim in the Enz. It was just like he was coming back. 'We'd got on like a house on fire, so I thought it would be fun – once I got over the thing of it no longer being the three of us. We thought, let's just do it together as a Crowdies thing, do a world tour and really take it out to 'em. I thought it could be great, because in Split Enz, Tim and Neil had never got to do it on a world scale. I still had a bit of nostalgia for the Enz. I was thinking, Tim and Neil – they're an almighty thing when they're together. Let's go, give it a whirl.

'Besides,' he added. 'Now we have someone to blame if the record stiffs.'

But Paul also recalls Nick not being so convinced. 'He's good like that, he tends to voice early on what you might not really want to hear. But he'll say it. And in retrospect he had good cause for concern.'

Nick was blunt about his opinion. 'When the idea first came up, I told Neil he was an idiot,' he says. 'I remember Tim saying, "I love these songs but I want to perform them," and me thinking, well he can perform them in the studio – but does that mean he's a member of the band? Will he have to be the boss, like he was in Split Enz? But then I went away and thought, perhaps we can have Tim guesting on the record and have him promoting it, because it's in his best interests as well. With Neil's all-or-nothing resolve, it seemed much easier to give the whole thing a shake-up – and it really did shake us up.'

In Los Angeles, Gary Stamler remembers getting a call 'out of the blue' from Neil, saying Tim was in the band. 'Neil was a little put out that I wasn't overly excited about hearing that news. It had really taken me by surprise. I said, it's just going to take some time to sink in. It's altering the chemistry of the band, and it could be great but it's going to be different. He put Tim on the line, and I was cautious about it, and he was very optimistic.

'The other members were told like I was told. I remember Paul being particularly concerned, because he said to me, "Well, you know, it's not like just any other guy is coming in. It's like, now there are two Neils!" '

For a quick east coast tour of Australia, Dror Erez was asked to fill in on keyboards. Three of the shows were to be in the tiny IDs, with Crowded House just taking the door. When Erez and his partners had expanded the club from 100 to 350, they'd neglected to apply for a licence to increase its capacity. 'We had all the other permits, but I thought the most that would happen would be a fine or a slap on the hand,' he says. The first night on 10 September, 1990, was also Erez's nervous debut as keyboardist.

'On the next night, about two songs in, my manager comes to the side of the stage and tells me I have to come off. The cops were downstairs. Our licence didn't suit the number of people. So between the second and third songs I walked up to Neil and said, "I have to get off stage." I didn't have time to tell him why. He looked at me shocked, and Hester couldn't believe it. I can still hear Paul saying, "Why do the bloody keyboard players leave us all the time!" He went on and on, speculating I'd gone to turn off the lights on my ugly blue Mazda.

'Anyway, Sir Eddie Rayner – known as a person who doesn't miss an opportunity – jumps up before my foot leaves the stage. So I think, not only are the cops here asking questions, bloody Eddie is here! They interrogated me and I got to finish the gig.'

A week later, Crowded House played a free outdoor gig for the public announcement of the city to host the 1996 Olympics. Melbourne was a leading contender. In the city square an audience of 70,000 people gathered to listen to the band – and hear the good news. Just as the gig began, Nick's amp blew up. Then Erez's Wurlitzer piano went out of tune. A few songs later, when the gig had gathered some momentum, word came through that Atlanta had won the Olympics. The mood immediately fizzled and the crowd drifted away.

Meanwhile, IDs had lost its liquor licence. When the club was shut down, the musicians who played there missed the relaxed venue, so they banded together to help with the legal battle. Crowded House, Tim Finn, Paul Kelly, Mark Seymour and Chris Wilson from Melbourne, plus Chris Bailey from Sydney, drew 2000 people to the Palace in November to 'Keep IDs Alive'.

It was a loose but special night; if the club was to lose its liquor licence, it was going to be dry when it closed. Crowded House were the house band, backing all the other musicians. Paul Kelly, who had broken his hand playing Australian Rules football, had recently moved back to the city he had so often written about. He sang two of his own songs, 'Careless' and 'Leaps and Bounds', the latter being the evocative ode to Melbourne which Crowded House occasionally performed: *'I'm high on the hill, looking over the bridge, to the MCG / And way up on high, the clock on the silo, reads 11 degrees.'*

Kelly returned the gesture by asking to sing 'Into Temptation'. 'It was the one and only time I played with Crowded House,' he says. 'It was fantastic. "Into Temptation" is one of my favourite songs.' Erez was also in his element, sitting in much of the night. After backing a garrulous Chris Bailey, a weary Crowded House had to perform themselves; by the end of the night, Paul had been drumming for three hours.

During the long gestation of *Woodface*, Crowded House were highly visible in Melbourne. 'We decided not to play ourselves up as pop stars,' Neil told Brett Milano. 'People appreciate us out here, but they can also say hello to us on the street. They get used to us being around. I think there are Australian bands that put themselves in the role of playing pop stars, like INXS for example – you always see Michael Hutchence in clubs with a large bevy of beautiful models. We're more part of the furniture.' Perhaps too much so; in Melbourne they began to feel 'benefitted out' and too available to the media: everyone wanted a piece of them. 'They were loved by everybody, not just the music industry,' says Michael Matthews, then promotions manager at EMI Melbourne. 'The sporting fraternity, the fashion people, everybody thought they were their property. They went from being incredibly accessible to not being accessible at all. The media felt they could ring them up directly, but didn't realise how hard they were working. When you're asked to do everything, you have to draw the line.'

Crowded House played some small warm-up shows near Sydney in November. One night, Tim and Neil went over to Ricky Fataar's house in the exclusive Sydney suburb of Double Bay. New Zealand film-maker Bruce Sheridan – shooting casual footage with Gary Stamler's assistant, Andrew Vogel, for use in the *I Like To Watch* video compilation – tagged along. The intimate scene Sheridan encountered meant the camera stayed switched off, but epitomised the Finns after-hours. 'It was the classic antipodean night,' he says. Everyone stood around in clusters, smoking and drinking, while the television, with sound off, showed a live rugby test from Britain. Ricky Fataar brought out a variety of percussion instruments, while Tim and Neil shared the guitar and piano. Also present were Lindy Morrison and Amanda Brown from the Go-Betweens. They played songs from musicals, old rock'n'roll tunes and a few of their own, 'but they never finished a song. Neil and Tim would sit at the piano together, one at the bottom end, the other at the top. The Go-Betweens would be singing, and Ricky sitting with his feet up on the coffee table, with this little scraper thing. They sang and played, then stopped, had coffee, watched the telly ... and it went on for hours and hours. It was Neil and Tim in their element because they can sing anything with anybody, whatever was thrown at them.' The Go-Betweens had just been dissolved by Robert Forster and Grant McLennan, so the conversation was this Australian music in-talk about who was going to do what with who. And the Crowdies were a bit fluid at that stage as well.'

The first Crowded House shows with Tim as an official member of the band took place on 'Ausmusic Day', 24 November, 1990. The band performed in both Melbourne and Sydney, flying between the cities in a private jet. 'I can retire now,' said Nick on television. 'Pop stardom is flying in a Lear jet. We've made it.' Performing their own songs on acoustic guitars, Tim and Neil come across like the Everly Brothers; but with both Mark and Arlo on stage as well, for much of the set, there is very little for Tim to do.

'There may be a familiar face with Crowded House,' Peter Green warned club members in his Christmas newsletter. 'He's been jumping onstage, singing "Chocolate Cake" and numerous other melodic ditties. Welcome to the House, Mr Tim Finn! The band prides itself in continuous changes and different directions. This is just another direction.' On 2 December, the fans were treated to a special show at the Prahran Town Hall, entry price: $10, plus a can of food for Christmas food parcels. Fans started lining up at 9.30am. When the show began almost 12 hours later, it was with 'Weather With You' – and the band was shocked by the number of fans who could sing along. Mark played keyboards, with Eddie Rayner also sitting in; Nick Seymour sang 'Ruby Ruby'.

The six months recording at Periscope in the last half of 1990 was the longest period Crowded House had spent in their home town for years, so it was a rare chance for some quality family time. Tim Finn – his relationship with Scacchi now over – had returned to Melbourne to live for the first time since 1984. 'Tim coming home was like a renewal of connection with his roots,' says Neil. 'He probably had the most difficult transition out of Split Enz of any of us, because he'd completely severed ties, though we were talking on the phone. Returning to Melbourne was important for him. It was the first time he had a community of people that he could rely on.'

'I had a great winter,' Tim told Mike Chunn in 1992. 'I got drunk far more than I should, but I was really enjoying myself – going out at nights, writing songs. I had refound Melbourne in a big way. We did the demos, I built the studio, experimented with dance music, met lots of musicians. It was great.'

The Shirley Grove house was like an open home at times, with Tim often staying and many friends passing through: the Split Enz clan, Jenny Morris, Jimmy Barnes, Paul Kelly, Bones Hillman, Debbie Harwood, Rikki Morris, and the comedy trio Los Trios Ringbarkus. Nick would visit to graze the refrigerator, Paul rarely. The grass court would be used for intense soccer or tennis matches and, in a throwback to Te Awamutu, the garden was a set for elaborate home movies with everybody's children. Parties became production numbers, particularly on New Year's Eve. *Spinal Tap* was the theme one year, the guests being filmed on arrival. Neil turned out in long white wig and tight cowskin trousers; Sharon as rock chick in leopard-skin bustier, bouffed-up hair and layers of eyeshadow; Nick's black trousers had the bum cut out. Heavy metal boomed around the garden, in which black lights were dotted everywhere. At the party's climax a biker in a skull mask roared up the drive on a Harley Davidson; Liam mimed to some music Neil had recorded; the club president Peter Green was the sacrificial virgin, dressed in suspenders and fishnet tights, cavorting on a burning dais. Fireworks exploded while a spotlight caught something moving up in the trees – a model of Stonehenge, descending to the garden like a UFO.

While the brothers at Periscope were experiencing a creative catharsis, harmony between Neil and Mitchell was at an all-time low. By this stage, Neil had been in the studio for almost a year, and the Melbourne sessions were going so well that he told Mitchell they were going to finish the record themselves. According to Neil, Mitchell was on the back foot after the disappointing early sessions – he had got word that people in the record company were giving him the blame – and 'got the huff, as if he was being excluded, having been judged as not being worthy. So for a couple of months there, we had a big falling out.'

Froom called Neil, offering to work on the extra tracks. 'That's the way it started,' Froom says. 'But then it got ugly somehow. He was unhappy, I was unhappy, and it got nasty. It's something that doesn't happen to me with people I work with. But he and I . . . at that point in my life, a lot of the best work I'd done was with them. And similar for him. So I'm too emotionally invested in it.'

Similarly for Neil, the estrangement was a new experience. 'It was the first time I'd had a friend tell me he didn't want to be my friend anymore. It was a big watershed for me. I had my back up a little bit, I probably fuelled it, but Mitchell has a strong-minded sense of justice, and if you cross it, or treat him unfairly in his view, he's very unforgiving.'

Froom describes it as 'a really bad conversation'. Neil describes it as '. . . one of those stupid conversations where someone makes an insulting comment and the other person over-reacts. He was insulting the original demos of "Whispers and Moans" and I said I liked it better than what we'd done in LA – and that "Don't Dream It's Over" was basically the way it had been written. He said, "What about that organ solo? That's the only thing your son knows how to play!"

'It was bad, bad, stupid stuff. He'd be equally disgusted with us now as I am. So, for a couple of months, it was all very strange, tense and weird. Then, in the end, I rang up, we made peace and said, let's finish it off. For the sake of good vibes, let's finish it together.'

For a while, Neil and Mitchell hadn't been speaking to each other. 'It got that low,' says Froom. But, at the beginning of 1991, he suggested that the band shouldn't give up on the original sessions, that Bob Clearmountain should mix a few to see how they sounded. When the results went back to Melbourne, everyone agreed they were excellent. 'Then the idea came up, why don't we all try and get together again,' says Froom. 'I'd heard what they had done, and thought, let's just work on the best of it – and make one really good album out of it.'

The last sessions of overdubs in Los Angeles 'were very, very positive and easy', says Neil. 'Apart from one or two casualties from the Finn Brothers sessions that Mitchell was very damning about. One song, he compared to "Silly Love Songs" – and you don't make those kind of comments without some kind of fallout.'

After carrying most of the production burden in Melbourne, Neil was happy to have Mitchell 'directing traffic'. 'It wasn't entirely without conflict – he liked some bits but not others,' says Neil. 'But he made a few finishing touches that were great, we were a bit limited where we were. He added all these little wild things on his old keyboards.'

'Chocolate Cake', in particular, got the treatment from Froom, even though he was dubious about the song. Any arguments, says Froom, were over which songs to use. 'I wanted to have quite a few less. But politically it was important that different ones made the record.'

Paul was pleasantly surprised that his song 'Italian Plastic' was included. Both Neil and Mitchell liked it, he says, 'treating it as a bit of a novelty song in the recording of it, adding a few sound effects. It was kind of cool. I thought, no way, how can we do that? It's too light. I didn't have to talk them into it, the only problem was me singing all of a sudden.'

Years later, he joked to the Melbourne *Herald-Sun*: 'I had to fight for it. The chips were down. Who did I have on my side? Nobody. Neil was sitting on the proverbial rock fence. He has his feet, bum, his whole bloody family up there. And some other bloke, I didn't know who he was, he could have been in the bloody Seekers for all I know. I threw a middle-class tantrum, and I might have threatened something, but it got in.'

The only song that gave them problems was 'It's Only Natural', which was being groomed as the lead single. 'We really chased that,' says Paul. 'It really excited everyone. It had much more of a funky, dance feel, but by the time we got to LA we'd been on it forever. I think we all just went safe on it, got a safe mid-guitar groove.' (The original version had a ringing guitar opening like the Jackson 5's 'I Want You Back'.) Blake says that they tried so many different rhythms for the song that the mood in the studio 'actually got nasty: tempers flared. Then they played that particular feel. We said "That's it!" – and everyone was finally happy with it.'

Stamler remembers debating with Tim that the bridge should be repeated; it was a bridge, said Tim, which only happens once. But they changed it, and sent a tape to Stamler. 'Tim called me, hoping I'd say, "You've nailed it." But I said there was still something wrong, that what I really thought was they had to recut it. Tim went off on me, in a mildly pleasant way, saying, "Recut it! That's not what I want to hear. Here, you better talk to Neil . . ."'

The most enjoyable part of those final sessions was putting the final gloss on 'All I Ask'. Tim and Nick had been lobbying for it to get a lush string arrangement. 'Mitchell suggested we went the whole way,' says Tim.

'To be completely honest,' says Mitchell, 'it just didn't have the substance to me. It had a charm about it, but I thought, this is too much like a guy sitting round in his smoking jacket and his ascot, saying, "*all I ask is to live this moment free from the last*". It's too removed. I thought it needed a bridge where the guy got real and said *why*. A little less flighty, give it more soul. At first he was into it, but then he resisted. He tends to want to just let things go, which works to his advantage and disadvantage. Okay, I said, if we're not going to do that, how about some really wild strings?'

Van Dyke Parks was unavailable, so Froom was recommended Jorge Callendrelli, an arranger from South America who lived in Hollywood and worked with many leading jazz musicians. He told him to 'take the song and go *out* – go somewhere and don't come back'. Tim remembers meeting Callendrelli, a 'somewhat kitsch character in a chintzy little flat. He could do the Hollywood string thing – we had to pull him back a little bit from his excesses, but eventually we got it right.'

Callendrelli's mock-up arrangement sounded terrible, says Froom, done on a bad synthesiser. 'The arrangement was hopeful, but there were some horrible moments. He was happy to get rid of those.'

Paul remembers the recording session with the orchestra in the large Ocean Way studio as 'a beautiful morning; the most fantastic day. We all dressed up in old '40s suits and nice ties. We got looking good, went out for a bit of breakfast, then went to the studio and hung out with these orchestra dudes. Once they have a run at a few things, when you're sitting in the room, it's wonderful – it just goes right through you. We hadn't felt an orchestra like that before, it was very emotional.

'It was a beautiful thing, a perfectly realised moment. We were so in awe of them – then, in one of the breaks, Neil and I were sitting in the lounge and we overheard a couple of the orchestra guys talking. One was saying to the other, "Oh man, did you see her tits, they were sticking out like a goddam icecream." It was such a shock, it completely ruined our whole image of them. They're a dime a dozen, there are a million orchestras overseas.'

Bob Clearmountain unravelled the maze of tapes with a bright mix that gave the kaleidoscopic sounds space to be heard. 'As usual, he made it sound pretty flash,' says Neil, 'and the record was finally finished to everyone's satisfaction. Considering the process, it's amazing the album is as good as it is.' His only reservation is that the prolonged recording 'smoothed out' the quirkiness of the album.

Froom points out that songs such as 'Four Seasons in One Day', 'Fall at Your Feet' and 'Whispers and Moans' came from the first session in Los Angeles, 'the one that was supposedly a disaster'. The only advocate for putting out 'Weather With You' as a single, he says, was Bob Clearmountain. Someone from the record company even tried to talk Froom out of putting it on the album. Both Froom and Tchad Blake feel the album is too long: the only people who heard such gems as 'She Goes On' and 'How Will You Go' were those who skipped the first couple of tracks: 'Chocolate Cake' and 'It's Only Natural'.

'The record came out and it ... failed,' says Froom. 'Even now people in America will say I screwed up on *Woodface*. Meanwhile, in England, it's a classic, "by far their best album". So there's no winning and no losing – and no figuring.'

When Hale Milgrim received a tape of the finished *Woodface*, he immediately called Neil. 'I told him I was ecstatic, over the moon. He'd delivered the songs that we would be able to have the success with. I really felt that – it wasn't lip service. When I'm excited about something I don't hide it.'

Milgrim and Jeremy Hammond then flew over to England, to see Paul McCartney and Pink Floyd perform at a large festival in the countryside. On the plane home, they plugged two sets of headphones into Milgrim's Walkman and listened to *Woodface*, taking notes. 'We loved it,' says Hammond. 'Paul's song "Italian Plastic" stood out as more off the wall than the others, but we understood the democracy. "Four Seasons in One Day" – so Beatlesque. "All I Ask" – Tim's vocal, sounding almost like a Frank Sinatra song. "Whispers and Moans" – a typical Neil feel. "Weather With You" stuck out a little bit. But "It's Only Natural" was the track we felt should be the first single.

'We were trying to work out how to position the band. There's a propensity in America to label or categorise everything. The hip thing at the time was to be an alternative band, and there was this quirky, wacky track called "Chocolate Cake", which showed the humorous side of Crowded House.'

Sink like a stone
• May 1991

'Every now and then the band comes up with an R&B gem. It's a new area for the band and one I hope we explore more.'

—Nick Seymour on 'Chocolate Cake', May 1991

Tell me about the discussions to release 'Chocolate Cake' . . .

Ha ha! All the fights, you mean . . .
– Julie Borchard, Capitol

That was tough, that was very, very tough. I didn't want to lead with 'Chocolate Cake', I didn't feel the song was indicative of the record.
– Hale Milgrim, Capitol

It's funny about 'Chocolate Cake'. I liked the song but I never in my life heard it as a single.
– Gary Stamler

I think it was Gary's call. If it wasn't his alone, he did it in conjunction with the American record company.
– Grant Thomas

There was a body of thought that Crowded House shouldn't be doing satirical material, it wasn't their area. But it was more surreal than satirical. I think it was Mitchell who said we should go with 'Chocolate Cake' . . .
– Tim Finn

I never liked the song. It was Crowded House figuring a different way of being uptempo. It was a new sound for them. Musically it's fine, but as a song . . . It sounded like Tom Lehrer political satire. I hate that shit.
– Mitchell Froom

Maybe Mitchell came in and hammered the point: it should be 'Chocolate Cake'. Maybe Gary picked up on that, and jumped on the bandwagon. Nobody else had a strong opinion. I don't regret it, none of us do.
– Tim Finn

I felt a little queasy about it, but not strongly enough to fight the system. I wasn't sure it was entirely right, but not sure it was entirely wrong either. And when you're in that position, you're buggered, you become ineffective because you can't really help.
– Grant Thomas

I'm not blaming anyone for it. In the end, I don't give a shit. But it was probably a bad commercial decision.
– Neil Finn

It was definitely something different for us, and I thought it was great.
– Paul Hester

In the studio in Melbourne, 'Chocolate Cake' had been one of the most exciting songs to record. Everyone who contributed to it enjoyed its rhythm, its edginess, its sardonic tone. And in Los Angeles, polishing the track with overdubs, even Froom agreed they had made a good *record*, even though he was still doubtful about it as a *song*.

The band were enthusiastic about it. The song's energy and attitude was so different to anything Crowded House had recorded before. 'It had more of a cynical lyric,' says Paul. 'It was good, poking a bit of fun. And it was very much the world we'd been travelling in: all that popular culture and those icons. We didn't see it as controversial. But the record company kept saying it wasn't happening. I thought it was a cool little song.'

Gary Stamler remembers the band responding badly to his negativity about the song. 'This was the first track, it was what the band wanted. Hale and others at the label were not into the song as a lead track. It wasn't representative of what people wanted to hear from the band. But the band made their opinions known on almost a daily basis. It was a song in which Tim could be the front person. I think he rallied everybody around the song.'

In Hollywood, from the point of view of both their manager and record label, the two songs most suitable for the first American single were 'Fall At Your Feet' and 'It's Only Natural'. Everyone involved was still not satisfied that 'It's Only Natural' had reached its potential. The camp was split about the song. Tchad Blake remembers one side arguing, 'We've got to take this to the height of singledom!'; to the others, it was just another candidate. Stamler says that at the mixing of 'It's Only Natural' with Bob Clearmountain, they were 'mentally trying to pull the song home, out of sheer frustration'. They even asked Tom Whalley – no longer at Capitol – for advice, playing 'Natural' to him over the phone from the studio monitors. 'We were wanting him to say, "Yeah, yeah, you're right, that's it". It was as though the "Better Be Home Soon" situation had been replicated. We were trying to somehow *will* this song into a hit single.' But Mitchell and Neil were second-guessing themselves. The song was that contradiction in terms: *too* catchy. They felt it didn't have enough substance to be a lasting hit single.

'It wasn't one of my favourites,' says Neil. 'It took such a long time to get it right. It seemed so obviously hooky. But that's what we were originally going to go with. Everybody who heard the mix said, "Oh, that's a smash" or "that's a radio song". So we thought we had it: "It's Only Natural" would be the first single.'

A promotional CD of 'It's Only Natural' was produced, with a sticker announcing it was the first single from the forthcoming album; the promotions department rolled into action, designing some 'natural' cereal boxes to give away when the single was released. Then Stamler, in conversation with Froom, started to have doubts about whether the song had 'legs'. Would it be just a 'turntable hit', that got lots of airplay but didn't inspire people to buy the record? That ran up the charts quickly but then disappeared just as fast?

'I began to doubt the song,' says Stamler. He thought they should be after something a little more provocative. 'Weeks before "It's Only Natural" was to be released, strangely enough, I started to think about "Chocolate Cake" as a first single – which is bizarre, because months before, I'd been more strongly against the song than anybody.' But, Stamler thought, the song was provocative, it might catch on with the college/alternative radio audience which was becoming influential in America, a radio format which was new territory for the band. 'It was a very strong format to build loyal record-buying fans.' Then they could follow with a more conventional song for Top 40 radio such as 'It's Only Natural' or 'Fall At Your Feet'.

Stamler called the band, and expressed his reservations about 'Natural', and his idea that 'Chocolate Cake' should be first. Their response was both 'shocked and elated', he says. 'I remember them saying, almost in a cheerleader fashion, "Yeah, that's what the band wants, Gary. Do what the band wants." ' He called Milgrim and said,

'I'm going to surprise you. This is fork-in-the-road number two on Crowded House for you. I think we should switch the single to "Chocolate Cake".' He tried to explain why; Milgrim said he'd think about it.

Twenty minutes later, Milgrim called back. He said he understood what they were trying to accomplish and that, reluctantly, he'd go along with it. 'So here we were,' says Stamler, 'two people who were passionately against the song, and several months later, we became passionate advocates for it.' Milgrim remembers meeting the band in his office at the Tower, after they had been 'vacillating back and forth' about the decision. They told him they had heard the negatives everybody had brought up, but they wanted to go with 'Chocolate Cake'. 'It wasn't like, oh this is going to be the worst thing that ever happened,' says Milgrim. 'But I always felt that, for a band still trying to open themselves up to radio, that first step is so vitally important.'

Surprising the audience and radio programmers with 'Chocolate Cake' was 'a smart move', reasons Julie Borchard, by this time working with Jeremy Hammond in the international department of Capitol. 'It showed Tim as an integral member of the new lineup. Coming after *Temple of Low Men* – which was a darker, more emotional record – it brought people back to the levity of Crowded House. It was one of those songs which had as good a chance as any to be a re-establishing hit.

'It created a lot of controversy within the company, which I loved: the fact that we weren't 100 per cent united, and we all had different opinions. That meant we had a strong record.'

How the song would be received by the industry could be gauged from the capsule review in *Billboard*, the influential trade magazine. It was perceptive but euphemistic; positive for all but Top 40 programmers reading between the lines:

CROWDED HOUSE Chocolate Cake (4:02)
PRODUCERS: Mitchell Froom, Neil Finn.
Musical influence of new member Tim Finn, late of Split Enz, is strongly felt on this lyrically quirky first single from the new *Woodface* album. Organic pop/rock instrumentation and tight harmonies should inspire both album rock and alternative airplay.

Capitol hoped to recapture the interest of MTV with the clip of 'Chocolate Cake', so it was given a budget approaching AUS$200,000. Neil later described the amount spent as 'outrageous', and would admit that they started talking ideas before costs. Mick Kleber, head of the Capitol video division, was a little concerned about the 'polyglot' of ideas from director John Hillcoat and producer Kit Quarry, so he flew from Los Angeles to Melbourne to oversee the shoot. 'I got the sense that people were calling around saying, "Hey, the Americans are here, and they've got *lots of money*. We're all in fat shape on this".'

The clip was like a set-piece from *Magical Mystery Tour*. The extravagant, busy production showing the band as tuxedo-clad entertainers in a sleazy nightclub while cockroaches play instruments, disembodied heads float about and Paul makes a cross-dressing cameo as 'Mrs Hairy Legs'. It closes with a chocolate cake of the Empire State Building melting.

At the end of the five-day shoot, Neil and Tim entertained the crew performing Split Enz songs on the piano. For Kleber, seeing the band on its own turf was a revelation. 'I liked the fact they all had rich cultural lives. There were artworks in their houses. When I went to Neil's there was a Billie Holiday record playing. There's depth there. With some bands ... you don't have a lot in common with a guy whose idea of art is a tattoo.'

Kleber had become a friend and confidant of the band. 'It was funny, each member would get me off by themselves and talk. Paul was bummed with the way things had been going in the band, like when Tim came in and Neil had never asked them. And he felt his material wasn't given the due it should be, despite "Italian Plastic". I sensed that he was chafing. He was absolutely hysterical, with a manic energy. I walked with him and his dog in the park, he had a joie de vivre, was really enjoying his life. The only thing he wasn't enjoying was that his creative contributions were being stifled.

'Nick was the hipster of the group, the R&B factor, the guy who worried about whether they were the happening thing, who was aware of what other bands were doing. I don't think Neil had a handle on that, he was much more in his own world, and more driven. Very much into his family.'

The cascade of creative ideas in the video 'confused and befuddled' viewers, says Kleber. It had cost more than Capitol had intended, 'even though nobody in the US was certain the song would hook in'. Neil agreed, telling Mike Chunn early in 1992 that the clip's budget was 'more than we'd want to spend again'. But, he said, 'Everything we did with *Woodface* was a saga; everything was a problem'.

Ice will melt • June 1991

'We had a wonderful time preparing for this new record. Another child was born. A house built. I went to Africa. Tim and I discovered we could write together.'

—Neil Finn, press release, 1991

The album was given the title *Woodface*, which the band claimed was French for 'hangover'. Paul grimly compared the impending campaign to promote the album to joining the Foreign Legion, though Neil joked that band should just send Paul out as 'Mr Crowded House'. The plan was to recapture the lost ground in the United States, and maybe establish a foothold in the United Kingdom. They began by returning to the low-key, high impact showcase gigs which had made such an impression around the world in 1986. Though it wasn't quite as humble as playing 'weddings, parties, anything', the first gig was a Valentine's Day love-boat cruise in Los Angeles. Each year on 14 February the radio station KROQ charters a boat to take dozens of engaged couples out into the Los Angeles harbour to get married; in 1991 Crowded House was the band. Neil was recruited to give away a bride named Thelma and, as he walked up the aisle cracking jokes to her, he heard the marriage celebrant starting his sermon. It suddenly occurred to him the bizarre occasion was actually *for real*.

The band was back in the States a month later, flying from Melbourne to San Francisco. As soon as they got off the plane, they went into the city to play a Gavin convention for leading US radio programmers. It was part of Hale Milgrim's plan to set the album up properly with a six-week promotional campaign prior to its release in July. 'Anything I needed to have done, they seemed to bend over backwards to do,' says Milgrim who, with his background in record retailing and marketing, was especially conscious of getting industry support beyond radio.

'You could tour the States on conventions and retail functions alone,' says Paul. The *Woodface* promotional tour of Europe and the US was a private, industry-only affair for retail, radio and record business. 'It was like a presidential campaign, constantly shaking hands, boozing, drinking, bullshitting your arse off. Trying to make one bit of human contact so there's a glimmer there, so that people know there's something remotely sincere about what you're doing.'

Having charmed so many industry people on the 1986 European showcase tour, though, a lot of them expected the same whole-hearted enthusiasm from the band. 'The first thing we got dubious about was the over-zealous promotional dude, with all these great ideas lined up,' says Paul. 'We knew what we were good at, and started to get a bit choosey.' But with Tim in the band, the mood was positive and they were all still enjoying the schmooze.

Mark, however, was a little in the dark. In late March, after the Gavin convention appearance, the band passed through Los Angeles. 'I knew the guys were in town and they hadn't called me,' he says. 'I thought, that's weird: it's not like I'm not in the band, it's my gig.' So he phoned Gary Stamler, whose wife Peggy answered. 'She said, "Well, I guess I'll see you tonight." I said, where? "Club Lingerie – the band's playing . . . oops."

'Then Neil calls me and says, "We're just going to get Tim to do all the keyboard parts. Give him something to do." Oh hell, here we go again.'

At the end of May, Crowded House launched 'Chocolate Cake' in Sydney and Melbourne. They had some costumes designed that were thought to reflect the song: powder blue tuxes in a sleazy Las Vegas style. 'In some cases, they came across with irony,' says Neil. One example was the Sydney record launch at the Rokoko Club on Neil's 33rd birthday. TV chatshow host Steve Vizard crossed live to find the band looking like Norman Gunston aspiring to be Dean Martin. 'It was one of the best pieces of television we ever did. We were all in our tuxes pretending we were at the reception for the record, and nobody had turned up. We were fagging, with drinks in hands, frilly shirts, tuxes. Tim was very funny, right on form.'

For the Melbourne launch, Peter Green suggested the Prahran Club as a venue. EMI promo man Michael Matthews got things organised: 'It's an old diggers' club, a dull little place,' he says. 'We decked it out, got the set designer of the video to do the stage, and we baked a big chocolate cake.'

There was plenty of free booze and food – the only thing not available was a copy of the single. A home video shot by Green captured the chaotic scene: EMI staff, media and fanclub members were packed into the club, the band trapped on the tiny stage. With the open bar, things quickly got very loose. The band played all the songs off *Woodface*, then the rest of their own repertoire and several old favourites as encores. But the drunken crowd refused to let them leave. Neil spotted Nick's mother in the audience and said, 'There's Paula

Seymour, ladies and gentleman. Nick's mum is going to sing a song for us now!'

'My mother was mortified,' remembers Nick. She wasn't the only one. 'I went with it, said, C'mon Mum ... But my brother, I've never seen him disappear so quickly. The family were all relaxed, standing a few people deep in the crowd. Mark just ducked and made a beeline out of the room. He knew what was going to come. Mum got up and sang a Clancy Brothers song from the record we had. So I knew it, and Neil was just revelling in it, he can play the chords to anything.'

Neil joined in, then Nick, slightly awkward but proud. Neil asked the crowd for 'The biggest hand of the night, please ... that was luxury indeed.'

'Next thing you know, there's a photo of Mum in the *TV Week*,' says Nick. 'To this day, whenever I jibe Neil about being a mummy's boy, he'll say, "Hang on a minute – your mother is the *only mother* of any member of this band who has sung with us on stage." It was a good moment.'

The evening didn't settle down, though. A few people started picking at the record-shaped chocolate cake, and the inevitable happened: a food fight started between retailers and record reps. A piece went flying across the room and hit Nick's mother in the head. 'There was no way I owned up to that,' says Matthews, 'she might have thought it was intentional.'

The promotional gimmicks could become a grind, or just downright embarrassing. Initially, says Nick, it was 'infectious' and the band were agreeable. At this time, he was asked by KROQ to judge a chocolate-cake eating contest in the San Fernando Valley in Los Angeles. 'It turned into a food fight with me wandering up and down the lines of these sugar-engorged teenagers with a loud-hailer, encouraging them. At the very end I caught myself and thought ... this is one of those situations that I'm going to look back on and wish that I'd never done. Another time it was walking behind a clown in a shopping mall, holding his portable PA for him while he yelled into a microphone, "Lookee lookee lookee, you lucky shoppers. I've got someone from Crowded House" ...

'There were so many rapid-fire situations they'd just breeze by you. If I could hear some of them back, I'd be mortified. Where you go to a radio stations and the DJ would say, "After the ad-break, when I turn to you guys and say, *I've got a crowded studio*, just go crazy, do your thing." And we'd instantly come up with some limp humour. It became a millstone, a hindrance, and we had to back off. But the most reticent to back off was ... Paul Hester.'

'On form,' says Neil, 'Paul was fantastic. He used to really undermine the situation. The biggest relief of doing promotion was that we could send it up, undercut it, give people shit without them realising it.'

Facing the media as a four-piece, they put a united, positive spin on the recruitment of Tim. Neil told *Pulse* he had thought about bringing Tim into Crowded House for years. 'I just didn't want to be half-assed about it, or have it look like a token thing. In the Split Enz days, we were still locked into younger brother/older brother-type of roles, but when we started writing together for the Finn Brothers album, we were a lot less guarded and the roles were less obviously stated. There was nothing to lose, and that was refreshing.'

In the same article, Tim said that 'Crowded House was my favourite band for years before I joined ... I don't think it was inevitable that I'd join the band, but the pieces fell into place very easily. When I think back on the number of times I'd worked with the guys, come to rehearsals or just hung out socially, there was a pattern developing. The energy of the band was already pretty high between them, so I knew I was joining something that was already established, and that I'd need to keep my distance for a while. And that's fine – it's a good feeling to be almost in a background role for a while.'

To the New Zealand *Listener*, Neil explained that having Tim in the band 'diffuses the tension between the three of us. Anybody else joining would have been much more difficult. I was in a similar situation when I joined Split Enz. I understood the aesthetic, and I think he understands the aesthetic very well. Tim is very mindful of absorbing himself into the Crowded House style of performance. He realises that's the only way it's really going to work. To Tim's eternal credit, he's totally aware of what Nick and Paul bring to the band, and of not affecting the chemistry to the detriment of the band. We're a fragile enough unit anyway, we always have been ... delicate, you might say.'

Nick – who socialised with Tim in Melbourne more than the others, sharing a fondness for nightclubs and dance music – would occasionally relax his natural tendency for public relations. He quipped to Canada's *Performer* magazine that when the band wanted to use Tim's songs for *Woodface*, 'It was like, it's my bat and it's my ball, so I'm the captain of the cricket team ... no, it wasn't like that, but it did force the issue in a way.' Returning to the diplomatic line, he recalled the occasion Tim had recorded with the band in Italy, and his backing vocals on *Temple*. 'So it made perfect sense to have him join the band. We've always respected his ideas. He's always been part of the family, more than just being Neil's brother.'

Contrary to his initial scepticism, however, Nick said he had found Tim didn't want to be the boss. He told *Pulse* that Tim 'has had to resign himself to a very fourfold combination of extremely strong egos, a genuine exchange of respect that takes place onstage and off.'

Tim had joined the band to sing harmonies on the brothers' songs, and play keyboards. Neil dwelt on the irony that he had joined Split Enz as a guitarist, having never played electric guitar before. Now Tim was joining Neil's band as keyboardist. 'Tim's a really good piano player but technology is not his strong point,' Paul acknowledged to Dino Scatena in *Juke*. 'We've been devising all these fail-safe methods for him with the crew. "Press one button man, and it's all there! Even Tim can work it." So it's been going well and it really resolves the problems of the floating fourth member/keyboard player.'

Tim said he was committed to getting his keyboards skills right. 'I have to be more disciplined', he said to *Pulse*, 'contributing to the music every night. If I'm not there, the music will suffer. I'll still have a few moments each night where I can get a bit demented. Otherwise, playing keyboards can be just as satisfying as doing a great frontman thing.'

Tim was aware that his presence meant that comparisons with Split Enz were inevitable. But, he told *Billboard*, 'Split Enz was burdened with good taste. This is 50 per cent different.' In a characteristic piece of Tim-speak, he elaborated on the contrasts between the two bands: 'In Crowded House, it's like group therapy, while in Split Enz, most things were left unsaid. And while that band was very patriarchal, this one isn't afraid of its feminine side, of talking emotionally about things. We're really organic and feminine, not wrapped up in male hardness and inflexibility. And Neil and I both write seductive melodies.'

In *Juke*, Paul said he was more comfortable with the idea than Nick, having worked with the Finn brothers in Split Enz. But, he pointed out, in a couple of ways, he was the odd-man-out among the quartet. 'Nick's a lapsed Catholic and so are Tim and Neil, so they really do form a tight little guilt group which I haven't had much to do with. But it's working out really well.

'It's funny, because Nick really relates to [the brothers syndrome] heavily because of him and Mark. He's always talking about the things they go through, the ups and downs of their relationship because they're both doing the same thing. Tim and Neil are the same again. There's a lot there that Nick understands just by being in that situation.'

Instead of the Finn brothers being a power bloc in Crowded House, there was a positive spinoff, said Paul. 'There are some things a big brother can say to a little brother that me and Nick can't say. It's a good dynamic, personality wise, now. Timmy can shed a look across the table now and go, "C'mon mate". And Neil sort of knows. That stuff is really good.'

Reaction from the media in the US was warm. *Rolling Stone*'s Kristine McKenna said Neil Finn's songs belonged to a tradition that began with Cole Porter and led to Buddy Holly, the Beatles and the Police. Their material always had depth, she said, though the treatments were usually conservative. Neil took from this that the review was written after only a couple of spins. 'That's an anomaly: to mention Cole Porter, and then say that's ordinary?' Yes, he admitted, 'I do read reviews, I take notice, and I remember names.' McKenna also took exception to the apparent hyprocrisy of 'Chocolate Cake', pointing out that the band that had shifted to Los Angeles to get their career off the ground was now 'lambasting America as a spoiled culture'.

But Capitol and the band's management took heart from the upbeat response of *Billboard*, the industry bible, read by radio programmers and record retailers:

CROWDED HOUSE Woodface
PRODUCERS: Mitchell Froom & Neil Finn
Capitol 70759
After slight misstep with sophomore effort, band from Down Under returns expanded to a quartet with the addition of Neil Finn's brother Tim. The retooled outfit now combines the melodic expertise of Crowded House and the quirkiness of the brothers Finn's previous band, Split Enz. 'Four Seasons In One Day' is probably the best Beatles song Paul McCartney never wrote. Facetious first single, 'Chocolate Cake,' is already climbing the album rock chart; the infectious 'It's Only Natural', beautiful 'Fall At Your Feet', and charming 'Weather With You' are likely follow-ups. This could be their year.

With *Woodface*, the band was determined to finally have a breakthrough in the English market. Crowded House had many supporters at Parlophone, their EMI label in Britain, particularly the head of marketing Tony Wadsworth, the head of promotion Malcolm Hill, and TV promotion Steve Hayes. Despite this, sales for the first two albums had been dismal – *Crowded House* and *Temple of Low Men* had sold only 18,000 and 12,000 copies respectively in the United Kingdom.

Nevertheless, says Wadsworth (later to become managing director of Parlophone), 'we felt a real affinity with the band. Though in reality, it was the American label who had the massive success with "Dream", and we were having no success.'

Malcolm Hill, long-serving Parlophone promotions manager, first met the band in Hollywood, while they were recording the debut album in Los Angeles. 'I warmed to them straight away, they were nice guys.' After the 1986 showcase in London, says Hill, and the exhortations of Heinz Henn, the commitment was there in Europe – but the band wasn't. They were in the United States, where the demand was. 'The forte of the band was live performance, which we never really got. I remember having a stand-up argument with Neil in a restaurant, because he was getting very 'oompy about it not happening in the UK. And I just had to say, well, you're never here. The regular punters can't see what you're about. People have to come and see you. That was pretty scary. I ended up shouting at Neil because he was shouting at me. If you think something, you've got to say it – and I did. He didn't end up hating me, which was good, because I was passionate about it – and I still am.'

Back in 1984, when Split Enz split up, Neil commented that they had a committed live audience in England, and steady radio play, but it didn't translate to record sales. 'I think England is a very difficult place to do well in, unless you're on the spot and "creating a buzz" within the industry, as they say, or you've got a record which is unstoppable, like Lionel Richie, which reeks of commerciality.'

David Hepworth, editorial director at Q and Mojo magazines, remembers that Split Enz's live following 'wasn't massive, though it was passionate – but it never grew beyond that. "I Got You" was a hit, but it didn't build a fan base or a cult, and there was no music paper interest.'

In 1991, there was even less about Crowded House and, motivated by Milgrim and Wadsworth, Parlophone set about changing that. At the time, the band could have played a 1800-capacity venue such as the Town & Country Club, but the audience would have consisted of Australian and New Zealand expatriates, and a few diehards who knew them from 'Don't Dream It's Over'. The band's English booking agency was Wasted Talent – who also represented acts such as Guns N' Roses – run by Ian Flooks and Emma Banks. With Parlophone, the agency decided to present a showcase gig to which both the media and the general public were invited. 'The record company wanted the Institute of Contemporary Art – a tiny little room which fits only 300 people,' says Banks. 'It's a bit staid, more for performance art. The Borderline seemed the right place. It's still very small – only 275 – but it's got that spit-and-sawdust feel and the right reputation. A lot of the club venues in the UK are geared towards indie bands, whereas Crowded House are in the 20 to 35 age bracket, rather than 14 to 18. It was an incredible gig, a very special event: it was mad.'

Mark Collen, product manager at Parlophone, remembers that as he accompanied the band to the Borderline, they were in a foul mood. They had just seen a remarkably frank Finn brothers interview by John Aizlewood in Q magazine. The article – headlined *Soap!* – dwelt on the anxieties beneath the band's sunny exterior. Tim discussed his reactions to Neil's success, Neil the guilt he felt during that success; together they gave a sombre account of the events that led to Tim joining the band. *Woodface*, they said, was important on two levels. If it succeeded, Crowded House would have cracked it for the second time. If it didn't, internal tensions would run their course.

'It's not like Split Enz, which began from a very strong camaraderie,' said Neil. 'Although we are capable of enjoying each other's company, it's not as intimate as Split Enz. It's fragile and volatile and at times it feels like it's going to end tomorrow.'

The article was quickly forgotten once the band arrived at the venue. Wearing their powder-blue tuxes, Crowded House captured the Borderline; so many people were out on the street, unable to get in, that the band went out and busked for them. And finally the press responded, Mat Smith writing in the hitherto sniffy *Melody Maker*:

For two nights last week, Crowded House were simply awesome. Now I'm surprised by that as you are ... [A] sustained roar of approval greeted the arrival and departure of every song they played these two nights. This was serious devotion time, with rumours that the Borderline had been deluged with more ticket applications than for the REM shows three months ago. And all this for a band that most of us have hardly heard of?

Like a less sentimental Squeeze, they're dismissed as AOR ['album-oriented rock', a conservative radio format, reliant on power ballads and stadium rock acts] by those who've not heard them, and they'd probably gasp if they were told that Black Francis and Dave Mustaine are fans. Crowded House are AOR in the way that the Beatles 'For No One' was AOR – bittersweet and capable of leaving an aching hole where your heart used to be. Chris Rea they ain't.

Live, they shake off the anally-retentive neatness and slavish adherence to song structure that characterises their vinyl output. They're visibly more comfortable with the puked-up designer glob of American greed that is the current single, 'Chocolate Cake', and the mucked-about jive of 'Sister Madly' than the more warmly cocooned comfort of 'Into Temptation' and 'Four Seasons in One Day'. In between, they piss around, tell a few crap jokes and get some funny looking f***er from Roxy Music [Phil Manzanera] up to jam on the first night and folkie Richard Thompson the next.

Crowded House are the wrong side of hip, the wrong side of 30 and come from the wrong side of the world – yet they're one of the best bar bands I've seen all year. The bleeding big limo waiting for them outside afterwards suggests a lot of other people think so too.

The promotional tour swung through Frankfurt, Amsterdam, London, New York, Baltimore (where Tim and Neil had an argument live on WHFS-FM) and Toronto before returning to the west coast. They gave a free show at Golden Gate Park in San Francisco, followed by another one in Hollywood, in the carpark of the Capitol tower at 1750 Vine.

Capitol occasionally used the carpark beneath its stack o'records tower to create a buzz around an act for its staff and the music industry. The two most memorable parties were for the Beach Boys (who didn't perform, but the company trucked in loads of sand to turn the parking lot into a beach) and Crowded House. 'We had the stage set up, food, booze and way too many people,' says Denise Skinner, a senior director of marketing at the time. 'It was out of hand – to the point where the fire-marshal turned up. They were going to close us down and the band hadn't even started. So I grabbed him, and took him into the building and started throwing product at him so he wouldn't close the performance down.'

Playing into the sunset, on a stage in front of the Capitol mural of jazz legends, Crowded House introduced the company to their new lineup. Mitchell Froom sat in on Hammond organ, cutting through the band's sound like Booker T playing Bach, filling in during breakdowns with lounge music. Tim continued the lounge theme, dressed in a frilly shirt open to the waist, with lovebeads and Raybans.

The company fired up, the band followed this with an appearance on the *Letterman* show in New York. With the Paul Shaffer Band, they performed 'Chocolate Cake' – but the lounge-lizard spoofing may have backfired. That was the low-point of that particular theme, says Neil: 'It was an absolute shocker. We had the pale-blue tuxes and we looked really flabby and horrible. On *Letterman* that's when we realised the whole thing wasn't working for us.' Just as well, then, that the company had politely forgotten about a publicity idea of the band's – to go on all the worst television shows in America. 'All the game shows, dressed in the tragic, Las Vegas tuxes,' says Neil. 'We thought of it as a way of getting into the underbelly of America, and it suited the song, the bad taste. The record company humoured us, said "We'll see what we can do!" – but they thought we were nuts.'

The only places 'Chocolate Cake' created any controversy were Australia and New Zealand: fans in both countries seemed worried by what the Americans would think, and how it would effect Crowded House. In Australia, there were discussions on talkback radio about whether the song was anti-American, and should the band be saying such things as *The excess of fat on your American bones will cushion the impact as you sink like a stone*.

'We didn't think about it twice, really,' said Neil. 'In America, people just laughed. I think it was far more important to them that we were talking about American icons than what we were actually saying about them. Building up that American junk culture – they love it. They're less sensitive to criticism than we think. Just because New Zealand says no to nuclear ships, and they say, naughty boys and slap us over the wrists, we think, Oh well, they're very sensitive, and petty. In actual fact, most people in America wouldn't even know New Zealand had said no to nuclear ships, it's a very low priority issue. America is a great steaming machine, and they're criticising it all the time anyway. They're aware of the junk culture – they thrive on it – but they can also see it for what it is, they laugh about it themselves.

'The song received a very polarised reaction. It surprised the hell out of me. I knew it was different for us, and it's unusual for us to be topical, but people who liked Crowded House in the past couldn't accept the fact we'd done the song. Whereas others, who had never liked us, really liked it a lot.'

Certainly the song had done very well at the alternative rock stations, as Capitol had hoped: the song reached number one on the alternative radio charts (for airplay) and stayed there for several weeks. But commercial alternative stations were just getting started in the States at the time, with KROQ being the leader of a format that probably only numbered 20 stations. It helped sell quite a few albums early on in the *Woodface* campaign, although the only actual sales chart on which 'Chocolate Cake' made any impression was the 'modern rock' format, where it peaked at number 20.

Gary Stamler explains that the original strategy of John Fagot, the head of radio promotion at Capitol at the time, had been to open up the alternative audience with 'Chocolate Cake', then take a more conventional song to mainstream radio. But after 'Chocolate Cake's success on the alternative stations, he decided to stay with it for the Top 40 stations. 'I was nervous about it,' says Stamler, 'I asked why he was changing his mind. He said, "Well, a lot of people are talking about it Gary, and there's a big difference between being in the Top 10 and being at number one – we have the big bold capital letters in the chart. When people see that song in big, bold type, it's so much easier to cross over."' Milgrim, too, was swayed by this argument – and the fact that the video was receiving heavy airplay on MTV.

'Yet despite the hopes, the song was an abject failure at Top 40 radio, and the record never recovered from it,' says Stamler. 'Top 40 radio is a format that's based on the sound of a song and how it fits between the song before and the song after. It's not band-based, it's song-based. The song clearly didn't work in between Madonna and Michael Jackson.' (At the time, Bryan Adams's '[Everything I Do] I Do It For You' had its stranglehold on the number one position.)

Rather than cause a controversy, 'Chocolate Cake' just baffled the Top 40 listeners, who really only associated Crowded House with 'Don't Dream It's Over'. 'Tim being in the band wasn't that confusing,' says Denise Skinner, 'there's always been the association between the brothers. But in performance it was: Tim was coming from a different space from the rest of the band. It wasn't the same band, it had a different feel than the three-piece. "Chocolate Cake" ... the band wasn't quite the same ... so the fans weren't sure what was going on.'

Two weeks after *Letterman* the band opened their Australian tour at the Palace in Melbourne. The month-long tour included many small venues and out-of-the-way places; it was a shaking-down period for the altered group dynamics. But the tour got off to a shaky start: the first casualty was Paul Hester, who broke his foot at the Ferntree Gully Hotel, Melbourne, playing basketball in the bandroom. The second casualty was an American soundman. 'The first few days were awful,' says Neil, who remembers a gig at the Frankston Pier Hotel, Melbourne, as probably the worst they ever did. 'We had this really dodgy sound until we sacked, ah, changed personnel.'

Angus Davidson, a sound engineer with many years experience in the Melbourne studio Sing-Sing, was in the bath when he got a call from Eddie Rayner. He asked Davidson if he wanted to mix a band that night. 'Who?' Crowded House. 'Sure, Ed.'

So on an hour's notice Davidson walked into Transformer's in

Melbourne when the band was doing its soundcheck. 'This American guy was still there, setting it up, and I was like, "Hi, I'm Angus, I'm mixing." It was pretty uncomfortable. But it worked out well for me because they were embarking on an Australian tour and didn't have a sound guy.' During the tour Davidson particularly hit it off with Paul Hester, who lobbied for him to get the job on the American leg. 'At that point Neil wasn't that confident in me, because we'd worked in the past and I was known to be pretty fractious and hot-headed and opinionated – and him too! But halfway through the Australian tour the reports about the sound had been very good, so they asked me to do the world tour. I said, Sure.'

A few weeks later, to the New Zealand *Listener*, Neil described this Australian tour as 'a role reversal in its teething period': Tim needed to get used to being on stage but not as the frontman, while Neil had to learn to be comfortable as the frontman while Tim was alongside. 'It took time to work out,' he said. 'I was initially feeling a little intimidated by having this presence standing next to me, whereas before I'd been calling the shots.'

A routine quickly established itself: Tim shifting between playing piano and acoustic guitar, singing duets on the co-writes, and a few of his own songs. That he relished being in the band was obvious early on in the tour when they played a couple of nights at the Metropolis club in Fremantle, in Western Australia. One of the concerts was filmed by the local television station, and it shows the two-Finn Crowded House at its best. Tim sits at a bank of keyboards, to Neil's left at the front of the stage. They make a spirited start with 'It's Only Natural' and a dramatic 'Mean to Me', which includes a tangential rap about the Nullabor Plains. On 'Don't Dream It's Over', Tim makes a tentative attempt at the famous organ solo. Neil is still in charge, but constantly looks over at his brother. A punchy 'Tall Trees' has Tim playing acoustic guitar while confined by the keyboard setup, looking caged. Then he comes out to turn the Finn Brothers into the Everlys with a double-acoustic 'Weather With You', then still new to the audience.

But 'Six Months in a Leaky Boat' is when the show really catches fire, like a rallying call inspiring the troops. Neil then quietly explores a lovely tune Phil Judd wrote for the Enz, 'So This is Love', until Tim takes up the thread and they send the gentle song back and forth, replying to each other, before heading into a medley of other obscure Enz songs. They have become brothers playing together at a party, once more leading the singalong, with Nick and Paul following, feeling their way. 'We'll have to teach you that one, Nick,' says Neil. 'Any requests before we leave this vein?' He then belts out 'Shark

Attack', with Nick deftly conquering Nigel Griggs's bass runs.

Tim then calls for Paul to join them at the front of the stage: 'Paul, throw down your crutches and walk.' As Hester struggles off the drum riser, Tim says, 'Get your arse down here – the best arse in Australia.'

'You'd know, you've been licking it long enough,' says Neil.

Paul: 'Just as mates do, as mates.'

The banter begins carefree and jovial then, the band enjoying themselves, ventures into the bizarre. Neil ticks off a roadie for wearing a paisley shirt – 'I find it scary. It reminds me of the moment of conception' – then Paul does some cathartic rebirthing as well. During 'This is Massive' he goes into a stream-of-consciousness rap: '*When I was 17, Dad told Mum where to go, so Mum left . . . the job, the house, the family . . . it hadn't been good for a long time . . . Dad hit the bottle . . . I went round and said, Dad, get your shit together.*'

It turns into instrumental madness, Paul hitting Neil's acoustic with his brushes, Neil hitting Paul's snare with his hands, Tim spouting nonsense through a megaphone: 'Paul, I liked that bit about your parents – a bit of therapy for you?' 'It's a true story, Tim.'

'Did you take after your mother or father as regards to your arse?'

Neil restores decency with a stately version of 'Fall at Your Feet', coaxing soaring harmonies out of Tim. Crowded House is on a roll, and say so with a loping 'Now We're Getting Somewhere'. A stray guitar line makes them segue into 'Spicks and Specks'. It's a significant moment: the brothers Finn returning to their childhood singalongs at the beach, and the harmonies of the brothers Gibb. It almost breaks down – 'Wouldn't you think we'd know the words?' says Neil – then Nick adds a falsetto, and it *does* break down. The Finns are stunned; it's an Australian anthem. 'Get her! Maurice!!' The Small Faces' 'Sunny Afternoon' gets the singalong rolling again, with everyone present exuberantly bellowing out the final chorus.

Neil restores order with 'When You Come', which slowly builds to a passionate, exhausting climax. Tim takes over, wandering the stage, microphone in hand, introducing 'Chocolate Cake' with a monologue ('They say when you eat chocolate, it releases the same chemical as when you fall in love. Don't eat too much'). In an instrumental break Neil, on rhythm piano, vamps 'Jumpin' Jack Flash'; Tim starts rapping Elvis songs – 'Suspicious Minds', 'Wooden Heart', 'It's Now or Never' – before kicking into the verse, '*I saw Elvis Presley walking out of a 7-11 . . .*' The song gallops along, the band thoroughly enjoying themselves. At the next solo, Neil plays two full choruses of 'Billie Jean'. This version of 'Chocolate Cake' has turned into an epic, which only comes to an end when Tim rolls around on the floor.

The first encore begins: 'Love You 'til the Day I Die', 'Money's No Object' , 'Sister Madly' . . . then the second: 'Four Seasons in One Day'. 'Get close to your friend with this,' says Neil, 'unless it's a mate, mate.' Tim follows with an excerpt from the Gershwin brothers' 'Summertime', which segues into an elegant 'All I Ask', accompanied by Neil's grandiose piano runs.

But the epic night in Fremantle isn't over yet. Neil strides back on stage, saying 'If you've got it in you, we've got it in us . . .' Tim takes the piano, starts a slinky 'Through the Years' (off *Escapade*) but loses the words, while Nick piggybacks Paul on stage. Paul rescues Tim with a kazoo solo on the megaphone. There's a great spirit in the large club, it is relaxed almost to the point of chaos. Calming the antics of his band (Tim hustles for an outing on someone's yacht the next day, preferably with an all-girl crew), Neil says, 'We've really set this song up . . .' as he begins a sombre 'Better Be Home Soon.' Nick rides out into the audience, held aloft by the crowd as he still plays bass. It has been a classic Crowded House gig: spontaneous, anarchic, moving, genuinely happy. The foursome can't leave the stage.

Water will boil
• August 1991

'There was actually a fourth Stooge, called Shemp. If you know the Stooges, Shemp had a very healthy head of hair, a bit of a widow's peak. Just like our Brian.'

—Paul Hester, 1996

The addition of Brian Timothy Finn to Crowded House inspired many debates among their fans and critics, wrote the *Sydney Morning Herald*'s Shane Danielsen when the tour played Selina's club in Sydney. The numbers seemed equally divided between those 'for' and 'against', but to Danielsen, it seemed an unlikely combination: the serious-minded Tim sharing a stage three self-deprecating pranksters. 'Something has changed in this House. Where once there was boundless energy and exuberance, on Friday their delivery seemed curiously flat, at times even leaden.'

For the Australian *Woodface* outing, Crowded House kept to small-scale venues. The itinerary included the Sundowner Hotel, Perth; the Beenleigh Tavern; Jindabyne Station Resort; Collonades Tavern, Adelaide; the Raiders League Club, Canberra; and the Shellharbour Workers Club, Wollongong. It was a settling-in period for the new line-up. While the audiences were receptive to Tim's inclusion in the band, on stage things weren't so relaxed. Tim was required to be the keyboardist, a crucial and demanding role which always seemed to cause problems for Crowded House. And while Tim was a competent piano player, his strengths were songwriting and singing – anything more than 88 ivory keys was a job for Eddie Rayner. 'That tour was difficult really,' says Neil, 'as everything was, at that time. It was an awkward situation for Tim and I to be in. I was having to say, "That's not right – play it like this." When you get a keyboard player in, you have to drill them. It was weird for both of us. Sometimes I'd be too unsubtle – and he'd be sensitive.'

Angus Davidson points out the difficult task Tim had been given. 'Tim took on a huge mantle as a keyboard player. No matter how good your backline technician is, no matter how well he puts together the equipment, you've got to have a grasp of the technology and subtleties of multi-keyboard set-ups – especially when you're trying to reproduce a record that was as complex as *Woodface*.'

There was a lot of pressure on Tim to be 'the classical musician, the keyboardist,' says Paul. 'And he'd never done that kind of thing. Tim and Neil went through some grief to get that all sorted out. There was a lot of them in rehearsal, with Neil leaning over to say, "Look, it's like this" to his older brother.'

Recalling the Australian tour to Mike Chunn in 1992, Tim said, 'We did some great shows, I liked it as a four-piece. But they reckoned I was lazy and didn't learn enough about keyboards. They were probably right – although I thought that was ironic coming from Paul – but I was more intimidated by technology. So I simplified things, which they weren't happy with.'

The keyboard issue became a crescendo which reached its climax on 13 August, two weeks into the tour. The setting was the 'love capital' of Australia: Byron Bay, a popular holiday resort and retreat for alternative lifestylers in northern New South Wales. 'It's full of hippies,' says Paul, 'peace-loving, muesli-powered Australia. And Tim and Neil have fisticuffs. They've never hit each other, I assure you – but they end up going to Byron Bay and belting each other.'

'I didn't play a keyboard part in "World Where You Live",' explained Tim. 'I'd pulled back and not played it because the sound I had was awful. It really threw Neil. But it was the culmination of him feeling paranoid and tense the whole time – just like me – and he came off stage and said, "You should have played it" – just like I did to Phil, all those years before. I said, "I'm the keyboard player and I chose not to do it, because it sounded fucking awful, alright?" He swung a punch and it hit me on the temple.'

They were in the dark backstage area; the lights were still down. Paul was standing in the middle, like a halfback between two, well, threequarters. He heard, 'I'm the fucking keyboard player, I'll fucking play how I want to play it!'

Then, says Paul, 'Bang! End of story. I ducked! Neil got Tim a cracker on the temple, a beauty in first, and Tim was stunned. It didn't knock him over or anything, he just thought, "My little brother – God, he got one in there." It was over as quick as it started.'

Tim remembers, 'The roadies were holding him back and jostling. I didn't want to hit him back, and I knew I wasn't going to. But they grabbed me, as well. My aggression came out: "Oh, yeah, come on . . ."'

Neil stormed outside. Paul will always remember what happened next. 'Nick turned to me and said, "I just can't believe we're not doing an encore." In all seriousness. I thought, Wow, what a funny way of looking at it. Then headed out the door to see if there was any more carnage.'

Out in the carpark, Neil got into the band's hire car and slammed the door. Paul, wandering around the carpark looking for him, saw 'a hippie woman from Rainbow Lake' standing outside the car, pleading with Neil through the window. He wound the window up, and the woman cried out, *'Release your anger. That's it. I can help you. Let me help you.'*

'Neil's going, "Just piss off!" And she says, "That's good! – you're letting it go. Release it." She'd been out in the carpark, checking the moon or having a spliff, and she'd seen something happen but not the actual fight. Neil couldn't believe it: he couldn't be left alone for five minutes.'

(In 1996, Neil recalled to *Goldmine*: 'I was stewing in my own juices, and this hippie woman [was saying] "Neil, I can help you. You've got to let your chakra go." And I wasn't in the mood.')

Paul went back to find Tim in the bandroom, having a medicinal scotch. 'His cheek was a bit red and rosey, and he was going, "Well, what about that, eh? A spot of bother, eh?" He was titillated a bit by the whole thing, being the older brother.'

The next gig was at the Queensland University of Technology, in Brisbane. As the band walked into the soundcheck, the keyboard tech started playing the theme from *Rocky* while two of the roadies simulated a brawl, and another one commentated through the megaphone, 'In the left corner . . .' The brothers looked appropriately sheepish.

'There was a real willingness in New Zealand for that to be the band,' says Neil. 'People were very accepting of it. In other places it had less support or impact.' In Australia, 'Chocolate Cake' reached No 20; in New Zealand, number seven. Two weeks after the Fremantle show, Crowded House were in Auckland, New Zealand, to play the Power Station, a small nightclub. It was a Monday night, and the band's last show before they embarked on a lengthy American and European tour – by Thursday they were to perform in Canada. In Auckland, the venue was just up the road from the coffee bar where Split Ends gave its first concert.

Every New Zealand fan wanted to see the Finn brothers together again, although Tim's recruitment in Crowded House actually received a mixed response locally. Most seemed pleased to see the elder Finn back in the limelight, while expressing concern that the three-piece was getting mighty crowded. Tickets for the one-off show were at a premium; the only recent event that compared was the triumphant return of Kiri Te Kanawa to an Auckland stage. Fans who weren't quick enough to buy tickets before they were snapped up by radio stations for competitions, phoned all their contacts looking for spares. Outside the gig, as hundreds of people waited for the doors to open, they were bombarded by the sound systems of two rival radio stations. Inside, the band endured the schmooze: there was family to greet and media to meet. 'I'm deeply flattered,' said Tim Finn of the radio stations outside trying to outdo each other in support. 'Fifteen years ago we were told, "We don't play that sort of stuff."'

On stage, the charm of the old trio remained – the acoustic busking, the rapport with the audience, the singalong melodies – but it was apparent the balance had shifted. The brothers didn't come across like an Everlys-style duo, as on the record; nor was it the old three-piece with a new supporting player. Instead, even in the duets, the limelight was firmly on Tim whenever he stepped forward, while Neil retreated back to his former sidekick role in the Enz. Neil was now the stronger singer, but the most magical moment belonged to Tim. 'Six Months in a Leaky Boat' was still fresh, nearly a decade after it was an inspirational chant for Split Enz: *The tyranny of distance / never stopped the cavalier. So why should it stop me?'*

There was a united, supported spirit in the audience; this was a bon voyage an Anzac expedition which seemed to have the odds on its side. Earlier in the day, Neil talked of the two-edged attitude New Zealanders have towards those achieving success overseas. They want them to take on the world and win – but still stay the same. When they've succeeded, the proper response is for them to act like an All Black after scoring: put their head down and walk back, impassive. In the morning's paper, Neil had noticed an All Black talking about the country's demanding relationship with its prominent citizens. 'The attitude seems to be, "Sure, we'll give you hero status, mate – *just don't stuff up."*'

It was time for the *Woodface* campaign to enter the northern hemisphere. The day of the Auckland concert, Neil referred to the imminent tour as 'the descent into hell'. To ease their burden, some fine-tuning needed to be done. During the Australian tour, Grant Thomas talked with Gary Stamler in Los Angeles, and reported that, 'On a musical level, with Tim on keyboards, the band was struggling. Because he wasn't embracing that side of the band. I mean, *Eddie Rayner* had been playing keyboards, so it left a void. So I said to Gary, for this American tour the band would have to be a five-piece. We needed Mark Hart in as keyboard player. Neil agreed.'

So did Paul and Nick. 'They were quite relieved,' says Neil. 'Grant was, and Tim in the end, because he was feeling the pressure of a role he was unfamiliar with – and getting the heat for it. It's a difficult job for anybody. We had four keyboard players – no, five – and Tim was by no means the worst.'

Neil found he was having to compensate for gaps in the sound, 'and it was making me more nervous on stage. Less relaxed. Paul wasn't getting the repartee happening as much as usual, because Tim was doing some talking. There was a different dynamic on stage. It was a bit uncomfortable. I was coming off stage most nights feeling strangely unsatisfied, anxious.'

Mark was playing scrabble at home in Los Angeles when the phone rang. His close friend Kenny had just asked him what he was doing for money. It had been a tough year. Every time Hart was offered work, it would fall through. His savings had dwindled to the point where he had started to sell equipment. 'My wife and I were quite worried. We had two kids, house payments . . . I said to Kenny, I don't know – something always seems to happen, I'm yet to be taken to the full ugly conclusion of having no money.'

It was Neil on the phone, offering him a place on the *Woodface* US tour. 'I said yeah, that sounds like fun, I'll do it. I was surprised they got as far as they did with Tim. He doesn't have the temperament for playing keyboards. Button pushing and standing still, concentrating – that's not his thing at all.'

As the band arrived in Canada, Capitol released 'Fall at Your Feet' as a follow-up to 'Chocolate Cake'; meanwhile, 'It's Only Natural' had started to receive airplay on the alternative stations. 'Unfortunately,' says Stamler, 'at Top 40 radio, the heat is on the first single. If that fails, the second single is much more difficult to launch. We had got ourselves behind the eight ball.'

In the four years since 'Don't Dream It's Over', says Jeremy Hammond, the band's audience had moved on. In 1991, the young fans wanted Nirvana, Pearl Jam. 'That was who we were competing against, and Crowded House was considered like an old-school band almost. The perception of the band wasn't in their favour, and it was hard at radio after "Chocolate Cake".'

Hammond remembers John Fagot championing 'Fall at Your Feet' to radio 'like there was no tomorrow, he did everything in his power. Hale was putting the thumb down so hard on John to get the record away. Because it was a personal thing for Hale – he'd come to

Capitol, and was going to do what they hadn't done on the second record, break Crowded House right open. He was going to make them REM. He wanted this record really bad – and so did we all. We felt we weren't doing our jobs unless we delivered on this record. It was the most frustrating time in my career, we all felt so strongly about it.'

The promotions department declared they weren't going to take off their Crowded House shirts until 'Fall at Your Feet' was on radio stations across the country. By the second week, says Milgrim, 'I was going, hey, a couple of you guys change your shirts – they're getting pretty dicey . . .'

In hindsight, Hammond considers that despite all the efforts of the Capitol team, 'Frankly, we didn't do a great job of marketing the record. There wasn't enough unity or focus. We relied too much on the fickleness of radio, which is a big mistake at any time. You've got to be incredibly well organised, and have a machine out there that markets records. Hale – who is considered one of the top marketing guys in the record business – was used to a different culture at Elektra, I was new in the job as the head of marketing. We were all on a learning curve, so I don't think that helped.'

The timing of *Woodface* was unfortunate: sophisticated pop songs appearing in the year grunge brought the alternative into the mainstream. In a review of their New York show at the Beacon – an article dripping with positive Beatles comparisons – Stephen Holden of *The New York Times* wrote, 'The main obstacle to mass American popularity for Crowded House is pop fashion. The group's sweetness and wit are simply too airy for a pop climate absorbed in darkness and aggression.'

But the alternative radio airplay of 'Chocolate Cake' did introduce a younger, hipper audience to the band, and across North America the daily newspapers were especially enthusiastic. For them, the arrival of Tim was just an angle, not an issue.

Three days after the Auckland appearance, the band arrived in Edmonton, Canada. They did a six-week tour that ventured down the west coast of the States, up through the midwest, back to Canada before finishing in the northeast.

Support act on the first leg of the US tour was Richard Thompson who, with Gary Stamler as a manager and Mitchell Froom as a producer, was like part of the family. Thompson would travel separately, in a car with his sound engineer. They would take back roads, exploring the culture and history of the areas they passed through. 'They'd go off like gentlemen and visit interesting places, having terribly philosophical chats,' says Paul. 'It was lovely to be around this English sensibility in the American midwest. We'd get him up to play – it was like having a child on stage. He plays so intuitively, putting so much heart and pure pleasure into it.' Thompson responded well to Paul's humour and pranks, even when he was heckled to 'down-trou' one night. 'He immediately dropped his trou and stood there,' says Paul. 'Legs abroad, big red hairy freckly thighs with these green jocks on. Nasty little tight pants! Quite a weird kettle of fish . . .'

The band and their crew travelled in two tour buses. For sound engineer Angus Davidson, after years running a studio, being part of a crew constantly on the move was a new experience. After a show had been loaded out, they would shower then get back on the bus. The promoter would provide a snack, usually pizzas, and a few beers left over from the rider. For a couple of hours, the crew would talk, discuss the show, watch videos, before turning in. At nine the next morning, they would wake to find themselves at another venue. A local crew would have arrived and started setting up the PA and lights. Soundcheck would be at five o'clock; there might be a couple of hours either side to themselves, before dinner then the show. Meanwhile the band would have a similar routine, only they would be doing promotion during the day, being live-wires at radio stations, answering very familiar questions for cub reporters. There might be some brief moments of schmoozing after the show, before showering and getting back on the bus.

Egos, fatigue, bad food: there have to be road rules to prevent the machine breaking down. Don't shit in the bus toilet – do that somewhere else. Don't leave your stinky boots in the aisle of the bus for people to trip over. And if you smoke, use the smoking lounge.

Before the show, the band would read over the fanmail which had arrived at their dressing rooms. Davidson particularly remembers a show in Salt Lake City, the Mormon capital of the world. 'I guess all bands get weird letters, but Neil gets his share from real space-cadets,' says Davidson. 'This letter was from someone who was clearly paddling with one oar in the water. On the one hand there was this kind of adoration, on the other, this condemnation of leading the world astray with his lyrics. Abject love mixed with murderous intent. So you'd read them with a nervous chuckle, it was a bit of free entertainment after soundcheck, but you'd be looking over your shoulder for this psycho element.'

Salt Lake City was very straight, with prohibitive laws about drinking, and the small theatre so tidy it could have been a chapel. 'It was pretty weird. The band were playing great, and the people were really getting into it. Neil goes off into one of his classic tangents while playing acoustic, and he starts playing this country-and-western, camp version of the Sex Pistols' "Anarchy in the UK": "I am an Anti-Christ". We were smiling, it had a jolly little feel to it. And I'm thinking, "Oh my God". To my right was a young mother, about 35, with a small child, and they're bouncing to the music, all jolly. Maybe they didn't hear the lyrics or chose not to work out what they said, but they were clear as a bell. It was really edgy. I'll never forget looking around the theatre waiting for someone to start throwing things, and this woman with her child, happily dancing, thinking, what a jolly, golly-gosh wonderful band.'

Back on keyboards, Mark found himself the man-in-the-middle of an unhappy band. He spent a lot of time in Tim's company during the tour, having built a rapport in 1989 when he was in his band promoting the *Tim Finn* album. 'Tim was telling me he didn't know what he was doing there,' says Mark. 'He was just playing acoustic guitar and singing harmonies. So he felt really awkward and out of place. Meanwhile, I'd hear the other three guys saying, in so many words, that it seems so awkward and wrong with Tim. "It doesn't feel right – the balance of the band has changed, the dynamics aren't quite right." It was hard for me: I couldn't be the mediator, but I knew what was going on. I was just watching it come to a head.'

The venues they played were slightly smaller than on the *Temple* tour, mostly theatres holding about 2000 people, with the exception of a packed Universal Ampitheatre in their second home, Los Angeles, and a large outdoor show near Chicago, where they shared the bill with the Smithereens and Richard Thompson. When the band left North America in early October, after six weeks of touring, over 30 shows, TV appearances such as *The Tonight Show* and countless radio and press interviews, *Woodface* was at 175 in the charts after peaking at 83, 'Fall At Your Feet' was about to peak at 75 – and 'Chocolate Cake' had disappeared.

Crowded House was about to make its first determined pitch at Europe. 'It was time,' says Stamler. 'We hadn't attended to the market at all. The English company was enthusiastic, and we committed early on to go there several times. The company had always said, to have success in England, you have to show the market that you're inter-ested. There's no replacement for being on the spot.'

Heading towards England, Neil admitted his confusion at the band's reception there. They had spent very little time in the UK, and the songs which had been massive hits elsewhere had met little response. But on the *Woodface* promotional visit, he'd been surprised by the impact *Temple of Low Men* had made by word-of-mouth. He found it perplexing that *Melody Maker*, for example, had 'slagged off'

Temple and *Woodface*. But in the paper's review of *Woodface*, the critic
– an Australian – said everyone should have been excited by *Temple*.
'It's bizarre,' said Neil. 'It's like they've suddenly turned around and
said the last album was great. We've had an on–off relationship with
England. The press over there is extremely unpredictable about us,
but I sense the last album created far more interest than the first one.
Temple had a certain underground status there which is actually significant. The guy from *Q* magazine asked me if I realised that. He said
a lot of people he'd interviewed over the last year had talked about
that album. Sometimes things reveal themselves over a long period of
time. You get the impression that something is a flop, but in actual
fact it does more good for you in the long term.'

The band now had many supporters at EMI in London, from Rupert
Perry, the head of the parent company in the UK, and Andrew Prior,
managing director of Parlophone, through the ranks to Tony Wadsworth, Malcolm Hill and Mark Collen. And the enthusiasm and exhortations of Hale Milgrim gave them the motivation – and the means –
to work the album. 'I went over to England several times for our
international meetings,' says Milgrim, 'and because I felt so strongly
about the album the band had delivered, I kept telling *everybody*. I had
discussions with a number of people who were very enthused, who
said, "Hale – we've got something happening, you've got to let us
have the group." So I was willing to take care of whatever was needed
financially. England put together a fabulous plan, and were working
so hard, I thought I'd take whatever positive they get and try to do
it in America afterwards.'

Milgrim was 'a passionate believer' in Crowded House, says
Wadsworth, then head of marketing at Parlophone. 'They were a very
special artist on his roster, probably more than they would have been
for their commercial performance at the time. He got a vibe that we
really believed in them as well, even though we weren't selling many
records. He was essentially a music guy and went along with and
supported our ideas.'

As Parlophone in London was preparing for the arrival of
Crowded House for the first leg of the *Woodface* tour, a very fortuitous
thing happened. A cover version of 'Don't Dream It's Over' by Paul
Young was imminent; at the time, the English blue-eyed soul singer
was still very popular, and he had made quite an impact performing
the song at the Nelson Mandela Freedom Concert at Wembley
Stadium in 1988. Gary Stamler had been contacted by Young's management, and Neil's publishers, about the song. 'We were trying to

get a fix on when his record was going to come out, because we had plans to put out "Fall At Your Feet".'

In the weeks before Crowded House arrived back in the United Kingdom, Young had a hit with his limp version of 'Don't Dream It's Over'. To capitalise on that success, the Parlophone marketing department had a couple of ideas that accelerated the momentum of Crowded House and *Woodface* in the UK. They placed the original of 'Don't Dream It's Over' on the B-side of 'Fall At Your Feet', took out advertisements in the music press to let people know the original was once again available, encouraged classic hits stations (for which the song was a playlist staple) to give it more airplay, and made sure their sales staff informed record stores about the B-side. They also placed stickers on the debut album saying it contained 'the original and genuine version' of the song. All this helped stimulate some life for 'Fall At Your Feet' in the UK charts. Stamler believes the B-side manoeuvre was as important as any hit potential the programmers heard in 'Fall At Your Feet', because the latter song 'got the usual lack-lustre reception from Radio One. We'd had no history there. But we thought it would be good to create some subtle competition between the versions.' As Paul Young's version peaked at No 20, 'Fall At Your Feet' started to climb.

Crowded House arrived in England in the first week of October. Having built up word-of-mouth with the Borderline gigs – which immediately doubled the early sales of *Woodface* from 11,000 to 20,000 – the band opened their European tour at London's Hammersmith Odeon. The 3000-seat venue was sold out.

In the audience was Miles Mendoza, a young producer at the radio station GLR. Since receiving an early tape of *Woodface* at the station, he had become a dedicated fan of the band, feeling 'a certain amount of smugness' at the Borderline when he was one of few in the room full of Australasians who could sing along to the new songs. But at the Hammersmith Odeon, he was one of several people who realised something was smouldering within Crowded House. Walking up the stairs to the bar afterwards, he noticed Tim in front of him, a little unsteady on his feet.

'The show wasn't very good, frankly,' says Parlophone product manager Mark Collen. 'The chemistry was wrong, and we sat there going, ''oo 'eck – something's wrong here, it's not working.'

'Tim wasn't at his best,' confirms Malcolm Hill. 'We were joking about him being the pub singer, which was a great shame – but that was how it was coming across.' The rest of the band, says Stamler, were concerned that the Vegas lounge-singer act – originally a parody for the 'Chocolate Cake' video – was becoming too real.

Now that Tim wasn't playing keyboards, there wasn't a lot for him to do on stage. Grant Thomas reflects his background as a tour accountant with some simple arithmetic: 'Tim had a duo-vocal role on half the songs off one album, in a three-album career. So he had a role to play in half of a third. Which means he was a participant on one-sixth of the band's material, or 15 per cent. So for about 85 per cent of the night . . .'

'Tim started to feel a bit left out and awkward,' says Paul. 'He was saying, "I feel like Stevie Nicks", banging the tambourine on the side, singing the occasional song. He was very funny. He's pretty good-natured.'

Immediately after the Hammersmith gig, the band headed for the Continent in an eight-berth bus, to play three weeks of dates in small venues. 'Some of the shows were better,' Neil recalled to Mike Chunn, 'but in others, Tim wasn't that happy. A bit moody. Paul and I had a couple of discussions, one in New York, one in Paris. In New York I said to Tim I wasn't sure if it was going to work. There was this "waiting for something to happen" thing. Tim wasn't verbalising it but subconsciously he was feeling pretty weird too.'

They needed to know how he felt, and decided the band would have a discussion when they reached Glasgow, where they had a couple of free days scheduled. 'We didn't want to talk to him and then play a gig an hour later,' says Neil. 'We wanted to have some time to let it settle.'

At the Paradiso club, a former church in Amsterdam, two fans climbed up on stage to sing an assured version of 'Better Be Home Soon'. Neil whipped backstage and emerged with a couple of Heinekens for them, saying, 'Here – you've earned it.' The last European gig before they flew to Glasgow was at the Theatrefabrik in Munich. For Tim, it was almost like a flashback to the Split Enz concert in Atlanta, in 1977, when the showdown with Phil Judd took place. He told Mike Chunn, 'I saw more clearly what was going on, and confronted it.'

In Glasgow, though, the band didn't manage to discuss the issue until a few hours before the show on 1 November. They sat in a hotel room and talked things out. 'He was immediately accepting of it,' says Neil.

'We laid our cards on the table,' says Hester, 'and Tim – graciously, as the rock gentleman that he is – just took it right on the chin and said, "Yes, I totally agree with you, let's nip it in the bud and get on with our lives." There was no bullshit, he just took his exit when the question was put to him.'

'He had to go, but it was very, very hard. For Neil and Tim to say "it isn't working", when it had actually worked beautifully. They had a great time in their lives, writing songs together, which they'd never done before. I don't think people realise that.'

(In 1994, Hester told Melbourne Tigers player Andrew Gaze, 'Neil couldn't say it. Nick was too scared to say it. I had to look young Timmy in the eyes and say: "You've been my landlord, you've been my soul brother, you got me into Split Enz and, well, you're sacked!" It was hard, but if we hadn't done it, we would've split up.')

Nick describes the meeting as 'impassioned and intense', but the issue was discussed 'maturely, objectively, succinctly. Everybody said their piece without actually alienating anyone. I believe that Tim became destructive, and forced the situation because he wasn't happy within the band.' Also present was Grant Thomas, who was impressed by how professionally it had been resolved. 'Everybody would like to think there were slanging matches – there were none.'

In Los Angeles, Gary Stamler received another 'out of the blue' phone call; he was used to them now. 'Virtually out of nowhere, almost as abruptly as it had started, it had ended. They'd resolved things, it was a mutual decision, and Tim and the band were going their separate ways.'

As Thomas took Tim to the airport bus, he thought what an odd position he was in. 'Here was I, taking an artist that I'm representing – and sending him on his way. And the next day, I would be organising what his next venture should be.' In the lift, Mark bumped into them. 'I said, "How's it going, Tim?" And he said, "Oh, good . . . they just sacked me", and he gave a little nervous laugh. He seemed surprised, but relieved. I said, "Well, now you can move on, do your own thing." It was the end of an awkward, intense time.'

Malcolm Hill had arrived in Glasgow on the same plane Tim was to take on the first leg of his journey back to Melbourne. 'As I walked into the hotel, they were all there, looking rather bemused. Grant pulled me to one side and said, "Well, we've had an interesting afternoon. Tim's on his way home." I said, "Is it permanent or temporary?" Grant said, "I think it's permanent this time." Then everybody seemed to shrug their shoulders and get on with it.'

Crowded House played two shows that night. The first was in the Glasgow club King Tut's, a dingy downstairs room that holds about 350 people. Angus Davidson remembers it as 'one of those gigs you don't look forward to'. Torrential rain was bucketing down as they arrived at the top of the rickety stairs to find the club jam-packed. 'There was a small stage and a dodgy PA and mixing desk, but the gig had so much energy. Because of what had happened, all the emotions were laid open. Everyone took a big deep breath. There was a great deal of relief – and also sadness. It was really emotional. The gig was phenomenal, the audience was singing louder than I could get the PA. It was a beautiful scene: full-voiced Scots singing along to all these songs. They'd caught on to this contagious atmosphere."

As soon as they left the stage, Hill drove them in a van the 40 miles to Edinburgh, where they appeared at an Aids benefit at the Music Box (Richard Thompson joining them for two songs). The show, which was broadcast live on the radio, didn't finish until 1.30am. Hill believes that the Aids benefit was instrumental in breaking Crowded House in Scotland. 'The fact that a band of that stature had done something like that really helped. A programmer from one of the Scottish radio stations opened up the floodgates to their music in Scotland. It was a big deal, playing two gigs, immediately after Tim left. They carried on, and they were capable of it.'

For Neil, it was a great relief to have the issue settled. 'Immediately, on stage, it felt more relaxed, more like it used to. Paul and Nick felt they were dealing with this brotherly thing, they couldn't really figure out this weird brotherly relationship. They were relieved.'

Paul points out that Tim had come into the band 'when we were floundering about, song-wise. He came in and inspired us. Then we took it on the road, and it was difficult to fit Tim in. We realised what we had: this intimate thing which had developed between us. Tim helped us appreciate that again. Even though at the time we might not have felt that way, in hindsight, it was a good thing.'

Also, says Paul, 'Tim and Neil had finally come back together to resolve something that didn't really get resolved in the Enz.'

'It was bad,' Tim told Mike Chunn, 'but I think our relationship would have deteriorated if we had been in the same band. It's the way we are. I've never doubted that it was the right thing to do. Maybe a little in the first week, because I was suddenly on my own again. I'm sure they were immensely relieved as well. I'd been a bit of a misery guts on the tour, especially towards the end."

Press release, November 5, 1991
Crowded House & Tim Finn
By mutual agreement of all concerned parties, Crowded House & Tim Finn have decided to go their separate ways.

The Finn Brothers and Crowded House were original entities and despite a great desire to blend the two, on stage, the four-piece ensemble ultimately proved too restrictive for everyone.

Neil and Tim will inevitably work together again.

Naturally Crowded House are as committed as ever to promoting

Woodface and future projects, while Tim is equally as eager to begin work on his next solo record.

Grant Thomas/Gary Stamler
Crowded House Management

The day after Tim's departure, Crowded House was in Dublin for the first time, 'endorsing everyone else's opinion of Guinness,' said Neil. He gave a hurried interview to New Zealand journalist Diana Balham, who filed her scoop home to the *Woman's Day* ('Why Tim Split . . . Neil Finn Tells'). 'Tim joined the band because we had written a whole lot of songs together and Crowded House seemed the best vehicle for them,' said Neil. 'It was good in context, but on tour Tim wasn't performing at his best. He didn't like taking a secondary role and we all felt restricted by his presence. It just wasn't feeling right. We did a lot of good shows, but it was a subtle thing. The positive side is that we are back to our old line-up, which we toured successfully for five years before Tim joined.'

That night at the Olympia Theatre, Neil told the audience, 'Tim says he's sorry he can't be here. He's down visiting a cousin in Cork.' A drunken fan called Joseph Moran passed the band a note, requesting they sing 'Better Be Home Soon'. Instead, they invited Moran up during the encore to sing it himself; he gave it 'a word-perfect, if slightly emotional reading'. But it was 'Don't Dream It's Over' which brought the house down. Paul could sense the crowd preferred the original version, but he reminded them, 'While we're asleep in bed with our ladyfriends, Paul Young's out there working for us.'

Like a bird released
• November 1991

'We haven't mentally given up on *Woodface* at all. It hasn't jumped out of the box, but it feels like success with it is in the realms of possibility.'

—Neil Finn, February 1992

Piggy-backing on Paul Young's hit of 'Don't Dream It's Over' was working: 'Fall At Your Feet' began to rise in the English charts. Because it now had a sales history, radio airplay increased – and it snowballed. Two days after the Dublin gig, the band was back in England, playing the Boardwalk in Manchester. In London, Mark Collen received the midweek chart: 'Fall At Your Feet' had reached No 27. They had expected only to enter the Top 40; this was the breakthrough they had been working towards. Collen drove up from London to tell the band the good news. 'This is it,' he said. 'We're off.'

When the official chart came out three days later, the news was even better: the confirmed position of the song was 22. At this stage, says Collen, 'there was overwhelming support for the band from the media and at retail. People wanted them to win.' Especially supportive were Chris Evans and David Hepworth at Greater London Radio (GLR) and Johnny Walker at the crucial national BBC station, Radio One. Help also came from unexpected quarters. On the Radio One programme *Round Table* – a show in which guests comment on the music played – Capitol stablemate Richard Marx and Australian compatriot Dannii Minogue went into a rave about Crowded House, Marx in particular enthusing about Neil's songwriting.

Mark Hart remembers that the band was relaxing in a coffee bar, playing pinball, when 'Grant came strutting in, goofy as ever. He told us that "Fall at Your Feet" had got to 17, then started giggling. We were very happy about that.'

'The band were working themselves to death,' says Collen, 'playing loads of acoustic sets on radio, doing the whole funny-guy routine. It worked a treat. I've never seen such a groundswell for a band. "Fall At Your Feet" took the album up to about 40,000 sold, but it was too late to get it into the shops in any great numbers before Christmas.'

('We did some appalling TV shows,' remembers Neil, 'such as *Pebble Mill* – a shocking blue-rinse lunchtime show. Because you're overseas, you don't know the territory, so you find yourself in these embarrassing situations ... perhaps I shouldn't be so precious.')

It was a frenetic week for Crowded House. The Manchester gig was on Monday; on Tuesday, they played Birmingham. On Wednesday, they made a quick visit to London to pre-record 'Fall At Your Feet' for the BBC's influential *Top of the Pops* television show, which screens to eight million people each Friday evening. The same night, they returned to Bristol, going on at the Bierkeller at midnight and playing till 2.30 in the morning. The following night, they were in Norwich, where a heckler harangued them about Tim's departure. The band responded by handing their instruments over to some fans during the encores, and leaving the stage. 'That was the ultimate,' Paul told *Q*. 'People pay to come in and see us – and end up playing the bloody songs themselves.'

While in London, Neil and Nick agreed at the last minute to perform on Greater London Radio, as the scheduled guest, Southside Johnny, had been delayed in Paris. In the studio was the young GLR producer Miles Mendoza, who put in a request for 'Mansion in the Slums'. Richard Skinner mentioned this on air, and Neil's response was, 'Wow – what a name. He should be a Brazilian pop star.' The next day, Mendoza was dubbing off a copy of the show, when a young woman visiting the station to be in a studio audience overheard it. She introduced herself as Lynn, a BBC-TV researcher who was a keen Crowded House fan and GLR listener.

That night, the English tour was coming to a climax with the first of two shows at the Town & Country Club in London, an old theatre with a large dance floor which had once been the orchestra pit. Everything was in place for two very special nights which have become legend, due to the release of a much-bootlegged promotional CD, and the use of many live tracks for B-sides. Angus Davidson was delighted to find a superb PA already installed in the Town & Country – for weeks, he had been grappling with an American system from Tasco, designed for heavy metal bands. 'Try Another Sound Company' had become his rueful joke. But the T&C system, he says, was 'second-to-none: a beautiful Midas XL3 desk and a whole lot of state-of-the-art stuff I'd never seen before.' By the second night, Davidson had it humming.

Most important, the band was relaxed, back to the Three Stooges again. Perhaps too much so, suggested *Melody Maker* reviewer Sally Margaret Joy, who found their antics undercut the emotions of the music. The songs, she wrote, make you 'close your eyes and let the thrilling feeling of loneliness surge up and overwhelm you'. But then the band pulled out a cardboard cutout of Rod Stewart and started to serenade it. Nick was the butt of all the jokes, smiling worriedly as he was hectored by Paul, and accused by Neil of 'moaning, woaning and whinging' throughout the tour. But, pointed out Joy, Neil's songs of hope and deliverance were perfect for unhappy people to sing along to. 'You spend a third of the evening with your heart in your mouth, another third fiddling with your watch, weeping crocodile tears of boredom, and chortling at their merry jokes in between.'

During the first show, Miles Mendoza failed to recognise Lynn when she said hello in the dark. Later that week, she wrote to ask for a cassette of the GLR session, and phoned a few times for research advice. 'Being the average bloke, the penny still didn't drop,' he says. 'I finally twigged that it might be a good idea if I asked her out. So I did – the gig was on November 9, 1991 and our first date was on November 30. Our son Henry was born on December 17, 1995 and we're getting married on July 12, 1996. Crowded House does this kind of thing to people.'

The Town & Country gigs finally laid a foundation in the United Kingdom on which Crowded House could develop a following. Once again, it was their intimate live shows that convinced both the record company and audience that this band was special; after a Crowded House show, those present felt as if they hadn't just seen the band, but had met them. Slowly, also, the music critics were getting the point. David Hepworth of GLR and Q (a convert since Temple) suggests that the same elements which won over the audience – the talking, skylarking and musical spontaneity – were those which prevented his colleagues from taking them seriously. 'Journalists looking for something to point at would very often say they went too far with all that arsing around,' he says. 'But the audience love it – it's been a really important part of their appeal.'

The week of the Town & Country shows, the band finally got a positive report in the usually dismissive NME: 'Crowded House are not bland,' wrote Stuart Maconie. 'They're not Nine Inch Nails (thank God); but they're a long way from the hollow, smoochy vapidity of your Simple Minds and your Phil Collins.' The headline: They Vegemite Be Giants.

In tapes from the mixing desk at the Town & Country, the band sounds weary but good natured. As Neil strums the swing rhythm to open 'Sister Madly', he threatens that the band will work its way through the Top 30, though they don't know half the songs. 'But God knows, that's never stopped us in the past.' Instead, after a slinky piano solo from Mark Hart, Nick slips into the seminal riff of 'Smoke on the Water': *duh duh duh, duh duh duh-duh* ... The others join in for a verse, then Paul throws it back at him: 'Well, Nick – you know the rules. You start 'em, you finish 'em.' So Nick obliges with the words, before Neil segues from 'This is Massive', to the riff of the '70s Jethro Tull standard, 'Locomotive Breath'.

'It's Only Natural' shows the band is still working out its arrangements and dynamics since the departure of Tim. With only one acoustic guitar – and despite Nick and Paul's backing vocals – without Tim's harmony to fatten the melody, the sound is sparse. Mark is exploring his parts on guitar and keyboards. A roar goes up as Neil begins the Maori strum to introduce 'Don't Dream It's Over'. 'In the words of Bono,' he says, 'this is a song that Paul Young sang – we're stealing it back.' That the band's close-knit camaraderie has returned is apparent on an emotional 'Better Be Home Soon'; feeling it, the crowd join in. They are not yet ready for a singalong on 'Weather With You', but the band gives them a go. Neil has to rescue them by improvising, 'On the other side of the world, the strawberries are about to be picked ...'

Crowded House had turned a corner in the *Woodface* campaign; they were on the home straight. England seduced, they were heading for their Christmas break. At the final farewells, Paul called to the audience, 'Thanks for coming down – we'll be back. We want to get in trouble and get locked up in this country. See you later.'

The band was on a roll, says Mark Collen. 'They were buzzing, really happy.' They were also worn out, and desperate for a holiday. First, however, there were nearly two dozen more dates to do in the United States. With one member less than on their earlier visit, the daily press in North America enthusiastically ran with the 'Crowded House Less Crowded' angle. In interviews, the band were frank about the reasons. Speaking from London a few days after Tim left, Nick told the Hartford (Connecticut) *Courant*, 'There's a lot more room now – physically, emotionally and musically. Now we can all fit into the rental car. It had been coming for about a week. It wasn't until Neil started feeling a sense of self-consciousness on stage that it became apparent. When he started to feel it, it was obvious we were going to change the onstage dynamic.

'Tim felt extremely frustrated. He didn't have enough to do in all of the songs. We'd come off stage after having a great night, and he would have had a terrible night. After we had a terrible night, he'd have a great night. I started putting two and two together that perhaps it was because we weren't connecting on stage.

'Tim never was much of an instrumentalist. That's probably what was at the bottom of the whole issue: how much he felt like a spare prick on a wedding night.' They had done some great shows with Tim, said Nick with the reviews and audience response all positive. 'But something was different.' Everyone was still good friends, he stressed, and Tim and Neil still brothers. They'd been through it once before in Split Enz ('a much stronger parting'). All it meant was that Crowded House was 'back to being Larry, Curly and Moe.'

After the Town & Country gigs, the band headed to Jamaica for a 10-day holiday with their families, during which Neil wrote 'Fingers of Love', inspired by the heavenly sight of the sun's beams shining through the clouds. Then they were immediately back on the road. The winter leg of the US tour began in Chicago, with School of Fish – a new Capitol Records signing – along as opening act. They headed down the east coast to the southern states. Tour fatigue was setting in. Neil describes the symptoms: 'too many miles, not enough sleep, wanking record company people, ignorant journalists, a record fading out of sight, crappy hotel rooms . . . a combination of factors, not just one of them on its own. People have different thresholds. I probably had more tolerance than Tim, but he'd been doing it longer than me. Phil Judd only lasted one American tour. Other people would say, how could you have a better lifestyle, it's ideal – Nick Seymour for one. It depends on your makeup.'

As the tour headed south, Neil got the flu. When the band arrived in Athens, Georgia, he was at a low ebb. Only half the tickets had been sold, and no-one from REM got in touch ('One of those things you think when you're in a dark mood already'). So he went out walking the streets, feeling sorry for himself. A man came up to him and introduced himself as a big fan of Crowded House. Mike Guthrie owned a small vintage guitar store, and invited Neil to come and have a look. 'He was a nice guy, and I saw this Gretsch I quite fancied, but thought, oh I shouldn't buy it, I'm feeling too pessimistic.' Back at the concert, just before the band went on, the guitar collector arrived, Gretsch in hand. Guthrie said to Neil, 'I want you to have this, I really dig your songwriting – write some songs on it.'

'It was a really nice gesture,' says Neil, 'it completely turned the day around. You can't wallow in your own misfortune for too long.'

By Memphis, however, the band were getting scratchy with each other. After the gig at the New Dixie, on Beale Street, local music critic Belinda Killough was alone at the stage door, planning to pass on the regards of mutual friends. But security wouldn't let her in. Later, the promoter told her why: Crowded House were having a heated argument in the dressing room.

'It had to be frustrating for the band – it was for me,' says Hale Milgrim. 'I don't remember Neil being uptight or upset other than saying, "Hale, what else should we be doing?" Which made it more frustrating for me, because he was bending over backwards. At the same time, I had them so busy in so many different territories, it wasn't like there was all this free time for them to figure out, well, why isn't it happening in America?'

The mood could shift from angst to anarchy day by day. The last gigs of the 1991 tour were in Los Angeles, in the week before Christmas. The support act School of Fish had entered into the Crowded House spirit during the tour, but it was a risk trying to play tricks with the masters. At the Wiltern theatre in Los Angeles they got in too far, playing strip poker on stage. Angus Davidson watched from the mixing desk: 'By the end of something poignant, like "Don't Dream It's Over", they'd got down to their jocks.'

As they left the stage, Paul wasn't that impressed. 'Well, that was hopeless,' he said, 'they didn't even get their clothes off.' Neil picked up on it, saying, 'Is that a challenge, Paul? You could have done better, eh?'

'Yeah, I reckon. I usually go all the way.'

'Go on, then.'

'No, no,' said Paul. 'I'll take my time.'

At the end of the show, while the audience was calling for an encore, Paul came out alone, wearing a red Santa Claus suit, playing heavy metal 'Star-Spangled Banner' licks on a guitar. Three-thousand people watched, transfixed, as he went into a rap and started to undress. Soon, only the hat remained – and the crowd was in an uproar.

'He was bollock naked,' says Nick, 'five feet away from the noses of all the young women that were crushed up against the stage, talking about what it's like to be in a band without any sense of self-consciousness. It was a sublime moment.'

From the mixing-desk, Davidson worried about what was going to happen next. 'Here's this skinny little guy with his willy sticking out. He takes the mike and says, "Angus, give me some reverb ... this is something I've always wanted to do ..." I'm thinking, Oh no – he's going to do a fart – this is like Jim Morrison. The cops are going to be here any moment ...

'But he sticks the mike in his groin and turns away from the audience. He started hitting the top of the mike, as if he's whacking himself off, while looking over his shoulder at the crowd. Everyone was in hysterics. He bowed, and walked off. It brought the house down.'

'I thought it went too far,' says Nick, 'but it came off beautifully. I knew he could go wherever he wanted, and we were happy to let him. But there were people at that show who were absolutely offended. I still thought it was the funniest thing. To have a mother and father watching the same band as their little boy, who thinks it's fantastic, while they're really pissed off. They hadn't paid money to see a grown man naked.'

Next day, the crew visited the Capitol tower, which was alive with gossip about the incident. Hale Milgrim had been at the show and when he saw Arlo and the lighting tech Steve Swift, he said, 'I can't believe what Paul did last night.' They waited for a scolding. 'I thought it was great!' Milgrim had videoed the show, and the tape was circulating the Tower to everyone's amusement. Others may have seen the striptease in a negative light, says Milgrim. 'I didn't – it was great, fabulous. Paul being Paul, taking it to the limit.'

'They loved it,' says Paul. 'Come on – if anything happens in that town, it's good news.'

An arduous but productive year had come to an end. Although the band hadn't recaptured its audience in the United States, they had finally made some headway in the United Kingdom and Europe. As they headed home to Melbourne for Christmas with their families, they determined that Europe was where they would concentrate their efforts in the next year.

Nick wrote to fans in the January club newsletter: 'Tis truly brilliant to be back home from the most gruelling tour ever. Five-and-a-half months, although we had 10 days off in sunny Jamaica. We have a month off in Melbourne. Off? We're rehearsing new material for the next lot of touring, February through April 1992, England, Europe and Australia . . . a new album commencing sometime this year as well. This, of course, being the album I ask *my* brother to contribute to.'

The next decision was crucial: which song would be best to follow up 'Fall At Your Feet'? 'Weather With You' seemed to get everyone's vote; the English record company was enthusiastic about the song, particularly Mark Collen.

Recharging back home in Melbourne after Christmas, Crowded House decided that the video for 'Weather' would show them going on a summer holiday. Compared to the baroque extravaganza of 'Chocolate Cake', the video had the production values of a home movie. If it looks like a Sunday picnic, it is because the shoot was exactly that. The band borrowed quirky classic cars from friends; the Fiat sedan driven by Neil is a well-known sight around the streets of

St Kilda. The director, Macgregor Knox, borrowed the humble caravan off his brother. 'That was probably the easiest video we ever made,' says Nick, 'because we were making it up as we went along. The way it looks is in fact what transpired on the day.'

It was like a day-at-the-beach for the extended family, with the band's partners (Brenda, Mardi and Sharon) taking part, along with the Finn children Liam and Elroy, plus the family dalmatian Lester. Noel Crombie directed the second-unit camera, his wife Sally Ann Mill organised the wardrobe. The location was the Bellarine Peninsula, near Queenscliff at the bottom of Melbourne's Port Phillip Bay. The unpretentious holiday resort there has the ambience of an English caravan park from the 1950s. Nick took his jet-black 1961 T-Bird convertible out for the day. 'It was the height of summer, but not too hot. With the top down, it's very pleasant, everything seems to be going in slow motion.'

The Queenscliff holidaymakers joined in the frisbee frolics and beach races; the local police became extras when they pulled Nick over for driving the unregistered left-hand-drive T-Bird, an 'unroadworthy' vehicle in the eyes of the state of Victoria. Of course, they had to take it for a road test, driving around the carpark, waving their hats; the footage made the incident look like something out of *Candid Camera*.

While making the video, Nick had visions of 'Something So Strong': that the image they were projecting was too tongue-in-cheek, too cute. 'But at that particular period of Crowded House, it was how we were living in Melbourne for the most part. Neil was very settled into his family life there, and there was the legacy of Split Enz families also. Very comfortable – possibly too comfortable. Nonetheless, it ended up being captured in that video quite nicely. The irony was, the American record company just didn't get it. They thought they'd sent us all this money and we'd kept it, just put it into our pockets and gone out with a Super-8 camera and filmed stuff.'

Back in Hollywood, Capitol executives – and Hale Milgrim in particular – hated the clip. Tony Wadsworth of Parlophone was in Los Angeles when the video arrived at the Tower, and watched it with Milgrim: 'He was viewing it with an American perspective, and he was furious. He was saying, "They've gone away and made a holiday video!" even though he passionately loved the band. He asked me what I thought. I said, well, we took delivery of it the other day, and it's already been played twice in the UK. To me, that says it's a great video. He said, "I still think it's shit."' Milgrim thought there was little chance of the clip getting played in the US. 'It just wasn't what MTV was showing,' he says. 'That was a very difficult video.'

Mick Kleber, head of video production at Capitol, says, 'It wasn't the kind of thing where you say, "Wow, what a video!" But it became a big hit in Britain, so maybe they were right. I have this theory, that in England, if you come in the winter with a video that's summery and makes everybody think, "Wow, I'm gonna get off on a great vacation", there's a real embrace of that idea. Here was a song and video that was mana from heaven to a British population in the depths of winter. I've never heard anybody talk about their vacations more than British people. For me, living in Southern California, *this* is where people come for their vacations. I walk out my front door and I think, Hey, it's great to be here. I don't even need to go on vacation.'

The British, of course, are notorious for an obsession with the weather. So perhaps they romanticised about the sunny mood of the video (which contradicted its lyrics, another reason Kleber was sceptical), and related to the Butlins-holiday-camp images of the clip. But another factor helped get the message across: Parlophone edited the song itself, so that it arrived at the chorus more quickly.

Mark Collen was the one who suggested the unthinkable to Neil. 'I said it needed an edit, it didn't work. Neil agreed, but didn't know how we should do it. I said, bring the chorus forward. At the moment it goes, *verse verse, chorus chorus chorus.* It needs to go *verse chorus, verse chorus, chorus.*'

Collen took the master into NoNoise Editing, put 'Weather With You' up on the computer, and digitally restructured it. The song remains the same length – 3'44" – but makes an abrupt change at the end of the first verse. It occurs at 1'13", after Julius Caesar and the Roman Empire fail to conquer the blue sky, and the 'While My Guitar Gently Weeps' guitar motif. Instead of the small china boat going nowhere on the mantlepiece, the universally identifiable chorus line makes its entrance: '*Everywhere you go, you always take the weather with you . . .*'

Collen sent the results over to Neil. 'He said, "Well, I don't like it but . . . you guys seem to know what you're doing, give it a crack." '

Mitchell Froom wasn't consulted – and wasn't impressed. 'Oh man, who did that?' he says. The industry-jaundiced Froom won't let A&R people have any input into his projects. 'They've never made a suggestion that's a good one. Suggestions happen after the fact, and usually they'll say something stupid. Like, there's an organ on the track – and they say, "Why don't you put an organ on the track?" The level of musicality we're dealing with is so low it's amazing.'

The English company was certain it had something building for Crowded House, and asked for financial support from Capitol for a marketing plan and a tour. Capitol had already spent close to US$1 million on *Woodface*, with the album's lengthy, complicated recording, and costly videos. Also, there was the cost of supporting tours in hitherto unresponsive territories such as the UK. 'Hale was responsible for financing all these expeditions,' says Stamler, 'and was willing to spend lots of money freighting gear from Australia to America and England and Europe, back and forth. That was horrendously expensive – on top of a horrendously expensive album that was really recorded twice. The amount of money spent to launch that album was astronomic, for a band with the sales of Crowded House. The problem we had was, with the exception of the UK, *Woodface* had gone backwards in every other market in the world. At that point, it had been a disappointment.'

Tension increased between the two managers, Gary Stamler and Grant Thomas, who had differing opinions about what the band should do next. Thomas was bullish about working the European market which was showing such promise; he didn't want the band to lose ground, as it had done in America. He also felt that the success of *Woodface* in Australia justified further investment from Capitol, even if the interest in Europe didn't develop into anything. Stamler agreed, but being in Los Angeles was sensitive about antagonising the company's relationship with the band.

There had recently been a series of high-level meetings at EMI, the parent company of both Capitol and Parlophone, to establish the priorities for the next financial quarter and the year ahead. At the time Parlophone wanted to mount their campaign, says Stamler, 'the climate around Crowded House and the success-for-dollars-spent was not very positive.'

Stamler had an awkward conversation with Milgrim and Capitol's head of international marketing at the time, Tom Corson. 'We were trying to talk Hale into allowing this project to go forward.' But neither Corson nor Stamler knew that Milgrim had just come back from an international meeting at which the sales returns of Crowded House were discussed. The pair tried to convince Milgrim to invest more money, 'in the face of this massive expenditure and this unsatisfactory result,' says Stamler.

At the end of the meeting, Milgrim asked Corson to leave the room. He turned to Stamler and said, 'I've got to tell you Gary, what I was told in this meeting about Crowded House. I was told in no uncertain terms not to spend any more money on this project. There was to be no discussion about it – this project was finished. And now you're asking me to spend probably another US$120,000 to support this single. What would you do if you were in my position?'

That put Stamler on the spot; he was as close to Milgrim as he was to the band. They were asking for a lot of money, with no guarantee of success. The English were enthusiastic, had a sound marketing plan and a lot of confidence. But there had never been any major success in England, a country with a volatile singles market.

'If I was in your position,' he said to Milgrim, 'I'd do it.'

'The full impact of that took days to sink into me,' says Stamler. 'I remember asking Hale if he thought he was doing the right thing, and he said, "Well, you gave me the opportunity to get this job." He felt he owed me this opportunity to follow out my instincts, and not to worry, we'd work it out some way or other.'

It was yet another fork in the road for Crowded House, a defining moment in the band's history. It's ironic, says Stamler, that Milgrim was involved in two of the most important decisions of the band's career: declining to put out the original *Woodface*, and deciding to go against his instructions to stop investing in Crowded House.

'To me, it just made sense,' says Milgrim. 'The British had a whole book of different market plans, so I just said, you guys stay out on the road and I'll continue to seed the money where it's needed. I felt I'd be able to take that story and translate it back to America. But we kept on hitting this invisible wall of radio not touching it. By that time we were quite a few months into it.'

'He trusted us, that's what it was,' says Mark Collen. 'It's very simple, we said, give us the band and we'll do this – and we delivered. That's how it works. You chase a hit wherever you can get it.'

In February 1992, Parlophone in England released the edited 'Weather With You'. There were two formats for the CD single, one offering three 'Byrdhouse' tracks recorded live back in 1989 with Roger McGuinn, the other with three live tracks from the Town & Country Club gigs, including the first official appearance of 'Walking On the Spot'. Parlophone was beginning to take advantage of the dedicated fanbase which was developing. Releasing several formats of a single which include extra tracks is a way of dealing with the fickle British charts. Companies can either go for a high chart entry in the first week by releasing all the different formats at once, or dribble them out to keep the single alive in the charts. Unless a single achieves massive success quickly, and crosses to radio, it may last only a couple of weeks in the upper reaches of the charts. As always, the idea is to get airplay to encourage album sales; in general, singles don't make a profit. The practice is seen as a necessary evil – it means the fans are compelled to buy three different versions of the same single – but Crowded House were insistent that the fans were given value for money. 'They can hold their heads up high, because everything we issued was worth having,' says Malcolm Hill of Parlophone. 'It wasn't just different mixes, but whole new songs, live songs – things people genuinely wanted.'

At the same time, Crowded House flew back to the northern hemisphere for three weeks of dates in the Netherlands, Belgium and Britain. (While touring *Woodface* they were to make six visits to England in a 12-month period.) During the UK shows – all outside London – it was apparent their audience had grown in size and fervour; fans such as Miles Mendoza were by now following them from gig to gig. *Vox* called the band the 'prank-playing Antipodean trio who attract teenyboppers and tactfully-tailored thirtysomethings in equal measure'; it was a ponderous but accurate description. Their reputation for unpredictable stunts intensified with mid-song phone calls, Paul stripping for a dare and cartwheeling across the stage and, most notoriously, appearing on the children's morning TV show *Going Live*. Host Phillip Schofield (an ageless elf who got his start on New Zealand television) asked the band to provide a question for a competition. To his horror, Paul suggested, 'Which member of the band is not circumcised?'

The band was in London, checking out of the Langholm Hilton, when they heard the news: 'Weather With You' had gone to number seven in the UK charts. Tim was back in Melbourne, working on his solo album. He was at Neil and Sharon's Murchison Street house – where he often stayed after leaving the band – when the fax arrived. Finally, a song he had co-written had entered the UK Top 10. It had even beaten the position of 'I Got You' 12 years earlier. Rikki Morris remembers being there when Tim heard the news. 'He was like a little boy, absolutely stoked. You could see it. I congratulated him and he said, "I've been waiting for this moment all my life, it's something I've always wanted. It's like a dream."'

'What a thrill,' says Tim. 'To have a hit single in England, of a song we'd written together – there couldn't have been anything better.'

They returned to Australia in mid-March for the Then There Were Three tour. The title said it was back to business as usual for the trio (plus Mark Hart), and acknowledged that the experiment with Tim hadn't worked live.

The tour began in Western Australia; the second show was in the spectacular outdoor setting of the Belvoir Ampitheatre, a natural soundshell in a field by a river, surrounded by bluegums. Next stop was Adelaide, for two appearances at the Womad festival, the annual celebration of 'world music and dance'. Also featured were acts such as Remmy Ongala, Nusrat Fateh Ali Khan, Voices of Georgia and Aboriginal singer Archie Roach (Tim and Neil had sung backing vocals on 'Down City Streets', on Roach's 1990 album *Charcoal Road*). The band were stunned by the diversity, colour and musicality of the performers. After their set, they phoned Tim from the dressing room to tell him about the South American bands on the bill. The next day, he arrived from Melbourne and joined the band on stage for a couple of songs.

Two sold-out nights at Sydney's opulent State Theatre showed the band was once again on a high. The spirit continued at the next gig, in Newcastle, just north of Sydney, which Crowded House regards as one of its most memorable (several songs from the night were included on the live 'bonus' CD which came with *Recurring Dream*). In 1996 Paul told Melbourne journalist Andrew Tanner, 'The Newcastle show really stands out in my mind as one of our best. We'd had an exceptionally good evening just on our own. We went down to the beach in the tour van – Nick put on his roller blades and we were towing him behind the van in the carpark, whipping him off into the corners. We were trying to hurt him – actually, in the end, we were trying to *kill* him – the whole affair became very feverish and out of control! Anyway, we went back to the theatre and the moment kind of carried on onto the stage – it was just a magic night.'

The tour continued up to the Gold Coast before returning to Sydney for the massive 'Concert for Life' benefit gig in Centennial Park. The outdoor concert was organised to raise funds for Aids research and the St Vincent's Hospital, but it later became controversial when the posturing of the headline act, INXS, led critics to question the benefit's expenses versus final proceeds. Besides Crowded House, other acts featured on the bill included Diesel, Ratcat, Yothu Yindi, Deborah Conway and Jenny Morris, plus cameos from Kate Ceberano, Chris Bailey, Jimmy Barnes and Richard Clapton. But unquestionably the stars were to be INXS, who arrived with a bevy of security guards, cordoned themselves off from the other acts and their families backstage, and were the only act permitted to use smoke machines and a light show. Perhaps time was up for INXS with the critics, but their behaviour didn't help. Michael Hutchence, dressed in white, struck messianic poses and finally deigned to speak to the crowd six songs in. 'Hello,' he said. 'You all turned up. Let's just play some fucking music.'

By contrast, Crowded House won over everyone present, forming a bond between band and audience. Not just content with leading the spirited singalongs, they orchestrated the Mexican waves, commentated as the crowd built human pyramids or engaged in blanket tossing, mocked the inclement weather, and threw drumsticks into the front rows. Wrote John Tingwell in *Drum Media*, 'Crowded House managed to whip up the spirits in an alarmingly short period of time, thanks mainly to the cheekiest man in rock, Paul Hester ... halfway through INXS's set, it was made painfully clear that it was Crowded House's day.'

Crowded House then headed to New Zealand for a two-week national tour, which was almost postponed when the band was invited to perform 'Weather With You' on a high-rating German television show. That plan was quickly scrapped when it turned out to be a game show for newly-weds. As the New Zealand tour began, the news arrived that *Woodface* was now at number six in the UK album charts, and had 'gone gold' there (100,000 sold). It was at number five in New Zealand but, per capita, the sales were far higher: the album was about to reach double-platinum (30,000).

In press interviews, Neil was fired up by the English success and looking forward to the band's return to Europe. 'The album has come back from the dead,' he told Wellington's *Evening Post*. 'I know people have always had their doubts about this album, but I've always had faith in it. For a while it seemed that we were beating our heads against a wall, but it's nice to be reassured that with hard work and perseverance that things can turn around.' Despite Tim's departure from the band, he was now in a 'sweet position', joked Neil. 'We're out here pushing the album, and he's sitting back at home raking in the royalties.' The fact that the split was amicable and mutual was made clear by the occasional 'guest appearance' Tim made during the tour to sing harmony on 'It's Only Natural' and 'Chocolate Cake'.

In several centres, second shows were added and new songs such as 'Dust From a Distant Sun' and 'Tail of the Comet' unveiled. While in Auckland, the band played a spontaneous lunch-time concert in Aotea Square to raise funds for the Maori band Moana and the Moahunters, who had been invited by the Neville Brothers to attend the New Orleans Jazz and Heritage Festival. The benefit was the first major concert held in the square since the 1984 event which had turned into a riot. Neil remarked that the venue should be used for more concerts – the good humour of the audience wiped the circumstances of the last one.

The band's two nights at the Founders' Theatre in Hamilton were a special celebration for Neil. It had been over three years since Crowded House had played Hamilton, on the Schnell Fenster tour. Now, Neil Finn was again returning on a high. New Zealand had never seemed so positive; it had been a nostalgic, uplifting visit. At the end of the first night, while he idly strummed an acoustic guitar, he shared his feelings with the devoted local audience.

'It's great coming home,' he said, 'seeing all the familiar places on the drive down from Auckland. Driving through Pokeno and Mercer. Past the Meremere coal mines and the Huntly power station. Bypassing Hamilton to visit Mum and Dad in Cambridge. Having lunch at my sister's. Having the Caseys and the Gallaghers round for afternoon tea . . .'

The nonchalant strumming evolved into the most basic of chord changes: C . . . A minor . . . E minor . . . G . . . then Neil croaked out the first line: *'Somewhere deep inside, something's got a hold on you . . .'* It was 'Better Be Home Soon'.

Four weeks' break were scheduled before the band was to embark on a strenuous but triumphant return to Europe. But there was no time for a holiday. Instead they rehearsed for the tour and spent a few days shooting a video for the next single, 'Four Seasons in One Day'.

For some years, New Zealand film-makers Kerry Brown and Bruce Sheridan had been lobbying Neil to have a video made in his birthplace. They were in the process of making a documentary about Split Enz, *Spellbound*, when one of their video submissions finally got the nod from Capitol in LA. Their vision – to emphasise the surreal, fantasy qualities of the song, using New Zealand landscapes – clicked with that of Mick Kleber, head of video at Capitol.

Brown and Sheridan spent a week travelling around the South Island, shooting background footage of locations such as the rugged West Coast and its wild beaches and dense native bush, the scorched plains of Central Otago and the preserved Victorian architecture of Oamaru. At night, Brown leafed through a book of Salvador Dali prints, getting ideas that could give the New Zealand scenery a psychedelic twist in post-production. They planned to use composite photography to blend their footage with shots of the band. Capitol was hesitant about having such a complex video shot so far away (Sheridan gasped as the vast contract spewed out of his fax machine, claiming such things as 'proprietory rights in all the planets in the solar system'), so Kleber went down to oversee the editing.

When the band arrived in Christchurch to begin filming, the atmosphere was tense. Brown was perturbed to see a fatigued Paul 'disappear into a black cloud' for a day, then bounce back the next. The band and the filmmakers were nervous about each other's ability to perform; the musicians were jaded after the solid touring, and jaded about making videos.

But things quickly thawed as the band was filmed in a range of dramatic settings and they all stayed in cheap smalltown motels. Stumbling across an Anzac Day dawn ceremony (which pays tribute to the war casualties of Australia and New Zealand) they made use of the iconography: marching girls, boy scouts and old soldiers congregating at a modest cenotaph. They filmed Nick painting at an easel, using chromakey technology to bring images of the band members through the canvas. Meanwhile, on the skyline, storm clouds loomed: they rushed the band on and off a bus at each location to stay a few hundred metres ahead of autumn downpours.

The result was a lavish, Dali-esque video, which won its makers an award from Australian *Rolling Stone*, and Kleber regards as Crowded House's best clip after 'Don't Dream It's Over'. 'Out of 700 videos I worked on at Capitol, it's one of the few I feel good about. But I don't know if anyone really felt *Woodface* was going to be brought back to life by it, that "Four Seasons" was going to be a radio hit.'

This time, Hale Milgrim felt the video was perfect for MTV and VH1, but neither channel was interested beyond a few isolated screenings. 'It just wasn't what they were showing. MTV felt the band wasn't having the hits, so they weren't going to go out on a limb and support it themselves. It was very frustrating for me.'

Woodface had achieved massive sales in the UK and in many European markets for the first time. But in the United States, the album had run out of steam. Stamler and Milgrim were watching the success of 'Weather With You', trying to think of ways to achieve the same results in the States. 'We thought we'd missed something,' says Julie Borchard. 'The record business has a saying – "A hit is a hit is a hit" – so we thought we'd revisit it. Unfortunately, it didn't manifest itself here.' Capitol sent copies of the song to TV weather shows, and picked up some airtime but couldn't translate it into sales. The marketing department sent out maps of the world, with flags signalling the countries where the song had been a Top 10 hit. But the reaction from radio programmers was cynical, says Stamler. 'They'd make typical disparaging programmer comments like, "When my antenna hits London, then I'll put the record on",' he says.

'Radio programmers don't care if it's a hit in England,' says Denise Skinner, 'They only care about what's selling in Des Moines, Iowa. And what people were interested in buying was grunge. It was just starting to happen. Hootie and the Blowfish would never have made it when *Woodface* came out because that's not what people were interested in. People who were going into the record stores weren't interested in that type of sound. The baby boomers were buying Bonnie

Raitt and a lot of catalogue, reissues – because radio wasn't exposing them to anything they liked.'

Grant Thomas describes the shift in US radio in the early '90s: 'Here we were with a song like "Weather With You", a really melodic, great pop song. And on radio you've got Pearl Jam, Smashing Pumpkins, Red Hot Chili Peppers and Nirvana: really aggressive, youth-driven, angry music.'

Most disappointed about the lack of success was Hale Milgrim. 'To me it just made sense, when you're having that kind of success, that you'd be able to translate that back in America. But every time I tried, we reached this invisible wall of radio not touching it. And it gets very difficult to continue a project that isn't getting a few stations in different markets really exploding it. And it just wasn't getting to that. I started going, okay, forget about the whole country, let's just pick some markets that we can get something going, then try and get it to the next level.'

Crowded House headed back to Europe in early June for two months of dates. To their relief, the hard work had finally paid off: they had developed a loyal fanbase and broken free of the expatriates. 'We're not letting any Australians in when we play London this time,' Paul said to Phil Sutcliffe of Q magazine. 'It's show your passports at the door from now on. Nobody with a smile on their face gets in.'

Their English record company had made sure everything was in place. 'Four Seasons in One Day' reached 17 in the charts, and major articles and advertisements appeared simultaneously in Q, Vox and Record Collector magazines. 'If there were a Booker prize for records,' gushed the Q ad copy written by Mark Collen, 'surely Woodface would win it.'

'The way the band seduced the company was great, and the way they seduced me was brilliant,' says Collen. The band had heard that Collen was about to get married, and asked Malcolm Hill for advice about a wedding present. When Collen drove up to Wolverhampton to see them at the Civic Hall, they threw a surprise party backstage, and presented him with a large barbeque umbrella. 'They'd had it trucked up to Wolverhampton, carried up six flights of stairs, and set it up in their dressing room. That's an example of what they're like: they're real people, always very matey. That was their magic, their charm.'

Everyone working with the band felt like part of a family, through good times and bad, says Emma Banks, their UK agent. 'They're great people to be with, all separate identities, friendly and involved.

There's a great atmosphere around them, even when they're falling out with each other, or locked in a huddle in a room because they're dissecting everything. They come out and they get over it. It's like being with your brothers.'

To *Vox*, Neil described relationships within the band as 'fragile', 'volatile' and 'hopelessly untogether'. He made a comparison to Split Enz, a band he saw as built on friendships and family. 'In Crowded House we're close, but the band didn't develop out of friends getting together.' The journalist, Steve Malins, surmised, 'Perhaps it's this uneasy combination of tension and humour which distinguishes Crowded House from yer average smoothly produced AOR act.'

One year and 12 days after the showcase gig at the Borderline, a London club holding not much more than 200 people, Crowded House filled the prestigious Wembley Arena with nearly 12,000 fans. To maintain some intimacy with the crowd, Neil and Paul popped up in the middle of the audience during the show, playing a couple of songs on acoustics standing beside the mixing desk at the back of the stalls. During the encore, they produced a surprise: Tim Finn, strolling on stage to celebrate his 40th birthday with a scorching version of 'Chocolate Cake' and a triumphant 'Weather With You'. The band then emphasised their camaraderie with a stirring 'Throw Your Arms Around Me'. At the backstage party afterwards, Tim and Neil displayed their harmonies for those present with an a capella rendition of the Irish ballad 'The Parting Glass'. Tim stayed on to be the support act at many of the UK dates.

They then headed for the Continent, where Crowded House was booked to perform at several summer festivals. Also on the bill was Little Village, the short-lived rootsy supergroup of Ry Cooder, John Hiatt, Jim Keltner and Nick Lowe. In Belgium they had a reunion with Keltner, Nick inviting him to share a few beers in his hotel room with Neil, Mark and Nick Lowe. Ironically, Keltner wanted to know how they got a good drum sound in the monitors; Lowe grilled Nick about his bass amp. Crowded House repaid the favour of Keltner teaching them how to play a shuffle by introducing him to their sophisticated style of making paper planes. The competitive launching of elaborate planes from hotel rooms was a legacy of Split Enz, says Neil. 'It's because you're in little cocoons all the time – hotel rooms, buses, planes – so the idea of sending something sailing off into the night is the best feeling.'

The tour opened up many new countries for the band, thanks to saturation radio play of 'Weather With You' in the influential German market. But, by the time they got to the last few dates, a series of gigs in Spain culminating in a performance at the World Expo in Seville, they were exhausted. They took a day off in Valencia and spent it at the beach. 'We had a great time,' says Neil. 'We ate well, drank well, and had a big crew/band extravaganza where everybody imbibed some substance or other. It was a wonderful, indulgent day on the beach for the whole tour party – except for Nick, who was traditionally hard to rouse. So he spent all day wandering along one beach down, looking for us. But it was 24 hours we paid for the next day.' The band caught a plane to the Expo at Seville, where the stage was set up in direct sunlight, beneath the biggest video screen ever built. 'It was stinking hot,' says Neil, 'and the very first shot of us showed Paul, telling the cameraman to *fuck off*. We'd had a really big spat that day. I was a little shell-shocked, and hadn't had any sleep – and he was really black, which was why he was yelling at the cameraman.'

Mark describes Paul's mood that day as 'really, really, *really* dark. We didn't even ask him along to do some interviews – "just stay at the hotel, please". He was having a really bad time, I don't know why. He wasn't being vocal about it, just physical – walking in, walking out, being rude to people. Not saying what he was upset about, but you definitely knew.'

The final gig of the *Woodface* tour was a television broadcast for MTV Europe in Barcelona. After the filming, Neil flew to Dublin to spend time in Ireland with his parents and Tim. The rest of the band headed home, weary.

'Things with Paul were beginning to get a little bit untidy,' says Gary Stamler. The band had been furiously promoting *Woodface* for over a year, and Paul had had enough of the gruelling campaign and the relentless travelling. The first the English record company became aware of problems with Paul was in September, when they asked the band to appear on *Top of the Pops* in support of the single 'It's Only Natural'. It meant Crowded House had to fly from Melbourne to London, just for the filming. 'There was always a reluctance to do *Top of the Pops*,' says Malcolm Hill, 'and it's a long way to come for a TV show.'

Feeling pressured, the band agreed, so the record company confirmed that they would be available. Then a problem arose: 'Paul absolutely refused to do it,' says Stamler, who was in London at the time. With Tim Finn, he was staying at Richard Thompson's house while Tim was recording his solo album. This put Hill in an awkward spot. 'I can't just turn up and say, I'm sorry but the band aren't doing it anymore. The show just doesn't wear things like that, and it damages the rest of my roster.'

Hill was on holiday when the crisis blew up. 'It completely ruined the holiday – I spent most of it talking to Australia and LA and

London, trying to persuade the band and trying to keep the TV show happy. They aren't the slightest bit interested in what your problems are – you've said you're going to deliver something, and you deliver it, mate – or your balls are off.'

The record company bombarded Stamler with faxes, 'imploring me to pick up the phone and call Paul, and try to talk him into coming to England. The UK company felt it was of extreme importance to the success of the record. I remember having a very difficult time with Paul. He was angry at me for twisting his arm. The rest of the band had resigned themselves to the fact that if they had to come without him, they'd come without him.'

Tim Finn even offered to sit in the drum seat if necessary – a personnel change allowed by the BBC rules, as he actually played on the original recording. 'I think at that moment, Paul got the full impact that these guys were serious,' says Stamler. 'So he reluctantly agreed to come.'

The band flew to London first-class, arriving on a Tuesday. They filmed the show the next day, then flew back to Australia on Thursday. 'When he was in England, Paul was a miserable human being,' says Stamler. 'He was impossible to deal with. You'd think, with the massive success in England, there was something to be happy about. Yet, for whatever reason, at that point Paul was reluctant to continue doing promotions for the record. As it was to unfold, he was also reluctant to do much more with Crowded House and be an active full-time member of the band. There was no talk of him leaving, but there was starting to be dissatisfaction with his commitment and his work ethic.'

After the *Top of the Pops* appearance, however, 'It's Only Natural' actually dropped in the singles charts. 'Paul was almost revelling in the fact,' says Stamler, 'and was making himself annoying in his revelry that the trip was a failure. He was extremely perverse about it. Very clearly, that was a defining moment which indicated that there were problems with Paul ahead.'

But the TV show did stimulate a rise in the album charts for *Woodface*. As 1992 drew to a close, it had been over three years since work began on the album. But there was plenty to feel happy about, says Stamler. 'We'd made great strides. I felt satisfied with what we'd all accomplished. I thought it was a very positive time. We'd come off on a high in Europe, we were able to get the Germans' attention for the first time, and had success. Unfortunately, there was some devisiveness within the organisation.'

In the October newsletter of the Crowded House club, Neil wrote to fans: 'Well we've come to the end of a brilliant year of touring with

Woodface and the brain is alive with a multitude of images and impressions from the gigs we did and the places we visited. I remember marrying a couple in Dallas on stage, not recognised by the law perhaps but sacred to us for sure. I remember a host of unknowns hoisted onto stage to sing with us, some brilliant, some appalling, all now legends! And there was the unforgettable sight of Paul Hester disrobing from a Santa suit and baring all for the good people of LA.

'And so we begin recording in NZ. The songs are pouring out, the band is still in high gear from all that touring . . . we will see you mid '93 with a new album, new haircuts, bulging muscles, glamorous new outfits and surgically altered faces: young, vital and slightly tragic but ready for anything.'

Seven worlds collide
• November 1992

'In a long forgotten place / Who'll be the first to
run?'

—'Kare Kare'

The band was eager to get started on the follow-up to *Woodface*. As far back as late January '92, while Neil was approving the edit of 'Weather With You', Nick, Paul and Mark had assembled in the pool-house of Neil's Shirley Grove estate to record demos of songs such as 'Fingers of Love' and 'Nails in My Feet'. But the continuing campaign in Europe intervened.

They also had to settle on a producer for the fourth album. It was time to cut the umbilical cord with Mitchell Froom. At the time *Woodface* was released, Neil expressed disappointment that the band playing live were that much 'wilder' than they were on record, where all the concentration was on getting the arrangements and structures right. 'One day we'll get into the studio and get across some of the tangents,' he promised. 'But mostly you want to get the song across faithfully, with as little distraction as possible for the listener.'

Neil describes Froom as 'very much the classic producer': he was a musician, who worked well on arrangements, was conscientious and never short of an opinion. 'That was great for me to encounter. I'd never struck somebody who was that fully rounded as a producer. But, after three records, we felt – and he did, too – that we needed to define ourselves outside his influence. We were looking for somebody completely different, whose personality would inspire us to be looser and experiment. We wanted to work with somebody wild, whatever that means.'

At Capitol, Hale Milgrim agreed. 'I was totally for it, even though I loved Mitchell. I felt maybe it was time for a change.' He put them in the hands of David Field, a young A&R man at Capitol, based in London. Milgrim had known Field at Elektra, where he worked on projects with the Sugarcubes and the London Beat. But internal politics led to Field's departure from Elektra; he found himself working with the president's son, and felt he'd got no credit for what he achieved. Milgrim, however, knew his capabilities and thought he had

243

been badly treated, so offered him a job at Capitol. 'Musically, he was very artist friendly, and he had strong feelings about things that he could articulate. I felt, if he and Neil could get along, there might be a good bond there.'

Field got to know both Finn brothers in 1992, developing a rapport with Tim during the convoluted and protracted recording of *Before & After*. Then, while Crowded House was on its lengthy tour of Britain in the northern summer, he acted as the go-between in the search for a new producer. He introduced a variety of candidates for the job to Neil, and escorted them to the band's gigs throughout the country. Among those considered were Steve Lillywhite, Gil Norton and John Leckie. They would hear the new songs the band included in their set, and afterwards would discuss their ideas with Neil.

Field says that towards the end of the tour, after seven or eight meetings, he had a clear idea of what Neil was looking for. 'I had this Youth idea. I'd met him and knew he was a character. He hadn't really done anything that was relevant, but I thought, this could be really interesting.'

Born Martin Glover, South London wide boy Youth first came to notice as the founding bass player in the uncompromising art-punk band Killing Joke (whose leader, Jaz Coleman, had settled in New Zealand). After leaving the group in 1982, he won respect as a producer/re-mixer, working with techno, dance and pop acts such as Brilliant, PM Dawn, Blue Pearl and the Orb. At the time he was approached by Crowded House, he had recently received his second consecutive nomination for producer of the year in the British record industry awards.

Field took the band to meet Youth in Brixton, where he has a couple of small studios in his house. The night before, Youth had held a summer solstice rave, so the garden was all trampled. 'Things were a little sombre in the studio that morning, a little delicate,' says Paul. 'We met him in the front room, sat down, had a coffee and proceeded to talk. It's early, and he's rolling joints the whole time, so we were all quite impressed. I thought, he's like Neil from *The Young Ones*. He just rambled on and it just sounded like fun: this guy's into a whole different thing. Let's do what he wants to do. We weren't too sure what that really was.'

Field says Youth was his 'usual cryptic self', but whetted the band's curiosity. Driving away, 'the conversation in the car was along the lines of, "You're fucking mad! The guy's wacky. But interesting. Did you see the size of that spliff? What was he going on about?"'

'Youth had heard a few of the new songs on tape, liked the music, and his ideas fitted exactly into what Neil had been thinking. Youth said he didn't want to think about it too much: "I want to explore". It was all very vague, suggesting we concentrate on atmosphere and rhythm and texture.'

Although nothing Youth had done in music suggested it was a good idea, something clicked straight away, says Neil. 'He's got a pretty nutty approach and attitude to things, and a great record collection. And he said some good things about music and passion, the sort of intensity he likes in music. So we took a punt on him.'

Youth's persona is very theatrical, says Field. Seeing him connecting with Neil was like 'the existentialist meets the sceptic. It was definitely two extremes, and the challenge was how they treated it, how they could bend each other in certain ways.' Neil's scepticism came out during a dinner, when Youth was waving a crystal above people's hands. Neil saw Youth's hand moving, not the crystal, and expressed his doubts. 'What about Stonehenge?' said Youth.

Club-hound Nick had most in common with Youth's musical tastes, although he couldn't stand Killing Joke. 'But I didn't associate him with the band. I thought of him as being a bass player, of about the same age, who was influenced by a lot of the same music in the late '70s and early '80s.'

Mark says they chose Youth because 'he was the most outrageous. He was the one who fitted the bill the least. As far as being a competent nuts-and-bolts producer, he was up in the stars somewhere. And that appealed to them in many ways, because Mitchell is very much a tight-fisted, cracking-the-whip kind of guy. With Youth, it's like "making a record should be like ... making a journey". He had all these little sayings, plus a really cool record collection, and they really hit it off. They all smoke a prodigious amount of pot, and I think this all led to some kind of camaraderie.'

Although Hale Milgrim was all in favour of the experiment – 'it was time for some walls to be broken down' – Gary Stamler expressed strong reservations about Youth's suitability. 'Having watched the recording process with this band from day one, I had learned what Neil responded to most,' he says. 'I felt he needed somebody who had a real strong sense of arranging songs. Neil had some brilliant ideas that, in some cases, needed restructuring. On several occasions Mitchell Froom actually took different songs and put them together. I was as willing as the next person to find someone who would be adventurous with the band – yet still had the skills to get the best vocals out of him, to organise his songs into good records.'

With an eye on the bottom line, Stamler felt that Neil – working with someone who wasn't strong enough to earn his respect – might produce work that was less commercial than its potential.

The other chance element in the experiment was the recording location. Neil wanted to avoid spending weeks in a sterile studio – be it in Los Angeles, London or anywhere – and realised that he had never done any serious recordings in New Zealand. During the April 1992 tour he sensed a positive mood in the country, then just emerging from a recession. He told BBC's Radio One, 'I just looked longingly at the country and thought, damn it – this is a really inspiring place, why don't we record here?'

When they couldn't find a studio in New Zealand that appealed to them, they decided to rent a house and set up their own. Recording the album on location also suited their experimental frame of mind. Neil's first instinct was to establish the studio on Great Barrier Island, an isolated alternative-lifestylers' retreat northeast of Auckland that is accessible only by plane or boat. He and Grant Thomas flew there for a recce, trekking through the native bush to look at several houses and the local rugby clubrooms. They soon came to their senses. 'We quickly realised it would be a nightmare getting supplies in, or if something broke down,' says Thomas. 'We were sleeping in a hut in the hills and it flooded overnight. I only had a pair of leather shoes, and Jaz Coleman piggy-backed me across a paddock covered in water so we could get out of there. It was no place to make a record.'

They then headed for the secluded, windswept coast 45 minutes west of Auckland, to visit houses recommended to them by Nicky Walker, a friend of the band who had worked in the area on film shoots.

At the end of a day visiting the western beaches, Neil, Grant and the videomakers Kerry Brown and Bruce Sheridan ventured down Lone Kauri Road, a daunting incline of hairpin bends through thick native bush, which descends to the Karekare valley. Only tarseal has improved the road since it was cut by the Shaw brothers, who farmed the area in the mid-1800s. The demanding road has claimed many cars. According to local legend, a rusting Mini with two skeletons lies near the bottom. If you stand near the top of the road and look west across many bush-clad ridges, a sliver of Karekare beach can be glimpsed in the distance.

Bob Harvey, now mayor of nearby Waitakere City, has been a dedicated member of the Karekare surf club for 40 summers. He says the beach is one of the 'smaller west coast gems, with all the rugged grandeur of the wild coast in a setting second to none'. He explains the way the environment changes its mood through the day. 'In winter, sea mist and light rain often hides the hills. In summer, the sun sets directly in front of the main beach, causing the legendary green flash the instant the sun sinks below the horizon.'

Tim Finn's former roommate Jane Campion made the beach famous in her 1993 film *The Piano*. The Maori name for the beach, Waikarekare, translates as 'rough, turbulent waters'. Overlooking the beach is the massive rock face Te Toka Matua, more commonly known as Watchman Rock. After losing a battle against the the musket-armed Maori tribes Nga Puhi and Ngati Whatua, survivors of the tribe Te Kawerau a Maki were hurled from the rock to their deaths. The small valley has a dramatic history of warfare, shipwrecks and tragedy, but for over 100 years has been a favourite picnic spot for Aucklanders – who enjoy the beach and its nearby rockpools and waterfalls – and an inspiration for painters.

Few people live at Karekare, even though Auckland city is a commutable distance away. The last house visited by the Crowded House scouts was a stark concrete structure, nestled in the side of a hill like a gun-metal grey bunker. It is the home of Nigel Horrocks, who in the mid-1980s designed and built it in the style of an open-plan studio suitable for performances. A floor-to-ceiling window slides back so the large living room is open to a southern view of the valley. A 10-minute walk along a bush track over the brow of the hill leads to a dramatic black-sand surf beach.

Horrocks – an enigmatic dilettante whom Nick Seymour describes as 'a Himalayas-climbing, Nepalese-loving ethnocentric chap' – was well disposed to the idea of renting his unique home for use as a recording studio. During the filming of *The Piano*, it had been the base of actor Harvey Keitel. Scattered inside the spacious living room are a variety of Pacific instruments which Horrocks has collected since childhood.

In November 1992, the band's technical coordinator Dugald McAndrew flew over to New Zealand to get things ready before Crowded House took up residence in the Karekare valley. They rented a couple of houses for accomodation, and Horrocks's forbidding home was set up for recording. Luckily, a new studio called Revolver was in the process of being built in Auckland. So with all their equipment in disarray, the studio didn't take too much convincing to hire it out. The old Neve console and 24-track Ampex tape-recorder, plus crates of effects racks and vintage microphones and a baby grand piano were put on a truck and driven over the narrow, winding road to the west coast.

Horrocks's house was across a creek and up a steep, treacherous gravel drive. In the recent winter the creek had flooded, swallowing the four-wheel drive Subaru of Horrocks's mother. 'So I thought it was time to stop being a romantic, and having a ford across the creek, and get started building a bridge,' he says. The band chipped in, as a crane was needed to get the equipment into the house. 'There wouldn't be many albums that have had a bridge-building/roading component in the budget,' says Grant Thomas. Horrocks's neighbours built a movable wall for the large living room, to separate the control room from the recording space. The main bedroom was used as a tape store and editing suite, McAndrew slept in another bedroom so he could keep an eye on the equipment at night, and a small room became the vocal booth. 'They had booths built all around the house,' says Horrocks. 'Out in the kitchen, in the bathroom, in the laundry. Because the whole band set up was here all the time, there was an incredible tangle of cables and equipment lying around.'

Arriving before Youth were his engineer Greg Hunter and programmer Matt Austin, who had flown from the congested grime of Brixton, South London. They were badly sunburnt from a brief stopover in Bali. Now, they found themselves in a tranquil, lush South Pacific valley. It was a bit of a shock. 'They looked like Dickensian waifs, punks from London,' says Hester. 'Long, thin hair, pale skin, sunburn, no shoes or socks. They'd arrived at this little house in Karekare, and were going, "Where the fuck are we? What have we done?"'

The band recorded six days a week for two months, quickly settling into a haphazard routine. The conscientious pair – Neil and Mark – would arrive at the studio at about 11am, then wait an hour or two for the others to arrive and start making tea. 'It was maddening, but you had to fall into this schedule we'd carved out for ourselves,' says Mark Hart.

Early on in the sessions, Mark wrote in his journal:

December 3, '92 – Thursday. Neil asked me not to go on tour with Suzanne Vega today. He says I'm part of Crowded House now and that I shouldn't have to do those kind of things. Nick's doing bass overdubs on 'Nails in Your Feet'. I took a walk up to the falls. It's very beautiful. Did keyboard overdubs. Started about 5.30pm.

As the days went by, they would start later – and finish later, not getting to bed till four o'clock some mornings. 'It got shifted to this weird zone where we were playing a lot at night.' The band's recording method changed. They worked up songs from lengthy jam sessions, having more say over their own parts.

The band lived in a house owned by John and Stephanie Lindeman, about a quarter of a mile away, high on a ridge overlooking the sea. At about nine o'clock each evening everyone would take a break and return to the Lindeman's, where a catered meal would be ready.

Left: The Mullanes in rehearsal, March 1985, Craig Hooper at right. *Neil Finn collection*

Below: The Mullanes on the St Kilda pier, Melbourne, 1985. *EMI*

Above: Performing 'Weather With You' for the cameras, Queenscliff, Melbourne, 1991. *Neil Finn collection*

Below: The big schmooze. Crowded House play Auckland on the showcase tour, October 1986. *Kerry Brown*

Opposite page: Tim and Neil at the Anzac Green, Te Awamutu, 1993. *Dean Taylor*

Opposite page top: A piece of 'Chocolate Cake', May 1991. *Peter Green archive*

Opposite page below: Wherever there is comfort, there is pain. A still from the 'Four Seasons in One Day' video, April, 1992. *Kerry Brown*

Left: At the waterfall, Karekare, 1993. *EMI*

Below: One last crowded house. Mark, Tim and Neil at the Corner Bar, the final Melbourne gig, 21 November 1996. *William West*

Left: Photo call at Bennelong Point, 24 November 1996. *Tony Mott/EMI*

Below: Farewell to the World, Sydney Opera House, 24 November 1996 *Tony Mott/EMI*

The dining room has a panoramic view, and the band, crew and their entourage would watch the sun go down and the waves sweep in, surrounded by ancient art from Tibet. (Lindeman and Horrocks had run an adventure company in the Himalayas together.) The evening meals grew into social events, with guests usually invited for dinner. Youth would put on Cat Stevens's *Tea for the Tillerman* and hold court, expounding on primeval belief systems, exotic cultures, mass hypnosis and the tribal nature of mankind – or just plain storytelling – while the red wine flowed and joints kept appearing. 'It was very convincing,' says Hart, 'but sometimes you felt he was improvising a lot.' Slowly the others would peel themselves away from the intense philosophical discussions, and make their way back to the studio.

The after-dinner walk was an exhilarating time of day, the band and crew feeling their way through native bush along a dirt track in the pitch dark. 'We'd try and get back without using a torch,' says Paul. 'It was scary because we'd walk along the side of this hill, with a sheer drop beside the track. It was great.

'One night we all got back to the studio and were all mooching around with cups of tea getting ready for the evening session and – there's no Youth! No-one had seen Youth. He'd been behind us on the track. So Youth had stumbled off on his own without a torch somewhere in the bush. We waited another half hour and then he finally showed up, covered head-to-tail in dirt and with a big stick in his hand. He'd gone over the side in the dark and grabbed this branch to stop his fall. He had used it to walk along the track and finally found his way back to the studio. He was totally shaken: "Oh man, I was lost in the darkness, this stick saved my life, man." For the rest of the album, he always had the stick with him – his sacred stick.'

Youth – the pagan/Celtic voyager – took to the area's primal atmosphere immediately. He would walk around barefoot, encouraging everyone to 'Take your shoes off, man – feel the path with your mind.'

Paul eventually got on well with Youth, after the requisite early altercation ('It was a domestic issue, which I had to raise, being the Mum of the house,' he says. The argument – about ashtrays and housework – led to the lines 'We left a little dust / On his Persian rug' in 'Kare Kare'). Paul liked Youth's spirit, his intuitive way of working. 'That's what we wanted to do and he certainly provided a lot of that. Sometimes you wondered, "Is this complete shit?" but you have to read between the lines with Youth. You don't take it all literally. He's also a mongrel for a joint and so am I.'

By all accounts, at the Karekare sessions there were few who didn't inhale. There was no shortage of 'electric puha'. When Paul arrived at the sessions he was asked, 'Have you seen the drawer? Go and have a look, third one down.' He pulled it out and found 'it was just filled with pot. It must have been well over a pound. We'd just go and dip into it. I thought, geez, we'll have to stay here for a year to get through that lot. But we did. We actually had to get some more in.'

According to Mark, the main difference in the recording of *Together Alone* was 'it was a real band effort. Everybody had their say. It's the way bands should be.' For the first time, says Seymour, 'we were all actually playing the parts we thought of, instead of having parts imposed on us. Especially with Mark Hart now playing on the record.' However, although Mark was finally confirmed as a member, he would occasionally be sidelined by Youth as well. 'It's partly a personality thing,' explains Neil. 'People who are reticent will be left out – it becomes self-fulfilling.'

Youth's contribution would be not so much arrangement in a literal sense, more an orchestration of the dynamics, conducting the spirit of the sessions with his enthusiasm. 'He definitely steered things in a completely opposite direction,' says Paul. 'Black and White Boy' is an example. When written, it had an almost bossa-nova groove, with a smooth soul melody. 'Youth just took that one to another place: *More buzz man, turn the guitar up. More fuzz, Neil – heavy. Yeah, heavy. Less notes, Nick – just that note, the whole way. All the way!*

'He was set up in the lounge room on a few pillows wrapped in his sari, with his ashtrays and his pot and his coffee and his books. He always had a novel on the go. So there would be this reading and rolling, then stopping to tell someone to turn their guitar up full. *More of everything!* And he would dance during takes, with headphones on. He would come up to you and conduct, just wave his arms at you and scream, *Freak out, man, freak out! More! More!*

'It was like a happening. It was great, totally the reverse from Mitch and Tchad. We would freak out and they'd say, "That was pretty good. Maybe you should come in and listen to it." Instead we got, "Man, that was *sublime* . . . a *paradox* of rock." '

Paul says Youth had a talent for setting up atmospheres in which the band could capture certain feels or work within. Then, he'd suggest other instruments to use. 'But once we started playing and jamming, he just let us go. Because he'd been in a band, he understood there were times to let us get on with it. If he wanted to make a suggestion, he'd put his hand up.' The band got used to Youth hippie-dancing in front of them as they recorded a take, headphones on, conducting. Meanwhile, Hunter would be headbanging behind the mixing desk, having fun turning up the volume and continually blowing speakers, creating 'zen mixes' in which only four knobs on the desk could be turned up at any one time.

Youth could recognise the character of the band and play with it, says Paul, 'introducing folklore and games to build up the band's spirit. I think he was subconsciously into that.' The mood created, the band were free to explore and run with it. Such an occasion brought about . . . Nude Night.

The exhilaration created by Karekare inspired the cathartic disrobing in the sessions for 'In My Command'. 'We wanted to be immersed in it somehow,' says Paul. The band had been playing a few takes which didn't seem to be going anywhere. 'It was like we needed to jump in a cold bath and get out and do one.' On the way back from dinner, Paul suggested the answer was to shed their inhibitions with their clothes.

'I thought we'd go nude, run around the house a couple of laps, then stand on the hill and howl and scream at the moon for a bit. Then we'd record a take. So that's what we did. But I remember Mark Hart farting around . . .'

'. . . within a moment everybody was nude,' says Mark. 'I was taking my time.'

'Me, Neil and Nick were nude within about a second, ready to go, and Mark was diligently taking off his trackshoes and socks, then putting his shoes back on – to run outside. He was being sensible, and we were going, Mark – *we're having a wild, abandoned moment here.* Don't get sensible. What are you doing? And he's going, "I-I-I'm putting my shoes on.' *We almost lost the moment.* Nude, you have to *act on it.* You can't be dilly-dallying, and Mark had this doubt about his nudeness. Eventually we got him out there.'

'So there we were,' says Mark. 'Neil playing keyboard, me playing guitar. Everything strategically placed. Of course, the real hippies – Youth and Greg – wouldn't have anything to do with it, being British and modest. They couldn't take their clothes off, even though they were adhering to this whole hippie philosophy. We played the song once, then all ran outside for some fresh air. It was like being stupid boys. Then we came back in, played it again a couple of times. But we didn't use those tracks! There might have been a bit of self-consciousness that you could detect. We ended up keeping a track we cut before dinner. It was funny – but we tried.'

They ended up listening to the takes – still nude – in front of the mixing console. 'It was great,' says Paul, 'we were all smiling, and someone snapped a couple of photos from behind: the true arseholes of Crowded House.'

Youth's experimental recording methods reflected pagan

spirituality. On 'Pineapple Head' he asked Mark to stand in a circle of volcanic stones while recording a guitar part. He obliged, stretching his lead 100 metres from the desk to the stone circle sited on the hill above the house, playing an ambient guitar part. Youth then gave Paul his instructions for recording the vocal.

It was at this point that Parlophone promotions manager Malcolm Hill, visiting from London, happened to call by to check out the exotic location. 'When I got there, they were going along with everything Youth suggested,' he says. 'As I arrived, Paul was sitting in an upright flight case, holding in his arms lots of crystals, singing backing vocals. I said to him, what the hell are you doing? He whispered to me, "Well, Youth wants me to. He's barking mad, but we're getting some great results." There was a lot of wackiness going on, but it was very funny.' Hill found when he went to the toilet that he had to share the cubicle with the Hammond organ's Leslie speaker. Youth didn't manage, however, to get Neil to hold any crystals.

Youth's friends who visited were always memorable. His cohort from Killing Joke, Jaz Coleman – who was living in New Zealand at the time, working out of York Studios in Auckland – called in occasionally for 'loud and brash visits', says Paul. Another friend had changed his name by deed-poll to 'something like ET. He owned this UFO shop and would drop around all the time to see Youth with crystals and things. We were chatting away one day and he said, "Oh yes, I've got a flying saucer." We all looked at each other and he said, "Yeah, I've got the plans for it in my car. I'll show them to you." He brought out these scrappy A4 pages of longhand notes and inscriptions – and I mean, who are we? We don't understand any of this. He's showing us proof and we're going, "Good oh".'

Youth was loaned a collection of very valuable crystals, which he was keen to place in strategic positions while the band recorded. One day he took them outside and buried them. 'Apparently that recharges them,' explains Paul. 'So he found a particular spot and buried them in a stoned stupor one morning. Of course, he could never find them again. They're still down there somewhere, buried in Karekare: $20,000 worth of borrowed crystals. Youth was lamenting for weeks having to tell the guy about his crystals. He was out there every other morning looking for them.' (When he couldn't find them, he would say, well they didn't want to come up.)

With the A&R direction coming from David Field, who was based in London, executives at Capitol in Los Angeles were concerned about the anarchic sessions, possibly fanned by Stamler's scepticism. Field was asked, were things out of control? 'From day one everyone at the label in America was adamant that Youth was the wrong choice,' says

Field. 'I was confident that things were fine. But it was a huge amount of pressure, a big responsibility for me, as I'd never worked with a band of that size before. It was a non-stop battle. So I felt I should go down to New Zealand and see how things were panning out. The responsibility for introducing Youth to the band was mine and my career would have suffered badly if things had gone terribly wrong.'

Field arrived at Karekare a day earlier than scheduled and found 'all sorts of strange stuff going on'. Many of those present were in a psychedelic frame of mind. Mark, who remained straight ('It's easy for me to be giddy when I'm around a bunch of giddy people') says Field seemed rather stunned by the scene. 'I remember him not reacting very enthusiastically. He was taken aback. I don't think he disliked it, but it was such a weird world to enter. Somehow we had developed this setting which we were very used to, but anyone coming into it from the outside world was surprised.'

But to Field, the music he heard coming out of the monitors was 'very, very exciting. An absolute thrill. I knew it was a serious departure – I thought, "My god, what are people going to make of this?" – but I felt it was exactly what they needed to be doing. It was adventurous, dynamic, so textured and atmospheric – much like Karekare itself, really. The place is very influential on the record.'

Mark says that occasionally he would get frustrated at the lack of progress being made – 'We'd just be getting ready to do something and a thunderstorm would roll in' – but then he realised, 'We were under the influence of the project: we weren't controlling it, it was controlling us.' Although Neil had most of the central ideas before they started recording, they started to change in character. Songs that were particularly affected by the climate at Karekare include 'Fingers of Love', recorded on a rainswept, melancholy day; similarly 'Distant Sun', with Nick and Paul in separate rooms inside the house, while Neil and Mark played acoustic guitars on the porch shrouded by a cold mist; 'Private Universe' changed from a swing song to a panoramic guitar wash; and of course 'Kare Kare', credited to all the band because it emerged during a jam. 'Locked Out', originally a slow ballad, became what Nick describes as a 'Mancunian thrash', at Mark's suggestion ('Which Neil regrets now,' he says, 'I don't remind him it was my idea'); 'Black and White Boy' was similarly delicate – like 'Into Temptation', says Mark – until one day Neil started playing it like the Ramones. 'We all jumped in and suddenly that was the new version.'

December 4, '92 – Friday. Because of technical difficulties we didn't really start playing until late afternoon, even though we got to the studio at noon. Some TV guys from Auckland came around and we did an impromptu interview. Started work on the 'Newcastle Jam' but gave up and went to 'Black & White Boy' which changed dramatically over the course of the day. It's now two electric guitars.

Both the physical and emotional climate at Karekare were always extreme, says Paul. 'Every day there was something going on, as people settled into the joint. They'd go off for walks and have these intense things happen. A lot of stuff has gone down in that area of New Zealand, and I think that rubbed off on us. The Maori folklore really made sense and we would dream about it at night.

'I remember Neil coming back from a walk and saying, "I went up to the ridge, round to that mountain, there's an amazing waterfall and this rock pool. I took all my clothes off and jumped in, screamed at the top of my voice." He was totally exhilarated with it, like he'd done an est course or something. Things like that were happening – it was very volatile.'

Nick describes recording *Together Alone* as a 'humbling experience, being in an area of the world so geographically dynamic and so incredibly removed from popular culture'. For Paul, that meant the penance of having no television to watch; for the British visitors, all sorts of luxuries they took for granted in cosmopolitan Brixton. Guitar tech Dugald found himself inundated with requests if he was making the 20-minute trip to Henderson, the closest town. 'Everybody would be aware he'd be going, and they'd say, "Oh good, he can get some supplies." This was very evident with the Poms, they were very separated from life,' says Paul. 'They'd be saying, "Oh, Dugald, can you get me some fags, can you get me some incense, can you get me a visa for India?"'

'Poor old Dugald, he had to do it all,' says Mark. 'He was our lifeline to the outside world. "Oh Dugald, are you going into town? Can you take this sample of, ah . . . shit to the doctor?"'

Neil had caught giardia from the local drinking water and, by the end of the sessions, weighed only 57 kilos. 'It took a toll on Neil,' says Paul. 'He was the man on the spot. There were all sorts of things to deal with: who was going to live where, for example. Everyone wanted their own space.'

'It was quite tough,' agrees Neil. 'It was a weird combination of people and there was quite a bit of stress around. But there were a lot of really good things about it too. There were very good days where we made some good music. But it was torturous to some degree.'

As the weeks dragged on in the intense environment, energy became drained and tempers frayed. 'Towards the end, Youth wasn't functioning particularly well, but then I'm pretty relentless,' says Neil. He started to feel he was being taken advantage of by Youth ('He was on a pretty good wicket, he got to go out to the other side of the world, smoke a massive amount of pot, was *very* well paid . . . there was a cynical edge to it'), and by hangers-on outside of the band enjoying the lifestyle. 'I regard the experience as a loss of innocence. It brought a lot of hostile things to the surface.'

'It was a struggle to make, no doubt about that,' says Mark. 'All these demons started expelling themselves, this ugliness started appearing. Everybody had their moments where they lost it. I remember Neil throwing a mike-stand at Nick, Paul screaming at Youth, Youth screaming at Paul, saying grow up, start being mature – that's coming from Youth. I had moments where I felt unwanted, unneeded, bored to death. Everyone went through different stages.'

'Man we exorcised some demons,' Nick told *Vox* with some braggadocio. 'We had some really big arguments. Everybody put their ego in, which was good.'

One night Mark, having had his fill of Youth's dinner-table theology, wandered back to the studio to 'do some homework', find a part for a song or play the baby grand which had been shipped in at great expense. Mark was playing his lap steel when Neil wandered in and sat down at the piano. He began to play 'Walking On the Spot', the Elton John-ish piano ballad that had been on the earliest Crowded House demos in 1985. The band had played it live a few times, but, despite several attempts, had never managed to record it satisfactorily. Then Paul arrived, and started playing a percussion part.

'All of a sudden, it started sounding good,' says Hart. 'I'd always wanted to do the song, it was lovely. So we said "Roll the tape, man" to Greg, who'd arrived by now, and we put it down, very humbly, in living-room style. Neil added an acoustic guitar, I added some strings and the lap steel, and Paul some percussion things. We finished it that night.

'Then Youth wanders in as we're finishing up. We're all excited: Youth, listen to this. And he was almost hurt. He was really solemn, unimpressed and unenthusiastic, as if we'd crossed some invisible line of respect, not having him there while he was talking to his friends.'

Another night after dinner, it was Youth who brought the normally reticent Hart out of himself. For a rap on Paul's 'Skin Feeling', Youth sat Mark in the vocal booth with a vintage '50s microphone, put some beads around his neck and lit incense and candles and told him to *go right out there*. Hart raved about motorbikes and horses and flying like an eagle. 'It was a side of Mark none of us had seen before. Youth did things like that quite often,' says Paul.

Nick found that, to his chagrin, Youth the dance/remix guru could be 'a bit of a dosser. He didn't really apply himself with much of a work ethic, it must be said. But I was very happy about the left turn Youth took us on, definitely. Before Youth I don't think Neil had even a tolerance for dance music. And Youth would play it an awful lot and Neil couldn't help but listen to it and realise there was room in this world for modal chant.'

To Paul, Youth and his cohorts seemed more open-minded in their approach to music, whereas the Americans seemed restricted, either by radio formats or self-imposed generic boundaries (such as being too 'black' or too 'country'). 'The Poms were much more into bastardising and taking and pillaging popular culture.' Everything was possible.

The usually disciplined Neil also found it unsettling at times, and tried to be relaxed about the fact more work wasn't getting done. 'I think Youth saw me as a bit of a schoolmaster or something,' he told the *NME*. 'He'd got his life to a point where he'd feel no qualms about indulging himself and doing a bit of work every now and then, while I like a little more order in what I'm doing.'

The solution was an 'uneasy trade-off. Some days he would prevail and some days I would. We got the work done in the end. Sometimes you'd get the feeling that you'd been goofing off and then all of a sudden at the end of the day you'd realise you'd got something really good down on tape.'

Despite their differences, Neil describes Youth as 'charming and intelligent'. Having Youth as producer meant they were less 'pedantic about the details' of what they were doing. 'That's what we wanted, and I wanted more of it. In the end, he was quite conservative with us. I was hoping he'd really challenge us, but he still made quite a "Crowded House-y" record with us. I don't think he really wanted to be the known as the guy who screwed up Crowded House.

'The album sounds really good in hindsight, it turned out really well. So in a way you can't knock Youth. Whatever he did, somehow it worked.'

The band went to Karekare with the intention of recording 12 songs; by the time they left the studio, a chart on the wall showed 20 titles with ticks beside them. The sessions took eight weeks, plus there were two weeks of overdubs and mixing to come in Melbourne. 'So it was actually pretty quick,' says Neil, 'compared to *Woodface*, anyway . . .'

In perfect harmony, he and Sharon finish the sentence together: '. . . it just seemed like a long time.'

Earth and sky
• January 1993

'Now is the hour / that we must say goodbye.'

—perennial Maori farewell song

The setting was idyllic, but the time at Karekare was no south-seas holiday. Working six days a week, the band only occasionally got outside the studio to enjoy the setting, swimming in the rock pools or being tossed about by the waves, playing frisbee, or teasing the pet pigs Madonna and Piggie Banks. When they had the time they also wound down by riding horses on the beach, getting lost in the bush, or playing Frisbee golf on a makeshift course. 'We had to play over Youth,' Paul joked to *Vox*, 'who would usually be rolling a joint on the fourth hole.'

Dugald found his duties expanded from equipment technician and runner to 'nurse, bum-wiper, lunch-maker, fisherman, whatever role needed to be filled'. For him, the only downside was sleeping in the actual studio, as the recording sessions often dragged on to the early hours of the morning. He would have to go out and say, 'Listen guys, it's four in the morning. You've been working on this for six hours. I think you should knock it on the head.' But there was often a chance to sneak away and go fishing off the rocks or surfing. With Nick, Dugald went surfing one night, and they had a good time yarning out on the water with a few guys from the Karekare surf club. But they were a little disappointed when they weren't invited in for a beer.

'They thought they'd been snubbed,' says Horrocks. 'In fact, all the locals were just giving them lots of breathing room. You don't come to a place like this to live or visit to get inundated by others. People here are very respectful.' The occasional gesture however showed that the band was welcome. 'Some of the neighbourhood womenfolk would come around bearing muffins or scones,' Nick told *On the Street*, '... it was very New Zealand.' Compared to the various films that have been shot at Karekare, the sessions had no impact on the community of 40 people. For *The Piano*, 180 people invaded the valley each day in huge trucks. At one point the shoot was joined by a couple of TV series and, says Horrocks, 'you couldn't drive your car anywhere. They were very polite, but we were glad to see the end of all that.'

As the weeks went by and moods changed as often as the weather, the dramatic valley made its presence felt in the music, and the songs changed personality or, in the case of 'Kare Kare', got written on the spot. One night, at one of the brainstorming dinner sessions, Neil got the idea to incorporate local and ethnic influences into the project. He decided to amalgamate the musics of the Pacific Islands, Maori and European New Zealanders on 'Together Alone', the final track they recorded, later to become the title of the album.

Through the contacts of his friend, the videomaker Kerry Brown, Neil invited members of the Te Waka Huia cultural group (a Maori choir), a team of log drummers from Auckland's Cook Islands community and a brass band quintet to perform on the track. He decided to make an occasion of it, getting them all out to Karekare to record their parts live one Sunday afternoon.

It was all organised at the last minute, Neil coordinating all the participants, while finishing writing the song with Bub Wehi of Te Waka Huia, and Mark was arranging parts for the brass band. To add to the pressure, the day before the epic session, another occasion that bordered on the surreal took place.

An assistant at Revolver Studios, charmed by the setting, belatedly asked the band if they would mind if he got married at the house the morning before the 'Together Alone' experience.

'I was flabbergasted the band okayed it,' says McAndrew, 'given the fact a record was being made there. But it was indicative of the mood: let's roll with it and see what happens. It was only a mild hiccup, but it was a very odd day.'

After venturing into the mystic with Youth, the scene gave Neil and Nick flashbacks to their childhoods. 'I didn't want the wedding, but Neil's conscience got to him,' says Horrocks. The 'small, private' wedding turned out to be a full Catholic nuptial Mass – outdoors by special permission – with the service being lead by an intimidating bishop. A large crucifix was erected, and seating for 150 people arranged. 'I think he was this travelling bishop who went around the world doing certain ceremonies,' says Mark.

Horrocks claims the bishop was 'the Pope's hatchet-man who goes around kicking people in line in Australia and New Zealand. He kept on saying marriage is a grievous occasion and that non-believers shall not be permitted to join in the ceremony.' Mark felt he was being condemned as a heathen; the band and its entourage felt they defined the Australian term spare pricks at a wedding (until they sang a couple of songs). Behind the rows of guests, says Horrocks, 'there was the rest of us in T-shirts and lava-lavas, with Youth up the hill sitting in the stone circle smoking a joint.' Nick told *Vox* he took one look and 'flipped out. The last thing we needed was a Catholic bishop putting a bad vibe on everything. He was giving us daggers. There was all this weird energy going on between Youth and the bishop and all these mums and dads sitting outside in their Sunday best.'

Neil tried to be the diplomat, and make small talk with the bishop, and got rebuffed. 'You could see that really flustered him,' says Horrocks. 'We all came away feeling we'd been treated like devil-worshippers. That felt a bit unfair. So the next day, with the "Together Alone" session, it was like a wonderful purging almost.' After a couple of hours, the intruders withdrew to a reception elsewhere, and life at Karekare got back to 'normal'.

The recording of 'Together Alone' was like a South Pacific production of Phil Spector's. By the fireplace stood the 30-strong choir from Te Waka Huia, conducted by Neil. On the porch were the Cook Islands drummers, taking their lead from Paul. Squeezed near the kitchen sink was the brass band quintet, playing Mark's arrangements. Conductor-at-large was Nick, and swanning about the proceedings enjoying the chaos was Youth. 'To Youth's credit, he thought that to get us into it, the best way was to get us directly involved, organising each group,' says Paul.

In a way, it would never have happened without the pantheistic chameleon from Sarf London. The appropriating of indigenous music for sampling is endemic in dance music, though the South Pacific has thus far been spared. To the *NME* Neil joked the session was 'a white urban attempt' to find another form of expression, but then elaborated, 'Most indigenous cultures like to work themselves into a trance state and that was something Youth's very into as well. The Celtic tradition is the closest that we can feel to native cultures, it's our pagan past, and he's very attracted to that. I'm quite interested in it myself, shedding the ornamentation and sophistication of music that Europe has provided.'

A few weeks earlier, Neil had taken the tune of 'Together Alone' to Te Waka Huia, asking the choir leader Bub Wehi to write the Maori words. The lyrics are based on the Maori legend about the origins of the universe. Rangi and Papa, earth (the mother) and sky (the father), were originally joined together in darkness. But the sun pushed them apart, so for eternity the father lived in the sky and the mother down on earth. They were separated, and could only look at each other with love and longing. 'The story appeared to symbolise the whole concept of the title *Together Alone*,' Neil told UK journalist Paul Tingen.

On the sunny afternoon itself, the studio and its garden were inundated with the musicians, cultural groups and their various entourages. About 200 people in all followed the signs that had been scrawled on drumskins and nailed to posts to lead to the studio. The lawn was swarming with extended families: grandmothers, aunties, cousins, and babies. Dick and Mary Finn were there, plus a film crew and photographers. The two fountains became paddling pools for the kids. Several barbeques were going. Nigel Horrocks recalls the sight as he came back from a swim at the beach: 'The place seemed to be crawling with hundreds of people on this beautiful day. Then, when a woman started to sing the karanga, it was a really powerful emotion. You could almost cut the air. I thought, hell, it's Sunday – what do the neighbours think? I looked over the valley and there were all these people sitting on their back lawns, enjoying it. It was an amazing experience.'

Getting ready was a struggle. 'I was as excited as hell about it,' says Neil, 'but all of a sudden there were 30 choir members there, log drummers and a brass band – and the song was barely written. Bub and I were trying to get the lyrics finished and a vague idea of the melody, Paul was rehearsing the drummers, and Mark still writing the brass parts he'd been working on for two days. I kept looking out at all these people watching on the lawn, with my stomach churning – massive, massive stress – but really determined to make it work.'

The night before, says Mark, while the others were talking after dinner, 'lounging around, smoking, having massages,' he was working intently on the arrangement for the brass, trying to capture a sound Neil had in his head. But Neil kept saying to him, 'Naah, it's not there yet, mate.' Mark would reply, 'Ohhh fuck', and go back to it. 'It got to the point where he was playing it to me over the phone,' says Neil. ' "Naah, it doesn't sound natural. Keep going." Finally, after working all night, about a half hour before the session was to start, he cracked it with this beautiful arrangement.' Mark had created the sound image Neil wanted, of a Salvation Army band's Christmas carols drifting lazily across backyards as they performed around the streets of Te Awamutu.

It took a few takes for the diverse factions to come together. Finn's taped guitar and vocal were accompanied, first by the choir, then the brass band. An anguished solo karanga brought everyone in together, then the Cook Islands drummers added their intense polyrhythms. 'It sounded terrible to start off with, the first few runs,' says Neil. 'Eventually it started to click a bit.

'Waka Huia suddenly broke into one of their own songs. Straight after that the log drummers hit their straps. Then we pushed the brass band into playing. They each did an item, spontaneously. The choir did one of their amazing action dances, it was *staunch*. Then the log drummers hit it in a really big way. It had become a playoff. And the brass band – these white guys standing there – we said to them, "C'mon you guys, you can't let us down!" They looked at each other and played . . . "Wipeout"! The choir and cultural group were going nuts.

'Then we hit a really good take, straight after that. By then, there was a huge will for it to work. We *had* to make it work – or else it would have been a joke. It came together, and it sounded really good. It was probably massively under-prepared and ill-conceived in some ways, but because of that giant will, it had this undeniable power. The song still gives me a thrill.'

Nigel Horrocks and his wife Jody were in tears. Building the exceptional house had been a longtime dream, and by opening it up to the band, this extraordinary event had taken place. To Paul, 'it was a fantastic, incredibly emotional day. I'd never been a part of anything like that. Afterwards, someone from the choir made a speech, then this old guy got up and said everybody should take this day on board with them, and continue it on. He said, even though we had done all the work, it was the beginning, not the end. Basically he was saying, don't let it go. They acknowledged it was a good thing for them to have done, too. It's Neil's baby, being the New Zealander: it's for him to run with now.'

Crowded House then replied with an acoustic rendition of 'Don't Dream It's Over'. The technicians collected the radio microphones they had placed on the other side of the valley, hoping to catch the echoes of the drums at the studio. Paul says when they listened back to the tapes, and isolated the tracks from the radio microphones, they found 'you can hear the Maori choir going, and the log drummers echoing across the valley – and it's really weird, all the birds and bugs and insects were buzzing in time with the rhythm of the drums, like a swell. It was amazing.'

As everyone was packing up, some council noise control officers arrived to close down the disturbance: a neighbour had finally complained.

That night, the band thanked the cultural groups, the Karekare residents and the diverse Auckland support network for their help with a party and concert up the road from the studio. Originally it was to have been held upstairs in a barn, but at the last moment they realised it would have collapsed with all the people, so the band's PA was moved in about five minutes by dozens of helping hands. They set up underneath a silver birch tree, outside the kitchen of a house.

'It was a far more idyllic setting,' says Horrocks, 'it meant beers could be passed directly out the window to the band.' Security was on hand as two Auckland radio stations tipped their listeners off to the party, but had only a vague idea it was somewhere on the west coast. Still, about 600 people were there, standing around the bonfire and barbeques, dancing as the band played songs from the album that weren't even finished yet. Mark Seymour and many others got up, and Andy Weatherall and Youth acted as DJs.

The party finished up at about four in the morning. For the key players, it had been nearly two days without sleep. Horrocks remembers Neil at the end, saying it had been a great day, but it was time to go to bed, relax and savour the experience. 'I thought that was a good idea. Then the next day I came across Neil. The only person who hadn't taken his advice was him. He'd stayed awake all night and was looking quite frazzled. But it was a beautiful night. To me that was really the first time you started to hear a really Pacific sound at a sophisticated level. You got the best of the European, the Polynesian and the Maori communities together musically – and it worked.'

The recording of 'Together Alone' provided an epic climax for the Karekare sessions, and an emotional release for what had been a tumultuous period in the band's history. 'It was a contrary experience,' Neil says. 'We went out to the country, to this idyllic place, and discovered there was more bubbling underneath the surface of everybody than we'd imagined.'

To Paul Tingen of *The Guitar Magazine* he said, 'The good thing about recording in amongst the elements is that it puts what you're doing in perspective. Karekare beach is a very wild and untamed environment where emotions are close to the surface all the time. It's a difficult place to live. The divorce rate in the local community is very high – seven out of 10 couples break up! – because the presence of nature is just absolutely overwhelming.'

The experience took its toll on the Crowded House organisation, as well. 'On the back of the *Together Alone* album,' says Grant Thomas, 'the only marriage or relationship that survived, out of everybody's, was Neil and Sharon's.' Nick's marriage broke up, followed shortly afterwards by those of Mark and Nigel Horrocks. Thomas himself was going through a divorce and, he says, 'while Paul's relationship with Mardi survived, his one with the band didn't, and neither did Gary Stamler's.'

In hindsight, says Neil, 'When I was making the album I was thinking, it's too much: this album is the last record. Together alone? Almost every theme on the record was about *loss*. Half of it was written as if it was already over. I sometimes wonder if the soundtrack of that record contributed to all those marriage bust-ups.'

Hit the ground running
• March 1993

'For Neil and I, it was a holiday from ourselves.'

—Tim Finn on the Split Enz renunion tour, 1993

Split Ends had given its first performance on 10 December 1972, in the tiny Wynyard Tavern on the edge of the Auckland University campus. Twenty years later, they returned to the same café to celebrate, play a short concert – and launch founder-member Mike Chunn's Split Enz biography *Stranger than Fiction*.

Squeezed onto the makeshift beer-crate stage was a respectable turnout of Enz members: Tim and Neil Finn, Mike and Geoff Chunn, Noel Crombie, Rob Gillies, Paul Crowther and Eddie Rayner. Their 90-minute set was equally respectable, hastily rehearsed but performed with humour and enthusiasm for the 80-strong crowd of family, friends and music industry stalwarts. In the audience, not wanting to take part, was Phil Judd.

But this wasn't the Enz of the '80s, playing pop hits for screaming teens. Instead, they went back to the eclectic art-rock of the Judd era. 'We were post-modern before it was a concept,' quipped Tim Finn. They began at the moment of conception, with the song 'Split Ends' – '*I'm writing letters to my friends, telling them about Split Ends*' – before moving on to the sprawling, skitterish songs from the mid-70s. 'Back then,' explained Tim, 'if a musical idea wasn't arresting in five bars, *out it went.*'

The quick shifts in the complex early songs – and the band's fading memories – made the set an exhilarating, edgy romp. As always, Rayner was the linchpin of the evening, calling out mid-song to warn that he'd forgotten bridges, choruses, chord changes – but managing to find them in time. His playing showed he was a one-man keyboard sampler before the technology even existed, deftly changing from Liberace lyricism to rock'n'roll boogie, with a detour into parlour jig for Crombie's inevitable spoon solo.

As the chaotic gig began, Neil was standing in front of the stage. Taking time out from recording at Karekare, he was beaming like the 14-year-old who wrote 'Split Ends' on his pencil case. Halfway through the set he once again got the offer to join the band for songs from *Dizrythmia*, and a passionate 'Message to My Girl'. But it was Tim who closed, with a symbolic 'Six Months in a Leaky Boat'. He threw in a chorus from 'In the Year 2525' to fool Rayner and, for his parents Richard and Mary, standing an arms-length away with their clan, a quote from 'Haulaway'. Strength through exhaustion had helped him bridge the tyranny of distance.

Afterwards, it was announced that an Enz anniversary reunion tour would take place early in 1993. Reunion? Had there ever been a life without Enz?

In 1993 Tim Finn was fond of quoting a Buddhist proverb: 'Before success, chopping wood; after success, chopping wood.' It would give him the title of his fourth solo album, released in the middle of the year. After his departure from Crowded House in November 1991, he had gone through a year of emotional and musical regeneration. 'When I got back to Australia, I did some work on myself,' he said in 1993. He went to the Blackheath centre in the Blue Mountains, outside Sydney, and attended a Buddhist retreat for 10 days of silence and meditation. 'It was the best thing I've ever done – and the hardest.' The centre had been recommended to him by *The Piano* director Jane Campion, with whom Tim flatted in London during the 70s. The Buddhist monks advised at the beginning that the retreat would not bring happiness, but it would provide a path one could choose to take. 'It will change you, but don't expect *bing* – suddenly you're happy,' said Tim. 'But I was happy, I came out feeling pure, cleansed. It was as though something inside of me snapped.'

Tim returned to Melbourne and started writing a series of songs which seemed to have a spiritual feeling: 'Protected', 'In Your Sway'. 'They're just songs, but they had some kind of essence about them that was pure. They were just popping into my head.'

For a few months after the retreat, Tim maintained the simple routine inspired by the retreat, rising early, swimming, meditating, not drinking or smoking pot. 'When you're meditating a lot and you're not using the usual props like alcohol, a lot of things emerge that we normally suppress: anger, fear, whatever. It's like they're centre stage, and you have to confront them. So it wasn't an ecstatic time, it was a weird, edgy time – and a lot of music was coming through.'

The technique Tim was taught went back to Siddhartha Gautama, the Buddha: 'a pure form of meditation, but not mantra or chanting. You're working in yourself, observing, noticing.' It propitiously provided another link with Richard Thompson, a Sufi who has practiced meditation for many years. In a tidy coincidence, Tim had been given a melody from Thompson's *Sweet Talker* soundtrack, with the suggestion he expand it into a song. Tim added lyrics and a bridge section, and 'Persuasion' – the delicate, affecting song which resulted – became the first single on *Before & After*.

The retreat was a powerful experience, giving Tim a sudden realisation that we can change and improve our lives. 'I wasn't suffering because Crowded House hadn't worked out, but because I felt a bit stuck. On about the ninth day of the course, when we could talk again, people said to me, why are *you* doing this? They assumed that I wouldn't need it, my life to them seemed a great one: I was lucky, touring, travelling, successful. I just said to them I was doing it because I wasn't happy, I needed something to change inside myself. I recommend it to anybody.'

In late 1992, he told his friend Mike Chunn, 'I hestitate to say, hallelujah, I'm saved, but it was a catalyst for change. At the moment I'm engaged in trying to change myself. I look back now on how I was in my twenties, and even my thirties, and I was so self-absorbed. I read about a character in a book who could never feel happy – or sad – for anyone else, because he was so self-absorbed. He never felt any genuine sympathy for anyone. I have to say that's partly where I was at for years.'

Tim's ties with Crowded House were never completely severed. Around the world the nomadic elder Finn would suddenly arrive and then there would be four again: Womad in Adelaide, the Dublin National Stadium, Wembley Arena in London on his 40th birthday, gigs throughout New Zealand. Paul Hester cracked that Tim was 'an awesome sight', thanks to the diet of 'no drinkin', no smokin', no pokin'.'

During the hectic year of *Woodface*'s European success, the Finn brothers had managed to do something they'd been promising for years: take their mother back to Ireland. It had been a family joke for a long time, Mary saying to her children, they couldn't go to Ireland unless they took her as well.

'It finally happened,' says Tim. 'It was so perfect, it was like a dream.' Mary and Dick Finn saw several Crowded House shows (with Tim as opening act) during the *Woodface* tour of Britain in July, 1992, including one at the National Stadium in Dublin, where Neil's encore was an a capella 'The Parting Glass'.

Then the band went off to play several dates in Spain. An exhausting trip reunited Neil Finn with his family: moments after singing a couple of songs for MTV Europe in Barcelona, he got on a plane for Dublin. He was met at the airport by his parents and Tim. They immediately headed for Galway on the west coast, with the boys driving the rental car while their parents were in the back seat. It was a reversal of their childhood roles in the summer holiday trips to Mt Maunganui.

A four-hour drive took them to a castle in Galway, where, after a late evening meal, the proprietors insisted on a singalong till the early hours of the morning. The Finns then explored the west coast, staying in pubs on the Dingle Peninsula, the Ring of Kerry, at Killarney and Tralee. The weather was perfect, and all the spontaneous decisions they made about their itinerary seemed to work out. They finished up in a Cork pub, being embraced by about 60 people who said they were relatives, from villages north of Cork such as Mallow and Doneragh. The singalong lasted till three in the morning. 'What a wonderful night,' says Mary. 'They played and played. Every man and his dog knew Tim and Neil were there, and they were all claiming to be related to me.'

'Half of them probably weren't,' says Tim, 'but by the end of the evening they were. It was like a film, discovering your Irish heritage and feeling, *this is my tribe, this is where I'm from.* Feeling comfortable, enjoying the whimsicality, the poetry, the musing. Sitting in the pub, chatting – not making points in the Anglo way, just meandering conversation. Just loving it, steeping yourself in it, responding to it.'

Tim Finn's immersion in his Irish heritage ('He's got quite a crush on the place now,' says his mother) was intensified when he returned to Dublin, and started making music with Liam Ó Maonlaí of the Hothouse Flowers and Belfast singer/songwriter Andy White. The trio had met in a London pub and formed an immediate bond, getting drunk together and having a baptismal water-pistol fight till 3am. Recording with his new Irish friends was 'a release from the neurotic obsession of "popdom" – of course, they're a band and their songs come out on records, and they want them to get into the charts – but that's not what they're about. They're Celtic musicians, carriers of the culture.'

Tim went to Lansdowne Road park to see the Irish rugby team play Australia. 'I was feeling totally Irish that day, surrounded by people, looking around at all these faces in the lovely soft light, thinking, these are my people. Being a New Zealander is still very strong, and I'll live there again, but another part of me will always be in Ireland now. The year I turned 40, I discovered Ireland. It was an enriching time for the family, and as an individual, too.'

After a night on the town in which they were denied entrance to a Dublin nightclub, White, Tim and Ó Maonlaí wrote the stand-out song on *Before & After*. 'Many's the Time (in Dublin)' is about wanting to belong, trying to find out where. 'In Ireland you don't have to try,' says Tim. 'Not just the people of Irish descent, everybody feels it's a special place.

'Music arises there spontaneously, it's no big deal. Everywhere Liam travelled, he had an instrument in his hand, a mandolin or a whistle. In the back of a taxi he'd be playing the mandolin and the driver would be happy, everyone's happy. It's just totally normal. They'd say to you, "What are you doing?" And you'd say, "I'm a musician" – and they'd say, "Oh, fair play to you."

'I do see it with rose-coloured spectacles, I know there's a lot of problems there too. There's a lot of unemployment, but a lot of emigrants are returning. They'd rather be unemployed in Ireland than London. Imagine the desolation of the Irish in London. I found it hard enough to feel I belonged, but the Irish – it's so weird. The English think themselves superior to the Irish. The mind boggles.'

The biographical songs of *Time & Tide* – 'Six Months in a Leaky Boat', 'Haulaway, 'Dirty Creature' – had been a removal of the masks Tim Finn hid behind in Split Enz. Seeing that band as a quest had provided the energy required, but later counting the costs, it seemed silly to think anything was that important. 'Once that left, I became more comfortable with myself. If I look at old footage of Split Enz, I see somebody who didn't really know who he was, clinging to the identity of the group. But now I feel, after everything I've been through, I've got less fear of showing myself and I think I'm a bit more lighthearted about it, too.'

Before & After saw the completion of two songs ('Strangeness and Charm', 'In Love With It All') which had been started at the 10 days of Finn brothers sessions which evolved into *Woodface*. Tim Finn recorded them in Dublin with the Hothouse Flowers, returned to Melbourne to add Neil's vocals, then took the tape back to Dublin for mixing.

When the album was about to be released, Tim was interviewed by the New Zealand *Listener*. He was asked about the line from 'In Love With It All' that went 'brothers come too close' . . .

'Brothers come to blows,' he replied. 'Did you think it was "brothers come too close"? That wouldn't have been a bad line actually. We just sang, "brothers come to blows". Damn. Why didn't we sing "brothers come too close"?

'Neil and I, that concept would have threatened us 10 years ago. We've been able to realise that, if we get too close, it can get a bit prickly, too much heat, like a hothouse. But the beauty of it is, we know if we don't work together all the time, when we do, it's exciting and something is going to happen. It's like we've got this secret kind of knowledge that, at little intervals, we can come together and write a song. There's no problems, no blocks. Even in Split Enz, we couldn't write together. I guess I was protecting my position: I'm the older brother, this is my band. I loved having Neil in the band, valued him highly, but still liked to keep everything as it was. He was very much playing the role of somebody who had joined the band, was in awe of the band, and just loved being in it. Those roles were going on, but they're gone now, and that's a very good thing.'

The much-anticipated Split Enz reunion tour of New Zealand took place in March, 1993; although they had recovened several times in Australia, this was the first time at home. Thanks to the band's iconic status in New Zealand, the week-long series of concerts had a celebratory air to them – a large proportion of the 55,000 who attended were under 25, so had never seen Split Enz in concert before. They had discovered them through their older brothers and sisters, since the band's demise nine years earlier.

The band responded with shows that were energetic and inspiring, with no effort spared to make sure they lived up to the myth. Noel and Sally Crombie designed fluroescent suits and a stunning *trompe l'oeil* stage set. Tim in particular relished being back in the spotlight, performing with a manic confidence that had been missing in his solo shows. Neil, also, was enjoying his different role, remaining in the background as he did when a teenager – while his brother threw himself about the stage like a man demented.

'It was a total celebration of the chemistry that's still there,' said Tim shortly after the tour. 'It was full on, it felt very comfortable and loose, I was able to achieve states of forgetfulness and ecstasy. For Neil and I, it was like a holiday from ourselves.'

Some shows in his solo career had been that intense, he said, but they had been in Britain or the States, never in Australia or New Zealand. 'I've found it easier to re-invent myself there because I didn't feel the baggage of the past. Here, I've always felt self-conscious. But with Split Enz, I was able to be completely natural.'

The band explored every era of their career, introducing songs from *Mental Notes* and *Dizrythmia* to their new young devotees, who drowned the band out on favourites such as 'I Got You' and 'I Hope I Never'. The shows climaxed with 'Six Months in a Leaky Boat', now almost a national anthem about New Zealand's pioneering heritage. Tim Finn took musical detours which explained his own chapters in the story: the Beatles' 'I Saw Her Standing There', Van Morrison's contemporary standard 'Irish Heartbeat' and, of course, 'Haulaway'. He resisted the band's request that he update the autobiographical shanty with the twists and turns of his life since.

Just prior to the tour, Tim was given a Maori welcome onto the Parihaka marae in Taranaki, to thank him for documenting the notorious conflict in his 1989 song (the Maori chief Te Whiti led his people in peaceful resistance to their lands being unjustly confiscated by the colonial government). The song had stimulated an interest among the tribe's young people in their history. Finn stayed on the marae for a few days, talked to the elders and went surfing with the young Maori. He felt his own sense of culture enriched, and also felt rewarded by the spiritual success of the song. 'I was so humbled by the welcome, they just wanted to say thanks. A lot of it was in Maori, so I didn't understand it, but I had people whispering a translation in my ear. I was very lucky to have that experience. It's rare to write a song, then return to the source. It was a great cyclical feeling.'

The tour was an uplifting experience for the band, a chance to get together for playing's sake only; there was no album to promote, a fresh audience, and a keener awareness among the Enz of their special bond with each other. It also provided an opportunity to unveil 'Best Friend', the first song Tim and Neil had ever collaborated on, in mid-1977.

There was a strong sense of homecoming during this reunion tour. Neil and Sharon had already made their decision to resettle in New Zealand even before the Crowded House sessions at Karekare. Immediately after the Enz tour they went house hunting in Auckland. Eddie Rayner and his wife, Enz lighting designer Raewyn Turner, moved back to New Zealand shortly afterwards, as did Dave Dobbyn and his family. They may have all returned for personal reasons, but to the small music community it was a statement, and an encouragement, to have the A-team back in their midst.

Tim was also feeling the pressure to come home, particularly from his nephew Liam, then 10, who asked if he was returning, too. 'I told him I wasn't sure – and he said, "I think you should." It really tugged at my heart strings.'

Tim had noticed that the climate seemed to have changed in New Zealand. There was a post-recession positivity about and, to him, the cultural mix was fascinating; he had been involved in numerous small projects with Polynesian artists over the years. The ingrained 'cringe factor' towards New Zealand culture also seemed to have dissipated. 'We noticed it in the young audience on the tour – they don't have the feeling that *local is suspect*. The young kids now seem quite cocky, in a positive way. If I thought that our music, or us as role models, helped show there's another way of being a New Zealander, then I'm very happy. It involves celebration, not introversion. Split Enz was about celebration, rebelling against that New Zealand tradition of the All Black scoring a try but showing no emotion.'

On 13 June, Tim gave a showcase to launch *Before & After* at the Borderline in London. Neil and Nick were present. In the encore, Neil joined Tim on stage for 'In Love With It All', 'Parihaka' and 'Weather With You'. While in London, it was announced the Finn brothers had been awarded the OBE (Order of the British Empire) in New Zealand for their services to music. Though the award bemused the brothers, and amused the other band members ('Does it get you a better seat in a restaurant, Neil?' quizzed Paul. 'Or faster through customs at Heathrow?'), it was a source of great pride to their parents. 'The smile on Mum and Dad's faces spoke volumes,' Tim told Mike Houlahan of Wellington's *Evening Post*. 'It means a lot in terms of credibility to that age group. But I can't help wondering about OBE being the first three letters of the word obedience.'

The brothers were unable to attend the investiture in New Zealand later in the year, but their mother told the *New Zealand Herald* they were 'quite honoured' by the award. However, added the Irish-born Mary Finn, she thought they might have been more excited if it had been a New Zealand award, rather than a royal honour.

Neil and Nick were in London to arrange the running order of the album recorded at Karekare. The title chosen was *Together Alone*. The album was still causing problems: Mark was on vacation visiting family in Kansas when he got a call from London to join Crowded House in the studio. They intended to do some more recording to complete 'Newcastle Jam' and add it to *Together Alone*. For family reasons, he was unable to make it, and the idea was dropped.

When *Before & After* was released in July, it confirmed the regeneration Tim had experienced. The album had the strongest selection of songs of Tim's solo career, and a more uplifting mood than its predecessors. All it lacked was a consistent flavour, due to the variety of producers – Langer and Winstanley, Mark Hart, David Leonard, Ricky Fataar. Tim then toured *Before & After* in Canada, the States, Britain, Australia and New Zealand. In Britain, the radio airplay, full houses and positive reviews were gratifying after the disinterest shown in *Big Canoe* and *Tim Finn*, but they didn't translate to sales (though it entered the UK charts at No 29).

In the United States, 'Persuasion' was the number one song on the airplay charts of the new Triple A (adult alternative) radio format for seven weeks, and 'Hit the Ground Running' for three, which would have justified extra promotional expenditure. However, Tim Finn was once again a victim of a changing of the guard at Capitol. In May, Hale Milgrim – a passionate believer in Tim as songwriter and performer, as well as a personal friend – had been deposed as president of Capitol. Milgrim came to see him backstage when the *Before & After* tour played Los Angeles, a guitar under his arm. Dror Erez, who was keyboardist on the tour, remembers thinking 'What bad luck. I wanted to see him in a suit and tie, not with a guitar.'

Erez also acted as tour manager, which made him aware of another problem. 'The hardest thing in the whole tour was trying to be a middle-man between Gary and Grant.' The two managers were finding themselves working increasingly at cross purposes.

Juggle like a diplomat
• June 1993

'There was a fear that this record wasn't strong enough to survive the Christmas rush ... that it lacked that clear-cut, obvious, classic Neil Finn mid-tempo ballad.'

—Gary Stamler, 1996

After the sessions at Karekare, film-makers Kerry Brown and Bruce Sheridan shot footage for use in an EPK ('electronic press kit'). Although Youth had been suspicious about Brown sitting in the corner with his little Bolex ('No cameras, man – bad vibes'), Paul and Nick hammed it up, while Neil earnestly wanted to explain why they had taken such risks. The mini-documentary shows scenes of the band rehearsing and goofing off, the recording of 'Together Alone', interspersed with interviews and dramatic shots of the coastal landscape. Using a camera on a remote-controlled model helicopter, they filmed an aerial shot which flew straight through Horrocks's house ('It was like having the band sitting around with a lawn-mower flying upside down beside them,' says Brown. 'If the operator got it wrong you could have decapitated one of them quite easily.'). And when an actual helicopter was used to film scenes of the band running down the expansive beach, Paul couldn't resist grabbing the director's headset and giving the pilot *Apocalypse Now* flying instructions. 'The pilot wasn't impressed,' says Brown, 'it was a very dangerous exercise. You don't want to get it wrong, and here's Hester on the walkie-talkie playing Vietnam.' But the risks were worth it: the EPK was shown many times on MTV Europe, captivating an audience whose curiosity had just been whetted by *The Piano*.

The *Together Alone* sessions didn't finish with the big day at Karekare. With Youth in tow, Crowded House made its way back to Melbourne, where they rented Platinum Studios to record overdubs, on 'Kare Kare' and 'Together Alone' in particular. They wanted to maintain the vibe of Karekare, so they virtually took the studios over. 'Neil asked the people at Platinum if they'd mind not working while we were there,' says Paul. 'So the receptionist and the manager left for two weeks, and we had the run of the joint.'

Youth's response to the studio was, 'Shrine it up, Neil, Shrine it up!'

To recreate the Karekare environment, the band brought in blankets, cushions, lava lamps, smoke machines, candles and incense. 'We turned it into our own little grot palace,' says Paul. The band had both large studios going simultaneously. While they recorded in dim light at one end of the building – with a psychedelic slide show against the wall – in the other studio, Bob Clearmountain made sense out of the Karekare tracks, mixing beneath bright lights. At some times, it was hell: there was very little order or cataloguing to the Karekare tapes.

Over an intense two weeks Clearmountain rapidly gave the tapes polish, turning the seemingly chaotic tracks into panoramic arrangements. Occasionally, though, the loose work methods of the British engineers got too much. At 'Fingers of Love', Clearmountain took his hands away from the computer keyboard and said it was impossible: he gave up. So Youth joined him at the console and talked him through the various bits and pieces, explained the abundance of drum parts and atmospheric sounds.

Since *Temple of Low Men*, the band had built a good rapport with Clearmountain; once more they were impressed by his determination and focus. This time, as he quickly mixed song after song – moments after they recorded the last notes down the hallway – they realised how far they were pushing him. But asking Clearmountain to come to Australia was like a safety net for the Karekare experiments – even though Youth's reputation had been built on remixing.

'We were able to be very loose and uninhibited with what went on tape,' Neil told *Vox*, 'because we knew Bob would sort it out. His mixes sound huge.' To video-maker Bruce Sheridan, he joked that Clearmountain 'went through all the tapes of the wild sounds we'd collected, and left most of them off.'

Several of those close to the band were disappointed by the results. The mixes were sparkling and expansive, but comparatively conventional compared to the recording sessions. Nick felt they should have used a mixer who had no preconceptions of Crowded House, so that the album reflected 'the integrity of the energies which had transpired in the studio and were on the tape. I think Bob glossed over a lot of those things, and made them sound a little FM-radio friendly. We'd gone on a journey, and made a left-hand turn with *Together Alone* – but maybe a lot of listeners would say it still sounds like a safe Crowded House record.'

Capitol's A&R man in charge of the project, David Field, says the album that existed before the Clearmountain mixes was 'very raw and dark, rhythm heavy and very unusual sonically. I thought it was a stunning record. It was exactly the record they needed to make. But Neil's confidence in Youth had been tested a little bit too often, and Youth was losing confidence in his own ability as well. They felt they needed to bring the record just a little bit back towards centre.' The track Field regards as most closely reflecting the original recordings is 'Private Universe'.

Hale Milgrim, who had been excited by the vitality of the early tapes, was also reluctant about the idea of bringing in Clearmountain, although he regards him as the industry's leading mixer. 'There's a little more of a sparkle to the early tapes. I feel they cleaned them up a little too much. They sometimes do – even on *Woodface*, which is so produced, it's unbelievable – but who's going to mess with *Sergeant Pepper*? When you saw them live, though, there was a spark that wasn't always on the record.'

Milgrim knew *Together Alone* wasn't the 'commercial, radio-friendly' pop album he thought *Woodface* should have been in the States. But, artistically, he felt it was a great step forward for the band and he was eager to start work on its promotion. With his usual ebullient hyperbole, he says it was 'almost as exciting as if there was a new Beatles record'. However, shortly after receiving an early tape of *Together Alone*, Milgrim's tenure as present of Capitol abruptly came to an end.

Nine months earlier, in June, 1992, Milgrim had been promoted to be chief executive officer of Capitol as well as president, and had signed an extension to his contract. 'I was going to be with the company for at least five more years – and hopefully, another two or three Crowded House albums,' he says.

The future looked good for Milgrim. As Capitol began celebrating its 50th anniversary, the company was emerging from the years of uneven results it had suffered since the Beatles heyday. Hammer's *Too Legit to Quit* had sold three million copies; Bonnie Raitt's *Luck of the Draw*, two million (on its way to five); and Bob Seger's *The Fire Inside*, one million. According to *Billboard*, in 1991, Capitol had the strongest sales year in its 50-year history, and its highest profits in over 20 years. Hammer's sales, however, were well down on the spectacular 10 million he had achieved with *Please Hammer Don't Hurt 'Em* – and then only after a massively expensive marketing campaign.

Milgrim had inherited the successes with Hammer and Raitt from the Berman regime, but promising artists he had nurtured included Blind Melon, Eric Johnson and Charles & Eddie. Due to the label's success with its established artists, heavily wooed acts such as Mazzy Star and the Butthole Surfers had chosen to sign with Capitol. The company became rather top-heavy with new acts, even though, since Milgrim had arrived in late 1989, he had cut down the roster of artists on the label from 150 to under 100. As 1992 began, nearly half of them had either never delivered a record, or had only delivered one record to the company. Among them were such non-starters as Levitation, Misery Love Company, Subject to Change, Meritt Morgan, I Mother Earth and the Cages.

In the publication to celebrate Capitol's 50th anniversary, Milgrim said that the company had got off the track at times during the '70s and '80s by being too hit-driven. 'I didn't think Capitol was developing as many artists for the long-term as a number of other labels in the business were. They were looking for that quick pop/urban hit. And they were having success with a number of acts that gave them that, which was fuelling that attitude.'

Early in his tenure as president, Milgrim had shuffled key executives and renamed their positions 'directors of artist development' or DADs ('Hale didn't like the term "product management",' says Denise Skinner of Capitol. 'He didn't like the term "product".'

In October 1992, further restructuring took place. Officially, these changes were made with the approval of Milgrim's superior on the corporate ladder, EMI Records Group North America chairman CEO Charles Koppelman. But it was more likely to be at his orders. Whereas Capitol had traditionally had some autonomy within the EMI group (compared to labels such as Chrysalis, SBK and EMI Records), after the departure of Capitol-EMI Music president/CEO Joe Smith, Capitol became part of Koppelman's empire. A cigar-chomping former music publisher, Koppelman's reputation was for wheeling, dealing and asset stripping rather than creative leadership. The artist-friendly Smith, a music industry legend, had employed Milgrim – one of the industry's biggest music fans. Koppelman's experience had been in the world of instant pop hits (Vanilla Ice, Wilson Phillips) and radio-driven strategies, rather than developing acts who may take several albums before their sales took off. Any young acts on Capitol's roster under Milgrim were likely to be in this slow-building category.

So when Capitol's executives were once more shuffled and renamed, there was industry speculation about Milgrim's own future under Koppelman. 'It's just another rumour,' Milgrim told Billboard in October, 1992. 'I don't think that has anything to do with what I'm trying to put together. I have been given a free hand by [EMI Music president/CEO] Jim Fifield and Joe Smith from day one.'

In his study of 1990s music industry politics, *Off the Charts*, Bruce Haring writes, 'Despite the public happy face, Milgrim was said to be not at all happy at the changes Koppelman wanted, which included dropping some of his favourite artists from the Capitol roster. But the sales of some of Milgrim's new artists were not great and EMI had a tradition of impatience.' The sales of new acts such as School of Fish, Phil Perry and Dave Koz, Milgrim told *Billboard*, were in the region of 200,000 on their first albums, 'which I'm very proud of.'

But Joe Smith, who had let Milgrim run Capitol in his own style, had left in January, 1993, when his contract wasn't renewed. By the end of February, rumours were again circulating within the industry that Milgrim was to be next – and that his replacement would be Gary Gersh, who had recently resigned from Geffen. However Milgrim was taken by surprise when, in May, Koppelman asked him into his office in New York and told him he was being dismissed.

The rumours were true: the day after the staff gave Milgrim a sad farewell, Koppelman had a meeting in the Tower with Capitol's senior executives and the company's new president: Gary Gersh. The appointment reflected Koppelman's feeling that Capitol's A&R department needed strengthening; he was keen to place 'creative' executives (those with experience in production or A&R) as EMI label heads. Gersh had made his reputation by signing Nirvana to Geffen, and opening up 'alternative' music to the mainstream; he was also instrumental in getting the retro act Counting Crows signed. In his late-30s, he was the youngest head of a major American record label.

Gersh quickly made an impact at Capitol. Just as newly appointed record executives prefer to sign their own acts than work with an artist roster they have inherited, they prefer to employ new people beneath them to do things their way. Within days Gersh installed a new A&R team, dismantled the DADs structure, sacked some staff and rear-ranged the duties of others. The changes caused unrest and resent-ment inside the Tower. Corporate counsellors, hired to calm the mood, found instead that group discussions intensified staff dissatisfaction. 'It was very unsettling,' says Julie Borchard. 'I felt most secure under David Berman and Hale. They were charismatic, open – you could respect the work they did as leaders. When the top leadership changes around, it's as unsettling for the employees as much as for the artists.' Long-serving staff members are suddenly embittered, after years of hard work – and the artists have lost their allies within the company.

Two Crowded House stalwarts were among those whose circum-stances changed. Mick Kleber lost his job as video and media vice president, while Jeremy Hammond was moved out of artist devel-opment and was given the task of marketing Capitol's celebrated back catalogue. Ironically, the man Gersh hired to re-establish, and lead a marketing department was Bruce Kirkland – a former New Zealander. Nearly 20 years earlier, Kirkland had started in the music business booking bands for the New Zealand university circuit, among them Split Enz.

It was during the changing of the guard in the Tower that Crowded House delivered the completed version of *Together Alone*. Gersh was going to Hawaii for a few days' break, and took a tape of the album with him. It was a couple of weeks before he reported his verdict. 'It seemed to drag on and on,' says Gary Stamler. 'I remember Neil getting very annoyed he hadn't heard back.' When Stamler got a call from Gersh, he was struck by its similarity to the the call he received from Milgrim in response to the original *Woodface*. Here was another incoming president, with a new Crowded House album, saying it wasn't finished: it didn't contain a hit single.

'Gersh wanted Neil to continue writing for the record,' says Stamler. 'He felt if he put this record out, it wouldn't sell 400,000 copies, and if we had the right song, we could sell one million copies. He asked, would I please communicate that with Neil.

'It was like *déjà vu*. As I called up Neil, I remembered the profoundly negative and angry reaction I'd got on the phone with respect to *Woodface*. But this time it was almost 180 degrees different. Neil started laughing on the phone, saying, "Here we go again. They want me to write another single." He asked me what I thought, then answered it for me: "It doesn't have a lead track." He was actually very mature, very controlled. It was almost as if he was half expecting to hear that, after two weeks, it's not great news. He said, "Let me think about it".'

Neil called Stamler back a couple of days later. 'He said, "No, I'm not doing it. I don't know how to do it. I tried it once, I can't do it. This record's great and that's the end of it. I want you to set up a meeting with Gary Gersh and I'll come up with Grant and we'll tell him that we want the record released."'

Neil and Gersh had first met nearly 10 years earlier, when the Capitol deal hadn't been signed yet. Neil and Stamler went to see Gersh at Geffen, and his response was the same Neil had heard from so many A&R men: 'He was into it, but not completely,' says Neil. 'He wanted to hear more. He also said, if we did the deal with him, he'd want to be heavily involved, in the studio with us. I remember being put off by that.'

Now Gersh was getting involved: he wanted them to go back and record some more tracks. 'And I said no, basically,' says Neil. 'Apart from the fact that I thought the record was good and finished, and it had been bloody hard work. I didn't know if there were any hit singles on it, I really had no idea. But I resented the fact that this guy who'd just started as president, and had nothing to do with the album, now wanted me to go and do a love song. He'd asked Gary Stamler if I could just write something like a "you-and-me" kind of song. I thought the album was full of them, just not the sort he was talking about. I just wasn't in the mood for it, so I said, we've finished it. I really like it. I think you should take it as it is.'

Gersh gave Neil a rundown of the album's expected sales figures. He did say, however, something which appealed to the disgruntled songwriter: that the best two shots at singles were 'Kare Kare' and 'Together Alone'. 'He thought the most exotic elements of the album were its most commercial possibilities, which was a good thing to say, because we went the safe route with our singles, as usual.'

Gersh simply said, 'We'll go forward.' But as Neil left Gersh's office, he had a feeling that his stand had probably cost *Together Alone* the push it needed in America. Next in line for a meeting with Gersh was David Field, who handled A&R on the album. 'Neil came out and huffed and blowed a lot. I went in – and got fired.' Field, who had reported direct to Milgrim from London, was shifted sideways to the English company – in reality a demotion. At the time he had two acts in the American Top 20, US3 and Radiohead. He describes Gersh as 'one of those people who think, you've got to do it my way, or nothing happens. The album wasn't something that was his, he wasn't inspired by it. He wanted to put his own stamp on it by saying go back and write more. When the band wouldn't, that was it.'

Capitol had changed since the heady days of 1987, when Crowded House felt that the Tower was their home-away-from-home. Nick, in Los Angeles to design the *Together Alone* cover, had it confirmed when the security guards wouldn't let him in the building. He told them he was a member of Crowded House, and the guards responded, 'What's a Crowded House?' Nick led them into the foyer, and pointed at the platinum album on the wall with the plaque reading 'Crowded House'. The guards then made a phonecall to see if he was a welcome visitor. 'When Hale got sacked, a lot of his administration got sacked,' says Nick. 'Ultimately, I think the security guards got the sack as well. Next thing you know, there's a new administration, and I couldn't get into the building. It was that simple: we'd gone off the boil.'

Over in England however, executives at their label Parlophone were thrilled with the album that was finally delivered. '*Together Alone* is a genius record, a piece of art you could hang on your wall,' says

Mark Collen, then marketing director. 'It was everything Crowded House represented: a sophisticated, classy band with great songs and a brilliant record from beginning to end. We always thought of them as REM. We didn't think there was no single.'

The English company thought the album was substantial, says David Field. The band hadn't revisited 'Weather With You' but it was going in the right direction. *'Together Alone* was serious and intellectual,' says Field. 'It went to a side of the band that was always evident, but was offset by the humour. It went more to the heart.'

Walking on the spot
• August 1993

'It seemed a bit vague as to what we were doing and why. I was living in Aussie and nobody else had been back here much.'

—Paul Hester, 1996

In May 1993 Neil and his family resettled in Parnell, a gentrified inner-city suburb of Auckland. He was home again, after spending 16 years – nearly half his life – in Melbourne, or in transit around the world. For years he had contemplated a return, but the time never seemed right. He had missed the landscape, the familiarity of being in his birthplace – but most of all, the couple had missed their extended family. Their parents were getting older. 'I wanted my kids to grow up with them a bit, a sense of family is important,' Neil told Australian journalist Peter Holmes. 'Also, Liam can go to school barefoot, just as I did.' He'd always felt a little displaced in Melbourne, and he wanted to return to New Zealand before the boys got old enough to miss it. 'Neil had talked about it, but I'd never wanted to,' says Sharon. 'It was too slow, too quiet – and we'd spent all that time in Australia, establishing friendships through our twenties. It was a big decision to make, and until we spent that time recording here, I wasn't into it. I said, okay, let's go: right now. Let's not talk about it. Because we talk about things all the time.'

His fellow band-members were sceptical about his return home. Nick was sure Neil would find his prominence in the small population claustrophobic. 'It must be difficult for him, because everybody knows him in Auckland,' he told Innes Phillips of *New Idea*. 'I don't know how he's going to get out the front door – he's the King of New Zealand.' Mark Hart remarked that if you wanted a place to hide, for him, that meant being in a big city in the States.

The band was now split around the globe; only Paul remained in Melbourne. Mark was in Los Angeles, Nick a citizen of the world after his marriage was a casualty of the Karekare turmoil. 'He's a vagrant who has this really forlorn notion that if he stays on the run then he won't have to end up paying tax anywhere,' Neil quipped to *Mojo*. 'He's in for a rude awakening.'

While the band was awaiting the release of *Together Alone*, they took the opportunity to road-test the songs in unfamiliar settings that suited the multi-cultural experiments on the album. They embarked on a two-week tour of South Africa – off the blacklist since the dismantling of apartheid – and then immediately joined the Womad bill touring through the United States.

The day the band left for South Africa, however, Neil hinted at the unpredictable nature of Crowded House to Australian journalist Dino Scatena. 'At times, it seems like the whole thing can fall apart. But when we actually play together – whether it's on stage or in the studio – it has an undeniable strength and power to it. It just sucks us in. On a good night, I think we're as good as anybody.'

South Africa was still a divided and violent country when Crowded House toured in August, 1993. Their minders drove them to see the stark contrasts between areas of white mansions and black ghettos. Finding 'the real South Africa' became a mission during their visit. When they asked to visit the townships, the nervous promoters always found reasons it wasn't a good idea, not out of racism but fear for the band's security. So, for information about the South Africa outside their cocoon, the band had to quiz their hotel maids, room service staff and the two black members of their stage crew.

Nick's fondest memory of South Africa was meeting Gough Whitlam, the former prime minister of Australia, whose Labor government was controversially dissolved in 1975. Seymour bumped into Whitlam's wife Margaret in a hotel lift, and was thrilled she knew about Crowded House. Next thing, he was being introduced to Gough and the Australian consul. But his imposing hero hadn't heard of the band. 'Well the Silver-haired Bodgie has,' replied Seymour, referring to Whitlam's rival, Bob Hawke. He immediately went to his room to phone his mother.

'The rest of the tour was pretty dreadful,' he told *On the Street*. He was particularly perturbed by the 'gun walk-up' at their concerts, where people deposited their guns before entering; the first night, 170 handguns were checked in.

The African National Congress was enthusiastic about the tour, feeling the visit would boost morale and confidence among South Africa's liberal whites, uncertain and worried about the new era. Thanks to *Woodface*, Crowded House was well known in South Africa, but the band was frustrated that so few blacks were in their audiences. For them, tickets were expensive (45 rand, about Aus$20), plus there was the cost and limited availability of public transport to the venues, which were a long way from the townships.

Hester in particular was determined to visit Soweto. He stayed behind when the others, frustrated by waiting for it to happen, drove to a wilderness park six hours out of Durban. 'In the evening we sat around, drank gin and tonics on the deck, watched the animals come in to the water hole and felt like real colonialists,' Neil told Samantha Trenoweth, who covered the tour for the Australian magazine *Juice*.

Eventually, Neil and Mark got to Soweto on the very last day, though not to play. Their black driver Joseph took the pair to his Soweto church group. They attended a 60th birthday party, and were treated like guests of honour as the intense traditional Zulu singing overwhelmed them. After the birthday celebrant had been blessed, it was time for the visiting musicians, who knelt on the floor while crosses were lain on them. They took part in a birthday feast and even received a couple of marriage proposals. Paul, meanwhile, was taken by an ANC member to his niece's party, which he described when he rolled back drunk as 'a real hoe-down shindig'.

The connections had belatedly been made, and, not for the first time, the band realised how divided society was at home. Crowded House had been involved in the Building Bridges concerts in Sydney, which featured Aboriginal and white Australian musicians on the same bill. 'The people in South Africa are so used to living separately that they're totally freaked out about how to live together,' said Paul. 'It's going to take them 10 or 20 years, like it will with us. There are all these incredible parallels.

'In the first Building Bridges concert in Australia, all the white musicians were standing around together at the Bondi Pavilion, and it dawned on us that we didn't have any connection to this community. We didn't have any Aboriginal friends. We didn't know where to start.'

Ten days later, Crowded House found themselves immersed in other cultures when they joined the Womad tour in upstate New York. With the Canadian dates cancelled (they filmed the video for 'Distant Sun' while in Toronto), the three-week musical caravan mostly played the midwest. Besides mainstream stars such as Peter Gabriel, Lenny Kravitz and Stereo MCs, there was a United Nations of musicians on the bill, among them Remmy Ongala from Tanzania, Indopop singer Sheila Chandra from Britain, violinist Shankar from India, the Terem Balalaika Quartet from Russia, the Drummers of Burundi and Tanzania's Orchestre Matimila.

In Los Angeles, Paul explained the ethnic diversity of Crowded House to reporter Jenny Cooney: 'We're sort of Antipodean with a little bit of midwestern influence and we've got Jewish and New Zealand management. The next thing we're trying to do is get a whole bunch of women on the road to run the tour. Otherwise it becomes too "Boystown".'

It was a relaxed tour, with Neil's family joining him for the last week. Everyone enjoyed the chance to cross musical frontiers. Since playing the Womad festival in Adelaide in 1992, the band's listening preferences on tour buses tended to favour exotica such as world music or Sun Ra, as anything more mainstream became an exercise in analysis rather than pleasure. If they listened to other pop acts, all they would hear were drum sounds or guitar effects, and wonder how they were done. Tim Finn – whose own musical tastes had been expanded through trips to Cuba and South America – joined them to sing 'It's Only Natural' at the opening gig in Saratoga, New York.

The European release of *Together Alone* was not due until October, with the American release delayed even further, till January 1994. The late American release was ostensibly to miss the Christmas rush of superstar albums, and also – the new A&R vice-president at Capitol, Perry Watts-Russell, told *Billboard* – to avoid the necessity, when an album gets simultaneous worldwide release and is successful, for an artist to be two places at once. Watts-Russell also acknowledged that the delay allowed a new promotional team at Capitol time to settle in. 'Because of the change in regime, we wanted to wait to get myself and other people in the company in place and get the campaign ready for the new year.' With so much of the A&R input to *Together Alone* coming out of England, Capitol in LA didn't feel in control of the project; it had been a long time since they had seemed like their house band.

Jeremy Hammond, now marketing the company's back catalogue, was at a lunch meeting with Gary Gersh, Charles Koppelman and all the Capitol vice-presidents. They were going through the albums on the company's release schedule; among them was *Together Alone*. Gersh turned to Hammond and said, 'Jeremy, what do you think of the record?' Hammond had listened to it 'backwards and forwards'; he loved the album. 'I think it's a great record,' he replied, then he admitted, 'but I don't hear any singles on it.'

Knowing what American radio stations were then playing – grunge, or ballads by superstars – like many in the company, he couldn't see any potential hits. 'I have to say, people weren't that excited about the record,' says Denise Skinner. 'They'd say it was a nice record but . . . in this country, it's such a competitive market. The band's fanbase had dwindled down to 250,000. And Capitol was spending a lot of money to market them, to only sell 250,000. At that point, with this regime, it was, "What can we afford to do with this record?" There were so many changes going on here at the record company that I think the record got lost.'

The lack of commitment is confirmed by Hammond, who was still the band's biggest fan at Capitol, but no longer in a position to do anything about it. 'The wind in the sails had left when the Milgrim regime ended.'

But another delay in the release of *Together Alone* was caused by Nick's sculpture for the cover: a gold-leaf tableau of Jesus, Buddha and . . . someone else, squeezed into a red 1964 Riley. It was inspired by all Youth's dinner-table talk about belief systems during the recording of the album at Karekare. Jesus and Buddha weren't the problem, it was the prophet sitting in the back seat: Muhammad.

When Gary Stamler saw it, he became anxious. Muhammad, sitting in a car with Jesus and Buddha? It seemed unwise, with Salman Rushdie so prominently under a *fatwa* death threat for writing the allegedly blasphemous *Satanic Verses*. He talked about it with Tommy Steele, the head of design at Capitol.

'Gary was thinking, this is an international act, what if it affects things? Why even take the risk?' says Steele. 'But rock'n'roll has always been about taking risks and it never seemed like a huge one to us. But he was worried, and that made the band worried. It didn't seem that irreverent to me: Muhammad with his arm sticking out of the car. Christians don't have a problem with it, but watch out for the irate Ayatollah. Why not be the Salman Rushdie of rock'n'roll?'

Stamler asked his other client, Richard Thompson, a follower of the Muslim mystic Sufi, who agreed that the image might cause offense. Then, says Paul, 'Gary put the wind up Neil and he started to freak out about it and finally we all talked about it. It was very stupid.'

So Nick agreed to hide Muhammad behind a curtain (with a Maori koru motif, which symbolises the frond of a fern). But his arm was still visible. 'Then the executives were afraid the Islamic community would see the striped sleeve and assume it was Muhammad wearing *pyjamas*,' says Nick. He was in no mood to see the absurdity of it. 'I'd just split up with my wife, and I'd gone to LA to bury myself in the artwork. I was working in Tchad Blake's garage, carving it using his power tools.'

Steele has seen sillier debates. When he started at Capitol, on his first day, he had a meeting with Poison. They wanted a cover which showed a girl with big breasts and a 10-inch tongue, plus long hair like Lady Godiva. 'I thought I was in *Spinal Tap*,' he says. 'It was hysterical – but it was *real*.'

The *Together Alone* album cover was a week away from going to the printers when another battle took place, over who would be credited as producer. Because Youth's contribution had been so erratic, Neil thought he or the band should share the production credit. Youth's manager threatened that, if it wasn't a solo credit as originally discussed, he would take out an injunction so that the record never came out. To Crowded House, it was more important to meet the release date than argue the point. 'It's not of much consequence. These credits get a bit lost,' says Grant Thomas. 'If you're trying to repeat the formula, you're never quite sure what the combination was in the studio.'

Dugald McAndrew, who as guitar technician/gofer was present throughout the recording at Karekare, has no doubt the band should have shared the credit. 'To say that Youth was the one who was running it all would be an untruth, to say the least. Crowded House have a very strong idea of what they're doing. Neil's been doing this for a long, long time. He knows what's working and what's not.'

When *Together Alone* was released in the UK and Europe on 11 October, it had the credit, 'Produced by Youth.' Grant Thomas adds, with a sardonic smile, 'I'm sure his career is huge as a result of the record.'

Crowded House headed back to Australia after the Womad tour. A week later they were in Europe to start six weeks promotion for *Together Alone* prior to its release, followed by the concert tour itself. Tim Finn's *Before & After* tour had also reached Europe, and their paths crossed in the Dutch city of Utrecht in late September. Neil, feeling weary, told Tim it was unlikely they'd be able to get together. Tim passed this on to the expectant crowd at his show at the Tivoli. So, when a jetlagged Neil jumped up on stage, it took everybody by surprise; even Tim took a moment to recognise him in his new blond fringe.

It was one of the few enjoyable moments on the European tour. A couple of days later, the band appeared live-to-air on MTV Europe's *Most Wanted* programme. 'Promo-wise, it was the straw that broke the camel's back,' says Neil. 'We were exhausted.' They cooked chicken satays, played bingo, sang four songs from *Together Alone* (and one composed on the spot called 'Most Unwanted'), and talked with host Ray Coakes. The bingo game involved drawing numbers, with questions attached. Paul was asked when he lost his virginity. 'When I was about 13, underneath my house,' he said. 'I got about 20 seconds. Her name was Robyn. She said there was a lot of room for improvement.'

Coakes asked if he had improved, then regretted it. Paul replied, deadpan, 'Yeah. I don't stampede the clitoris anymore.' Nick looked at him, stunned. That was the end of the questions.

From Amsterdam, Paul wrote a card to the Crowded House club newsletter: 'Hello thrill-seekers, it's Paulo here. I'm sitting in a coffee shop in Amsterdam with Mark Hart. We've just had eggs on toast and a cup'o'Joe! Feeling good, feeling sassy! I wish you all good health for the new year. Be kind to your mothers (read *The Kitchen God's Wife*, by Amy Tan).'

But, soon after this, Paul had soured on the whole idea of doing the promotional tour. This stint on the road had already lasted six weeks, and it was still another five before they were going to start performing again. From the delays in the record's release, it seemed obvious to him that the American company's commitment was lacking, and that the US tour would be a long grind to no avail. The experience of flying around the world to do *Top of the Pops* and then seeing the 'It's Only Natural' drop in the UK charts (even if the album rose) had made him very dubious about the value of doing promotions in territories that had gone cold.

He made no secret of his opinion that Stamler was the problem. 'The situation with Paul and myself had deteriorated,' says Stamler. 'He forever held it against me that I forced him to do *Top of the Pops* and threatened him that the band would do it without him. I think he magnified that beyond reasonable proportions.'

'Things weren't adding up,' says Paul. 'I was starting to say, "Look, we've actually gone backwards." All that promotion and touring in the States for *Woodface* – and we sold less. Neil was aware of it, but it hadn't been talked about. I was seriously beginning to doubt Gary and obviously we weren't getting along. I was thinking management should be going about things differently. I wanted us to concentrate on the areas where we were strong and forget about the other shit for a while. I'd be shooting questions and that became a noise after a while. If someone doesn't know the answer, it's a real pain in the arse to keep asking questions. Then, if someone's in a bad mood or a bit upset, all sorts of other things get raised. The other guys would just be trying to get through the day, hanging onto something positive. The longer you have a band, the harder it gets – you've got so much history and any bastard can pull a bad day if they want.'

Paul also felt that Stamler had 'divided and conquered' the band, by phoning each of them, saying other members had agreed to do things. However, Stamler felt he was getting the runaround, and was talking to each of them separately because they weren't talking to each other, if only because they were scattered around the world. Even when Neil and Nick lived around the corner from each other, Stamler would occasionally get asked to tell the other something. 'Rather than shouting it out the back window, a call was made to LA to phone back to Melbourne. It was a very bizarre band in a lot of ways. There was never a lot of communication among the guys. Band meetings were almost never held. It eventually got to a situation that they were all living on different continents. That's a difficult band to keep together.'

'Then there would be another silly argument and I lost the plot,' says Paul. 'Everyone was so aware of me blowing up and being in a bad mood; it became like I was being treated with kid gloves. So we all lost our innocence through all that. It got to a point where we'd fall in and out. We'd get together before tours and rehearse and resolve a lot of things by being together. We had to rely on ringing each other up, because we ended up living quite apart. Neil moved back to New Zealand, Nick was going away more, Mark was in LA and I was just hanging around Melbourne.'

It came to a head on the European promo tour, when Paul said he didn't want to take part in the video for 'Nails in My Feet'. It was to be shot by Evan English, who directed the cheesy 'Something So Strong' video which still makes them cringe. This time, English's concept was dripping with Catholic imagery, even though the song's title actually came from sandals with nails in the soles, which Neil bought at a garden shop to aerate his lawn.

The band had a discussion in their London hotel. Paul told the others he couldn't keep doing the promotional tour: he had to go. 'I had just switched off, I'd had it with everyone. It was no longer me and Neil organising things, the power had shifted to record companies, Gary, Grant and Neil. When I got into it, I became very confrontational. I was pretty hard to handle on that tour. I was acting like an arsehole. The guys put it to me, perhaps I should have a bit of a break and they'd do the next leg and the video – "See if you can get your head together, Paul," sort of thing. So I took that on board and went home, happily, and sat on my bum. It was a mutual thing. I had no idea what was going to happen.'

Grant Thomas had gone back to Australia, leaving a tour manager handling the European campaign. On the Friday night he arrived back in Sydney, to a dinner party at his house. The phone rang from

London: Paul had left the promotional tour. Thomas had to ignore his guests to spend the evening on the phone. At seven o'clock the next morning, he flew straight back to London. 'I managed to keep him there for three more days. We convinced him to come to Cologne and do some German showcases, then he jumped on a plane and left.

'So we battled on, but it really wounded us a great deal. The other three guys were having difficulty doing the promotion without him. This was a team, and now suddenly part of the equation was missing.'

On form, Paul was the master when it came to promotion. His deadpan wit and outrageous antics were an asset to the band, as were Neil's songs. The difference was, Paul didn't get any royalties for his personality. With so much money being spent on recording, shooting videos, touring, freighting gear all over the world – all of which comes out of the band's advance – there was very little left for those who didn't write the songs.

'Neil was generous about it – some of his money would end up in the band's account – but still there was an enormous disparity,' says Stamler. 'The band was still essentially unrecouped [ie, hadn't earned back its advance] so they never got recording royalties and their touring – with the exception of that one tour in the UK – wasn't prof-itable enough that it would make a difference to their lifestyles.

'Some of the investments Paul had made in the early, good days, had gone south with the real estate market. I think he got to the stage where he felt, professionally, that every time he got on stage or went on TV he was enhancing the value of Neil's publishing catalogue.'

At times, Paul and Nick found it difficult to pay their mortgages. 'Paul and I were just getting by at home, on the places we'd bought,' says Nick. 'I could fare it a lot better, but Paul was under pressure. He used to ask, "What the fuck am I doing this for? Why am I on the road second-guessing every decision by management, when I know not to trust their judgement?" If management had made sure that we would be looked after on the home front, while they were putting money into videos, recording budgets, etc, then I don't think Paul would have left.'

Another issue discussed in London was the role of Gary Stamler, who flew over for the meeting. The band decided he would remain as their lawyer, but Grant Thomas would handle the management alone. Once that change was made, says Nick, 'We seemed to have more sense of control, we were talked to a lot more about finances. But Paul and I have to take responsibility for allowing that situation to happen.'

Although Neil still had a workable relationship with Stamler, Nick and Paul's had become quite destructive. 'Gary was passionate about the band,' says Neil, 'and he had a key role in the first album. He did a lot of work, and it worked very well. Paul always tended to look for somebody to blame for his angst in the band. And it was always Gary and Grant ringing him up saying you've got to go and do this, it's so important. To Paul that was like a nightmare: "Oh no, I just want to be home and watch the telly." They were like the devil incarnate for him, ringing him up and dragging him off on these trips he thought were crazy.'

Nick was lobbying for them to cut the stick with Stamler, but saw it as Neil's call. From his perspective, Stamler's first priority wasn't the band. 'It was a very single focus he had, and that was Neil Finn.'

'Nick and Paul would feel like accessories after the fact in a lot of the decision making,' says Neil, 'and to some extent, that was true.' There was also a constant battle of communication between Stamler and Thomas. 'It was consistently bad,' says Neil, 'and in the end, we had to choose between one or the other. Because Grant was close to us, and more involved in the day-to-day running of the band, he came out on top.' The band's key territory was now Europe – a strength of Thomas's – whereas the United States had stayed in Stamler's hands. 'You couldn't apportion blame to either party,' says Neil, 'they just had contradictory traits rather than complementary. Gary was good at working the upper levels, but a lot of details got missed.'

The promotional campaign continued, with the occasional hint of the unease within the band emerging in interviews. 'We don't even know if we'll make another album,' Neil told *Arena*. 'Crowded House is very much a volatile situation. We look enviously at other groups who seem to have such seamless organisation, whose careers seem to have this logical trajectory. We stumble along, and sometimes we're hanging by a thread.'

Meanwhile, Paul went home for a month and thought about the pending *Together Alone* tour. 'To leave the band at that point would have really stuffed everyone up. So I thought I should do the tour, it was important. I went into it with all the best intentions, of finishing off the tour. But it actually got worse. I just switched off.

'It was a two-month tour, which is a long time when you can hardly get through one day. It's not two months in one spot, it's two months all over the world . So I developed a serious anxiety towards travelling. Not a flying phobia, but a leaving phobia. It strung me up, the day before I left I'd be in depression. Then, at the end of a tour when it was time to come home, I'd be freaked out about not being able to leave. I would think every minute that something was going to happen and we'd have to stay. A few times that did happen, we'd be asked to stay another day, and it would completely freak me out and I'd lose it. So I became very unreasonable to everyone else. It seemed like my panic upset everyone and this was another thing to contend with.'

Paul went to an analyst about his anxieties and depressions. 'I recommend it to any 30-year-old man. Once you get to 30, you've got a bit of emotional baggage and I think you owe it to yourself to go and dump it – your mates can't help you.

'I went to a psychiatrist. It was great, I could get all the money back on Medibank, so it was only about $20 a session for this guy who was really good. I'd go and see him once a week and tell him all my most outrageous deadly thoughts. It was amazing. I had to get it off my chest with a completely independent person. He had no concept of Crowded House, hadn't really heard of us. I'd have to explain to him all about the band, and that was really boring for me. But it helped me work a few things out.'

When the band returned to Australia briefly before the tour proper began, it was time to talk seriously with Paul. 'We questioned him fairly in depth,' says Thomas. 'We said, we're going to do this touring – can you do it? Because if you can't, give us an opportunity to get someone else. But he was totally into doing it, saying "Yeah, absolutely." '

After the four Top 30 singles off *Woodface*, British fans were eagerly awaiting the release of *Together Alone*. The album entered the UK charts at number four – outselling current releases by superstars such as Prince, U2 and Nirvana – and journalists devoured the dramatic anecdotes about the exotic Karekare.

In Britain, the years of critical condescension finally gave way to reviews that were uniformly positive, some of them even adulatory: 'Pop is far from dead,' declared Peter Paphides in *Melody Maker*. 'It'll die when someone wears out the last copy of *Together Alone*.' 'Ambitious and impressive,' said the *NME*; 'Finn is a bona fide classic pop songwriter,' said the *Independent*. 'Stylish rock music with genuine emotion,' wrote Laura Lee Davies in *Time Out*.

However, many of the fashion-conscious critics felt they had to apologise for liking such an unhip act, as if Crowded House were Cliff Richard. *NME*'s Ian Fortnam spoke of a 'negative credibility quotient' and the *Telegraph*'s critic asked why people were embarrassed to admit they liked the band: 'Is it because they're too mainstream for cool people to like? I shall certainly play this record again. But only when my trendy friends aren't around to laugh at me.' *Time Out*'s Davies insisted, 'This is mainstream music as something *good*.'

Back home in the South Pacific, critics evocatively understood the impact the album would have in the environment where it was created. 'The fruits of last summer at the beach seem likely to make this summer a better place to be,' wrote Russell Brown in the New Zealand *Listener*. Lawrie Zion in the Australian *Rolling Stone* predicted, 'Soon the melodies of *Together Alone* will be oozing from the next car at the traffic lights, leaking out of cheap transistors in shops, and drifting across beaches. There is no safe level of exposure if you want to avoid getting hooked.' Brown was one of several critics who thought the loose atmosphere wasn't reflected in Clearmountain's crystal-clear mix: 'Crowded House, presumably, are not yet ready to make their woolshed recordings. The final mixes are huge and colourful, but sometimes it feels like walking in the sand in expensive shoes.'

The European leg of the *Together Alone* tour began at the National Stadium in Dublin on 5 November, and ran through to 19 December. Paul was feeling good when it began: 'We had a new batch of songs to play, we got ourselves some sleazy new costumes and a whole lot of new gear. I got a new drum kit and we bought some toys, like samplers. So it was pretty positive. We started in Dublin with "Black and White Boy". It was great. It rolled on pretty good at the start.'

The band played 34 gigs in 44 days, as autumn turned into a particularly cold northern winter. London came early in the tour, with three nights in the Hammersmith Apollo. The stage set – an imposing 3D purple backdrop, with coloured lights shining through windows – placed the band in a large circular room. Writing in the *Times*, David Sinclair considered the irony that, on their last tour, Crowded House could win *Q* magazine's best live act award – ahead of U2, Springsteen and Guns N' Roses – without elaborate props, light shows or pyrotechnics, and a lack of heroic rock'n'roll gestures. He found their 'laddish banter' pointless, although it gave the band a strong sense of identity, and the 'unaffected and convivial approach worked wonders on an audience doubtless accustomed to the rather more aloof behaviour of most major league rock acts'. At the party after the three-night season at the Apollo, Neil took a bar full of people to a small basement room, and led them in a singalong of Beatles tunes.

During one of the London shows, the band probably wished they were more aloof when a very drunk Scot got out of the audience and started to do a striptease on stage during 'Four Seasons in One Day'. 'It was very funny, and the band enjoyed it to begin with – but he wouldn't go away,' remembers Miles Mendoza. 'It was a real shame because they'd been going really well and they lost their concentration.'

The band were enjoying themselves, their impromptu play-acting making the shows teeter towards chaos. Yet Paul's behaviour was becoming increasingly erratic. At another London show, he drank a large mug of tea then, to the annoyance of the others, abandoned the stage to go to the toilet. Neil sat at the drums and accompanied himself singing 'Where is Love?' from *Oliver*. At the encore, Paul cartwheeled back on stage to begin 'Sister Madly'. In the north, fan Catrin Hughes mentioned Paul's shifting moods to the Crowded House fans on the internet. At the Manchester Apollo, he was subdued, and quickly disappeared after signing a few autographs, while Nick and Neil shared a packet of pineapple lumps (New Zealand chocolates) with the shivering fans waiting at the stagedoor. In Bradford, on the other hand, Paul wouldn't stop talking during the concert. A farewell London show was added on at the Town & Country, now re-named the Forum. After a two-and-a-half hour show, the audience still wouldn't leave, so the band came out in their dressing gowns for an extra encore.

Paul remembers the launch of the album, and the tour starting well, 'but after that it gets a bit grey. Because I started to lose it. My mind began to wander because my heart wasn't in the performance any more. I was too troubled by the whole picture of it, so that I couldn't focus just on the gigs. I wasn't actually tuned in, and after a gig I'd feel, "That wasn't very good" – and the others would be saying, "Where were you?"

'That started to happen a lot. I'd say, "I'm sick of having to be funny" until it became a bit of a cliché, whereas I never really had to be funny at all, I just had to be true to the gig. That's all the guys ever wanted. So I let myself down in the end. I was just sick of being the funny, wacky guy. It was never really a problem, it was just at the end that I lost my way.'

Paul became increasingly vocal about his dissatisfaction: they weren't doing the right promotion, or playing the right gigs . . . 'Whatever the reasons were,' says Nick, 'he'd always tag it with, "I'm going to leave the band". Finally, I pinned him down one night, when he threatened again, and I said, "When? I want a date." And he wouldn't ever say. He got angry with me trying to pin him down. I wanted to be able to project into the next few months.'

To the crew, it was very noticable. Paul had talked about wanting to stop being the class comedian, and just be a musician, but it couldn't happen overnight; the expectations of the band and audience wouldn't let it. 'The more he wanted it, the more pissed off he became,' says sound engineer Angus Davidson. 'It really affected his performance. He stopped singing harmonies, he stopped caring about shows. The more that happened, the more Neil felt the pressure. He was annoyed he was having to make up all Paul's slack. The drummer whirls a big stick in a band – if he decides to get lazy, it doesn't matter what you do, it's hard.

'Everyone in the crew recognised what was going down, and there was a real effort to try and support Paul, to help him out and make him feel okay. To the sound engineer, when someone isn't trying hard it's really obvious. As hard as it was for Neil, it became that hard for me to mix the show each night, because you can't polish a turd.

'I was really passionate about the band. But I probably have too much to say, so I ended up at loggerheads with Paul. I was saying things like, "If you don't like it, just leave, because right now all you're doing is giving everyone fucking grief". And I started having huge arguments with Nick because he also felt like he was carrying the show, which he was. He was actually quite shy on stage, but his performance became better, he started exchanging patter with Neil because Paul just wouldn't talk. Paul just disappeared off the back of the stage – he was there but he wasn't. He didn't want to be there. So Nick started taking on his role of banter with Neil. Nick had always been the fall guy, he'd open his mouth and Paul and Neil would just cut him down. All of a sudden Nick had taken on this role where he probably should have always been: a really talented and funny guy.'

The tension simmered as the tour continued through Scotland, England, Wales, Holland, Germany and Switzerland. Nick and Davidson started to argue. 'It's not an ego thing,' says Davidson, 'you're all dependent on each other. It's a symbiotic relationship – when one link fails, the whole thing falls apart. Nick felt the crew were all pandering to Paul, who was being a pain in the arse. We had this big blue. He was saying, "Fuck you guys – you're only in it for the money." And I told him, if I didn't care, we wouldn't even be discussing this. I'd be out in the bus, drinking and smoking and laughing about the band. But we're here, arguing.'

Ironically, at Eindhoven the crowd tried to cheer Paul up. During the show he'd been given a cigarette from someone in the audience. After smoking it, he complained that he felt sick. The audience responded by singing to him, 'Always look on the bright side of life . . .'

In London on 27 November, Neil had a day off prior to a show at the Forum, so he fulfilled a childhood dream: he played for the All Blacks at Twickenham. New Zealand's national rugby team was playing England at the hallowed ground. He rang the team for tickets and they said sure – as long as he came back to say hello after the game. To Sean Fitzpatrick, the All Black captain, Split Enz were heroes: they were in their prime when he was a schoolboy at Sacred Heart College.

A week earlier, the All Blacks had beaten Scotland 51–15, but against England they lost 9–15. Reluctantly, Neil went beneath the grandstand to the dressing room. He described the scene to David Hepworth of *Mojo*: 'It was gloom and despair, all these semi-naked All Blacks with their heads between their legs and the smell of linament.'

Eventually, some of the All Blacks started to talk to him. Then he was handed a guitar: 'Everyone was looking at me as if to say, "This is a national disaster, man, do your stuff, turn it on for the All Blacks". You can't say no to All Blacks. They're physically very intimidating. So I sang a few songs and the mood lifted and they started singing. It was like a scene out of a movie.' They wanted to hear his own songs, and every one he chose – 'Better Be Home Soon', 'It's Only Natural', 'Don't Dream It's Over' – seemed pointed and poignant.

'I got pissed and I went back into town on the bus with them. I felt like I'd walked into sacred territory.'

The pressure inside Crowded House finally exploded in Milan. Neil and Paul had earlier come to blows in Milan during the showcase tour in September 1986. But this time the argument took place Kinks-style: on stage. Everything was wrong about the gig from the moment they arrived. Gary Stamler admits, 'That was one show we shouldn't have booked. It was a fiasco waiting to happen.' The band had turned down a television appearance to a massive European audience to play the Zimba Club. Dugald McAndrew says that when the crew arrived in the afternoon, they found a 'pokey little shit-hole, with a tiny concrete stage and a horrid band room'. A plastic-strip flyscreen divided the audience from the backstage area. The crew had to scale down the band's backline equipment to fit them on stage.

There were only about 40 people in the audience. During the show, as the band began its busking routine, Paul started complaining about the sound. McAndrew watched from the side of the stage: 'He was hitting the snare, saying "listen to the boink", then going *bang, bang, bang*. Neil turned around to me quite innocently and said, "Can I have my spare guitar?" I handed it to him, wondering why he wanted it – maybe he was going to give it to Paul to play.'

Neil took the guitar by the neck and smashed it onto the snare drum a couple of times, then handed it back to McAndrew. 'There's a tape of that show,' says Neil, embarrassed. 'It's not pleasant listening. Paul yelled at me, we went backstage, had a short brief sharp exchange . . .'

Paul: 'It got a bit verbal when we got off stage, and Neil felt this shove . . .'

Neil: '. . . and as I left he pushed me through this weird screen, while saying "Come 'ere!" at the same time. I ended up flying through it and landing at the feet of these people waiting to say hello to the band. Hardcore Italian fans, and the lead singer comes blasting through a screen. I just walked off. It was a disaster.

'The crew were very dark at us after that, they lectured us for about three hours about how they'd done the set up, and it'd been really hard, and it was bad for them and the show, and we'd let them down. I can remember feeling pissed off and thinking later, fuck you – this was a really tough day for us, the last thing I need is to be lectured by our own crew.'

The tour had four days to go before going home for a Christmas break. 'Everyone had just had it,' says Angus Davidson. 'After the show I got completely drunk and basically confronted Neil and said, "This is crap. You've got a whole crew wanting to leave. All this shit's going down." I just didn't want to be there. I had been looking forward to this tour for so long and it turned out to be a complete nightmare.'

McAndrew: 'We had a pow-wow in a hotel suite that evening. A few spleens were vented, some hot air blown off. It was the darkest period I ever spent with the band. It all blew over in about 24 hours, but the repercussions were felt for some time. Decisions were made there that I was not privy to, concerning other people's roles within the organisation. There was a bit of ugliness.'

The last thing the band had scheduled before leaving – though their flights home weren't booked yet – was a television show in Paris. Paul bailed out early, leaving the drummer Alister from Frente, the support act, to fill his seat for the filming. 'A lot of stuff got sorted out and Nick and I resolved everything and it was all hugs,' says Davidson. After the Christmas break, he got a phone call from Paul, who told him the band had a meeting in Paris, and had decided to let Davidson go. They needed a tight crew for the upcoming tour, said Paul, which was going to be tough. When push came to shove, if a choice needed to be made between a disgruntled drummer or an outspoken sound engineer, Davidson knew what the answer was. He went fishing in Tasmania, got married, and thought, Paul won't survive another tour.

The Shadows of night
• January 1994

'I'd given up on Britain. I thought you were weird and unknowable and scene-obsessed and dismissive of colonials. But in the end people are won around.'

—Neil to *Q*, February 1994

Crowded House were in separate countries over Christmas. Mark and Nick were in Los Angeles, while Neil and Paul preferred a Christmas at home in the sun. In Melbourne, Paul and Mardi adjusted to the idea that they would be parents in a few months. In Auckland, Neil once again performed at the Christmas party of his friends, the video-makers Kerry Brown and Bruce Sheridan. At the previous year's carpark party, Tim Finn had joined him; this year it was Dave Dobbyn and the rhythm section from local industrial funksters the Headless Chickens.

Meanwhile, Capitol in LA prepared for the American release of *Together Alone*. In music-biz jargon, the capsule review in *Billboard* provided positive clues for radio programmers: 'Still looking for a hit single to help duplicate the success of its 1986 debut album, Down Under unit regroups slightly – and dishes up a platter of typically well-crafted pop songs. Sparing but intelligent use of unusual instrumentation and stirring presence of the Te Waka Huia cultural group choir adds life, as does addition of new member Mark Hart. Among the many sterling numbers – most penned by Neil Finn – [is the] impressive title set-closer. Top 40s and modern rockers alike should sample from this feast.'

An accompanying article signalled that this was virtually a relaunch for the band, almost seven years after 'Don't Dream It's Over' had been a hit. It was also the initiation for yet another Capitol promotion team under a new presidential regime. The company was targeting 'Locked Out' at commercial alternative and adult alternative stations, which they hoped would crossover to pop stations. Brian MacDonald, Capitol's new director of alternative promotion, said, 'If "Don't Dream It's Over" is the only Crowded

House track that can go to pop radio, there's something seriously wrong with pop radio.' Yet *Billboard*'s pre-release articles usually discuss marketing ideas for albums; that Capitol had lost touch with the group's fans was reflected by the limpness of their strategy: 'bounce back' postcards placed inside albums and on seats at the band's concerts, so the company could build up a data base of fans.

Capitol were, however, running a competition to send a US fan to a Crowded House benefit concert for Amnesty International, to be held in Wellington, New Zealand, on 25 February. The concert had come about through the tenacity of Lorna Leydon, at the suggestion of her son Mark, a dedicated fan of the band. For 18 months she had been discussing the possibility with Grant Thomas; the intention was always there, if the band was able to do it. But as the concert drew closer, he discreetly admitted the delicate position the band was in. Due to illness, he said, it wasn't clear whether Paul would still be in Crowded House by then.

In public however, it was business as usual: interviews which determinedly emphasised the positive. 'The band feels stronger than it has for years,' Neil told Samantha Trenoweth. 'We've had our seven-year itch, but we're through that. It's solid.' In Sydney's *On the Street*, Paul said world domination was no longer on the agenda: 'Old Crowded House have been having some pretty serious talks. We're pulling back and saying we're going to tour where we're really liked and feel successful. We're regaining control of the band.'

The future looked a breeze: a short tour of Australia and New Zealand, six weeks in North America, then time off for fatherhood. 'We'll have a few months off and I'm going to do the John Lennon thing – stay home and look after the kid, bake some bread, watch the telly,' said Paul. Maybe he would even write a song, which he hadn't done for several years, as 'Skin Feeling' was written at the same time as 'Italian Plastic'. 'I've got a bunch of stuff. I'm going to launch my own career when I'm about 40. I reckon your best years are between 40 and 60. I think you need to live a bit first.'

Paul stayed home while the others headed back to the northern hemisphere for promotion, performing on the television shows *Music Scoupe*, *The Late Show with David Letterman* and MTV's *Alternative Nation*. On the Toronto television station MuchMusic, Neil explained Paul was 'at home dealing with a pregnancy', and dedicated 'Black & White Boy' to him.

A week later, they were back in Australia to begin a two-week tour. As the entourage assembled in Melbourne, a package arrived at the band's PR office, containing an unidentified statuette. Peter Green placed it on the mantlepiece and used it to crack open cashew nuts. It turned out to be a Brit award: Crowded House had been voted the best international act in the forthcoming annual bash of the UK music industry. A few days later, the band was filmed accepting the statuette *in absentia* on St Kilda Beach; Nick insisting the cameraman wait until sunset, Paul hiding an arm inside his jersey, spoofing Def Leppard's one-armed drummer.

The Melbourne concert was at the Myer Music Bowl, with Yothu Yindi, the Sharp and Ed Kuepper. In the buildup, a relaxed joint interview between Paul and Andrew Gaze, hero of the Melbourne Tigers basketball team, appeared in the *Herald-Sun*. Hester, a Tigers fanatic and season ticket holder, described himself as 'the Jack Nicholson of Melbourne. I've got my shades. My hair's falling out. I'm there every week.'

Gaze: Is Crowded House a New Zealand or Australian band?
Hester: Two of us are Aussies. Neil is a New Zealander.
Gaze: Does he claim that?
Hester: Oh definitely. Neil claims everything (both laugh). Neil claims me and Nick as dependents.
Gaze: What about day-to-day. You're working on a song and you really want a drum solo. You get knocked back. What do you do?
Hester: A middle-class tantrum (both laugh). Middle-class tantrums rule music. It's whoever can throw the biggest middle-class tantrum gets their way. The other thing is, in the '90s with the new age muso, the male thing, everyone has still got their huge ego, but they're appearing not to have an ego. The whole thing is language now.
Gaze: Ah, diplomacy.
Hester: Right. You hide it in language. If you want a drum solo, you say something along the lines of 'I think we need some African tribal rhythms, or an indigenous rhythm background' when basically it's still some little white guy who wants to do a drum solo (laughs). Backstage, behind the scenes, it's sort of like a cross between *The Young Ones* and *Home and Away* (both laugh).

During rehearsals, Neil sat the extended family, band and crew, down together to talk tour politics. 'Being stuck on the road with a group of people for months at a time can bring you close to killing someone,' Peter Green wrote in his club newsletter tour diary. 'A few words of wisdom from the Finn makes us aware . . . well, a little bit.'

Opening night was in Adelaide. Then the band returned for a large outdoor show in their former homebase, Melbourne. Several days of rain finally came to a halt 15 minutes before the gates opened; the band arrived by helicopter. Green remembers standing in the mud listening to 'Private Universe': 'It had the most brilliant natural setting one could ever want. A full moon, dark purple clouds speedily heading eastward, the band playing their hearts out under the billowing white sails of Myer Music Bowl, the city of Melbourne lit up like a beacon behind the Bowl.'

The night the Brit awards were made public in England, Crowded House was playing the Barooga sports club on the Murray River. The world's 'best international act' was also the biggest ever to play Barooga; all six hotels in the town were booked out. Neil Finn thought the irony of playing a country town, when they had just been voted ahead of U2, Nirvana and Pearl Jam, 'sublime'. That night Paul found a raffle wheel in the sports club, and brought it on stage for 'Paulo's Lucky Wheel'; prizes included a piece of chocolate cake, a guitar pick and a dance with Nick. On the drive to Canberra the next day, Mark, Neil and Peter Green took an unfrequented route through the outback. Green turned off his mobile phone, Mark put on a tape of music from Mongolia, Zanzibar, Morocco and Sardinia and they drove by flooded canals teeming with wildlife. They were surrounded by flat plateaus, with families of ibis in the sky above. 'Without the aid of any artificial stimulants we were in a complete trance state,' Neil told NME, 'driving 50 miles past our turns and stuff. It was really quite profound.' Stopping at an isolated roadside café for breakfast, they looked through the video titles (Hot Babes from Hell; Bikies' Playground – 'This video is banned in Queensland') while the owner tried to sell them a whistle that stopped birds flying into the car window.

When the tour reached Sydney, the band gave a free lunchtime concert at Martin Place, in the heart of the city, for 5000 shoppers and office workers; it was a fundraiser for the City Mission, which Triple-J broadcast live-to-air. Their gig at the Horden Pavilion was packed and stifling. Roadies doused the audience with buckets of cold water and Paul declared the venue should be renamed the 'Whore Den'. In his review for the Sydney Morning Herald, Bruce Elder was amazed the band kept their sense of humour as they baked under the stage lights to deliver 'a truly great, uplifting show'. He detected a revitalised spirit in the band, possibly due to the energy of the now-permanent Mark Hart. 'Never has Paul Hester hit the drums with such enthusiasm as when the band launched into a wonderfully hard-edged version of "Mean To Me".' Old favourites sounded fresh, and the band conveyed a sense of genuine joy and unpretentiousness, said Elder. 'Crowded House are simply a bunch of good mates having a great time and playing music of transcendental beauty.'

The rare chance to hear three of New Zealand's most accomplished performers together packed Wellington's Town Hall for the Amnesty International 'Freedom Concert' on 25 February. On the bill was vocalist Annie Crummer, whose operatic soul relects her Rarotongan heritage; a political 'Pacific folk' set from Dave Dobbyn; and Crowded House, unveiling the inspirations from Karekare for the first time in New Zealand. It was an unusual set, which avoided *Woodface*, and mixed dark and lesser-known songs from *Temple of Low Men* with the expansive, summery *Together Alone*. Two years since they last played New Zealand, the band seemed 'raw and looser than ever before,' wrote Nick Bollinger, 'thanks largely to recent recruit Mark Hart's grungy guitar and organ textures. Finn's melodies still leapt out like lost Beatle records.'

They followed this, two days later, with a free concert in South Auckland, to support Maori and Pacific Island musicians in the community. 'There's a great resource in South Auckland that's not recognised by the rest of New Zealand,' said Neil. Two young Polynesian men were plucked from the audience so Paul could take a pit stop: Billy played Neil's acoustic guitar while Amos drummed, leading the 6000-strong crowd in a version of Bob Marley's 'Exodus'.

While in Auckland, the band was filmed for the video of 'Private Universe', once again directed by Kerry Brown and Bruce Sheridan. A local metal-work artist, Sean Kerrigan, made some exotic instruments and furniture out of scrap-metal for the shoot. In a helicopter, Neil was taken alone to White Island, a small active volcano off the coast of Mt Maunganui, where he'd spent his childhood summers. The island has a dramatic, desolate landscape, reinforced by the occasional belch of volcanic rock and poisonous gas. 'It's a very difficult filming environment,' says Sheridan, 'because of the acidic, sulphuric air. It eats into your throat, and cameras can die in a day. So here we are with one of the world's major recording artists, risking life and limb with the danger of rocks falling out of the sky.' The return journey, by sea, was equally hazardous, as the tides were wrong. The small launch – a scrap-metal chair strapped across its bows – had to battle across turbulent waves breaking against an off-shore bar. The boat was almost swamped. 'We decided to give it a shot, and surf in. It was very scary. Neil went white as a ghost. It'd be wrong to say we didn't all go white.'

Back in Auckland, a studio session took place to film the others playing the bizarre instruments in front of a chromakey screen. Paul was in high spirits at the session, giving the impression to crew-members that this was his last task before going home for good: he was about to leave the band.

The two benefit gigs were the only concerts in New Zealand during the *Together Alone* tour. In two weeks, the American campaign would begin, with Sheryl Crow as the support act. But Stamler remembers receiving 'a very strange phone call from Paul' at this time. 'Most of the phone calls I had with Paul trying to set up the tour were very negative. There was a lot of hostility, I felt, towards me – and between Paul and Nick. It wasn't a very healthy situation. The two of them weren't getting on well. In fact, they weren't even talking at one stage.

'About two weeks before the tour went out, Paul actually told me, "It wouldn't be the dumbest thing in the world to start looking for another drummer." He didn't know if he was going to pull out. I called Neil, and he was both surprised and disgusted at the same time. He basically said, "If that's the way he feels, we'll leave him alone." That temporarily resolved itself, but he was miserable.

'The band started to spin down with the lack of success again. Gersh's prophecy was realised, not surprisingly: the record wasn't happening really anywhere to the extent we expected. In England, it went to platinum, but very slowly.

'So the band was in a very dysfunctional state. The whole operation was. Communication was virtually non-existent, there was a lot of anger at shows, a lot of dressing room blow-ups.'

Just as the tour opened in Phoenix, Arizona, an interview the group had given in London appeared in the US magazine *Creem*. Neil was telling interviewer David Konjoyan that the title of *Together Alone* 'suggests what a lot of the songs are about, which is the contradiction of being close to somebody and being distant at the same time – which is what relationships are all about.'

'If you're in a band,' chimes Hester.

It's unclear whether Hester's passing comment is in reference to his personal life or life with the band, but it becomes increasingly evident that the happy-go-lucky Crowded House is a band with its own inner-demons and inter-personal tensions ... The latest debacle for the band revolves around the relatively recent development of Finn moving back to his native New Zealand, Hester living in Melbourne, and Seymour and Hart spending most of their time in Los Angeles. It's an arrangement Finn fears may not work out, maybe even split the band, as he and Seymour have a playful go at one another over the topic.

Finn: 'We're all strung out over the four corners of the globe. It's weird, nobody lives near anybody else.'

Seymour: 'Well, we all lived in the same city until you decided to move to New Zealand.'

Finn: 'Well, you moved first, man. Anyway, when I moved to New Zealand, you weren't living in Melbourne anyway.'

Seymour: 'No, you gave us *carte blanche* to live anywhere we liked.'

Finn: 'I couldn't control where you lived.'

Seymour: 'You rang me one time when I was in LA and said, "Why are you there? You have to be in the same city if you're in the same band."'

Finn: 'Well, that could well prove to be true (laughs). We haven't tested the theory really, we've just been touring. But can you have a band that lives in different countries?'

The early reports of the US tour noticed the spark was absent. Reviewing their shows at the Wiltern Theatre in Los Angeles, the *Los Angeles Times* carefully said Crowded House was straddling 'the very fine line between being consistent and being static' and wondered why the early hits were missing from the set list. *Music Connection* said that they were 'just going through the motions'. Two weeks later, at the Agora Theatre show in Cleveland, Ohio, *Scene* reviewer Pete Chakerian reported: 'Everything sounded *great* – but just the same, something was *still* missing.' The crowd didn't know the new material, which destroyed the momentum. Two audience members invited onstage to sing with the band turned 'Fall At Your Feet' into 'karaoke with the stars'. Disappointed fans were still calling out for the hits as the lights went up. Support act Sheryl Crow, however, was 'thoroughly enjoyable,' said Chakerian. 'I expect she won over more than a few fans on this night.'

Paul's behaviour was more erratic than ever. Early on in the tour, at San Diego, he left his drumkit in the middle of a show, followed two women fans into the restroom and returned with a rubbish tin, which he emptied on stage. A gulf between Paul and the others began to be noticed; after gigs, the band and crew were perturbed by the way he'd disappear into his hotel room for a smoky session watching basketball videos. 'I thought he'd gone mad,' says Nick, bluntly. 'I thought he was allowing the dark Paul to take him over. He had Mardi there, so I didn't think I needed to go to his room and counsel him or anything. I thought he really needed help, but it wouldn't have been appropriate because his girlfriend was there.'

David Field caught up with the band in Providence, Rhode Island, on 5 April, and found them utterly dispirited. 'It was bad,' he says. 'Neil was angry because no-one seemed to know the band was there. Nobody had shown up from the record label, or even called. It was appalling. And Paul was up to his shenanigans, grumbling and moaning. His girlfriend was there, too, and she was the same. It was grim.'

Two days later, Paul's demeanour spoilt an *Intimate and Interactive* show they did on Toronto television. 'He wouldn't even talk,' says Mark. 'Someone called in and asked him about something and he was really dismissive of him and really short. He was drifting. It wasn't like at one point you knew; each day you knew a little bit more. People began to ask what was wrong with Paul. We were embarrassed by the whole thing, we didn't know what to do. What can you do, say "be happy"? He didn't look that way.'

He certainly didn't: in all the photos taken to promote *Together Alone* and during the tour, Paul's face is drawn, his mouth downturned, his expression haunted, exhausted.

My second life has just begun • April 1994

'If You Leave Me, Can I Come Too?'

—Mental As Anything song, 1981

In Britain, *Together Alone* had been in the charts for more than six months; in the States it slipped out of the Top 200 after only seven weeks. But the US tour continued: New York, Philadelphia, Washington DC, Norfolk, Charleston. They were playing a different city every day, then jumping on their tour bus to travel to the next one overnight to save money. David Hepworth, who flew from London to Washington on 10 April to write a cover story on the band for *Mojo*, recalls the mood he encountered: 'They were playing to good, enthusiastic audiences, but their record was barely out. The record company wasn't doing anything, they were working very hard, but they were banging their heads against a brick wall. They were clearly not happy campers.

'Kurt Cobain had just died and that really disturbed Paul, though it wasn't obvious to me why that would be. His girlfriend was pregnant and about to go back to Australia, which can't have helped: she was going back to have a baby and he was going to be slogging his way around America to no great purpose. The shows were great, but they were not enjoying themselves offstage.' Hepworth didn't get to the bottom of the tension he sensed – Paul, while amicable, wouldn't give him an interview – but suspected it was a combination of tour organisation and 'a career not going quite right'.

Australian journalist Lawrie Zion, who had a close rapport with the band, was in the States, and was invited to join the tour for a few days. A producer at the national youth radio network Triple-J, he decided to make a short documentary. He joined the tour in Atlanta, where the band had been a couple of days, and immediately got an odd feeling. He met the band at 'modern rock' the radio station 99X-FM, where they were doing a 'live to air' set. Paul wasn't with them, he was seeing a doctor. For his documentary, the 99-X programmer told Zion that, although the station played many tracks off *Woodface*, she 'didn't know who was to blame for the fact it wasn't a huge success in the States. I know "Chocolate Cake" wasn't a favourite of radio at the time, and it's almost like a lot of radio stations are afraid to play a second cut off an album if the first one is not a hit.' But, said the programmer, the new AAA stations (adult alternative) meant there was finally a home for 'bands like Crowded House, who make great albums but have had very little radio airplay because there hasn't been the format for them'.

At the station, says Zion, the band were very welcoming and in good humour, making a few jokes at the absent Paul's expense. He caught a taxi back with Nick, and then went his own way for a few hours.

When the band arrived in Atlanta, Paul had got very sick. 'I had this migraine thing and went down big time,' he says. 'Mardi was due to leave, and she stayed back a couple of days to nurse me. My whole body just went *poof*. It just gave up, like it was saying, "Nah – I'm not going any further." No doctors would come to the hotel, so we had to drive across town. This guy looked at me and said, "You should just go home. Whatever you're doing, you're fried." It's like my body started the whole process off. Because I had no mental intention to leave that day, it was just a sequence of things.

'I was angry at everything going on around me, it just got a bit too much. Mardi and I were just walking around, trying to find something to eat, not doing much. All of a sudden everything went very quiet and incredibly dull and really obvious. It was like something was being laid out in front of me. There were no people around, I couldn't find anyone. Neil came back in the afternoon, and I'd been lying on my bunk in the bus, tossing and turning. I realised, if it kept going – things had been bad enough – I could see what was coming. In the psycho-analysis I'd had, I had learnt to recognise things about me. I realised that if I didn't get out then, something would go really bad, there would be a huge falling out. The penny dropped, I thought, "Everything could change by tonight, if I just spoke up".'

Just before soundcheck, Paul walked into the grim backstage area of the Roxy in Atlanta, where Neil and Mark were sitting in the dressing room. 'He said he wanted to talk to us,' says Mark. 'He said, "I can't do it anymore. I'm leaving. I'm leaving tonight. Tomorrow, when Mardi goes home, I'm going too." She was having a baby, and he wanted to be there – though this was April the 14th and she wasn't due until mid July. He couldn't face the fact she was going to go back to Australia by herself, pregnant. He was really dissatisfied with the band and he looked dead. He was spiritually dead – he couldn't take it any more, even if he wanted to. It took a lot of courage.'

'It was a huge release,' says Paul. 'Neil was incredibly good about it, he was taken away with the moment. In his eyes, it looked like he was thinking, "I'd love to do that". He was hugging me, saying all this stuff, it was great.'

Nick heard when he arrived to prepare for the show. 'I didn't fight it, I said, "Congratulations – you've done it. You've somehow turned a corner in your own mind. It's a good decision, for your own creative growth." Then I thought, "Ah ... tomorrow night ... what are we going to do for a drummer?" It was the middle of a tour, we'd sold the tickets, that takes priority.'

Lawrie Zion was in the dressing room just before the show, but hadn't been told yet. 'Nick was in a really foul mood. I didn't feel I could go up and ask, what's wrong. The rest of them were pretending to me that nothing was wrong. It was quite strange.'

Zion's *radio vérité* documentary captures a moment backstage. Neil says to him, 'Are you riding on the bus tonight? It'll be fun. We're in the heart of the tour, Lawrie. Join us. Mid-tour, where reality is blurred. The tour manager is pissed, half the band is pissed. Reality is suspended.'

On stage, it turned into a marathon gig. 'Even before the encores, they had the place on fire. It was a great show, but there was something strange about it,' says Zion. 'Neil provided cryptic clues as to what was really happening.'

From the stage, Neil told the audience the band were doing all their own favourites, there would be no requests. 'That's what is different about tonight's show, in case any of you go home saying, "Oh, the bastards didn't play my song".' The banter was more surreal than humorous, covering Neil's academic relatives, New Zealand's health system, and American politics.

From the moment the concert opened with 'Kare Kare' an extra intensity and focus was apparent. There was an edgy commitment to Paul's drumming, Neil's singing and all the backing vocals. 'Distant Sun' in particular took flight.

'In a funny way,' says Paul, 'me going to them before the show provided the gig with an incredible impetus of real emotion. It came out in the songs, and the crowd saw a doozey. We had a lot of things going on that night.'

As the encores began, Neil and Nick put their heads together at the microphone, like George and Paul – or Liam Clancy and Tommy Makem – and started to sing, a capella.

Of all the comrades that ever I had
    they're sorry for my going away ...

It was 'The Parting Glass', the old Irish drinking song about saying farewell to a friend. Mark Seymour had taught it to Neil and Paul; Crowded House had sung it when they bonded with Paul Kelly and his gang; Neil had sung it in Dublin the night his parents were in the audience.

> ... And of all the sweethearts that ever I've had
> they wish me one more day to stay.

'I couldn't even look,' Paul told Zion. 'I was just broken up. That song was a big thing between us which was unspoken. We went into the encore, looking down the last 100 metres of Hessie's career with the Crowdies, and somehow it was overwhelming. I got a real insight into myself and into those guys that night. It was like a swansong, a testimonial. I didn't know what to expect, it could have been an anticlimax. The boys let me call the encores.' For well over an hour, Paul shouted out his favourite songs for the band to do, 14 in all. 'Sister Madly' turned into a marathon, with detours into 'I've Got to Be Free' and 'Born Free' – and the old New Zealand placename trick, used by pre-war All Blacks overseas when they were asked to say a speech in Maori: '*Waikato, Te Awamutu, Taumaranui, Te Kuiti, Rotorua, Maunganui* ... ' Finally, they came back to earth. Neil said, 'Paul Hester, ladies and gentleman!'

When their repertoire seemed exhausted, Neil waited for the elation to subside. Quietly but emphatically, he made a statement. 'I'd like to dedicate this song to a man I love, Paul Hester.' He then picked out the simple opening of the song which described the hazards of life on the road; the song which marked the reversal of their fortunes in America: 'Better Be Home Soon'.

Paul later told Australian journalist Peter Wilmoth that Neil had been euphoric that night, 'taken with the idea of me escaping. It was like we were back at the start again. He embraced Mardi and said, "I love you and I love Paul and good luck." It was really heartfelt and I'd never felt closer to Neil.'

Also that night, Nick noticed a curious thing: Paul's face had altered shape. The fatigued, unhappy look of the past 18 months had gone, replaced by one of calm and relaxation. 'He had been holding himself a certain way for about a week before he made his decision. And when he'd made it, his face had changed, he was holding all his muscles differently. I was happy to see that.'

The band was leaving immediately on the bus to drive overnight to Nashville, about eight hours away. They dropped Paul and Mardi off at the Atlanta hotel to pick up their luggage. The pair were going to catch a cab to stay in an airport motel before leaving for Australia the next day. 'It was like a scene from a Southern play or the end of a film,' says Paul. 'Atlanta is so hot and humid. The moment they drove off on the bus, it was really like a complete full-stop, it was so still and quiet. There was no traffic around. Me and Mardi were sitting on the kerbside, our suitcases behind us, and we were waving at the bus as it took off towards the city and then petered out. We thought, "Wow, this is really finished." It was euphoric, like a trip, it was so warm and humid, not uncomfortable or cold. There was a sweet smell in the air, and we just got a cab and went to this shitty motel and felt *fantastic*. We checked in, then went straight out the door to a 24-hour waffle joint, where we had pancakes and coffee, and then went to bed. It all felt like a dream, the peacefulness of it was so special.'

On the bus, the euphoria had turned to exhaustion. Neil offered Zion a cup of tea; Zion gave Nick a sleeping tablet. 'They were very hospitable. Nick was still playing the perfect host. They explained to me the rules of the bus, to treat it like their home, how you're always quiet in the sleeping quarters, where you could talk, where to go to smoke. They didn't get excessively drunk, there was an air of relief. They said to me, this is bad *now* – but you're lucky you didn't come a couple of weeks earlier, because Paul's moods would control the bus.' Neil put on a tape of African music and tried to relax; he contemplated the irony that 17 years earlier, he got his career break when Phil Judd had abruptly quit Split Enz in Atlanta.

The most immediate problem was to find another drummer. 'I was daunted by the prospect of doing a tour not knowing who was going to be drumming,' says Nick. 'It was a very big call. But it seemed like a burden had dropped off my shoulders, of not being able to predict what Paul was going to be like, whether I'd have to stay out of his way. The gigs that followed, we engaged the audience in the excitement of flying the show by the seat of our pants.'

Wally Ingram, drummer with the support act Sheryl Crow, enthusiastically agreed to fill in. 'It was a do-or-die thing,' he told Zion, 'but it was definitely a day of neurosis for me.' Luckily he had been enjoying watching Paul's drumming over the last few weeks, 'and the band is so tight, you just sort of jump on and go for the ride. It was a lot of fun, and the nerves went away after the first song.'

Jules Bowen, who had joined the crew as a keyboard tech only three weeks earlier, says Neil worked hard at keeping everybody up. Just before going on stage at Nashville, he gathered the band and crew together backstage. He produced a large bottle of scotch, poured everyone a stiff shot, and insisted they drink it. 'Okay,' he said, 'this is it. We're still all in this together.' Adrenaline also helped pull them through the Nashville show, in front of about 3000 people in the 328 Performance Hall (among them was Barry Coburn, Split Enz's first manager, now a Nashville publisher). Neil introduced Wally to the audience, and explained, 'Paul has gone back to Australia. He couldn't cope with touring and we'd like to wish him well as he speeds his way across the Pacific Ocean.'

On the bus between Nashville and Dallas, Nick sat with Ingram and went through a tape of a show, listening to Paul's drum patterns. At the gigs, the audience would become involved as Nick coached Ingram through the songs over the microphone. 'I'd tell him, change to the chorus on a certain word, break down our songs in a way which delighted the audience. They felt they understood how we arrived at arrangements. We ended up pulling it off every night.'

Ingram kept it up for a week; his only disappointment was the non-eventful bus rides afterwards. 'I'm used to riding with Sheryl Crow and nine party animals, going wild, cranking up the music – and here's Neil Finn offering me a cup of tea.'

Just after making his decision, Paul had phoned Grant Thomas, who was in Los Angeles, and told him. With the time difference, there was nothing Thomas could do: by the time he got there, the gig would be over and the band on their way to Nashville. 'Paul was resolute: he was going home. The next time I talked with him, he was ensconced in Melbourne. By that stage, I was fielding phone calls in LA, while Neil and the band were trying to find drummers on the road.'

Paul's decision wasn't a surprise, says Thomas. 'What hurt was, here was a guy who was part of a team. We'd asked him if he could make it or not, and he'd given us his iron-clad guarantee that he could do it, and would. Four weeks in, he jumped, in the middle of an American tour. It was pretty devastating.'

It also hurt that no-one from Capitol in Los Angeles made contact with the band (Jeremy Hammond was out of the country). From England, David Field rang Neil to commiserate; Parlophone in London offered help if needed. 'It was clearly obvious the Americans weren't even vaguely into it,' says Thomas. 'So we battled on for another six weeks across Canada and America.' To cancel the tour would have angered promoters; to reschedule would have caused just as many difficulties as continuing. 'They had to keep going, for the band, for the record. They were heading back for England, where the record was blowing up. The band had a serious future.'

On the bus, two days after Atlanta, Neil said to Zion, 'In a way, we feel slightly liberated, because there's been a pall hanging over the band. Paul's been so miserable that it cast a shadow on all of us. Now he's gone there's possibly a lot more unity of purpose. It's a shame it didn't happen when we were off the road and could have rehearsed, but we had a great gig last night with Wally. It's rough around the edges, but we proved to ourselves that we're a band still.'

Zion had a scoop, but was determined to handle it sensitively. 'I felt a bit odd, but the band were saying, "No, we're glad it's you that's here: a friend." I got a big run with the story, talking live-to-air back to Triple-J. The reaction seemed to be, Oh the band has split up. But being there, you could see that wasn't the issue at all. It wasn't about to split.

'If anything, I was spoken to a great deal more than if I'd been on a normal tour. Neil and Nick were very open and talkative, expansive. Nick was far more annoyed than Neil. He was saying, "Life's full of people who can't last the distance. Of course it hasn't been working, but that's not the point." Neil was much more, "Oh, let him go, if he wants to go." But a day or so later he was saying, "Well actually, now that I think about it, I'm quite annoyed." '

In Dallas they performed at the Edgefest. By now they were drained; reality had kicked in. The festival featured a lot of young British bands. In England, Crowded House would have been the headlining act, but to this college-radio oriented audience, their music was unknown. Sheryl Crow's star was rising, although her breakthrough hit 'All I Wanna Do' hadn't been released yet. (Crow's debut *Tuesday Night Music Club* eventually became one of the year's biggest-selling records. But, due to the high drama, the two acts became close on the tour. Crow later hired long-serving Crowded House production manager Paul 'Arlo' Guthrie to become a member of her crew.)

'Sheryl Crow was just at the beginning of her meteoric ascent,' Neil told *Goldmine* in 1996. 'We noticed the difference between what her record company was doing in every city, and what ours was. We'd arrive in towns and there'd be big window displays of Sheryl's record and we would struggle to find ours in the shops at all. That was discouraging, to say the least.'

In the weeks following Paul's departure, the band heard nothing from Capitol in Los Angeles. The only person from the record company who contacted them had been David Field, who himself felt out in the cold in Gersh's regime. He was still based in London, spending 'six months in purgatory' until his contract was up. 'I just called Neil and congratulated him for sticking with it, because a lot of bands would have cancelled the tour and come home. But he wouldn't stop. The amount of courage it must have taken him to do that was huge.'

The band started to audition drummers on the road, rehearsing six numbers with them at soundcheck, then playing those songs together at the concert, with Ingram doing the rest. The drum technician Craig Bird would sit beside them on the drum riser, tapping them on the back when it was time for a drum fill, or tugging their sleeve to get them to ease off.

'Sometimes you'd get people in the audience, waving drumsticks,' says Jules Bowen. 'Dougs used to pull 'em on stage and put 'em on. The great thing was, they were actually drummers, they were alright. The good thing about drums of course is you can't play out of key.'

The drummer who seemed likely to get the position was Andy Kubiszewski, formerly with The The. He played drums as they crossed Canada (including a gig at Toronto's famous Massey Hall, where – perversely – the band perfomed Paul's 'This is Massive'), but the 'chemistry' was lacking, so Seattle was his last gig. The band had flown him in from the midwest and, thinking positively, had only bought him a one-way ticket. Grant Thomas, who had joined up with the tour in Seattle, provided his airfare home. 'One minute he was there, part of the furniture,' says Bowen. 'The next thing he was gone.'

Gary Stamler and his wife Peggy also flew up to the Seattle show, bringing Hale Milgrim. It was almost a year since Milgrim had been removed as president of Capitol; in semi-retirement, he worked on various charitable causes. After the show – which Stamler says 'wasn't memorable for being good or bad, just okay' – Neil suggested they have breakfast next morning. In the hotel restaurant, says Stamler, 'Neil was very nervous, there was something on his mind. He was smoking cigarettes, having a very difficult time getting it out. He finally said, "This is where we terminate our artist/manager relationship." I said, what for? Neil basically said the level of communication had been non-existent recently and there was no vibe in America. He asked, "What else does there need to be?" then said, "I've got to catch the bus now . . . can you cover this, I'm a bit short." '

Stamler was shocked: a 10-year passion had come to a sudden end. He told Neil it was crazy – he was about to start working 'Distant Sun' in the States; Gary Gersh was on the verge of spending money on it. 'Neil said, "I realise I might be making a mistake, but I'm willing to live with that." '

Stamler told Neil he thought his dismissal was unwarranted and inadequately explained. He found it so hard to accept, he offered to keep pushing the single while it still had a life. 'He was stunned by that, and said, "You mean you'd really still work the single? That's great – then there's no real risk. If you want to do that, that's fine." '

The band had two more shows before heading off for Europe, Portland and Vancouver. In Portland, a fan improvised a song for the band, 'Paul is Free', sung to the tune of 'Mean to Me'. 'Distant Sun' peaked just on the verge of entering the US Top 40.

In Australia, the dramatic departure of the much-loved Paul Hester was big news. Grant Thomas's comments to the *Sydney Morning Herald* were a characteristic mixture of candour and damage control. 'Paul's in a good frame of mind, but wants a few day's break before talking to the media . . . He's been battling with this for a while. Basically it's come to the point where he's not happy doing it, so there's no point in him doing it.

'I don't think the band has any desire to become deep or introspective or moody, or to escape from the lightness that Paul brought – I just think we're going through a different phase.'

When Paul emerged, it was on the national TV chatshow *Denton*. Introducing him, the host Andrew Denton asks, 'Why would a man give up the rock'n'roll stardom we all crave? Here's the man himself: Paul Hester!'

The audience responds with a noisy, supportive ovation. Paul still looks a little shell-shocked.

> *That applause may never happen again for you, Paul.*
> This is true, and that's a risk I want to take.
> *Three hours before a gig? That's pretty drastic.*
> Yeah, I was sick. I wasn't well that day. I'd been to the doctor's, had a Vitamin B shot in the bum . . . [to the audience] We've all got one, it unites us all.
> *An interesting concept of world peace, there.*
> I didn't feel well, so I left – rather quickly – that day. Nick had gone somewhere, I found Neil and Mark Hart and dragged them into this room, and I had a bit of a chat. It was very emotional, a big outpouring, a few tears, like the America's Cup in reverse . . . Then we went on stage about 10 minutes after that.
> We didn't tell the crew, just did this gig that lasted about three hours or so – next week it'll be four then six – the story will get bigger.
> *Paul, I have to get a bit Willessee with you now, a bit tough. Why?*
> Why not? I've got a lot of things I want to do. Being in a band takes you away all the time, I was leaving places, moving through, waving . . . when you're in perpetual motion, it's an illusion that

you go to all these places and see all these things, because you don't actually get very much time to connect. And it's all one way traffic, everyone just tells you how great you are all the time, and you don't get to get off that and have something happen that's real.

I can fix that: you're rubbish.

I just wanted to come home, I've got a great home, and I just wanted to be there [his voice starts cracking] and I'm going to be a father in a few months ...

Being in a band, what's that relationship like?

I don't know what anyone else's is like, but ours is pretty much psychotherapy while getting paid to do it all the time. It was weird. I like those times we had, great memories, but you get kinda married, and it's unusual. For a split second everyone gets what they want. When things go your way and the band is on a roll, it seems like everyone's getting what they want. Then, after some time, that changes and you struggle to get things right, or how they were, or how they could be.

Everyone struggles with all this: Farnsey, Barnsey and Warnsey ...

So rock'n'roll stardom is not what it's cracked up to be.

I think everyone knows that ...

No we don't: you're on the road, groupies, it's out of control ...

I gave up rock'n'roll so I could take up sex, drugs and rock'n'roll ... does that make sense?

It does, in a tragic kind of way. The press release says you felt you'd been drifting apart from Neil and Nick.

Yeah, a bit. And it was a great thing we had, so to see it getting to a point where they were going to do these promotional tours – grinding forays into the world of TV hell, Andrew ...

What are you going to do now?

Get together with some friends of mine, down in Melbourne, try and produce a few records, play on some people's stuff, open a café, hopefully. Sleep and read a few things, watch TV.

You're a free man, Paul Hester – welcome back to the human race.

Waiting for the thrill to return • May 1994

'Paul is working on a TV pilot, a show for overseas music fans called *Walkabout*.'

—club newsletter, September, 1994

While the band was in Seattle, Nick put a call through to an old friend in Melbourne. Peter Jones was just off to play drums with Australian jazz singer Vince Jones when the phone rang: would he be interested in joining Crowded House for the tour of Europe?

The offer was everything Peter could have wanted, as he was already saving to go overseas. 'Now I was about to get paid for it, playing fantastic songs, with a great group, to thousands of people. I thought, what did I do to deserve this?' Neil had been something of a hero to Peter since his teens. 'I can still remember the moment I heard "I Got You" for the first time, the room I was in, the radio it was on. I went, what the *fuck* is this?'

Peter, a sought-after drummer in Melbourne, first met Nick at the Victoria College of the Arts. Studying jazz, he was only on the outskirts of the rock scene, although he regularly attended gigs at the Crystal Ballroom, and his older brother Philip was in Nick's band Bang. Peter had been asked by Nick to join Plays With Marionettes, but he was sceptical about the seedier side of the St Kilda scene. Instead, he drummed for a variety of bands. Repeat Until Dead's music he describes as 'subterranean: a mix between Stockhausen, Schönberg and weird pop music, with very strange rhythms'. They did more rehearsing than actual playing. Harem Scarem was a swampy blues band, and he played jazz with Vince Jones and Kate Ceberano. His musical tastes broadened thanks to his older brother, who in the late '70s would bring home the latest records from Britain. 'So I got this really weird mixture, listening to jazz, trying to understand and play it, while learning about punk bands through my brother.'

In the '90s, Peter was a working musician in Melbourne, juggling sessions for people such as Deborah Conway with his only longterm commitment, to the R&B/reggae band Dynakiss. Fronted by Ross Hannaford, formerly with Daddy Cool, Dynakiss have a long-established Monday night residency at St Kilda's Esplanade Hotel. The

'Espy' is a local legend, a proudly rundown symbol of the area before gentrification. The pub's variety of acts – jazz, metal, R&B, punk, comedy and singer-songwriters such as Paul Kelly – attracts a crowd which is equally diverse.

After getting the call, Peter went around to see Paul Hester. 'We had a chat, and he took all these tapes out and briefed me on the songs. He was very friendly.'

Peter played his last gig with Vince Jones in Perth, then flew straight to London to meet up with Crowded House. They rehearsed for a couple of hours, then it was off to Germany to begin playing the European festival circuit, to crowds sometimes as large as 80,000 people. 'The whole tour was a blur,' he says. 'I was thrown in the deep end, but tried to make the most of it. I learnt the songs on stage. Filling in for Paul was one of the hardest things you could do, because he was such a big part of the group. But they were very positive and encouraging, which was good, because I was shit scared.'

To bring the atmosphere of Karekare to the shows, a group of Maori singers and Cook Island log drummers toured with the band in the United Kingdom. Thirty members of the London Maori cultural group Ngati Ranana took to the stage in traditional grass skirts for 'Together Alone', 'Catherine Wheels' and 'Private Universe'. After a shaky start at gigs in Glasgow and Whitley Bay, rehearsals at sound-checks and on their bus meant the large troupe was ready for the climax of the tour: two soldout dates at Wembley Arena, and a head-lining appearance at the Fleadh, London's Irish festival.

Neil's family had also joined the tour; during his daily phonecalls home from America, he had seemed miserable to Sharon. But when she arrived with Liam and Elroy, the mood of the tour became light-hearted and fun. Peter Jones was installed and Paul's departure already seemed a long time ago. Weary of continual questions about Paul, Neil's responses became increasingly frank. To Andy Fyfe, an expatriate New Zealander on the *NME*, he said, 'The worst thing has been the last six months, where Paul was totally unpredictable and casting a shadow over the whole organisation and making us doubt the future. But he's always been a bad-tempered little bastard.

'As much as he's incredibly funny when he's up – totally funny and an incredibly gifted sense of humour – the other side of that is very black and it became that we would wake up on any given day and not know whether we would find him up or down. It was quite a burden.'

The Fleadh festival, at Finsbury Park, was originally a celebration of Irish music, but has evolved to include mainstream performers such as Bob Dylan, Sting and The Beautiful South alongside traditional and cutting-edge Irish acts. When Crowded House headlined the Fleadh, Christy Moore, the Cranberries and Shane McGowan were also on the bill.

Crowded House took the stage as the sky was turning navy-blue, quickly setting the tone with an atmospheric 'Fingers of Love'. To the crowd of about 50,000, Neil said, 'When I told my mother we were playing an Irish festival, she wept over the phone. Her younger son was going home.' Despite the size of the audience, the band's performance had an intimate, amongst-friends spirit; the banter with the crowd was genial rather than pointed. Neil took the role of MC, introducing Peter Jones, saying hello to Paul 'who's watching us on live TV'. After a cacophonous 'Locked Out', Neil lamented, 'That song started out slow and acoustic and went through a magical metamorphosis.' He demonstrated the song in its original form, more like a country ballad.

The climax of the evening was a throbbing, transcendent 'Private Universe', with the log drummers hitting a groove, syncopated by Peter Jones, and the harmonies of the Maori choir providing a rich bed for Mark's frenzied guitar work. The drummers and choir were a spectacular sight, in lava-lavas and grass skirts, with garlands of flowers and sharks'-teeth necklaces standing out against their chests. Recruited to join the drummers was Liam Finn, determinedly keeping rhythm as the talking drums brought a moving 'Together Alone' to its climax. An a capella verse of 'The Parting Glass' from Neil brought the evening to an appropriately Celtic conclusion. By mixing their Pacific and Irish influences so seamlessly, Crowded House proved they belonged at the Fleadh.

While in London, Tim caught up with Neil at his hotel, and they talked about the future. They found they were both thinking along the same lines: when the tour was finished, the brothers would record again.

In Melbourne, Paul wrote an open letter to the *Herald-Sun*. He confessed to missing Crowded House, particularly around eight o'clock each night when it was time to go on stage. 'I have felt a few pangs of sadness and loss, but nothing I can't deal with. I thought I would be shattered, but at first I was overwhelmed by being at home and what was in front of me. I felt euphoric. Now it's died down a bit and I know I've got to keep busy.' In the club newsletter, he thanked fans for their support, and for helping him live out a dream. 'My life is now returning to a local abnormal lifestyle as compared to an overseas abnormal lifestyle.' On 29 July, a Friday, Paul's partner Mardi gave birth to a girl, whom they named Sunday.

Neil also wrote a letter to the fans. 'The band has adapted to a new phase and feels very strong as a result. Some of you, I'm sure, will miss Paul and what he brought to the band – humour, good grooves and a touch of anarchy – but I'm sure you won't be upset when you see the new model perform and hear the next album. We are highly motivated and re-energised by the change. Expect a new album early next year – we want to get into the studio really soon. In the meantime, thanks for your energy and encouragement through the chaos of the last few months.'

A few days after returning to New Zealand, Neil began producing *Twist*, an album for Dave Dobbyn, at Revolver studios in Auckland. In 1987, Dobbyn's song 'Slice of Heaven' had been a huge hit in Australia and New Zealand, but since then, his career had been languishing. Creatively he was recharged by recording an album in Hollywood produced by Mitchell Froom. (Froom had always loved hearing Crowded House play Dobbyn's 'Whaling', during pre-production for the band's first album.) *Lament for the Numb* was dark in content but rich musically, displaying Froom's developing taste for raw sounds and natural recording techniques. As with *Temple of Low Men*, it was critically acclaimed but a commercial disappointment.

Neil and Dobbyn spent six weeks on *Twist*, with Tchad Blake engineering and the Muttonbirds' Ross Burge and Alan Gregg on drums and bass. As producer, Neil brought to the studio a different take on the musical heritage he shares with Dobbyn, plus everything he had gleaned from Froom and at Karekare. The album is a mix of careful arrangement, found sounds and experimental jamming, the raw sitting comfortably with the delicate. Dobbyn says that in the studio, Neil is 'intensely busy and very easily bored. But he doesn't wallow in it, he just finds another path. He has so much energy – and a lateral abandon. He helped me get rid of the shackles, stopped me being precious about my songs.'

Blake remembers the sessions, fuelled by Cardhu whisky, were a lot of fun, the ease and spontaneity coming through on the completed album. At various moments while they were musically doodling, Neil would nod to Blake to press the record button. Then they would reshape what had been captured into a song. Dobbyn says Neil 'knows how to turn the corner in a song. He knows how to distract you just enough to lead you to the next bit, but it's a little out of the ordinary. You find these little devices being used to get from one section of the song to another. He's very inventive and playful in the studio, he approaches any instrument as if it's the first time he's played it, he drops all his preconceptions.'

After the exhilarating sessions for *Twist*, a remarkable reunion took place in a school hall in Glen Innes, Auckland. The Sacred Heart College old boys who had made such an impact on New Zealand rock'n'roll returned to their alma mater to raise funds for the music rooms. In a wild three-hour show, the Finn brothers, the Chunn brothers, Eddie Rayner and Wally Wilkinson from Split Enz, Dave Dobbyn and Peter Urlich from Th' Dudes, and Rikki Morris, entertained other old boys and their partners with chaotic versions of their own hits and, it seemed, everyone else's. The night emphasised the golden era for music at the college as the '60s turned into the '70s.

Neil and Tim then spent 10 days writing songs together, in Neil's basement studio and at Bethell's Beach, on Auckland's west coast. They would establish an atmosphere, find a verse and a chorus, then put the results to one side as sketches rather than completed songs. Then, with his family, Neil headed to Rarotonga for an extended holiday while the Pacific Arts Festival was taking place. Also on the trip were Tim, Dobbyn and his family, and several other close friends. While there, the brothers listened to their demos, strummed through the songs, and checked out the music of the Pacific Islands at the festival. One night, Tim came off his motor scooter – the local method of transport – and as his wounds were dressed, a barefoot nurse told him, 'You kissed the road of Rarotonga'. The brothers gave a loose concert at the local pub, Trader Jack's, unveiling a few of their new songs. Tim turned the nurse's phrase into an off-the-cuff jam.

Returning to Auckland in November, the brothers entered York Street studios in Parnell for sessions which would reflect their recent recording experiences, and that of co-producer and engineer Tchad Blake. Like Neil, Tim had been experimenting. Relaxed sessions with his Irish friends Andy White and Liam Ó Maonlaí had seen the musicians picking up unfamiliar and exotic instruments, and Tim taking the drum seat. (In 1995, as Alt – Andy, Liam, Tim – the trio released *Altitude*, more a diversion than an album). Similarly, Blake had recently emerged from the Latin Playboys, his after-hours low-fi combo with Mitchell Froom and Los Lobos's David Hidalgo and Louie Pérez.

The Finns' sessions lasted a month, with the brothers playing virtually all the instruments themselves, including old Chamberlain and Mellotron keyboards, and a tea-chest bass given to them by a Tongan friend, Sifa. 'Playing the drums was it for me,' says Tim. 'I've never felt so needed. You are the engine, the motor, instead of this fey creature, waiting to apply his tune.' Before and after takes on the drums, Neil saw Tim shift between 'terror and jubilation.'

For Neil, collaborating with Tim lacks the pressure of working with others. 'With somebody else, if it's crap, you get discouraged and close up. With Tim, it doesn't matter. There's enough empathy between us that something will happen. We have a chat for a while, talk about a book one of us has read, and let ourselves drift off together.

'We wanted to take the atmosphere of the writing to a recording stage,' says Neil. 'We weren't labouring on structures, and we only had a month, so there wasn't time to go and sit by a beach and think about the last two lines.' On the last two Crowded House albums, Neil had spent an agonising time rewriting lyrics when recording was nearly over. 'In the early days I was more interested in there being a literal sense that flowed through a song. These days, I think a series of images is good enough for me, with a certain essence about them that seems rooted to the melody. It's a springboard for people's imaginations, hopefully.'

The songs were usually completed with Tim on the drums, working out a rhythm while Neil played around with chords. 'Last Day in June' was several years old, dating from before *Woodface*. Neil had written it on Tim's piano in Melbourne. ('Locked Out', another song which took years to emerge, came from the same session.) The presence of a ukelele on the languid 'Paradise' and 'Mood Swinging Man' was only the most obvious influence of the time in Rarotonga. 'But I make no claims for it being rootsy or authentic,' says Neil. 'It's a kind of kitsch Pacific that us white Te Awamutu boys grew up with: the nostalgic view, "Bali Ha'i" and shell mirrors.'

Neil finished 1994 with a couple of appearances as sideman to help launch Dobbyn's album, and at a TV awards show to back Maori singer Emma Paki singing 'Greenstone'. Neil had produced Paki's single, adding a rhythm loop, vocal harmonies and guitars beneath her soaring rendition of a rather shapeless melody. He also performed 'Together Alone', accompanied by Te Waka Huia, before 250,000 Aucklanders at a Christmas in the Park concert. Although he had been 'home' for nearly two years, Neil was only just beginning to make his presence felt.

When the *Together Alone* tour came to an end, Nick had based himself in Dublin for five months. 'I've been sitting by a turf fire,' he wrote to the club newsletter, 'venturing to Europe, skating in Greece, France and Spain, haircuts in London, Paris and Berlin – and finally I've written a couple of songs. I've had a totally inspired time. So – Paul finally left the band, and now Pete is playing with us. Also pint-sized, he has brought a wonderful energy to the boundless possibilities that is our future. Can't wait to record with him – he has eyes like Steve McQueen!'

Mark went back to Los Angeles; Peter Jones to Melbourne. Peter had been invited to join a group put together by a friend, Barry Palmer, formerly with Hunters and Collectors. Called Deadstar, the group slowly recorded an album. Paul, too, had been re-establishing himself in Melbourne, writing songs with his Deckchairs Overboard friend John Clifforth, recording with Deborah Conway's Ultrasound, and opening a café on Elwood Beach with musician Joe Camilleri.

Crowded House reconvened in mid-January to take part in a short Australian concert tour called 'The Breaking of the Dry', with Midnight Oil, Hunters and Collectors and the lesser-known Electric Hippies. Although it was a stress-free and convivial tour for the musicians, and the audiences were enthusiastic, the numbers were disappointing for such leading acts. In Brisbane, several members of the 'Crowdies, Oils and Hunters' gathered in the studio for a jam, but the session was more fun than productive.

During the tour, Neil mentioned the intention of Crowded House to take a break for a couple of years. They looked enviously towards REM, who had managed to have their two biggest albums without touring. REM was now back on the road, and on 28 January, the two bands shared the bill at a large outdoor concert in Auckland, with up-and-comers Grant Lee Buffalo opening. Neil was at home; in a relaxed set, he proudly introduced his fellow bandmembers to the audience of 30,000. The spectacular natural ampitheatre of Western Springs Stadium was where, at 14, Neil had witnessed Elton John play.

Several dates in the New Zealand provinces followed, including a free outdoor show in Christchurch, attended by 80,000 people. Afterwards, Neil took a hurried trip back to Te Awamutu to attend a reunion of his classmates, 20 years after they left high school, then rejoined the tour in Palmerston North. The concert in the local showgrounds demonstrated how Crowded House had weathered the departure of Paul. It was Waitangi Day, a public holiday in New Zealand, and 5000 people attended the informal, outdoor event. With so many children present, Neil stopped the show halfway through to organise a running race around the grounds. Nick gave a race-caller's commentary, Mark played the theme from *Bonanza*, and a roadie and two policemen were enlisted as judges. Then it was the parents' turn to race. Later, Nick climbed the scaffolding and did a death defying ballet high above the stage. But apart from the antics, it was Neil's passionate singing and the band's increasing taste for psychedelic, jamming fadeouts which showed they were not going through the motions. Introducing 'Mean to Me', Neil gave a lengthy explanation of the song's connection with the city.

The brief tour concluded with two nights in Auckland at the Power Station. New Zealand royalty was present – Rachel Hunter, with consort Rod Stewart – but the guests of honour were Neil's 16 former classmates from Te Awamutu College. The band's new dynamic was in place: Neil and Nick shared the banter, Mark was now the fallguy, and Peter was heard but not seen. The reticent drummer was uncertain of his tenure; at one of the Auckland shows, he was criticised for leaving the stage when the others took their bow. 'I was told I was a member of the band now, not a sideman,' he says. 'But other times, I was treated like a sideman. I was confused about where I was supposed to be.' He was more than happy, however, to miss the sometimes testy band meetings.

If Peter was unclear about where he stood, it was a reflection of Neil's ambivalence about the band's future. Early in the year, Neil told Auckland magazine *Metro*, 'We're in a sort of rethinking phase and I don't know what will emerge from this. If we get some new songs together and it's feeling good, we'll go in and do another album pretty soon. If we haven't found a motivation to do anything in the short term I'm sure we're not going to break up, but we might put everything on hold. Being in a band is a kind of regime which I'm keen to break away from now. It's like being married to four people and I'd like to be married to just one person for a while.'

While the others in the band dispersed around the world, Neil kept a low profile in Auckland. In March, he emerged when Pearl Jam visited for a concert. Their lead singer, Eddie Vedder, turned out to be a dedicated Split Enz fan and collector. In Auckland, Pearl Jam asked Neil and Tim to join them onstage in the encore to perform 'History Never Repeats' and 'I Got You' to a delighted audience. (Neil reacted angrily when a local reviewer suggested their guest appearance made the ending an anti-climax; when his combative fax was leaked to a gossip column, many were surprised by his sensitivity to criticism.)

The next day, before Pearl Jam's second show, there was the obligatory pilgrimage to Karekare. First stop was the studio, where Tim, Neil and his son Liam jammed with Vedder and Stone Gossard (Pearl Jam's guitarist) for a couple of hours. 'We banged a few drums and played a few guitars,' says Neil. 'It was just a fun afternoon. Tchad taped it, but I don't think anything will ever come of it.' Afterwards, they inflicted an arduous bush walk on their visitors, then Tim took Vedder into the wild surf for a swim. The Karekare undertow got hold of Vedder and took him 80 metres out to sea, requiring the local surf lifesavers to get him back to shore.

Neil returned to Nigel Horrocks's Karekare studio for a week to try out writing songs with Jim Moginie, the guitarist in Midnight Oil. He was interested in collaborating with someone, finding 'an equal partnership' which would be inspiring. 'I don't crave it,' says Neil, 'but I'm into the idea of it happening with somebody I could learn from.' The pair had a rapport, and Neil found inspiring the way Moginie always plays 'to the edge of his ability, pushing his boundaries.'

Horrocks was now using his home permanently as a studio and had started his own label, Greenstone, for an album by Emma Paki. This led to Neil, Mark and Paki being filmed performing for a natural history television programme, *Deep Blue*. On a catamaran anchored in cathedral-like caves in the Poor Knights Islands, north of Auckland, they recorded 'Private Universe' and a song of Paki's. The music echoed around the caves and was relayed under water through hydrophones, the fish reacting by dancing in formation. Mark then spent seven weeks producing Paki's album, which was released late in 1996. 'It was really enjoyable, but it wasn't easy – nothing at Karekare is easy,' he says.

At the time of Pearl Jam's visit, Tim and Neil were taking a break from finishing the Finn brothers album, which was being mixed by Blake. Neil wrote to the fans, 'It's great to be home with very little to think about other than family, friends and songwriting. This may seem unexciting to those of you who crave our presence on your stages, but believe me, for the soul of the band and the ultimate good of the music, it is a great position to be in.' He said the band was trying to put out *Paul is Dead*, a live CD of Paul's last show in Atlanta, but 'it's been bogged down in record company bullshit'.

A priority for the year was to settle the relationship between Crowded House and Capitol. The band wanted to leave the label, and Gary Stamler offered to negotiate a release from their contract, which still required two more albums. Stamler felt his raport with Gersh would enable him to get them released without penalty. The band's disappointment with the label had been intensifying since the failure of *Woodface* in America, in fact Grant Thomas had been arguing with Gary Stamler that they should try and leave Capitol before *Together Alone*. 'There was no point in giving the Americans another record,' he says, 'because they just did not get it. Gary thought that contractually, we were bound – which of course, we were – but I would have been interested in having the disagreement with them at that point. But his opinion was that Gary Gersh was now the president, he had great A&R skills, had signed some very successful acts, that there was a commitment from the guy to do the job – and that we shouldn't shortchange them.' Inevitably, Capitol's lacklustre performance during the US *Together Alone* tour only confirmed their disatisfaction.

Stamler spent months trying to diplomatically negotiate the departure of Crowded House from their Capitol deal. At first, the company didn't want to lose Crowded House, he says. 'Gersh very clearly wouldn't go out on his own.' However Jeremy Hammond suggests that, inside the label, there was a sense that time was up for Crowded House. 'Gersh had his vision for where the label was going to go. I don't think he saw Crowded House as part of it. That's all – and that's understandable. He didn't have the desire to continue the relationship.'

In other territories, however, EMI affiliates were very keen to hold on to the band. Late in 1995 it was decided that Crowded House would leave Capitol in the States (several Sony labels were interested), but stay with EMI elsewhere. In the United Kingdom, their albums would continue to come out through EMI's Parlophone which, as the Beatles' label, has a strong tradition of links with Capitol. Part of the exit package was the release of a greatest-hits album, despite the band's reluctance that it was too early in their career; Neil's preference was for a live album, from the hundreds of tapes they had recorded at their shows.

Meanwhile, in July, Nick, Mark and Peter gathered in Auckland to record demos for the next Crowded House album. The month-long sessions were in York Street's B-studio, an old radio studio in the centre of the city. The environment was against them. It was the middle of a particularly wet winter, the studio was large, dank and cold, the engineer was inexperienced, and Neil's commitment was lacking. 'Things had been happening in Auckland that were interesting to me,' he says. 'I had thought, it might be good not to be in a band for a while, and take a break. Inevitably, when you take a break, you start to enjoy certain aspects of your life – and then you start to resent having to give them up and get back into the band.'

For Neil, the sessions were 'tortuous, just hard work. I didn't enjoy it socially, and I didn't enjoy it musically'. The others were happy with the results, though the poor quality recordings prevented them being taken further. (Among the songs is an early version of 'Instinct'.)

'The tracks are quite a few notches back from where we had peaked,' says Mark. 'Some of the songs were beautiful: good arrangements, well played.' Both he and Nick felt they had more input into the music. 'Neil seemed relaxed, it was nice,' says Mark. 'He was taking ideas on board and really trying. I thought, with this kind of communication, and belief in each other, it's going to be a great record.'

Nick enjoyed playing with Peter Jones on drums. The band's layoff had been frustrating to Nick at first, but then he found it helped his own focus on music. 'I rediscovered the rhythms I've always wanted to try and perform in a band – there's an aspect of the raw groove Crowded House didn't take advantage of.' Nick felt several songs from the winter demos showed promise in that direction. 'They didn't sound self-consciously like reggae or dub, but because it was Neil playing guitar, and Mark lap steel, they had this really interesting marriage of styles. And Peter Jones was drumming, with a hiphop shuffle – a very different style to Paul Hester.'

Paul's drumming was one of the things Neil missed. 'Paul's got limitations technically sometimes, but he gets there eventually, and he played my songs very well. He plays a shuffle the same way I play the guitar. There was a certain chemistry in the band. And I didn't want to go out with the baggage of that, trying to do the same thing and not quite getting there. I thought it was better to quit while we were ahead.

'All during the rehearsals, I thought, maybe this is the time I should make a break. But I resisted out of loyalty and a bit of stubborness. Everyone was saying, the band is poised, one more album would be all it might take. All those things – even though that's not the major motivation to write a song – they play on your mind. The machine was built up, and you've got this idea of responsibility to all these people, the roadies and management. But in the back of my mind I was thinking I'd love to just be free of of it. I was as envious of Paul as anything for leaving, thinking, I wish I could have that luxury.'

The *Finn* album was prepared for release in October. Having paid for the recording, the brothers had control over the tapes. In Britain, Tony Wadsworth was keen to have it out as soon as possible, so it didn't clash with the next Crowded House project. In Los Angeles, to Jeremy Hammond's disappointment, Capitol decided against releasing the *Finn* album. He set about finding an independent label which was interested.

Crowded House devotees warmly embraced the album for what it was: an uncommercial diversion, maybe, but one which was charming and musical. Wrote David Hepworth in *Q*, 'The hardcore Finn fans – the kinds of people who troop after them on tour like sensibly dressed Deadheads – will adore this most warm and loose of records.'

It didn't have the finely honed sibling harmonies many expected; rather it was like leafing through the Finn brothers' scrapbooks, with the songs left in a raw state.

'It was pretty effortless,' says Tim. 'I think we've been making it for quite a while. But I think people expected that, when we finally got around to making a record, it would be the great summing up: the Finn Brothers. It's not like that, it's just what was there at the time. We were just off in our private space, making it.'

Although Neil admitted to having 'very modest expectations' of the album's reception, he also said, 'I don't want people to think this is a bit of a dabble before I get back to the real stuff. This is part of a continuum, and we're very pleased with it.'

On 29 October, the Finn Brothers opened a brief Australian tour at the National Theatre in St Kilda, Melbourne. A brief European tour followed, with Dave Dobbyn as support act. Hepworth was right: the concerts were sold out, and the audiences enchanted by the act the brothers had developed. It was like psychedelic cabaret, an intimate romp through 20 years of songwriting. The brotherly repartee was now unmistakeable as banter rather than oneupmanship.

While on the road in England, they played a tape which had just arrived from Eddie Rayner. It was a demo of Rayner's orchestrations of Split Enz songs, for an album with the New Zealand Symphony Orchestra called *Enzso*. The Finns had been sceptical about the idea, the history of orchestrated rock music being littered with failures or plain bad taste. But the brothers were excited by Rayner's arrangements, and called him on a cellphone to report back.

The Finns' trip north turned awry, however, when they arrived at a Liverpool television studio to appear on *This Morning*, a daytime TV show. The interview consisted of gormless questions along the lines of, 'Tim: have Crowded House broken up?', then as the brothers began a song off *Finn*, they noticed the credits rolling. An argument ensued, which was reported in the English tabloids. The fight with the hosts 'Richard and Judy' made more impact than their appearance on the cutting-edge show *Later With Jools Holland*.

That night, the first of two concerts in London took place at the Union Chapel. The formula for 'An Evening With the Finns' was in place: a flexible songlist, harmonies, digressions and *Morecambe and Wise* humour. The gothic architecture of the former church made Neil realise that 'every song has some kind of religious reference. I was expecting a bolt of lightning to come out of the sky.' The pulpit became part of the act.

When the topic of Crowded House came up in interviews, Neil hinted at the uncertain future for the band. In the Netherlands, where they were playing at the legendary Melkweg (Milky Way) club, Neil surprised fans by telling journalist Jip Golsteijn that Crowded House had virtually broken up after the *Together Alone* tour, and that he would get some outside musicians involved for the next record. Golsteijn's headline was 'Tim en Neil Finn sollicietern bij eigen broer' ('Tim and Neil Finn apply for a job with their own brother').

While in Ireland, the brothers were approached to take part in a compilation album of modern Irish music. Produced by Donal Lunny, *Common Ground* features artists such as Bono, Elvis Costello, Sinéad O'Connor, Liam Ó Maonlaí and Christy Moore. 'We jumped at the chance,' says Neil. 'We don't get to do those sort of records, because we're in this part of the world. There was a good cast of characters, and we were allowed to be different.' As descendants, the Finns felt apprehensive about performing a traditional Irish song, which the others were doing, so they wrote their own song based on their mother's emigration from Ireland at the age of two. The song was written in about four hours, using an old melody of Tim's, and Andy White helping with the lyrics and title. A slow waltz, 'Mary of the South Seas' was recorded in Dublin that night, with some overdubs done in London. 'From woe to go, it was very satisfying,' says Neil.

On the way back to New Zealand, Neil stopped off in Los Angeles and spent a few days recording overdubs for Sheryl Crow's second album. (Crow ended up only using some backing vocals on 'Everyday is a Winding Road'.) Other collaborations had also taken place during the year when the timing was right. On request, Neil had sent some music to Shawn Colvin, who added lyrics to create the song 'What I Get Paid For' (on her album *A Few Small Repairs*). And for singer Annie Crummer, of Rarotongan/Tahitian descent, he wrote the music to 'Here Come the Gods'; Crummer's mother Tania wrote the lyrics, giving the album *The Seventh Wave* its most Polynesian flavoured song.

Back home for Christmas, Neil was facing a flurry of diverse activity in 1996: more touring for the Finn Brothers, some dates performing with his Split Enz colleagues and the New Zealand Symphony Orchestra to promote the *Enzso* album, the recording of a couple of new tracks for Crowded House's impending 'best-of' compilation and a promotional trip upon its release. Sometime in July or August, the real work could begin: the recording of the fifth Crowded House album. In January, Mark and Nick were asked to go to Auckland to rehearse. For Nick, it was inconvenient as, ironically, he was in the middle of helping his brother record a solo album. 'Neil got really pissed off at me when I actually complained about it,' he says. It emphasised the difficulty of having the band spread around the world, and idle for so long. Inevitably, the other band members would also get involved in their own projects.

In February, Neil and Tim returned to the *Finn* album, embarking on a month-long tour of Australia and New Zealand. Performing together had been 'a novelty and a joy,' said Neil. They wanted to give the show wider exposure 'before we kissed off the record'. The tour was a close-knit operation, with Sharon operating the lights and Dave Dobbyn once again playing solo support.

'An Evening With the Finns' had settled into a comfortable, stress-free act which showed the brothers playing with their relationship, making music and making fun of each other. They skated between their private and public lives, flirting with the audience's desire for revelations. In Melbourne, they unveiled a trump card. Dugald McAndrew walked out with a projection screen; it was home movie time. The flickering Super-8 footage showed a sunny childhood recognisable to audiences on both sides of the Tasman: barefoot Christmases, birthday parties at the beach. The joke was on themselves, the images sentimental but universal.

Tim gave a running commentary to one of his father's production numbers, a carefully choreographed nativity scene. The neighbourhood children walk by in formation, with towels on their heads, their hands in prayer; they present gifts to the Holy Family. 'That's our sister Carolyn, playing Mary,' he explained. 'There's me: I'm Joseph. And here comes Neil, as baby Jesus.' The audience swooned at the shared nostalgia. 'Ah, Neil,' said Tim, 'how come we've got all the lead roles?'

A New Zealand tour followed, with the final night taking place at the Founders Theatre in Hamilton. The extended Finn family and lifelong friends turned out in force; Tim greeted the audience saying, 'It's going to be an emotional night.' For him, settled in behind the drumkit, it was the realisation of a dream. 'I've always wanted to be a drummer who sang,' he said, telling the story of seeing the Dave Clark Five at the same theatre. Someone called for 'Glad All Over', and the brothers obligingly pumped it out.

By now the act was finally honed, an invitation home to witness a family singalong – or a family fight. 'We haven't had a decent row on this tour, yet,' said Neil, turning to Tim: '. . . you bastard.' 'Bugger you,' came the reply. 'Up yours,' said Neil. The audience held their breath, then realised it was part of the routine, a spoof of the sibling rivalry chestnut. Some nights, they even offered to take requests.

When passing through Los Angeles a few months earlier, Neil had met with Mitchell Froom and told him about the new songs Crowded House were to record for the compilation. Froom offered to produce. 'I always had a thing about that band,' he says. 'I said, I wasn't presuming anything, but at this stage it felt funny not being involved. I thought they should get Paul and Nick back together, do the songs and put a period at the end of the sentence. There was less chance of the project being a struggle, without a new drummer and producer looking over their shoulders, trying to emulate their predecessors.'

For Neil, it made sense to have the old team back, for consistency and a sense of conclusion. 'I also thought, maybe this is a chance of finding out if there's some life in the old bones.' He was also keen to involve Paul. 'He'd been gone for two years, and I thought, well, maybe something's changed. He's had a bit of time to think.'

Nick was dubious at first. 'But Mitchell pitched it to me as a way of tidying up the relationships we had forged and bringing them to a nice resolve,' he says. 'And he was absolutely right. He'd been so positive that everyone came into the studio with a healthy attitude to each other.' Froom says that Nick agreed 'almost immediately. They weren't communicating at all, it was just assumed Nick would say no.'

Speaking to Australian journalist Ed St John about the impending sessions with Paul, Neil warned, 'I don't want anyone to read anything into this ... I'm not about to speculate on the future line-up of the band; there's always been a faint air of impermanence and fragility about Crowded House, and there have certainly been times when we barely existed at all. All I can say right now is that we definitely do exist, and we will be making a new album at some stage this year.'

In March 1996, Crowded House gathered in Auckland for the two weeks of sessions at York Street. 'It's great returning like this,' Paul said. 'I'm back in the studio with my mates. It's only for 10 days, so there's no pressure: it's like I'm having a dirty weekend with my ex-wife.' Paul was in good spirits, and playing well. 'He was his lively, bouyant, funny self,' says Mark. 'But he could see an end in sight: it was going to be 10 days, then he was done with it. Why not be happy?'

Mark, however, was disheartened when Froom took him aside as the sessions began, and said, 'Just let them do their special thing, then we'll go in. There's no ego involved here.' To Froom, the band was still a trio, which meant Mark once again had to take a back seat. 'I didn't feel comfortable, as if it was my project.'

Froom and Blake arrived in Auckland with several flight-cases containing the secrets to the anti-technology production style they had developed since *Woodface*. Both men had become dedicated collectors of discarded instruments, strange percussion gadgets and archaic recording equipment such as valve compressors, tube amplifiers and trashy "stereo wideners" made for home use in the '70s.

'Instinct' was recorded first, based on a rhythm track Finn had recorded at his home studio. The band then got distracted by a dark, heavy song that wasn't working. With only five days to go, they abandoned it to concentrate on 'Not the Girl You Think You Are'. Recorded in only one-and-a-half days, the song was an overt Beatle tribute from a band for which the adjective 'Beatlesque' had long ago become an albatross. But, says Neil, 'It wasn't deliberate, or tongue-in-cheek. It was Mitchell who gravitated towards the song.'

Froom thought it was one of the best songs Neil had yet written. 'We don't say, let's go for this Beatle thing,' he says. 'It's never worked out.' A combination of effects pulls off the illusion. Neil wrote the song in 10 minutes using a piano loop he found on an Optigon, a keyboard from the '60s which reads optical discs, like a primitive sampler. But mostly it's in the melismatic vocal, which is double-tracked, just as John Lennon always insisted. Both voices in the bridge section are Neil's, although the strained higher harmony uncannily echoes Paul McCartney. 'A lot of people assume it's Tim,' says Froom. 'We've never been that successful double-tracking Neil's voice before, but it's a nice rough double. You can hear the seams. I couldn't get the song out of my head.' With the recording of 'Everything is Good For You', a song which Neil says is 'about not letting regrets ruin your life', the sessions were completed. 'We had a lot of fun,' says Froom. 'Three songs in a week – that's a pretty good week.'

Over the first five days, Neil had felt the sessions were going nowhere. 'In the end, it turned out really well,' he says. 'Everybody played well, but it wasn't substantially different. Paul was still Paul, wanting to make coffee and have a bit of a joint and a break in the middle of a take. But he was great, everything was great – it just didn't get there.'

'Really, I was looking for some revelation, to be knocked out by playing with them and realise what I'd been missing. It was a lot to expect. So I agonised a bit, and didn't come down on anything definite. I thought, oh well, we'll make an album. What the hell, we better go ahead.'

During the recording sessions, Mark Collen of Parlophone arrived from London to discuss the release of the greatest hits album; it was his second trip in a matter of weeks. 'I was living and breathing the project,' he says, 'in contact with Grant on a daily basis. But I was worried throughout that period, I knew something was wrong. There was a lot of indecision, a lot of vaguery. I thought, oh well – this is Crowded House. It's not like they're all sharing a big house together. They live on three continents.'

Collen found the mood in the studio convivial and welcoming. But when Neil told him the final mixes had been done, he was surprised: to Collen the production was 'understated'. There were two singles for the compilation, 'Not the Girl' and 'Everything is Good For You', plus a song called 'Instinct' which was unlikely to be used. 'They were all but refusing to play it to me. I thought it was great, but said to Neil, if he didn't want to release it, fine, it was his call.' Neil had been vacillating about promoting the compilation album, to be called *Recurring Dream*. By Collen's second visit, Neil had changed his mind: the band wouldn't be involved.

'I lost my temper, which I never do,' says Collen. 'Certainly never with artists, and people I love and respect like those guys. They've been an integral part of my life, of my career. I said, listen – I've come down to Auckland for 24 hours from New York, then I'm back to London. Tell me if I'm wasting my time. I go away, you tell me one thing. I come back, you tell me something else. What gives?'

The discussion became more frank. Afterwards, it was agreed that in June, Crowded House would do a few showcase gigs in Europe to promote *Recurring Dream*, starting in a small London club on 3 June. Parlophone also wanted the band to return in November, not to tour but for seasons in Glasgow and at the Albert Hall. They would be billed, 'A Special Evening With Crowded House'.

Recognise a nervous twitch • May 1996

'] hear voices leading me on/the wise and the strong'

—Neil Finn, 'Voices', 1984

When Parlophone promotions manager Malcolm Hill heard 'Not the Girl You Think You Are', he baulked. The song may define 'Beatlesque', but Hill felt it wouldn't get any radio play in Britain. The Beatles themselves had just been spurned by Radio One with their 'Real Love' off *Anthology 2*. In the era of Oasis, Hill thought the raw, swampy 'Instinct' had more chance. He called Neil, who agreed. So did Collen, who was exasperated but relieved.

Nick went to London, to work on the artwork for *Recurring Dream*. Meanwhile Neil toured New Zealand as part of Enzso, Rayner's orchestrated-Enz project. At this time, Paul Du Noyer of *Q* interviewed Nick and Neil on opposite sides of the globe. From the impression they gave, Crowded House was listless, unfocused. 'When you see Neil,' Nick said in London, 'Ask him if he's writing some new songs. I'm not going to ring him up and nag him.' Neil took Du Noyer out to Karekare and said, 'There's been a lot of emphasis on the past for me recently ... Now there needs to be a redefining of Crowded House. There's a point we'll be at soon where it's all just a blank new piece of paper. We'll start recording soon. There will be a Crowded House. We just don't know what it looks like yet.'

Deciding who would make the videos for the new songs on *Recurring Dream* was the next hurdle. Neil was keen for a New Zealander to direct one of the clips; Nick wasn't. So they went with Jeff Darling, Parlophone's choice as director. In mid-May, Neil, Nick and Mark assembled in Sydney to shoot two videos over two days; Paul was also present to play a cameo role. 'Instinct' and 'Not the Girl' were filmed simultaneously, using a large cast and crew. The lavish approach seemed at odds with the low-fi nature of the songs – and the prevalent fashion of music television. The rent-a-freak extras of 'Instinct' made the band feel like aliens in their own clip. To Neil, 'It was somebody's advertising impression of what we should be doing.' But neither he nor Nick had the energy or inclination to insist on changes. 'Every step of the way, we'd stressed and agonised about things,' says Neil. 'It's usually been the right thing to have done. This time we let the guy have his run, and I hated the result. So I had a couple of major anxiety attacks during the course of it.'

With his scenes completed, Paul hugged the others and left to fly home. Meanwhile, in the Sydney alleyway, drizzle intermittently fell on the video shoot as it extended into the evening. The trip to Europe was imminent. Neil was considering the idea of Paul coming; for the brief reunion he had been in good spirits. Mark felt 'it was too soon'; Nick says, 'It would be more of the same: enthusiastic when it suited him, but massive mood swings.'

Neil returned to New Zealand, and spent the next few days in his basement studio at home, having a 'big listen' to tapes of music he had recorded over the last six months. Most of it he had rejected when it was recorded, but listening over the tapes, he found he had written 'tons of stuff – and it just didn't sound like Crowded House. It wasn't finished, but it didn't have anything to do with Crowded House or my perception of the band.

'I just thought, I'll break the band up. It was like a lightness descended on me. I felt a silly grin on my face, went upstairs, stood by the fire and said, "I'm going to break the band up."'

Sharon will always remember that moment. 'He looked liberated, completely liberated. I just said, "Yeah, sure."'

'I did feel liberated,' says Neil, 'from myself as much as anything.' If he had done it earlier, he could have avoided so much of his angst, and it would have been easier on the others. 'But things take as long as they take. All the reasons I stuck with it were the right ones – it was only out of loyalty – but I haven't had a moment's doubt since. Not even a second of doubt.'

An hour later, Neil's phone rang. It was Mark, calling from Los Angeles to suggest some equipment they should take to Europe. 'He seemed completely uninterested,' says Mark. 'I sensed there was something troubling him, but didn't ask. Finally, he said, "Well Mark, I may as well tell you this while you're on the phone – I've decided to knock the band on the head. I just can't do it anymore."

'I said, "Oh? Okay. Whatever you think, it's your life." It was everybody's lives really, but we didn't come into it. I said, we're not really a band anymore – do what you have to do to give everyone a life. I'd survive, but it was a shame.'

Nick was at home in Melbourne where, with a couple of friends, he shares a renovated stables on the edge of a large estate. They were just sitting down for a dinner party when the phone rang. 'Neil's not much of a communicator. Whenever he rang, I'd immediately get butterflies in my stomach, thinking it was bad news. Nine times out of 10 it was. It was seldom he'd ring just to stay connected.

'Neil said, "I've got some news . . ."'

'And by the way he said it, I knew he was going to say, "I've decided to leave the band." '

'. . . I've decided to leave the band,' said Neil.

Nick replied, 'Well, you'd be absolutely sure, otherwise you wouldn't be saying it. He agreed. I said, alright, I'll talk to you soon.' (Nick later told David Hepworth of *Mojo*, 'I could tell he was really captivated by the very words, he was enjoying breathing them into life. I was quite happy for him.')

Nick then went into shock; just two weeks earlier, Neil had talked enthusiastically about the next Crowded House album. Nick told his friends, then got in his car and drove around to see his brother. The next evening, he called Neil, who seemed in a good mood. 'I asked if he was happy about his decision. He said he felt great about it. That was all I needed to know. He wasn't going to change his mind.'

Peter Jones was in Sweden, living with his girlfriend, whom he had met during the *Together Alone* tour. When the band had recorded 'Instinct' with Paul, Neil had called to let him know what was happening. As much as Peter wanted to record with them, he understood: true chemistry was the hardest thing for a band to find. Since then, he had been getting the occasional message regarding the promotional tour. 'It had been on-again, off-again for me. It would have made perfect sense if Paul had done the tour as well. Then I got the call: it was on again.'

Two days before leaving for London, Peter heard from a friend in Melbourne that Crowded House was splitting up. Then Nick rang and confirmed. To Peter, it wasn't a surprise. He had been waiting for it since being asked to join the band two years earlier.

Grant called Tony Wadsworth at Parlophone and told him Neil's decision. 'There has always been interesting emotions flying around Crowded House, and you get used to that,' says Wadsworth. 'But I was shocked: why didn't it happen before, two years ago, when Paul left? I was surprised it happened when it did. The timing was impeccable. My immediate thought was, well that's a real shame.'

Then the ramifications came to him: as a record company CEO, as a friend of the band members. What would Nick and Mark do? Who will Neil work with? Would he keep the name Crowded House? 'He made it clear he wouldn't, which is his decision but makes my job more interesting. This is why Neil is so great and so frustrating at the same time. Because he's totally and utterly true to himself and his emotions and he can't hide it. That's what makes him a great artist.' Wadsworth told Malcolm Hill, and they agreed to keep it quiet until the band arrived. 'The promotion was falling into place nicely,' says Hill. 'In fact, I'd worked this band for so long that I thought, something's going on here – this is far too easy.'

In the next few days, the promotional tour was almost cancelled. Neil offered to do it on his own, but Parlophone had too many things organised which needed the whole band. The first opportunity for the band to discuss the decision was when they gathered in London on 2 June to start the tour. Nick was determined to talk about it, knowing it would be very likely the issue would be avoided.

'Neil, in his earnestness, wanted to announce to everybody straight away that he'd left the band, the band had broken up. I thought that the media only needs to know what it wants to hear, and usually makes up its own story. We didn't owe them anything to be this honest. I wanted to work out a way of using it as a tool to our advantage, to help sell the "best of". I felt it would be best to have a meeting to work out what we were going to say to the press.'

Neil, Nick, Mark, Grant Thomas and tour manager Bill Cullen met in Thomas's hotel room. Neil didn't want to elaborate on his decision, saying that if he did, the reasons would be hurtful. Nick forced the issue, thinking he had nothing to lose, the band was finished. It turned into an argument – and he was indeed hurt. 'He told me I was an okay bass player, but that was it. That was all I had going for me. And he added that I had an overinflated sense of my own talents. He can be quite eloquent at times, and extremely hurtful. I thought it was completely unnecessary.'

To Hepworth, Neil said, 'We had a couple of meetings and a bit of personal stuff came out. We shouted and yelled and said a few things. But once we got into being a band we just clicked back in and wanted to enjoy it.'

Monday, 3 June, was the day of the 'secret gig' to launch *Recurring Dream*. Crowded House club president and PR man Peter Green had also come over from Australia. At 10.30am he was called into a meeting with Thomas and Cullen. Green wrote in his diary, 'By midday my world is picked up and thrown about – Crowded House are calling it a day. We work out our battle plan – and Neil arrives.

He sounds excited, happy, fired on adrenaline and probably needs a good sleep. We work out a rough press release.'

The Hanover Grand, a small club off Oxford Circus in the heart of London, was the venue for the concert. Thanks to Green, of the 600 people squeezed in, fans outnumbered the media and industry free-loaders by two to one. That day, the decision had been announced to Parlophone staff. But among the audience, very few were aware of the press release which had just been sent out:

'Neil Finn of Crowded House will announce tonight at their show in London that the band as it currently exists is not to continue after their present three-week promotional tour ... Neil feels that after a highly successful 10 years with Crowded House, it is time for a change creatively and [he] is excited about continuing his recording career within a new context. It is too early to say whether this will be under a new name or under the Crowded House banner.'

Crowded House took the stage in lurid Polynesian shirts. The band took quite a while to gel, then it became like an exorcism for them. The jams at the end of songs became longer and more aggres-sively cathartic as the evening went on. 'Don't Dream It's Over' was greeted with screams, and faded out to the Beatles' 'I've Got a Feeling'. Mark Hart emphasised the raw passion of 'When You Come' with power chords; 'Distant Sun' concluded with a improvised rant; the confidence of 'Locked Out' was bloodletting. By 'Private Uni-verse', they were playing like a band proving it had a reason to live.

Neil stopped the show for a chat. It was time to announce the breakup of the band. He spoke of *Recurring Dream*, saying it was 'both a blessing and a curse ... we are looking forward to the future with relish'.

But he couldn't bring himself to go any further. They went on with the show, which turned into an epic of improvisations, musical quotes and noisy extended codas. Afterwards, the 'meet-and-greet' was so packed that most in the room didn't hear the news.

The Crowded House internet page *Tongue in the Mail* was given the scoop; London radio stations started announcing the breakup while the concert was still on. Because of the time difference, the news spread more quickly on the other side of the world. By the time English fans were waking up, Australians and New Zealanders had seen their evening papers. The headline was usually, 'Don't Dream, It's Over'. When Paul heard the news, he laughed wryly, imagining an anguished scene in a hotel room. Then he sent a congratulatory fax to Neil: 'Great move, Fang. Love Hess.'

The next day, another press release went out, in which Neil said he had intended announcing the breakup during the concert.

'. . . In fact, I said nothing on stage. I couldn't bring myself to be that dramatic. I do, however, confirm that the band is indeed over and the name too. We have had many moments of great intensity between band and the audience and I will always value that, but there have been creative frustrations lately – I think we were beginning to repeat ourselves. I crave a new context to draw something fresh out of me as a songwriter . . . there are no plans to tour. No farewells for us. I need to get on with it, the future, that is.'

By the afternoon, Crowded House was back at work, being filmed by MTV Europe in their studios at Camden Town. Their voices were shot; Grant Thomas had spent the night harrassed by his mobile phone. He became so bamboozled by the frenzy of calls, at one point he tried talking into his electric shaver.

The band ran through its hits for the cameras, wearily spreading the word about the compilation which had suddenly become an epitaph. There was a lump in every throat, and the occasion altered the subtext of the songs. 'Private Universe' now spoke of burdens to be shed: '*And I will run for shelter, endless summer, lift the curse.*' Unable to reach the high notes, Neil sang 'Don't Dream' in a lower key: '*Get to know the feeling of liberation and relief . . .*'

The jocularity was sluggish. Looking around the studio, Neil noticed a mural on the wall, with Elvis Presley prominent. 'Can't we find another icon?' he said. 'All around the world it's the same: Elvis, Marilyn, James Dean . . .'

The others thought about it a moment. Then Nick laconically said, 'I guess you've gotta be dead, mate.' Meanwhile Mark familiarised himself with the hired Wurlitzer, giving a slinky feel to a James Brown song: '*You've got to live, for yourself / for yourself and nobody else.*'

Afterwards, the TV crew wanted a photo-shoot, and a few autographs. The band obliged, like amiable politicians kissing their last babies as the polls closed. They watched an early cut of the video for 'Everything is Good for You', which had arrived by courier. Made with a handheld camera, it was very arty and very cheap. Then they headed for the BBC-TV studios in Shepherds Bush. In the van, Thomas stayed welded to his mobile phone. Neil thought aloud about the six-figure expense of the recent video shoot. It had been Capitol's idea, even though he felt a US$5000 video was all that was needed. Now the band had split, perhaps the company should adjust the royalties, and share more of the cost? 'Maybe if I called Gary Gersh direct,' he mused, '... though they probably wouldn't put me through. But there's going to be some major sales on this record.' Meanwhile, Nick laughed at his politically staunch brother Mark's response to the news. 'Do a farewell tour, mate,' he had advised. 'Go for the vulgar dollar.' Mark Hart joked, 'My band is splitting up? How am I going to get back to Oklahoma?'

The band was at the BBC for the filming of *Later with Jools Holland*, the hippest music show on British television. The guests enjoy playing live rather than miming, and parrying the edgy quips of its suave host. On this show were the Fugees (then at number one with their rap cover of 'Killing Me Softly'), Richard Thompson, Patti Smith and Tom Verlaine. Top of the bill was Crowded House.

Thompson was greeted like an old friend; in the presence of Verlaine, Neil became a nervous fan. He talked with an approachable Smith instead. She had recently returned to performing, and said during the show, 'Artists don't retire. They just shift conditions.'

Recording the programme took over three hours. During dinner, Tim Finn finally reached Neil on the phone. Tony Wadsworth arrived, staying till the end of filming, about midnight. The mood was one of the family rallying after a bereavement. Crowded House played through 'Instinct' several times for the cameras, its chorus now steeped in significance: *I felt the burden lifted from my back / Do you recognise a nervous twitch? ... It's nearly time to flick the switch.*

The last promotional tour got rolling: three weeks of whistlestop visits to Germany, Belgium, Spain and Holland, before returning to Britain. Each day there would be soundchecks, rehearsals, showcase gigs, TV run-throughs, recordings, interviews, radio live-to-airs – then travel, to do it all again somewhere else. Mark says the trip helped the band understand the decision to quit, as they listened to Neil's explanations get clearer in interviews. 'But they were long, tiring days.' On 21 June, they said goodbye to Europe with a performance broadcast from the Greater London Radio basement.

The band then flew to Toronto for more of the same, plus a final showcase gig on 24 June. A 'who's who' of Canadian musicians were among the 350 people who packed the legendary Horseshoe bar for Crowded House's swansong. The atmosphere was charged; tense before the show, Neil did most of the talking on stage. The tone was more earnest than humorous. To a cry of 'Where's Paul?', he gave his standard reply: 'Curled up in front of a TV with a fat joint and a cup of tea.' He encouraged Nick to explain his Canadian ancestry. 'They were transported to Australia from Calgary for stealing a loaf of bread. They were Protestants, but in Australia became Catholics.'

'. . . and wrote songs like this,' said Neil, as he began 'Into Temptation'. In 'Hole in the River', Neil jumped into the dance floor as the jamming became a psychedelic expedition. It calmed down with an effortless segue into 'Don't Dream It's Over'. The dignified pace made certain no one missed the emotion or significance of the moment: it was the band saying farewell to the song.

'Well,' said Nick as the last chord faded, 'I hope we did it justice.' Everyone present felt they had, though Neil responded with a hurt look. 'I think so,' he said. 'It's taken me 10 years to get it that good.'

Nick lightened the mood by answering Neil's 'Give us a C' with a boogie bass solo that turned into the disco hit 'Born to Be Alive'; it was the spontaneous moment the night required. Neil looked lost as he tried to find a gap to add some guitar. With 'It's Only Natural', they all hit the same groove. 'Neil – you rocked,' said Nick, whose own playing was rising to the occasion. Neil suggested a future career for the band's bass player/artist: 'a travelling revue: half disco, half naked performance art. Beret bohemians.' Mark was relishing exploring Hendrixian feedback on his 12-string guitar. 'Better Be Home Soon' closed the set, the crowd cheering the lines, '*It would cause me pain, if we were to end it / But I could start again, you can depend on it.*'

In the seven-song encore, they finally cut loose. A hint of Bach fugue from Mark inspired the band to scat like the Swingle Sisters, before a Pentecostal fervour seemed to possess Neil. Suddenly he became a leprechaun improvising an Irish jig, speaking in Celtic tongues. (It was a parody of the German-Irish band Paddy Goes to Holyhead, who supported them in Hamburg.) 'I'd like to see Bryan Adams do that,' he said, puffed out.

Neil began the slow crescendo of 'When You Come', enjoying a sudden clarity in the sound – until he noticed Mark had left the stage. When he returned, Neil said, 'I was describing the birth of the cosmos, orgasmic delights – *and you were having a piss?!*'

After a team discussion, farewells and thank yous, the last song was an epic 'In My Command'. They stood together at the lip of the stage and gave a dramatic, united bow, saying goodbye to Toronto, and Crowded House. It was a gesture borrowed from Split Enz; however the tendency of the Enz for regular reunions seemed unlikely.

Liberation and release
• November 1996

Nick: One day it might be cool to have a Crowded House record, as it is with the Velvet Underground. Neil: They were shit. Nick: So were we.

—interview on ME Sounds, Germany, June 1996

Less than two weeks after the Toronto finale of Crowded House, the Finn brothers were back in the city, performing and promoting their album. When the band dispersed, Neil and Grant Thomas had gone to Los Angeles for a week. They met with various industry contacts, and prepared for a short North America tour by Tim and Neil. The brothers' album had found a home at Discovery, a boutique label distributed by Warners. The album's release had been held up when a British band called Fin threatened a lawsuit. The brothers couldn't be bothered fighting a legal battle, even though it was likely they would win, so in the United States the album was named *The Finn Brothers*.

However the album was scheduled to come out almost simultaneously with Capitol's release of *Recurring Dream*. In the Tower, Capitol's international product manager Scott Greer spoke for many when he said, 'Why are we having a Finn record at the same time as a Crowded House record? What's that going to mean? My conversation with Grant was: *why?* It's almost a false start for *Recurring Dream*.'

Resigned to losing Crowded House, Greer had seen the compilation as an opportunity for the band to clean the slate in the US and start afresh. With the new triple-A format (adult album alternative) it seemed there was finally a radio outlet for their catalogue of sophisticated pop. 'You couldn't put Crowded House up against Mariah Carey or Michael Bolton – pop radio staples of the last few years – it just doesn't fit. I have a theory. For records in the US to be successful, they have to have that element of mediocrity.'

Recurring Dream entered the British charts at number one the week of its release. In the States, Capitol decided not to put out a single. With the relationship over, and costs recouped, and new acts such as Radiohead and Everclear on the way up, there was no point. 'You have to have every gun loaded when you come into the market in America,' says Jeremy Hammond. 'More than 30 new records a week are going for three new slots at radio.' *Recurring Dream* didn't reach the *Billboard* Top 200 chart.

After Toronto, Nick flew to Dublin, where he had bought an apartment, and Peter went back to Stockholm. Both returned to Australia to become the permanent rhythm section of Deadstar with Barry Palmer (ex-Hunters and Collectors) and Caroline Kennedy (the Plums). Mark went home to Los Angeles. Within a few days, he was offered two jobs: touring in Sheryl Crow's band in support of her second album, or rejoining Supertramp, who were about to record and tour. Crow would be on the road for two years; Supertramp's schedule was a lot more palatable, and he got on well with the band. He chose Supertramp.

In July, Neil and Tim Finn played nearly a dozen dates around the States, with Sharon, Liam and Elroy joining them on the tour. Then Neil and his family returned to Auckland, where he finally had a chance to reflect about his decision. He had ended up carrying all the responsibility for the band, as songwriter and leader. The whole organisation depended on his creativity, and his decisions. 'By doing things on my own, I know I'm not bound into so many other people's lives. If I make an decision, I do it because it's important to me, not because it's feeding the machine.' Now, he could ask himself, 'Does this have more weight than staying home with my family? In the past it was: does this have more weight to the whole Crowded House machine. Though for all the angst I've created for other people, and all the times I've been a pain in the arse, I can honestly say it's been for the music.'

In the end, he missed having the stimulation of another strong creative, musical partner in the band. Paul hadn't written a song for years; any ideas Nick brought to the studio were 'virtually instrumentals' which required a lot of work but didn't inspire the desire in Neil to do it. 'If somebody gives you a set of chords and you say, well, I could have written that – well, what's the incentive?' says Neil.

The band had coined a phrase about themselves, Neil told Peter Wilmoth of the Melbourne *Age*: 'Two dorks and a dictator. As a joke, but it became stuck for a while. A very bad thing to say. We all laughed about it. They saw me, I think, at times as being a bit of an intimidating presence, and I wanted to get things my own way, but that was only because I wrote the songs I wanted. To some extent those guys were on a pretty good wicket.

'They may have their own spin on this, but it was a pretty good run. They'd turn up to the studio, there'd be a whole bunch of songs written for them, they'd get a lot of directions, between Mitchell and myself in terms of what might work in the arrangement, they'd get to work for a couple of weeks on 11 tracks, then muck around for four or five weeks in the studio, we were living in LA, they'd be off having long coffees and breakfasts and bookshops and clubs and cafés, you know. So to some extent I felt quite justified in, at times, putting my foot down and saying, "This is the way it has to be", because I was in the studio all the time and making the phone calls and making the rehearsal tapes and going home and editing them up and turning up the next day with the edited tapes.'

Paul agreed that the criticisms were fair. 'Neil's approach to song-writing has always been pretty much on his own. He would come along to rehearsals sometimes with quite completed ideas ... there wasn't any real drive for me and Nick to write songs with Neil.' But when the *Age* comments reached Nick, he was 'really pissed off. He accused us of not doing any work, being basically lazy. I've worked hard in the last 10 years, really hard. Neil says, well, he could have been a lot harder, but that's not the point. If you want to be in a band, you've got to have a relatively thick skin to cope with the pressures and compromises that have to be made.'

However, to Neil, he was the one feeling the pressures and making the compromises: 'I was prepared to take that responsibility and the other guys were prepared to let me do it. They had a bit of an attitude about their importance in the whole thing, but they weren't coming up with the goods as far as assistance when I needed it. I was really getting stressed. I've got an overdeveloped sense of responsibility, it's a kind of neurotic thing.'

In the months after he got home, Neil relaxed with his family and prepared his studio to record an album. He was joined briefly by Jim Moginie and Tchad Blake for separate sessions. Meanwhile, Grant Thomas wanted to close the chapter on Crowded House prop-erly, particularly in Australia, where their following was at its most widespread and loyal. The ending had seemed rushed and, while the promotional tour and announcement had lifted the band's profile, it had only directly reached the media and a few hundred fans at each city. Neil was reluctant about giving a final concert, the big gesture; he wanted to bow out quietly. If it had to be done, he wanted it small scale, the way they had begun: a private house party for a few friends, possibly filmed for a documentary. 'Eternally humble,' jokes Neil. 'But it was achievable, we'd definitely have a good time, and it would come across well. We were one of *the* unplugged bands of the last 10 years, but we never used it for a record, or a TV show.' But Thomas had other ideas. Crowded House and its fans deserved a big send-off; a free, charity concert would say thank you and goodbye without the exploitation overtones of endless farewell tours.

By late October, after intense weeks of lobbying sponsors, council bureaucrats, TV producers and the band members themselves, Thomas had his grand scheme underway. A free farewell concert would take place in front of the Sydney Opera House on 23 November, with the proceeds benefitting a Sydney children's hospital and blood bank.

For Neil, the idea seemed just a bit too grandiose, but Thomas pushed it 'like a bull terrier'. By the time Neil arrived in Melbourne, a week before the show, he agreed it would be a good ritual to say goodbye in such spectacular circumstances. The ending at Toronto hadn't been as emotional as he'd expected. 'We'd just done a three-week tour. We'd been talking about the breakup all the time, so it didn't feel that real – just a little gig in Toronto. None of the factors made it seem like a definitive ending.' The week building up to the Sydney finale was intense: reunions and farewells with the extended Crowded House family, rehearsals, a private dinner party, a press conference at Paul's Elwood café, and two warm-up shows at a small pub.

Paul was on top wisecracking form, breaking old habits – and unsettling Neil – by turning up early for everything. At the press conference, they entertained those present with one last round of humour and sincerity. Paul said he hated being called the court jester of the group; Neil the way he was always on time and the others always late; they all hated the term 'Beatlesque'. Nick said that the band was breaking up too early, he wanted to record one more album and turn the band into the biggest in the world. Neil said, 'We're not the all-for-one, one-for-all body that we used to be. You have to be actually hanging out in the same town, you have to be a bit of a gang – then it's a real band.' When asked the highlights of their time together, their different aspirations showed. Neil said eating porridge and bus-jogging after gigs in the Midwest; for Nick, it was winning the Brit award ahead of U2, REM and Nirvana.

The two warm-up shows were held at the Corner, an old pub in Richmond. The first night, it was packed with fans, hanging on every note and joke; the second, the audience was even bigger, swollen by a guest list which had grown out of control. Here was Crowded House at its most intimate, delighting in playing together again, feeling all the same musical and personal bonds return within a few songs. For Paul, it was an emotional and triumphant return to the stage. It was reflected in his playing; head down, sticks flailing, he didn't just provide the rhythm but got *inside* the songs.

The stage patter and anecdotes became increasingly barbed and confessional. 'Did I make a mistake? Blame me,' said Paul. 'We have been for the last 18 months,' quipped Neil. 'Deserter.' Nick cracked up, whereas moments before he had almost cried during 'Don't Dream It's Over.' With the original band, the extended psychedelic jams made sense, whereas when Peter Jones sat in on drums, the slinky R&B groove he instantly found with Nick revealed the pair had an equally strong rapport in a different genre. When the jams became too black, Neil seemed lost, closing them down to begin something folkie. Inevitably, Tim joined the stage, to cheers which lasted well into 'Weather With You'; though the others became sidemen, the magic was undeniable. After a crazed 'Sister Madly' rap from Paul, Neil ceremoniously knighted his colleagues with a bunch of gladioli from the dressing room.

By the time they arrived in Sydney on the eve of the show, media saturation had set in – and the skies had opened with a tropical rainstrom which lasted hours. The big farewell was postponed. The band headed for Randwick Children's Hospital to play a set – and highlight the cause of the event. After one last busk, before children in their hospital beds or wheelchairs, wrapped in bandages, linked to drips or machinery, Paul left the room rapidly, to be found later having a sob.

Postponing the concert had upset the plans of fans who had flown in from as far away as Perth, New Zealand, Britain and America. Those who couldn't stay an extra day milled about the venue: a stage facing one of the world's most spectacular views, the Opera House, Harbour Bridge and Sydney harbour all in one panorama. The band arrived for a soundcheck and gave an impromptu concert, an hour of music and comedy, for the few thousand present. Among them was Neil's family, his parents and sisters, over from New Zealand. Marvelling at the crowd, the setting and the atmosphere, was Dick Finn. 'Split Enz were ahead of their time,' he said, 'and Crowded House were different to all those other bands. You often don't know what you have until you lose it.'

On the following night, the weather was perfect. At 8.00pm, Crowded House ran on stage to a brass band fanfare. The view from the stage was breathtaking; in the crowd, it was suffocating. Squeezed onto Bennelong Point were 150,000 people; 100,000 more were on the harbour and in the surrounding streets.

Neil opened alone with 'Mean to Me', pausing dramatically at the line, *'and the sound of Te Awamutu . . .'* Instantly, the audience replied: '. . .

had a truly sacred ring.' The concert was alive, a family singalong magnified to stadium level. Onstage, there were few smiles, the band concentrating hard against being overwhelmed by the occasion. With Paul utterly immersed in his playing, the band's telepathy and chemistry was once more effortless. The audience was just as involved, swaying, waving, surfing, catching line after line and echoing them back to the band. As the show gathered momentum, the bond increased, every song taking on a special significance: 'Four Seasons in One Day', 'Better Be Home Soon', 'Distant Sun', 'Something So Strong' . . .

Peter Jones sauntered on stage, giving 'Sister Madly' a relaxed swing to accompany Paul's manic antics. At Neil's call for 'a brotherly presence', Tim joined them, his harmonies emphasising the sense of celebration: *'Do I sing like a bird released?'* Strumming their acoustics, Neil and Tim waltzed around each other, while Nick and Mark sang at the same mike, finally breaking out in smiles. In the photographers' pit below the stage was Peter Green, watching 16 years of Enz/Finn/ Crowdie evangelism come to a climax; by the mixing desk were Sharon and Liam, both in tears; at the side of the stage was Mardi, taking photos; pausing momentarily to take it all in was Grant Thomas, beaming.

During the encores, Neil struggled to thank everyone he could remember who had helped over the last 10 years: 'Too many notes, songs, decisions – and only one brain. This feels more like a celebration than a funeral.' Neil grabbed the chance to sing alone. It was the song which had come to symbolise their Anzac mateship, 'Throw Your Arms Around Me'. Nick joined in, standing to attention as if it were the national anthem. By the chorus, 150,000 others were singing, bonded by the sentiment of a final goodbye amongst friends.

'Thanks,' said Neil. 'It's been a blast.' He then scratched out the strum he had learnt in Te Awamutu singalongs. It was as if all of Sydney squealed, cheered, then sang: *'There is freedom within . . .'* Everyone knew 'Don't Dream It's Over' would be last. Paul played with his head right down, his face crumpled, tears dripping onto his snare drum, not missing a beat as Neil advised, *'Get to know the feeling of liberation and release . . .'* By the end, the crowd had taken over. The band hugged each other, waved, and gave a theatrical, emotional bow. Neil was the last to leave the stage; as he reached the bandroom he said to Peter Green it felt strange he didn't cry. 'You did enough of that at the Enz With a Bang shows,' said Green. In the sky above the Harbour Bridge exploded Aus$20,000 of donated fireworks. Over the PA came the cheesy strains of *The Sound of Music* children's choir: 'So long, farewell, it's time to say goodbye.'

Coda–Together, alone •April 1997

'We'd put 10 years of our life into it, and we gave it its due. We went out and had a sacrament of sorts.'

—Neil Finn, 1997

The view from the stage was 'awesome, overwhelming,' says Neil. 'I was concentrating on playing well, because it was being filmed. There wasn't much banter, but we would have miscued if we'd tried to make it the definitive night of Crowded House spontaneity. We all went through our own internal journey on stage. I was trying to take mental snapshots all the time, to tell myself *I've got to remember this*. The sense of occasion was palpable.'

The farewell show turned out to be grander than any of them had thought necessary – it was the biggest concert anywhere in the world that year – 'but it ended up being the best thing to do,' says Neil. 'It was a dramatic event. A lot of people don't bother splitting bands up, they just let them go into cold storage and bring them out every now and again. For some reason I was attracted to the idea of making our intentions clear and letting things be. I think it's done some good for the legacy of the band. If the shine had gone off it, I think it might have made the whole thing seem less special. The way we finished with the last concert, was pretty emotional, for us and the audience. That's all you can ask for.'

When the crowd eventually dispersed from Bennelong Point, the band left its bare caravan – no-one remembered to organise drinks – and went up the road to join the party at the Royal Automobile Club. Arranged by EMI, it turned out to be one last 'meet and greet', with the presentation of gold records, photos and autographs, a few speeches and hundreds of industry guests the band barely knew. The next day, travel arrangements were similarly not quite how they had intended. Neil's family were seated separately, dotted about the plane, surrounded by passengers wearing their farewell concert t-shirts.

Based in Sydney, Grant Thomas continues to manage Neil Finn, Tim Finn, the Finn Brothers, any loose ends from Split Enz and a few

Australian bands. He is well past his second million in frequent flier miles. 'The music business is not about being safe,' he says. 'There's always a song that defies logic. That's what's exciting for me. You can work a formula, but the great music comes from people who don't – be they the Beatles or Smashing Pumpkins,'

Gary Stamler is in Los Angeles, giving legal advice to a variety of acts. A few days after Crowded House released *Recurring Dream* and announced its breakup, another act he had been close to, Van Halen, also released a greatest hits. Simultaneously, their lead singer, Sammy Hagar either quit or was sacked by the Van Halen brothers; David Lee Roth was invited back, temporarily. 'Well Sammy,' counseled Stamler on the phone during interviews for this book, 'you get involved in bands with brothers . . .' His wry humour came at a very sad time for Stamler; shortly afterwards, his wife Peggy died of a rare blood condition.

Hale Milgrim is semi-retired and working on environmental causes. He lives north of Los Angeles, and made a pilgrimage to Kare-kare in 1997. He wore a *Together Alone* t-shirt when interviewed, and proudly showed his hall-of-fame: guitars signed by Richard Thompson, Paul McCartney, Bonnie Raitt, Ry Cooder and Neil Finn, in gratitude for his efforts and enthusiasm.

Tom Whalley is president of Interscope in Los Angeles, and regarded as one of the most astute A&R men in the music industry. During his tenure the label has released or distributed an eclectic roster of cutting-edge acts including Tupac Shakur, Snoop Doggy Dogg, Primus, the Wallflowers, Marilyn Manson, Nine Inch Nails, Bush and No Doubt. Controversial because of its catalogue of gangsta rap, Interscope is nevertheless the spectacular success story of the 1990s. Whalley, a golfer and a surfer rather than a music biz scenester, doesn't give interviews; he doesn't need to.

At Capitol, Gary Gersh has had success with Everclear and the Butthole Surfers, and in 1996 the company spent $10 million to acquire 49 per cent of indie label Matador (Liz Phair, Bettie Serveert). Matador co-owner Christopher Lombardi told *Billboard*, 'Capitol has shown us through their experiences with acts like Radiohead and Mazzy Star that they are committed to working acts over the long haul.' Capitol's parent company EMI Music is itself for sale, but with the lowest market share of any major (8.2 per cent in 1996), the asking price of US$8 billion is thought to be $2 billion too much – especially now that the mining of the Beatles vaults is over.

The week Crowded House announced its demise, Jeremy Hammond decided to leave Capitol after 16 years. For him, the Gersh regime was an 'adverse culture'. He had just put an early dub of

Recurring Dream in his car tape deck. 'It has been very therapeutic,' he says. ' "Don't Dream It's Over" ' – *"there are shadows ahead"*. What was Neil doing when he wrote this? *"You know that they won't win."* Songs like that – that's one of the reasons I'm in this business.'

Mitchell Froom is based in New York, where he lives with his wife Suzanne Vega. 'In this age of over-information, nothing can have the impact it used to. There's no next Bob Dylan, no next Beatles. Politics tends to dictate more and more what you hear, and the cream is not rising to the top. Whenever anybody makes any decision that's actually a bad business decision but a good music decision, I'm with them. I turn down big groups all the time, groups that I could make a lot of money doing, because I just don't like them. You can't think that way, because then you're cynical about music – and if you're cynical about music, you have nothing.'

In Melbourne, Paul Hester holds court in the Elwood café he owns with Mardi and several others, daughter Sunday on his knee. His humour remains disarmingly honest. 'People say "Black & White Boy" is about me,' he says, 'I'd be rapt if it was.' He continues working on music projects, thinking of schemes to put his talents to use – a radio sports show? A television music and chat show? – without leaving the inner-city pages of the Melbourne street directory. As 1997 began, he emerged to perform his own songs – and chat – in a series of shows at St Kilda's Esplanade Hotel. The evenings were billed as 'Hessie's Shed'; he named his band the Largest Living Things.

Tim Finn worked on another solo record through 1996, with the occasional in-concert appearance as a Finn brother or with Enzso (which Neil nicknamed 'never againzo' when the success of Rayner's symphony project looked like becoming a permanent career). He is still capable of outrageous showmanship and music-hall antics. In the last Finn Brothers show for 1996, while Neil earnestly tuned up, he stole the show with a manic, unaccompanied rant through 'I See Red'; at the final Enzso show, when rain drenched the crowd, he came out in his suit and tipped water over his head. 'It's only fair,' he explained to Neil. When interviewed for this book – the agreed topics were growing up with Neil, and writing songs for *Woodface* – he said goodbye with, 'I want to say that at all periods of the band – before I was in it, during and after – I was always a big fan of their music and their stage show. I'd go every night when they were in Melbourne.'

After the Sydney finale, Mark Hart joined up with Supertramp to record a new album, *Some Things Never Change*, and tour. With his partner Sylvie – who worked for EMI in Europe – he became a father again.

Nick Seymour and Peter Jones also went back out on the road, touring Australia and Europe with Deadstar. Nick called on his mobile phone: 'I stayed in a hotel two nights ago with four other people in the same room. It's back to grinding the old pub-rock again. Starting out with Deadstar has brought the reality of the whole thing screaming back into perspective, and I think Neil's lost that.'

He says that Neil closing down Crowded House was 'a lifestyle decision, which he's able to afford'. But the worldwide sales of *Recurring Dream* – approaching 2.5 million early in 1997, with Neil sharing part of his publishing royalties with the rest of the band – and the audit of Capitol's bookkeeping which was being done through 1996, may bring a belated windfall to those who weren't songwriters.

At home in New Zealand, Neil says he feels 'in a strange no-man's land. I'm quite alone, I don't live among the people I'm competing with, so I have this disconnection to the whole thing as I'm not part of the New Zealand scene.' He has the occasional pang that he's so far away from the world's music industry that he misses out on tempting opportunities to collaborate. Although he's the most well-known musician in the country, he gets the occasional reminder what that means. While lobbying government for a public youth radio network, he met the prime minister, Jim Bolger, who greeted him with, 'And you are?'

Neil turned his basement from a room for recording demos into a proper studio. He immediately started work towards another album, for which there is no deadline. In April 1997, he faced a completely clear schedule for the first time since he was 18. He made the occasional live appearance at benefit gigs, but mostly stayed at home, recorded with a variety of visitors, and saw a lot of his family. Although Sharon, Liam and Elroy were often on tour with the band, Neil acknowledges that at some periods of Crowded House, it seemed like she was bringing the children up alone. Sharon jokes that his big comeback line was, 'It could have been worse, I could have been Captain Cook.' And when he returned, she says, 'there was always a coming-down period. Domestic things don't enter his head. At various times, he'd be drifting off and I'd say, what are you thinking about? It became a joke, because it was always *the band*.'

Coming home, it always takes a while to fit back in, says Neil. 'I wander around and can't even get into the idea of doing the dishes. I get back into it eventually, but Sharon sits there and says, "What's this mess? This mess wasn't here last week."'

'For me, the great thing about Sharon is she's so rooted in the here and now, she doesn't get lost in the ethereal anxieties like I do. It's a good balance. We're mates, we're good friends. That's a large part of any relationship succeeding. There's a mutual respect. We've got two really good kids. And we've worked really hard to make it work. There were any number of things that conspired to push us apart. It's not like a denial, of not allowing the possibility of it not working. It's more like, whatever it takes to make it work, we'll commit ourselves to.

'We've been through as many ups and downs as any other couple, but we just have a certain determination to make it work. I like the idea that it goes against the grain, it's the perversity in me. Rock'n'roll marriages are not supposed to be possible. The lifestyle that I see other musicians having – freewheeling from resort to nightclub to musical happening – occasionally I'm envious of. I feel stay-at-homeish and boring, but I like the idea of carving out my own experience of being a rock musician. Within a home and a family, there's the full gamut of human experience, just as much as there is having a wild time.'

Now, family and music can be the motivation, rather than keeping the Crowded House machinery moving. But, says Neil, 'for all the angst I've created for other people, and all the times I've actually been a pain in the arse to myself, I can honestly say it's because I've had the music in mind, rather than wanting fame or a glamorous life.

'There have been times when I've been making all the decisions on my own. It's almost something I do to avoid writing a song. It's a fearful moment, when you're sitting down to a blank page, there's nothing scarier. People say, oh you'll be okay, you've been doing it so long – but it's not like that. It doesn't get any easier.'

But he remembers something his mother Mary once said: 'Neil, you'll always do alright, a good tune is always in short supply.'

Afterword

I first discussed the possibility of a book on Crowded House with Neil Finn in August, 1988, just after the release of *Temple of Low Men*. He said he was flattered, but felt it was too soon. When Pan Macmillan in London brought up the idea in mid-1995, Neil's response was similar: it was too soon, the story was only half over. But eventually, after the winter demo sessions in Auckland that year, Neil agreed – though he hadn't had a chance to talk about it with the others. Then he asked what 'authorised' meant. I explained that an authorised biography gave the approved version, that its contents went through the filter of its subject; it would be like a coproduction between the Crowded House organisation and the author. I could feel his eyes glazing over and he said, no, we don't want that. Just get around everyone and talk to me last. All that meant was, the less he had to be involved, the better it suited.

I started interviews in March 1996 and, thanks to Neil's okay, everyone approached agreed to take part. It was perturbing, though, when the first subjects said, So you think the band is still going? It had been three years since the *Together Alone* sessions, and two since Paul had left in Atlanta. But there were plans to start another album in July, 1996.

So it was a shock, but not a surprise, when Neil shut down Crowded House at the time *Recurring Dream* was released. But it meant that the book would now be complete and, better still, interviews a little more direct, if still discreet. Like Split Enz, the Crowded House organisation is an extended family – and with that comes a staunch loyalty. Everyone involved wanted the book to be honest, but it took a lot of cross-checking to fill the gaps, eliminate the faulty memories and make the generalisations specific.

There was no reason for Paul Hester to be so obliging, other than to put across his point of view. But his frankness in many sessions went beyond self-interest or justification. He knew he had a good story to tell and he loves telling stories. He had had time to reflect on his experience, and his love of the others meant that he was usually the butt of his own critical comments. Still in the band when we first talked, Nick Seymour's conversations reflected his conflicting natural tendencies: to be the band's ambassador and image guardian while maintaining his sardonic humour (which emerged in the months following the split). Tim Finn didn't really want his life to be part of a book ('I've been talking to the press for 25 years') but nevertheless agreed to discuss his childhood and time in Crowded House, and gave permission for me to use unpublished interviews done by Mike Chunn for *Stranger than Fiction*, on events after 1984. Mark Hart and Peter Jones calmly told their stories, while the frankness of everyone else depended on how connected they still were to the organisation. To the

Americans, the Crowded House story was mostly a long time ago, while the English company was on its way to selling a million copies of *Recurring Dream* by Christmas. And when the interviews with Neil finally took place in August and October 1996, it seemed he was still coming to terms with his very fresh decision. The interviews would shift from anecdote to analysis, as if he was working out what had happened while he spoke.

The key players did read the manuscript, and found the occasional flaw in the memories of others or themselves, or the odd myth which had been taken as fact. But there was no exertion of control or late attempt at spin-doctoring. I was glad to be alerted to any errors; my own decisions of interpretation or emphasis were made after comparing divergent viewpoints with concrete evidence. As historian Michael King has said, writing biography is like trigonometry: where the different viewpoints intersect, that is where the facts should be.

I regret that I missed out on interviewing two people who would have made a valuable contribution: Craig Hooper and Youth. Leads to Hooper proved fruitless, and I spent months getting the runaround from Youth's 'management'. When I got to London for the Hanover Grand gig and the UK interviews, I found out that Youth was in New York. He was to get back the day I was leaving, ironically for New York and an interview with Mitchell Froom. I then spent many winter nights waiting up to call the UK trying to set up an interview with Youth, or get a straight answer from his entourage. One night he actually answered the phone and said, sure, he'd talk, but not right now. Unfortunately our planets never connected again. The last couple of times I tried, the phone number was disconnected. (When Crowded House asked Youth in mid-1993 what he had learnt from the Karekare experience, he allegedly replied after a long pause, 'Unconditional love'.)

Crowded House may be no more, but the story is indeed only half over; the participants have futures to unfold, and even the past has a tendency to keep evolving. Two days before sending this afterword and discography away, someone mysteriously dropped a package at my doorstep which had originally been posted to me a year ago. Inside was a letter, and a tape labelled 'Neil Finn – early samples'. The letter was from Chris Ampleford, who had met Neil in 1976 when visiting Martin's Refrigeration as a rep for Pye Records. The boy behind the counter wanted to know if Ampleford had any Split Enz posters, and explained his brother was in the band. Ampleford next saw Neil a few weeks later, on stage at His Majesty's supporting the Enz. He called Neil to say how impressed he was, and invited him to record some demos on his home reel-to-reel, which were then rare in New Zealand.

When Ampleford next visited Te Awamutu to discuss the idea, Neil invited him to dinner at his parents' house. 'He showed me his room and it came as no surprise that it was packed to capacity with musical instruments. It was quite a small bedroom and the largest item in it was an upright piano. There was an assortment of stringed instruments, a piano accordion and, among the clutter, just enough room for a bed.'

At dinner, Neil's parents talked of how proud they were of Tim, not just for what Split Enz had achieved in New Zealand, but early reports from England suggested things were going well there, too. 'I remember Mrs Finn asking me if I thought there was a future for Neil in the music business,' says Ampleford in his letter. 'I told her that he was, without doubt, the most gifted entertainer I had ever met.' The recordings Ampleford made show Neil in '70s singer-songwriter mode, delivering his Carole King/Elton John songs in a reedy voice which was still developing. Among his own originals are versions of 'Blackbird' and 'Cry Baby Cry' off the Beatles' 'White Album'. But Pye wasn't interested in the demos. 'I was bitterly disappointed,' says Ampleford, 'probably more so than Neil, who looked a little dejected but soon shrugged it off. He was only 17, had bags of talent and his head screwed on. This wasn't going to be a major setback.'

Acknowledgements

Grateful thanks to the many people who were willing to be interviewed for the writing of this book and for earlier articles over the years: Emma Banks, Tchad Blake, Julie Borchard, Jules Bowen, Kerry Brown, Geoff Chunn, Mike Chunn, Mark Collen, Noel Crombie, Angus Davidson, Peter Dawkins, Dave Dobbyn, Dror Erez, David Field, Neil Finn, Richard and Mary Finn, Sharon Finn, Tim Finn, Mitchell Froom, Ivan Gannoway, Rob Gillies, Tom Gorman, Scott Greer, Jeremy Hammond, Debbie Harwood, Mark Hart, Bob Harvey, David Hepworth, Paul Hester, Malcolm Hill, Nigel Horrocks, Peter Jones, Paul Kelly, Roger King, Mick Kleber, Paul Kosky, Walter Lee, Geoff Lloyd, Dugald McAndrew, Paul Martinovich, Michael Matthews, Miles Mendoza, Hale Milgrim, Jenny Morris, Rikki Morris, Greg Perano, Eddie Rayner, Nick Seymour, Bruce Sheridan, Denise Skinner, Gary Stamler, Tommy Steele, Dean and Robin Taylor, Grant Thomas, Tony Wadsworth, Rob Walker, Lawrie Zion.

Several people have been especially generous with their advice, encouragement and tangible assistance: Arthur Baysting, Kerry Brown, Mike Chunn, Robin Dudding and Tom McWilliams. Peter Green at the Crowded House club in Melbourne (P O Box 333, Prahran, Melbourne VIC 3181; enclose two IRCs) was endlessly patient with my queries, and willingly gave me access to his archives; Mark Goulding helped me sort through hours of video and audio tape, and read the manuscript with a scrupulous eye for detail. Grant Thomas and Hayden Yarrall at Grant Thomas Management responded cheerfully to many trans-Tasman inquiries. Kerry Brown, Mike Chunn, Neil and Sharon Finn, Richard and Mary Finn, Peter Green, Paul Hester, Hale Milgrim, Nick Seymour, Amanda Urquhart, Mardi Summerfeld, Grant Thomas, William West and Lawrie Zion generously made their photo archives available.

Many friends in New Zealand and overseas offered support including accommodation, technical advice, conversation and research legwork: Christina Asher and Catherine Madigan at the Pa, Clare Avery and Jon Feidner, Tony Backhouse, Babs Baker, Nick Bollinger, Russell Brown, Bill Cullen, Jonathan Doolan, Devta Doolan and Devie Hopkins, Stephanie Bauer, Claire Bourke, Tim Bourke and Sam Beilby, Paul Ellis, Kevin Ireland and the New Zealand Society of Authors, Sarah Kennedy and Wayne Anderson, Mark Leydon and Rose Travers, Simon Lynch, Ian Morris, Hazel Stewart, William West, plus the staff of the New Zealand *Listener*. Assistance with the arduous task of transcription came from Catherine Callen, Tricia Clareburt, Mary Dobbyn and Libby Giles. Those whose past generosity directly contributed to the book include Tim Byrne, Murray Cammick, Maxine Morris, the Kennedys and McCartins of Utiku, Stratford Productions, Ken Williams.

Thanks also to staff at EMI New Zealand: Kerry Byrne, Chris Caddick, Ben Hill and Bruce Ward; EMI Australia: Amanda Urquhart; and Parlophone UK: Malcolm Hill. Crowded House fans who shared their memories or tape collections: Chris Ampleford, Matt Browne, Eelco Doornbos, John Johnson, Keith Wilkinson, Mark Leydon, Stefan Warnqvist.

At Pan Macmillan, Ingrid Connell of the London branch started the ball rolling; in New Zealand, Joan Mackenzie and Jill Rawnsley were constantly supportive; in Australia, James Fraser, Amanda Hemmings and Tom Gilliatt showed unwavering enthusiasm and remarkable patience.

Appendix 1:
live surprises

During their concerts, Crowded House often performed songs by their musical antecedents or peers – or just made them up on the spot. The following list is mostly taken from tape logs of live shows, which were only done regularly from 1989.

Cover versions: 'Leaps and Bounds', 'Brady Bunch theme', 'Kingston Town', 'Irish Heartbeat', 'Little Sister', 'Anarchy in the UK', 'Walk on the Wild Side', 'Age of Aquarius', 'Throw Your Arms Around Me', 'Get Back', 'I've Got a Feeling', 'Born on the Bayou', 'It's Only Natural' (Ramones version), 'I Should Be So Lucky', 'I've Been Everywhere', 'Rocky Raccoon', 'Blue Moon', 'The Mighty Quinn', 'One Fine Day', 'Don't Be a Stranger', 'Roadhouse Blues', 'Pale Blue Eyes', 'Born to Be Wild', 'Seven Times Champion', 'Riders on the Storm', 'Sunny Afternoon', 'Play it Strange', 'The Nips are Getting Bigger', 'I Can See Clearly', 'Still in Love With You', 'Blue Suede Shoes', 'Frank's Dark Past', 'Not Fade Away', 'Till We Kissed', 'Cry Baby Cry', 'Be My Guest', 'Forever Friends', 'You Sexy Thing', 'The Letter' (with Sheryl Crow), 'Louie Louie', 'Those Were the Days', 'Walk Tall', 'Leaving on a Jet Plane', 'Spicks and Specks', 'Whaling', 'Hit the Road Jack', 'Love in a Fowl House', 'Road to Nowhere', 'Smoke on the Water', 'Wild Thing'.

Instant songs: 'George With the Green Nose', 'Two Mistakes is One Idea', 'Seymour Clan', 'The Tennis Song', 'Make Your Preparations', 'Paris Song' (by Mark), 'Get a Little Washing Done', 'Chicken Song', 'Darts', 'Manchester International Airport', 'Peter Seller's Girlfriend', 'Last August I Left Auckland'.

Unreleased songs by Neil: 'I Love You Dawn', 'The Burglar Song', 'Lester's Song', 'Time Immemorial', 'Tail of the Comet ', 'Good Luck Morning', 'Convent Girls', 'Money's No Object'.

Split Enz songs: 'Message to My Girl', 'Hello Sandy Allen', 'Split Ends', 'Six Months in a Leaky Boat', 'I Got You', 'I Walk Away', 'History Never Repeats', 'Giant Heartbeat', 'Shark Attack', 'The Devil You Know', 'Sweet Dreams', 'One Step Ahead', 'Time for a Change', 'Hermitt McDermitt', 'Log Cabin Fever', 'Missing Person', 'Serge', 'Kia Kaha'.

Songs by Paul: 'Worms', 'I'm Still Here', 'Signs', 'My Telly's Gone Bung!', 'Six Feet Under, 'Thank You Anne', 'Me on Drums', 'I'm Still Emotional'.

Appendix II: Crowded House-a discography

Vinyl and CD releases in the United States, United Kingdom, Australia and New Zealand; not including promos. All tracks by Neil Finn, unless otherwise noted (exceptions only listed at first mention). Information from Peter Green's 1994 discography of Split Enz, Crowded House, Tim Finn and related releases, the discography compiled by Marck Bailey and Lisa Kempner for the *Tongue in the Mail* Crowded House home page – www.etext.org/Mailing.Lists/house/ – and my own research.

ALBUMS

Crowded House
Mean To Me / World Where You Live / Now We're Getting Somewhere / Don't Dream It's Over / Love You 'til The Day I Die / Something So Strong (N Finn, M Froom) / Hole In The River (N Finn, E Rayner) / Can't Carry On / I Walk Away / Tombstone / That's What I Call Love (P Hester, N Finn)
  UK LP EMI EST 2016, April 1986; CD EST 2016, 1987
  World Where You Live / Now We're Getting Somewhere / Don't Dream It's Over / Mean To Me / Love You 'til The Day I Die / Something So Strong / Hole In The River / I Walk Away / Tombstone / That's What I Call Love
  US LP Capitol ST-12485; Aus LP EMI ST240555; NZ LP Capitol ST-12485, June 1986
  Second issue of the debut album has 'Can't Carry On' added. US LP Capitol ST12485, CD Capitol CDP 7466932; Aus CD EMI CDP7463172; NZ CD Capitol CDP 7466932

Temple of Low Men
I Feel Possessed / Kill Eye / Into Temptation / Mansion In the Slums / When You Come / Never Be the Same / Love This Life / Sister Madly / In the Lowlands / Better Be Home Soon
  LPs: US Capitol C148763; Aus EMI RP 168; NZ Capitol ST 748763 (July 1988); UK EMI EST 2064 (August 1988)
  CDs: US Capitol CDP 7487632, Aus EMI 748763, NZ CDP 748763 (July 1988), UK EMI CDEST 2064 (August 1988); EMI CDP 7487632 (1991 reissue)

Woodface
Chocolate Cake (N Finn, T Finn) / It's Only Natural (N Finn, T Finn) / Fall At Your Feet / Tall Trees (N Finn, T Finn) / Weather With You (N Finn, T Finn) / Whispers and Moans / Four Seasons in One Day (N Finn, T Finn) / There Goes God (N Finn, T Finn) / Fame Is / All I Ask (N Finn, T Finn) / As Sure As I Am / Italian Plastic (P Hester) / She Goes On / How Will You Go (N Finn, T Finn) / I'm Still Here (*unlisted track, no composer credit*)

   LPs: US Capitol C193559; Aus & NZ EMI 7935593 (July 1991); UK EMI EST2144 (June 1991)

   CDs: US CDP 7935592; US DPRO 79759 (*special diecut package*); Aus & NZ EMI 7935592 (July 1991); UK EMI CD EST2144 (June 1991)

Together Alone
Kare Kare (N Finn, N Seymour, M Hart, P Hester) / In My Command / Nails In My Feet / Black & White Boy / Fingers of Love / Pineapple Head / Locked Out / Private Universe / Walking on the Spot / Distant Sun / Catherine Wheels (N Finn, T Finn, N Seymour) / Skin Feeling / Together Alone (N Finn, B Wehi, M Hart)

   LPs: UK Capitol 8270481 (October 1993)

   CDs: UK Capitol 8270482; Aus & NZ EMI 8270482 (October 1993); US CDP 82704829 (January 1994)

Recurring Dream – the Very Best of Crowded House
Weather With You / World Where You Live / Fall at Your Feet / Locked Out / Don't Dream It's Over / Into Temptation / Pineapple Head / When You Come / Private Universe / You're Not the Girl You Think You Are / Instinct / I Feel Possessed / Four Seasons in One Day / It's Only Natural / Distant Sun / Something So Strong / Mean To Me / Better Be Home Soon / Everything Is Good for You

   CDs: UK, US, Aus, NZ Capitol CDEST 2283 (June 1996)

   LPs: UK Capitol EST 2283 (June 1996)

Recurring Dream – bonus live album
(tracks marked * are from Newcastle, Australia, 20 Mar 92)

   There Goes God* / Newcastle Jam* / Love You 'til The Day I Die* / Hole in the River* / Private Universe (Birmingham 18 Nov 93) / Pineapple Head (Manchester 23 Nov 93) / How Will You Go (Glasgow 12 July 92) / Left Hand (Gent 18 Oct 91) / Whispers and Moans (Philadelphia 3 Oct 91) / Kill Eye (Philadelphia 3 Oct 91) / Fingers of Love (Atlanta 14 Apr 94) / Don't Dream It's Over (Cambridge 6 Mar 92) / When You Come* / Sister Madly

(Portsmouth 23 Nov 93) / In My Command (Munich 12 Dec 93)
   LPs: UK Capitol ESTX 2283 (June 1996)
   CDs: UK, US, Aus, NZ Capitol CDESTX 2283 (June 1996)

SINGLES

7-inch singles
Aus '87 EMI CP 1769 World Where You Live / Hole in the River
Aus '86 CP 1778 Mean To Me / Hole In The River
UK '86 CL 416 World Where You Live / That's What I Call Love
US '86 B-5575 World Where You Live / That's what I Call Love
Aus '86 CP 1822 Now We're Getting Somewhere / Recurring Dream (N Finn,
P Hester, N Seymour, C Hooper)
US '86 B5614 Don't Dream It's Over / That's What I Call Love
UK '86 CL 438 Don't Dream It's Over / That's What I Call Love
Aus '86 CP1842 Don't Dream It's Over / That's What I Call Love
NZ '86 F5614 Don't Dream It's Over / That's What I Call Love
US '87 B5695 Something So Strong / I Walk Away
UK '87 CL 456 Something So Strong / I Walk Away
UK '87 CP 1945 Something So Strong / I Walk Away
NZ '87 F5695 Something So Strong / I Walk Away
NZ '87 CP 657 World Where You Live / That's What I Call Love
US '87 B44083 Now We're Getting Somewhere / Tombstone
US '88 B44164 Better Be Home Soon / Kill Eye
NZ '88 CP 2100 Better Be Home Soon / Kill Eye
UK '88 CL 498 Better Be Home Soon / Kill Eye
Aus '88 CP 2120 When You Come / Better Be Home Soon
US '88 B44226 Into Temptation / Better Be Home Soon
Aus '88 CP 2128 Into Temptation / Mansion in the Slums (live) / This is
Massive (P Hester) (live)
UK '89 CL 509 Sister Madly / Mansion In The Slums
Aus '89 CP 2206 Sister Madly / Love This Life
Aus '89 CP 2278 I Feel Possessed / Mr Tambourine Man (Dylan) (live with
Roger McGuinn)
Aus / UK '91 CL 618 Chocolate Cake / As Sure As I Am
UK '91 CL 626 Fall At Your Feet / Don't Dream It's Over
Aus '91 2640-7 Fall At Your Feet / Whispers and Moans
UK '92 CL 643 Weather With You (single edit) / Into Temptation
UK '92 CL 655 Four Seasons in One Day / There Goes God
UK '92 CL 661 It's Only Natural / Chocolate Cake
UK '93 CL 697 Distant Sun / Walking on the Spot

UK '93 CL 701 Nails In My Feet / Don't Dream It's Over (live)
UK '96 CL 776 Not The Girl You Think You Are / Better Be Home Soon (live)
UK '96 CL 780 Don't Dream It's Over / Weather With You (live)

12-inch singles

UK '86 12 CL 416 World Where You Live (ext) / Can't Carry On / That's What I Call Love

US '86 V-12485 World Where You Live / Mean To Me / Something So Strong

NZ '87 GOOD1311 World Where You Live / Mean To Me / Something So Strong

UK '87 12 CL 438 Don't Dream It's Over (ext) / Don't Dream It's Over / That's What I Call Love

US '87 V-15292 Something So Strong / Can't Carry On / I Walk Away

NZ '87 GOOD179 Something So Strong / Can't Carry On / I Walk Away

UK '87 12 CL 456 Something So Strong / Something So Strong (live) / I Walk Away / Don't Dream It's Over (live)

Aus '88 ED 354 Better Be Home Soon / Don't Dream It's Over (live) / Kill Eye

UK '88 12 CL 498 Better Be Home Soon / Don't Dream It's Over (live) / Kill Eye

Aus '88 ED388 Into Temptation / Mansion In The Slums (live) / This Is Massive (live)

UK '88 12 CL 509 Sister Madly / Mansion In The Slums / Something So Strong (live)

Aus '88 ED509 Sister Madly / Mansion In The Slums / Something So Strong (live)

Aus / UK '91 12 CL 618 Chocolate Cake / As Sure As I Am / Anyone Can Tell

10-inch singles

UK '94 10 CL 707 Locked Out (live) / Distant Sun (live) / Fall At Your Feet (live) / Private Universe (live)

UK '94 10 CL 715 Fingers Of Love (live) / Love You 'til the Day I Die (live) / Whispers And Moans (live) / It's Only Natural (live)

UK '94 10 CL 723 Pineapple Head / Weather With You / Don't Dream It's Over / Together Alone

CD singles

(New Zealand CD singles were imported from the UK and Australia, with the exception of a NZ-only release of 'Together Alone')

US '87 Cap 5614 Don't Dream It's Over / Something So Strong / World Where You Live (CDV: 'Don't Dream' video and audio, in NTSC format, other tracks audio only)

UK '86 CDCL 416 World Where You Live (ext) / Something So Strong / Don't Dream It's Over / That's What I Call Love

UK/Aus/NZ '88 CDCL 498 Better Be Home Soon / Don't Dream It's Over (live) / Kill Eye

Aus '88 CDED 383 When You Come / Better Be Home Soon / Something So Strong

UK/Aus '88 CDCL 509 Sister Madly / Mansion In The Slums / Something So Strong (live)

Aus '88 CDED 388 Into Temptation / Mansion In The Slums (live) / This Is Massive (live)

US / Aus '89 CDP 7154902 I Feel Possessed / Mr Tambourine Man (live) / Eight Miles High (Clark/McGuinn/Crosby) (live) / So You Want to Be A Rock'n'Roll Star (McGuinn/Hillman) (live) (live tracks with Roger McGuinn)

UK '91 CDCL 618 Chocolate Cake / As Sure As I Am / Anyone Can Tell

US '91 C 215738 Chocolate Cake / As Sure As I Am / Anyone Can Tell

Aus '91 25902 Chocolate Cake / As Sure As I Am / Anyone Can Tell US '91 C215757 Fall At Your Feet / Whispers and Moans / Six Months in A Leaky Boat (T Finn/Split Enz) (Tim & Neil, live)

Aus '91 26402 Fall At Your Feet / Whispers and Moans / Six Months in A Leaky Boat (Tim & Neil, live)

UK '91 CDCLX 626 Fall At Your Feet / Six Months in A Leaky Boat (Tim & Neil, live) / Now We're Getting Somewhere (live) / Something So Strong

UK '91 CDCL 626 Fall At Your Feet / Don't Dream It's Over / Sister Madly / Better Be Home Soon

UK/Aus '92 CDCL 643 Weather With You (single edit) / Mr Tambourine Man (Byrdhouse live) / Eight Miles High (live) / So You Want to Be A Rock'n'Roll Star (live)

UK/Aus '92 CDCLS 643 Weather With You (radio edit) / Fall At Your Feet (live) / When You Come (live) / Walking on the Spot (live)

US '92 C 215734 Weather With You (Radio Edit) / Walking on the Spot (live) / Don't Dream It's Over (live) / Better Be Home Soon (live) / World Where You Live (live)

UK '92 CDCLS 655 Four Seasons in One Day / Dr Livingston / Recurring Dream (1989 version) / Anyone Can Tell

UK '92 CDCL 655 Four Seasons in One Day / Weather With You (live) / Italian Plastic (live) / Message to My Girl (live)

Aus '92 8801452 Four Seasons in One Day / There Goes God (live) / Tall Trees

Aus '92 8801072 Four Seasons in One Day / Italian Plastic (live) / Love You'til the Day I Die (live) / It's Only Natural (live) / Four Seasons in One Day (live)

UK '92 CDCLS 661 It's Only Natural / It's Only Natural (live) / Hole In The River (live) / The Burglar's Song (medley, live)

UK '92 CDCL 661 It's Only Natural / Sister Madly (live) / There Goes God (live) / Chocolate Cake (live)

Aus '92 26522 It's Only Natural / Dr Livingston / Fame Is

Aus '92 4360122 It's Only Natural / Recurring Dream (1987 version) / Hole In The River (live) / Better Be Home Soon / I Walk Away

UK/Aus '93 CDCLS 697 Distant Sun / This Is Massive (live) / When You Come (live)

UK/Aus '93 CDCL 697 Distant Sun / Walking on the Spot / Throw Your Arms Around Me (live) (Seymour/Archer/Crosby/Falconer/Howard/Miles/Waters) / One Step Ahead (live)

Aus '93 8809962 Distant Sun / Walking on the Spot / When You Come (live) / Skin Feeling / Weather With You (live)

Aus '93 8811772 Nails In My Feet / You Can Touch / Zen Roxy (instrumental)

UK '93 CDCLS 701 Nails In My Feet / You Can Touch / Zen Roxy (instrumental)

UK '93 CDCL 701 Nails In My Feet / I Am in Love / Four Seasons in One Day (live) US '93 C2-72438 Locked Out / World Where You Live (live) / It's Only Natural (live) / Weather With You (live)

Aus '94 8816992 Private Universe (radio edit) / Nails In My Feet (live) / In My Command (live) / Whispers and Moans (live) / I Am In Love USA '94 85813627 Distant Sun (remix) / Pineapple Head (live) / Locked Out (live)

UK '94 CDCLS 707 Locked Out / Distant Sun (live) / Hole in the River (live) / Sister Madly (live)

UK '94 CDCL 707 Locked Out / Private Universe (live) / Fall at Your Feet (live) / Better Be Home Soon (live)

Aus '94 8811802 Locked Out / World Where You Live (live) / It's Only Natural (live) / Weather With You (live)

UK '94 CDCLS 715 Fingers Of Love / Skin Feeling / Kare Kare (live) / In My Command (live)

UK '94 CDCL 715 Fingers Of Love / Catherine Wheels / Pineapple Head (live) / Something So Strong (live)

Aus '94 8816992 Private Universe (Radio edit) / Nails in My Feet (live) / In My Command (live) / Whispers And Moans (live)

UK '94 CDCL 723 Pineapple Head / Weather With You / Don't Dream It's Over / Together Alone

NZ '95 8770272 Together Alone / Kare Kare

UK '96 CDCLS 774 Instinct / Recurring Dream / Weather With You (live) / Chocolate Cake (live); second CD: Instinct (alternative mix) / World Where You Live (live) / In the Lowlands (live) / Into Temptation (live)

UK '96 CDCLS 776 Not the Girl You Think You Are / Instinct (live) / Distant Sun (live) / Fall At Your Feet (live); second CD: Not the Girl You Think You

Are / Private Universe (live) / Fingers of Love (live) / Better Be Home Soon (live)
Aus '96 8830212 Everything is Good For You / History Never Repeats (live, Crowded House with Pearl Jam) / Chocolate Cake (live) / Into Temptation (live) (also slimline CD 8830502)
UK '96 CDCLS 780 Don't Dream It's Over / Weather With You (live) / Into Temptation (live) / Locked Out (live); second CD Don't Dream It's Over / Four Seasons in One Day (live) / In My Command (live) / Pineapple Head (live)
Aus '97 8834482 Instinct / Private Universe (live) / Fingers of Love (live) / Better Be Home Soon (live)

Other Crowded House releases
The Crossing soundtrack (features Crowded House version of the Zombies 'She's Not There') – 1990. Aus Regular TVL 93336 (LP), TVD93336 (CD); UK CCD1826 (CD)
Tequila Sunrise soundtrack (features 'Recurring Dream') – 1988. US CDP7911852
Rikky & Pete soundtrack (features 'Recurring Dream') – 1988. Aus EMX790678 (LP); US SBL12593 (LP), CDSBL12593 (CD).

VIDEOS

I Like to Watch – all Crowded House videos up to 'Four Seasons in One Day', plus extra footage shot by Andrew Vogel (UK, 1992: Capitol/EMI MVP 9913413, PAL format; Australia: EMI 15040; also released in France on Secam).
Farewell to the World – the November 24, 1996 final concert at the Sydney Opera House, Australia, plus behind-the-scenes footage shot by Kerry Brown (Australia: 1996, PolyGram PVA 1392).
Split Enz 1972–92 – collection of Split Enz videos (Australia: 1993, Mushroom V81363).

CONNECTIONS

Split Enz on CD
All original Split Enz albums were re-released by Mushroom Records, Australia on CD in 1991: *Mental Notes*, 1975 (D19217); *Second Thoughts*, 1976 (D19218); *Dizrythmia*, 1977 (D19219); *Frenzy*, 1978 (D19474); *The Beginning of*

the Enz, 1979 (D19220); *True Colours*, 1980 (D37167); *Corroboree*, 1981 (known as *Waiata* outside of Australia) (D19473); *Time & Tide*, 1982 (D19475); *See Ya 'Round*, 1984 (D19540). *The Living Enz* is a live double from the 1984 'final' tour (Australia: Mushroom CD D45029/30); *Enzso* is Eddie Rayner's orchestration of Enz songs, performed by Split Enz with the New Zealand Symphony Orchestra (1996, New Zealand: Epic 4838870.9).

Tim Finn
Solo albums on CD
Escapade, 1983 (Mushroom D19230); *Big Canoe*, 1986 (Virgin 4320742); *Tim Finn*, 1989 (Capitol CDP7487352); *Before & After*, 1993 (EMI 7949042).

Finn Brothers
Album
Finn (1995, UK, Aus, NZ: Parlophone 8 35632 2; 1996, US: Discovery 77043)
Only Talking Sense / Eyes of the World / Mood Swinging Man / Last Day of June (N Finn) / Suffer Never / Angels Heap / Niwhai / Where Is My Soul / Bullets in My Hairdo / Paradise / Kiss The Road of Rarotonga (All songs by T Finn/N Finn except where indicated) Singles
(extra tracks are demos recorded in Melbourne, 1989)
UK '95 82438 Suffer Never / Strangeness & Charm / In Love With It All / Four Seasons in One Day
UK '95 82436 Suffer Never / Prodigal Son / Catherine Wheel / Weather With You
UK '93 82585 Angel's Heap / It's Only Natural / Chocolate Cake
UK '93 82586 Angel's Heap / There Goes God / How Will You Go

Neil and Tim Finn's song (written with Andy White) 'Mary of the South Seas' appears on the compilation *Common Ground: Voices of Modern Irish Music* (UK, 1996: EMI/Premier 7243 8 37691 2 4).

Tangents
Hunters & Collectors: *Collected Works* is a compilation featuring 'Throw Your Arms Around Me' and 'Talking to a Stranger' (1990, Australia: White Label/Mushroom TVD 93338; NZ: CD 53338).
Paul Kelly: his Australian trilogy consists of *Post* (1985, Australia: Mushroom CD D19811), *Gossip* – a double album with 'Leaps and Bounds' (1986, Australia: Mushroom L45961/2, CD reissue D19811; in the US, A&M CD-5157), *Under the Sun* (1987: Australia, Mushroom CD 53248).
Dave Dobbyn: *Lament for the Numb*, produced by Mitchell Froom (1993, New Zealand: Trafalgar 450992330-2); and *Twist*, produced by Neil Finn (1994, New

Zealand: Epic 477792.2). *Twist* was released in the US with three tracks from *Lament* (1995: Tristar WK35025). *Dave Dobbyn Collection* features 'Whaling', 'Slice of Heaven' and Th' Dudes' 'Be Mine Tonight' (1990, NZ: Festival 30733.

For quick overviews of New Zealand mainstream pop since the 1960s, two double compilation CDs are available: various artists, *25 Years of Kiwi Rock* (1990: EMI NZ, CDTP38; recommended) and, dominated by middle-of-the-road pap, *25 Years of Kiwi Pop* (1990: EMI NZ, CDTP 40). The post-punk boom in New Zealand music is well represented on *It's Bigger Than Both of Us: NZ singles 1979–82* (1988, NZ: Propeller/Festival, LP L60037/8 [2REV 210]).

Bibliography
Books

Chunn, Mike, *Stranger than Fiction: the Life and Times of Split Enz* (Wellington: GP Publications, 1992) (a second impression is available from P O Box 74–321, Remuera, Auckland, New Zealand)

Chunn, Mike & Jeremy, *The Mechanics of Popular Music: a New Zealand Perspective* (Wellington: GP Publications, 1995)

Dannen, Fredric, *Hit Men: Power Brokers & Fast Money Inside the Music Business* (New York: Vintage Books, 1991)

Dix, John, *Stranded in Paradise: New Zealand Rock'n'Roll 1955–1988* (Wellington: Paradise Publications, 1988)

Doole, Kerry, and Chris Twomey, *Crowded House: Private Universe* (London: Omnibus Press, 1996)

Grein, Paul (ed.), *Capitol Records Fiftieth Anniversary 1942–1992* (Hollywood: Capitol Records, 1992)

Haring, Bruce *Off the Charts: Ruthless Days and Reckless Nights Inside the Music Industry* (New York: Birch Lane, 1996)

Hoskyns, Barney, *Waiting for the Sun: Strange Days, Weird Scenes, and the Sound of Los Angeles* (New York: St Martin's Press, 1996)

Hutchison, Tracee, *Your Name's On the Door: 10 Years of Australian Music* (Sydney: ABC Enterprises, 1992)

Knoedelseder, William, *Stiffed: a True Story of MCA, the Music Business, and the Mafia* (New York: HarperPerennial, 1993)

Marsh, Dave, and James Bernard, *The New Book of Rock Lists* (London: Sidgwick & Jackson, 1994)

Smith, Joe, *Off the Record: an Oral History of Popular Music* (London: Pan, 1990)

Walker, Clinton, (ed.), *Inner City Sound* (Sydney: Wild & Woolley, 1982)

Articles

Adams, Steve, 'Crowded House', *Record Collector*, June 1992

Aizlewood, John, 'Soap!', *Q*, July 1991

Applefeld, Catherine, 'For Crowded House, Plans Come "Together" At Last *Billboard*, 14 January 1994

Azerrad, Michael, 'House Party', *Spin*, November 1988

Baillie, Russell, 'A big "hi" from the Low Men', *Auckland Star*, 12 January 1989

'Finn's bit of Kiwiana', *Sunday Star*, 31 January 1993

Baker, Barbarina, 'Ain't Nothing But a House Party', *Shake!*, November 1986

'Across a Crowded Room', *Shake!*, August 1987

Balham, Diana, 'Why Tim Split . . . Neil Finn Tells', *Woman's Day*, 4 December 1991

Bliss, Karen, 'No Vacancies Please', *Performer*, September 1991

Bourke, Chris, 'History never repeats', *New Zealand Listener*, 10 November 1984

'Crowded House at State Theatre, Sydney', *New Zealand Herald*, 26 August 1988

'Eddie Rayner interview', *Rip It Up*, September 1988

'Nice Place You've Got Here', *Rip It Up*, September 1988

'Crowded House in Sydney', *Shake*, October 1988

'Spirited Harmonies: Mitchell Froom & the Brothers Finn', *Rip It Up*, June 1989

'A New Lease for Crowded House', *New Zealand Listener*, 21 October 1991

'Twists of Fate', *New Zealand Listener*, 3 December 1994

'Brothers of Invention', *New Zealand Listener*, 2 March 1996

'Finn de Siecle', *New Zealand Listener*, 15 June 1996

'Inside the Dream Machine', *New Zealand Herald*, 18 July 1996

Byrnes, Terry, 'Three's Not a Crowd', *RAM*, 2 July 1986

Casimir, Jon, 'Alterations & Repairs', *RAM*, 13 July 1988

Catlin, Roger, 'Finn's splitends association with Crowded House', *Hartford Courant*, 25 November 1991

Clark, Alix, 'Burning Down the House', *Who*, 25 November 1996

Creswell, Toby, 'True Storeys', *Rolling Stone Australia*, September 1988

Danielsen, Shane, 'No room for inspiration in this House', *Sydney Morning Herald*, 11 August 1991

Darling, Cary, 'The House that Roared', *BAM*, 27 March 1987

DeCurtis, Anthony, 'Temple of Low Men', (US) *Rolling Stone*, 14 July 1988

DeYoung, Bill, 'The Finn Brothers', *Goldmine*, 13 September 1996

Du Noyer, Paul, 'Pets Win Prizes!', *Q*, July 1996

Eliezer, Christie, 'Get up, I feel like being a mean machine!', *Juke*, 12 July 1986

Ellis, Paul, 'Crowded, but back to reality', *Auckland Star*, 6 April 1986

'Crowded Life for Neil Finn', *Auckland Star*, 25 August 1988

Fahey, Jude, 'Split Enz – setting trends', *Press*, 4 March 1976

Fyfe, Andy, 'The House that Roared', *NME*, 11 June 1994

Gaze, Andrew, and Paul Hester, 'One on One', *Herald-Sun*, 10 February 1994

Gee, Mike, 'Tearing Down the House', *On the Street*, 20 November 1996

Gifford, Phil, 'Enz of the world', *New Zealand Listener*, 23 May 1981

Harvey, Bob, 'Karekare, Mon amour' (unpublished mogograph, 1996)

Heal, Andrew, 'Neil Finn, the *Metro* Interview', *Metro*, February 1995

Hepworth, David, 'Crowded House', *Mojo*, June 1994

'Did you think I would leave you crying . . .', *Q*, December 1995

'The Best Part of Breaking Up', *Mojo*, January 1997

Hester, Paul, 'Why I quit', *Herald-Sun*, 12 May 1994

Hill, Robin, 'Just a Fraction of Brotherly Friction', *Good Weekend*, 29 August 1987

Hogg, Colin, 'Finn in new waters', *New Zealand Herald*, 20 February 1987

'Kiwi flies to the top', *New Zealand Herald*, 27 March 1987

Holden, Stephen, 'Crowded House at the Beacon Theatre', *New York Times*, 10 October 1991

'That Old Sweet Song Again', *New York Times*, 24 July 1988

Holmes, Peter, 'Neil Finn's Homecoming', *Sydney Morning Herald*, 5 February 1994

Isler, Scott, 'The Ant-Man Cometh', *Musician*, October 1988

Kay, George, 'Getting Mighty Crowded', *Rip It Up*, June 1987

Konjoyan, David, 'The Dream Isn't Over', *Creem*, March 1994

Leser, David, 'The Finn Review', *HQ*, Winter 1993

Lloyd, Robert, 'Crowded Housewarming', *Spin*, June 1987

Maconie, Stuart, 'The Fine Art of Surfacing', *Q*, February 1994

Malins, Steve, 'Deeply Drippy', *Vox*, July 1992

'Inside the Green House', *Vox*, November 1993

McArthur-Byrnes, Terry, 'We'll Meet Again', *Countdown*, July 1988

Milano, Brett, 'Three's a Crowd, Four's a Crowded House', *Pulse!*, July 1991

O'Donnell, John, 'House on Fire', *Rolling Stone Australia*, July 1991

Pond, Steve, 'Following Up is Hard to Do', (US) *Rolling Stone*, 17 November 1988

Presland, Gerard, 'Paul Hester: every man needs his shed', *New Zealand Musician*, June 1996

Reid, Graham, 'Finn and fame', *New Zealand Herald*, 26 August 1988

'House on the Move', *New Zealand Herald*, 3 April 1992

'Home thoughts from abroad', *New Zealand Herald*, 29 October 1993

Scatena, Dino, 'Just Like Firewood', *Juke*, 13 July 1991

'The Living Enz', *Rolling Stone Australia*, May 1993

Scoppa, Bud, 'Chairman of the Board', (US) *Rolling Stone* 4 December 1986

'The View from Crowded House', *Music Connection*, 23 March 1987

'Mr Whalley builds his dream house,', *Music Connection*, 23 March 1987

Smith, Byron, 'Split Enz/Crowded House', *Juke*, 14 June 1986

Smith, Mat, 'Crowded House at the Borderline', *Melody Maker*, 22 June 1991

Staunton, Terry, 'Kiwi's Pig Adventure', *NME*, 6 November 1993

Sutcliffe, Phil, 'Don't dream it's over', *Q*, July 1992

Taylor, Greg, 'The Once and Future Enz', *RAM*, 4 January 1985

Thomas, Deborah, 'Out to Lunch', *Cleo*, September 1988

Tingen, Paul, 'A Maison Grace', *The Guitar Magazine*, December 1993

'Froom at the Top', *Sound on Sound*, November 1994

Tingwell, John, 'Temple of Four Men', *Drum Media*, 26 October 1993

Trenoweth, Samantha, 'Crowded House: Together Alone in South Africa', *Juice*, January 1994

Watt, Andrew, 'Three's Company in Crowded House', *Beat*, 30 July 1986

Wilmoth, Peter, 'A House Divided', *Sunday Age*, 11 August 1996

Young, Charles M, 'Crowded House', *Musician*, May 1987

Zuel, Bernard, 'The Homecoming', *Age*, 3 February 1996

Index

Crowded House
  audience: English 132, 198–201,
    214–15, 229, 237; moved on 211
  benefits: 'Concert for Life' 233; Aotea
    Square 234; NZ (1994) 301–2;
    Sacred Heart College 319
  final days: decision to disband 334–40;
    press releases 337, 338; MTV
    filming 338; member criticisms
    342–3; farewell concert 344–6
  image: name selection 78–9; the look
    85; fun-loving 117–18; availability
    180; alternative band 186;
    compared with Split Enz 197
  members: abilities 77; keyboardists 89;
    biographies 91–2; keyboardists
    105, 132, 141, 142–5, 154; bass
    players 155–6; Tim joins 176–8;
    relationships 196–7; Tim's role
    203, 204; Tim's public acceptance
    207; Tim on keyboard 210–11; Tim
    leaves 216–18, 219–20;
    relationships 237–8, 255; effect of
    Karekare 262; relationships 287–8,
    295–6, 302–4; drummers 309, 312,
    315; new dynamic 322; reunite
    329**press releases:** 91, 219, 337, 338
  promotion: launching parties 90; slow
    sales 102–3; *Temple of Low Men*
    129; North America 137; band
    absent 139–40; in limbo 152;
    Woodface tour 193; gimmicks 195–6
  radio: NZ 7, 8, 14, 112–13; English 23,
    236; Eon FM 90; US 92–3; GLR
    221; Radio One (BBC) 221; US 237;
    AAA (adult album alternative)
    306, 341
  recording sessions: debut album 71;
    Temple of Low Men 122–7; *Woodface*
    168, 170–1, 183–5; after Finn
    brothers' 175; *Woodface* 183–5; with
    orchestra 184–5; Karekare valley
    248, 259–61, 259–62; 1995 demos
    324–5; reformed band 330
  reviews: debut album 93, 100–1; Roxy,
    LA show 108; *Temple of Low Men*
    124, 130–1; Pantages Theatre
    shows 148–9; *Woodface* 198;
    Borderline venue 200; *NME* 223;
    Together Alone 291–2
  shows: Melbourne debut 89; Paritai

Drive, Auckland 99–100;
    Melbourne party 115; 1988 State
    Theatre, Sydney 133–4; 1989 New
    Year's Eve 165–6; Split Enz/CH
    167; 1996 Olympics announcement
    179; IDs rescue 179; first with Tim
    180–1; Prahran Christmas (1990)
    181; Valentine's Day cruise 193;
    Fremantle 204–6; Power Station,
    Auckland 209–10; pre-show
    routines 213; Olympia Theatre,
    Dublin 220; Barooga Sports Club
    300; last with Paul 307–8;
    Waitangi Day (1995) 321; Hanover
    Grand, London 337–8; farewell
    concert 344–6
  style: banter 23, 52, 205–6, 223, 344;
    busking routine 96; cuppa-and-
    joint band 109; Beatles influence
    124; limelight on Tim 210;
    camaraderie returns 224
  television shows: the Mullanes 52;
    Rock Arena 104; *The Joan Rivers
    Show* 107; *Solid Gold* 107–8;
    presentation on 111; *The Factory*
    129; David Letterman show 137,
    201–2; MTV awards, LA 137; *MTV
    Unplugged* 169; appalling 222;
    Pebble Mill 222; *Top of the Pops* 222,
    239–40; *Most Wanted* 286–7;
    northern hemisphere promotion
    298; *Intimate and Interactive* 304;
    Later With Jools Holland 326; *This
    Morning* fight 326
  tours: European showcase (1986) 96–9;
    US showcase tour 102; Orchestral
    Manoeuvres in the Dark 103–4;
    Bruce Hornsby 107, 109; plane
    mishap 112; first North American
    114; first in NZ 115; Australia
    (1987) 115–16; North America
    (1987) 116; Europe (1988) 131–2;
    North American promotion 135,
    137; *Temple* US, cancelled 137; two
    more cancelled 138; NZ, January
    1989 141–2; US *Temple* tour 149;
    Woodface promotion 193, 198–202;
    Australia (1991) 203, 204, 208, 232;
    North America (1991) 212–14;
    Europe (1991) 216; US, late 1991
    225–7; early 1992 234; Europe